The Last Time When

By George Gipe

To Alan —
with Thanks for your
help and intelligence

George
10/19/82

WORLD ALMANAC PUBLICATIONS
New York, New York

To My Mother

Cover design: Cris Grana
Interior design: Donald C. DeMaio

Copyright © 1981 by George Gipe

First Published in 1982.

Paperback edition distributed in the United States by Ballantine Books, a division of Random House, Inc., and in Canada by Random House of Canada, Ltd.

Library of Congress Catalog Card Number: 81-52843

Newspaper Enterprise Association ISBN: 0-911818-24-3

Ballantine Books ISBN: 0-345-30391-1

Printed in the United States of America

World Almanac Publications
Newspaper Enterprise Association
200 Park Avenue
New York, New York 10166

Table of Contents

But First...

Last, as Shakespeare said in two of his plays, is not necessarily least.

Having made "last" the first word of this book and thereby fulfilling a creative impulse (without yet deciding how to make "first" the book's last word), I can now proceed to an explanation of my desire to write about last things.

The study of firsts has produced several books, deservedly so, as a first is generally innovative and symbolic of progress and the human race's unwillingness to accept defeat. Yet while the term "end of an era" has come to be part of the language, no major work has been dedicated to the study of lasts. I feel this is a regrettable oversight because lasts often make better reading than firsts and in many ways illuminate the human condition with more clarity, poignancy, and realism. After all, few of us are likely to invent the first phonograph, be the first to walk on the moon, or run a sub-four-minute mile. But Edison, Armstrong, and Bannister share with every person the inevitability of facing life's last moment, of having to live with the surety that a decline in our faculties will lead to a personal "end of an era." Thus I believe we are more inclined to identify and sympathize with Joe Louis's last fight than his first, simply because the over-the-hill-but-struggling-mightily figure of Louis, circa 1951, is closer to what we are than the dynamic Louis of 1934.

It also occurred to me a book of lasts could be a handy reference tool for someone researching a subject who did not want to pore through indexes or countless books and encyclopedias. Many of the lasts contained in this book were not listed in other references so that they could easily be found. Others were not accessible at all, but had to be dug out.

Try, for example, to discover the names of the last people condemned to death by the notorious "Bloody" Queen Mary of England. The standard biographies of that monarch, especially the shorter ones in encyclopedias, do not mention names.

Speaking of Queen Mary, try to locate the exact moment those two majestic liners, the Queen Mary and Queen Elizabeth, passed in mid-Atlantic for the last time before they fell victim to the jet age.

And, speaking of Queen Elizabeth, try also to find a list of national leaders who were excommunicated by popes in order to find out who was last. Such a list does not exist. Many of the books or articles dealing with the subject mention medieval monarchs who incurred papal wrath, but invariably fail to describe Juan Peron's 1955 interdiction by Pope Pius XII. I am at a loss to explain this omission.

4

Writing of Juan Peron forces me to describe exactly what a "last" is, and is not. In the context of this book, it is simply something interesting or significant that can never happen again, at least not without miraculous intervention. Peron's excommunication is not a legitimate last, in my opinion. Because the papacy is still intact, there exists the possibility that another national leader may be excommunicated by the present or future pope. Therefore, Peron's punishment was, and remains, only a "most recent."

Occasionally, I have violated my own rule of what a last should be, in the above case because I felt that the Peron incident had sufficient historical importance (especially in view of the fact that Pope Pius XII did not excommunicate Adolf Hitler or Mussolini) to be included. Only rarely in this book does such a violation occur, however, and when it does, the text contains explanatory material.

Actually, my criterion for a legitimate last is too strong. Babe Ruth's 714th career home run, struck on May 25, 1935, certainly qualifies as a legitimate last because Babe Ruth is deceased. Someone who wanted to be difficult, however, could argue that another baseball player might come along, take the name Babe Ruth and hit some major league home runs - thereby making this book not only erroneous but, even worse, obsolete.

That's a rather obtuse argument, of course. Ruth's last homer is a logical entry, as is - to remain in the sports area - Charles Leander "Bumpus" Jones' 1892 feat of pitching the last major league no-hitter from a distance of fifty feet. It may be argued that at some future date the pitching distance will be changed from sixty feet, six inches back to fifty feet, but one must concede that such an event is highly unlikely. When one considers how long the National League has resisted the designated hitter change, we are truly heading into the realm of miraculous intervention.

With these checks and balances and exceptions firmly in mind, I set out to write a book of last things not only because I felt there was a need of such work, but because I was fascinated with the subject and possibilities it presented. After all, just as historic firsts are inevitable and desirable in the recounting of the human situation, so are historic and personal lasts. All good things must come to an end, we are told (most appropriately by Jules Renard, who wrote, "There are moments when everything goes well; don't be frightened, it won't last"); likewise, most bad things end , too.

For this reason, most "lasts" have an aura of sadness about them, but there are exceptions. Contemplating the cruel and unusual punishments man has inflicted on his fellow man in the past, and the subsequent abolition of these atrocities, brings a certain feeling of relief. It is pleasant to know that at least one infectious disease, smallpox, has claimed its last victim. And, let's face it, the fact that Maurice Chevalier will never again turn up live on television or make another movie has got to warm the heart of someone besides the author of this book.

Finally, in cataloguing last events, people, and places, it should be pointed out that there are many traps in addition to the above-mentioned tendency to describe a "most recent" as a "last." Some lasts, it turns out, are not really that. Witness Harper's magazine, which died in 1980 only to be quickly reborn; the liner France was thought to have made her final journey in 1974, but was then reno-vated as a cruise ship (and may soon prove uneconomical again); the Spanish monarchy, thought extinct, was recently restored; even some varieties of birds and animals, once thought extinct, have turned up to prove the accounts of their demise were hasty and exxagerated. In addition to circumstances such as these, there is confusion created by deliberate human manipulation.

The last words of Rudolph Valentino, for example, may never be known because there were simply too many people involved who wanted their own piece of the action brought about by the actor's death. Several books specializing in "last words" state that Valenti-no's final statement went something like, "I want the sunlight to greet me - don't pull down the shades." In fact, soon after the man's death, Oscar Doob, a Hollywood press agent, announced solemnly that Valentino's last words were, "Let the tent be struck!" Doob no doubt thought this phrase was not only noble but a gentle reminder to the public that Rudy's last movie (yet to be released) was Son of the Sheik, which featured several tempestuous love scenes in Arabi-an tents. But when it was pointed out to studio officials that the words were almost identical to the deathbed utterance of General Robert E. Lee, the story was retracted and an explanation added that the intern who heard Valentino's final words had but a slight familiarity with the English language. Yet another doctor who attended the star said that he did not speak a word of English after 6:30 a.m. on 23 August 1926, the day he died. Finally, another publicity group composed of gentlemen seeking to promote the career of actress Pola Negri started the rumor that Valentino's last words were, "Pola, I love you, and will love you in eternity." The group produced its own doctor who was with the patient at the end, of course, which leads one to the conclusion that the poor man's hospital room must have resembled the Mark Brothers' ocean liner stateroom in A Night at the Opera.

Except to a few devoted fans, of course, it doesn't matter a great deal exactly what Valentino said before dying, if indeed he spoke at all. I mention this controversy only to show that sometimes uncover-ing even the simplest historical fact can be extremely complicated. Which is really another way of saying that if an error or two has crept into this book, I humbly beg your indulgence even as I know the mistakes are unlikely to be my last.

Chapter One

Lasts in The Lively Arts

Chronology

458 B.C.
The last dramatic work by Greek playwright Aeschylus (525-456 B.C.), *The Oresteia*, is performed in Athens.

408 B.C.
At the age of seventy-six, Greek tragedian Euripides completes his drama *Orestes*, which is the last performed in Athens during his lifetime.

406 B.C.
Last play of Greek playwright Sophocles (496-406 B.C.), *Oedipus at Colonus*, is completed before the author's death and first performed in 401.

388 B.C.
Last play of Greek writer of satirical comedy, Aristophanes (448-380 B.C.), *Plutus* ("Wealth") is performed.

404 A.D.
Called entertainment by some and a form of capital punishment by others, Rome's last gladiatorial shows are probably held during the reign of Emperor Honorius.

1576
(Aug. 27) Ninety-nine-year-old Venetian painter Tiziano Vecellio (Titian) is at work on his last painting, *La Pieta*, when he falls victim to the plague. The work is completed by his assistant.

1613
English playwright William Shakespeare (1564-1616) completes his thirty-eighth and last play, *The Two Noble Kinsmen*, in collaboration with John Fletcher.

1633
A Tale of a Tub, the final play of Ben Jonson (1572-1637) fails to excite audiences as did his 1606 masterpiece, *Volpone*.

1642
(Autumn) The last opera of Claudio Monteverdi (1567-1643), *L'Incoronazione di Poppea*, is first presented at Venice.

1668
Rembrandt Harmens van Rijn, famous Dutch painter, completes portrait of the *Family Group* of Brunswick, his last work before his death a year later.

1673
(Feb. 17) French actor-dramatist Moliere makes his

final appearance onstage in his own comedy *The Imaginary Invalid* (which deals with a hypochondriac), is seized with a convulsion during the performance, and dies soon afterward. (see p. 20)

1686
(Sept. 6) The last opera of Jean-Baptiste Lully (1632-1687), *Acis et Galatee,* is produced at a gala held by the Duke of Vendome, then is given eleven days later in Paris. In 1687, Lully stabs himself in the foot with his baton while conducting and dies shortly afterward of an infection.

1694
Last produced play of British author John Dryden (1631-1700) is *Love Triumphant*.

1707
George Farquhar (1677-1707) finishes his last play, *The Beaux Stratagem*, on his deathbed, even though he has been paid in advance.

1710
Elizabeth Barry (1658-1713), the first great English actress, retires from the stage. During her career, she created 119 roles.

1727
(May 17) Giovanni Bononcini (1670-1747) writes and producs *Astianatte*, his last opera, for the London stage. Grand finale occurs on closing night when a tremendous battle onstage takes place between rival singers Faustina Bordoni and Francesca Cuzzoni.

Bidding farewell to her admirers, English actress Anne "Nance" Oldfield (1683-1730) appears in the last new part created for her, that of Lady Townley in *The Provoked Husband*.

1730
Artaserse, last opera of Leonardo Vinci (1690-1730), is produced at Rome. Composer dies four months later.

1733
Antonio Stradivarius, famous violin-maker, constructs his last instrument, dies in 1737 at the age of ninety-three.

1735
(Autumn) *Il Flamminio*, the last opera of gifted but short-lived Giovanni Pergolesi (1710-1736), is produced at Naples.

1740
Last of the Amati violin-makers (from about 1564), Girolamo Amati, dies at the age of ninety-one.

1741
(Jan. 21) Last opera of George Frederick Handel (1685-1759), *Deidamia*, is given at London. It is not a success, running only three nights.

1745
(Feb. 15) English actor Colley Cibber (1671-1757) makes

his final stage appearance as Pandulph in his own play, *Papal Tyranny in the Reign of King John*, at Covent Garden.

The last, and greatest, of the Guarnieri violin-makers of Cremona, Giuseppe (born 1687), dies.

1756
(March 27) The last opera of Karl Heinrich Graun (1704-1759), *Merope*, is given at Berlin opera as the final stage work prior to the Seven Years' War. On 19 March 1764, it becomes the first opera to be performed after the fighting ends.

1764
The last print of English artist and satirist William Hogarth (1697-1764) is appropriately titled *Finis*, or *The Bathos*.

1773
Ther last play of British author Oliver Goldsmith (1730-1774) is his best, *She Stoops to Conquer*.

1774
(June 6) *Il Trionfo di Clelia* is the last opera produced during the lifetime of Niccolo Jommelli, who dies on 25 August at the age of 60.

1776
(June 10) One of the English stage's greatest actors, David Garrick (1717-1779) makes his final stage appearance, playing Don Felix in *The Wonder, a Woman Never Vexed*.

1778
Irene, the last play of Francois Marie Arouet, better known as Voltaire, is produced at Paris, the audience applauding the eighty-four-year-old author rather than the play.

1779
(Sept. 24) The last opera of Christoph Willibald Gluck (1714-1787), *Echo et Narcisse*, is given in Paris. It is not a success.

(Dec. l4) *Amadis de Gaule*, the final opera from the pen of Johann Christian Bach, shares the fate of Gluck's last work, also unsuccessfully produced at Paris

1784
(Feb. 26) *Armida*, the last opera produced during the lifetime of its composer, Franz Josef Haydn (1732-1809), is given at the Esterhazy estate in Austria.

1789
(May 7) In his final stage appearance veteran Irish actor Charles Macklin (1700-1797) plays his favorite role, that of Shakespeare's Shylock.

1791
(Sept. 30) The last opera of Wolfgang Amadeus Mozart (1756-1791), *Die Zauberflote*, is premiered at Vienna.

1812
(June 29) Considered by some the greatest actress of the English stage, Sarah Siddons (1755-1831) makes her final appearance as Lady Macbeth. She "unretires" seven years later to perform a benefit for her brother and his wife, then returns to her secluded life.

1820
Suffering from terminal tuberculosis, poet John Keats writes his last poem, "Bright Star, would I were steadfast as thou art," only a few weeks before his death in Rome on 23 February 1821, at the age of twenty-five.

1822
(Feb. 6) *Aladin*, or *La Lampe Merveilleuse*, finally produced in Paris, proves to be the last opera for two composers -- Niccolo Isouard (1775-1818), who dies before completing it; and Angelo Benincori, who finishes the work, but dies on 30 December 1821, before it's produced. Ironically, the opera is very well received.

1825
(Sept. 9) Composer Ludwig van Beethoven makes his final public appearance two years before his death, attending a performance of his own String Quartet in B Flat, Opus 130, at the Hotel Wildemann in Vienna.

1826
(April 12) First production of *Oberon*, or *The Elf King's Oath*, takes place at London. Opera is the last of Carl Maria von Weber, who dies soon after the premiere, at the age of forty.

1829
It is a good year for last operas by renowned composers. On 20 May, the final stage work of Francois Boieldieu (1775-1834), *Les Deux Nuits*, is given at Paris. On 12 June, *Agnes von Hohenstaufen*, last opera of Gasparo Spontini (1774-1851), is produced in Berlin. And on 3 August, the final song of the "Swan of Pesaro," Gioacchino Rossini, *William Tell*, is given a lavish premiere at Paris and is quite successful. Ironically, then thirty-seven-year-old Rossini lives another thirty-nine years without writing another opera, a combination of laziness, financial success, and declining health depriving music lovers of additonal scores by this merry master.

1833
(March 25) Playing Othello to his son's Iago, celebrated actor Edmund Kean collapses onstage at Covent Garden and dies two months later. (see p. 21)
(May 16) *Ludovic*, the last opera of Louis Joseph Herold (1791-1833), is com-

pleted by Halevy and produced at Paris.

1835
(Jan. 25) The last opera of Vincenzo Bellini (1801-1835), *I Puritani di Scozia*, is given at Paris.

1844
(Jan. 18) The last opera of Italian composer Gaetano Donizetti (1797-1848), *Catarino Cornaro*, is produced at the Teatro San Carlo in Naples. (see p. 22)

1845
(Jan. 1) The final opera of Ludwig Spohr (1784-1859), *Die Kreuzfahren*, is produced at Cassel. So famous during his lifetime that he is ranked with Beethoven in William Gilbert's lyrics to *The Mikado* (1885), Spohr is a virtual unknown by the turn of the century.

William Friedrich Ernst Bach, sole surviving direct descendent of composer Johann Sebastian Bach, dies in Berlin. (see p. 23)

1849
(March 9) *Die lustigen Weiber von Windsor*, the last opera of Otto Nicolai (1810-1849), is premiered at Berlin, and eventually establishes his reputation as a composer.

Following his concert tour of Great Britain, Polish
composer-pianist Frederic Chopin plays his final concert, a benefit for Polish refugees.

1865
Often billed as "The African Roscius," America's first great black actor, Ira Frederick Aldridge (1804-1867), makes his final stage appearance, in England. French dancer and pantomimist Celine Celeste (1814-1882) , makes her final American appearance. At least that is what the audiences hope, for Celine's "farewell" appearances outnumber even those of Charlotte Cushman, who gives them regularly from 1852 to 1875, the year before her death.

1872
Hans Christian Andersen (1805-1875) writes the last of his popular fairy tales, a series which he began in 1835.

(April 2) Renowned American actor Edwin Forrest (1806-1872), makes his final stage appearance at the Globe Theatre in Boston. Forrest is most remembered, however, not for his acting but for the riot at New York's Astor Theatre in 1848 when his fans clashed with those of rival actor William Macready.

1875
(March 3) The last opera of Georges Bizet (1838-1875),

Carmen, is produced in Paris. Bizet dies after the twenty-third performance.

1879
(Oct. 25) Veteran American actor John Brougham (1810-1880) outlives a pair of acting wives to make his final appearance on the stage of Booth's Theatre in New York.

1880
(Feb. 21) *Donna Juanita*, the last successful operetta of Franz von Suppe (1819-1895), is produced at Vienna.

1881
(Feb. 10) The last of some 100 stage works composed by Jacques Offenbach (1819-1880),*The Tales of Hoffman* is premiered shortly after his death. Orchestrated by Ernest Guirard, the famous drinking song and barcarolle are taken from Offenbach's 1864 opera, *Die Rhinenixen*.

1882
(July 26) *Parsifal*, the final music drama of Richard Wagner (1813-1883), is produced at Bayreuth.

1887
The last play of Alexandre Dumas, the Younger (1824-1895), *Francillon*, is produced; it fails to match the previous success of the author's *Camille*.
(May 18) *Le Roi Malgre lui*, last of his operas produced during the lifetime of Emmanuel Chabrier (1841-1894), receives its premiere in Paris.

1889
At Sundown, John Greenleaf Whittier's final volume of verse, is printed privately just three years before the poet's death at age eighty-five in 1892.

1890
(July) Artist Vincent Van Gogh, while at work on his last painting, *Wheatfield with Crows*, becomes increasingly despondent and fatally shoots himself. (see p. 25)
The final "big show" produced by celebrated showman P. T. Barnum comes at the end of a triumphant run in England. (see p. 24)

1891
(April 4) Famed Actor Edwin Booth gives his final performance, as Hamlet, in New York. (see p. 26)

1893
(Feb. 9) The last opera of Giuseppe Verdi (1813-1901), the comic *Falstaff*, is premiered in Milan. Verdi, at seventy-nine, has written only three operas during the last quarter century.

1896
(March 7) *The Grand Duke, or The Statutory Duel*, the final collaboration of William Gilbert and Sir Arthur Sullivan, is produced at the Savoy, London.

1898

The "Waltz King," Johann Strauss Jr., writes his final waltz not long before his death at the age of seventy-three. (see p. 27)

1899

The last play of Norwegian dramatist Henrik Ibsen (1828-1906), *When We Dead Awaken*, is produced.

1903

Artist Paul Gauguin (1848-1903) paints his last important picture. Entitled, *Where do we come from? What are we? Where are we going?* it shows his depressed state of mind.

1904

(March 25) *Armida*, the final opera of Czech composer Antonin Dvorak (1841-1904), is premiered at Prague.
(Oct 7) The last opera of Nicolai Rimsky-Korsakov (1844-1908), *The Golden Cockerel*, is produced at Moscow shortly after the composer's death.

1910

More famous for his *Cyrano de Bergerac*, French playwright Edmond Rostand, who is plagued by ill-health during his entire lifetime (1868-1918), finishes *Chantecler*, the last play to be completed and performed during his lifetime.

1912

(Feb. 17) *Roma*, the last opera produced during the lifetime of Jules Massenet (1842-1912), is given at Monte Carlo. Massenet leaves four works behind which are performed after his death.

1914

(Oct. 20) At the age of seventy-one, internationally famous soprano Adelina Patti (1843-1919) makes her final public appearance, on behalf of the Red Cross.

1916

(Jan. 28) The last opera of Ennrique Granados (1867-1916), *Goyescas*, is given in New York City. Returning to Europe, Granados is amoung those lost on the *Sussex*, which is torpedoed by a German submarine.

1920

(Dec. 13) The last opera produced during the lifetime of Ruggiero Leoncavallo (1858-1919), *Edipo Re*, is performed in Chicago, but fails to repeat the success of the composer's *I Pagliacci*.
(Dec. 24) The world's most famous tenor, Enrico Caruso, sings for the last time at the Metropolitan Opera, then returns to Italy ill with pleurisy. (see p. 27)

1922

The death of Alexandro Moreschi brings the age of the *castrati* singers to a close.

1923
Just four days after completing the movie *La Voyante*, actress Sarah Bernhardt (1844-1923) dies of uremia.

1924
During her final tour of America, Italian actress Eleanora Duse appears in New York in Ibsen's *Lady from the Sea*, then is caught in a downpour in Pittsburgh, where she appears in Marco Praga's *The Closed Door*. Already afflicted with tubercular lungs, Duse dies shortly afterward.

1926
(April 25) Left incomplete at the death of Giacomo Puccini (1858-1924), *Turandot*'s last duet and finale are completed by Franco Alfano. With Arturo Toscanini conducting, the final opera of the master of *verismo* is given in Milan.
The Son of the Sheik, the last movie starring Rudolpho d'Antonguolla, otherwise known as Rudolph Valentino (1895-1926), appears just as the sex symbol for millions of women dies of peritonitis caused by a bleeding ulcer.

1927
Veteran vaudevillian Eddie Foy (1856-1928) makes his last onstage appearance with his seven children.

1928
The last production of American impresario David Belasco (1859-1931) is *Mini*, an adaptation of the play, *The Red Mill*, by Ferenc Molnar.

1930
(Jan. 18) After nearly a half-century as New York City's leading musical comedy house, the Casino Theatre at 39th Street and Broadway, is closed. The final performanc: *Faust*.
(Dec. 13) Ballerina Anna Pavlova dances for the last time, at Golders Green, in England. (see p. 29)

1931
The final edition of the *Ziegfeld Follies* produced during the lifetime of the master showman features a narrator for the first time as well as Florenz Ziegfeld's last personally selected beauty, Gladys Glad.
(Dec. 10) American composer John Philip Sousa conducts his last march, "The Circumnavigator's Club" in New York. Three months later, just after rehearsing his most famous march, "The Stars and Stripes Forever," Sousa dies of a heart attack, in Reading, Pennsylvania. (see p. 29)

1934
Betrayed by an unattractive voice that sabotages his switch from silent films to talkies, actor John Gilbert (1893-1971) appears in what turns out to be his last movie, *The Captain Hates*

15

the Sea. Also starring Victor McLaglen, Leon Errol, and Akim Tamiroff, the zany comedy deals with crime on an ocean liner.

1936
The Boy David, last play written by James M. Barrie, is premiered a year before the master of whimsical comedy dies.

1937
(Feb. 24) Elsa Olivieri Respighi completes the last opera of her husband, Ottorino (1879-1936), so that *Lucrezia* can be given its premiere at Milan.

Although only twenty-six, platinum-blonde leading lady Jean Harlow appears in her last film, *Saratoga*, dying of uremic poisoning before the shooting is actually completed. A double is used for many of the scenes with Clark Gable.

The second and last opera of Alban Berg (1885-1935), *Lulu*, is premiered in Zurich.

1938
(April) The final production at the Shubert Brothers 49th Street Theatre in New York is a modern dress revival of Ibsen's *The Wild Duck*. The house then becomes part of a growing trend by being converted to a cinema.

Purgatory, the last play of Irish author William Butler Yeats (1865-1939), is given its first production.

1939
The last musical stage show of American composer Jerome Kern (1885-1945), *Very Warm for May*, is produced. During the last six years of his life, Kern writes for the movies.

In operation since its opening on October 26, 1903 (with King Edward and Queen Alexandra in the royal box) London's Gaiety Theatre offers its final play, *Running Riot*, and then closes for good.

Author of the play *The Silver Cord*, as well as the screenplay for the movie *Gone with the Wind*, writer Sidney Coe Howard's last play, *Madam, Will You Walk?* is completed only days before he is killed in a freak accident at the age of forty-eight.

(June 30) The end comes for the Federal Theatre Project, since 1935 the nation's first government-financed dramatic group.

In his last Broadway stage appearance, actor John Barrymore plays himself, an over-the-hill tragedian. *My Dear Children* is a success partly because audiences came to see what ad-libs he invents. (see p. 30)

1940
Veteran showman-author George M. Cohan (1878-1942) makes his final stage appearance in his own play, *Return of the Vagabond*.

1941
In *Two-Faced Woman*, Swedish leading lady Greta Garbo tries to be gay and modern, but the movie sinks beneath a leaden script and proves to be her last.

1942
In *I Married an Angel*, the famous singing team of Jeanette MacDonald and Nelson Eddy appears together for the eighth and last time. The movie is not a success. (see p. 31)

1943
Thank Your Lucky Stars, an all-star wartime musical, is the ninth (and last) film in which both Errol Flynn and Olivia de Havilland appear. They do not have any scenes together, however.

1946
More famous for his Academy Award-winning short subjects, writer-comedian Robert Benchley (1889-1945) makes his final movie appearance in a faded comedy entitled *Janie Gets Married*.

1949
The tenth film in which Judy Garland and Mickey Rooney play opposite each other, *Words and Music*, is also their last.

1949
The last West End production of a new George Bernard Shaw play is the first in nearly a decade. The play, *Buoyant Millions,* runs only five weeks, which does not disturb the ninety-three-year-old Shaw. "At my age,' he says, "you are either well or dead."
(June 26) Fred Allen's last regular radio show is aired.

1950
Appearing together as a team for the last time in *Love Happy*, the Marx Brothers end a long movie career badly. (see p. 35)

1951
American novelist Sinclair Lewis (1885-1951) completes *World So Wide*, his twenty-second and last novel, which deals with Americans living in Italy.
(August) The last "March of Time" short subject appears in American movie houses, ending a fifteen-year tradition. (see p. 32)

1953
Playing himself in a cameo role, veteran actor Lionel Barrymore (1878-1954) appears in *Main Street to Broadway*, the last movie of his career.

1954
(April 5) After seventeen years with the NBC Symphony Orchestra, eighty-seven-year-old conductor Arturo Toscanini leads his final broadcast concert. During the program, the maestro's mind seems to wander and a

17

few observers think he is having a stroke. (see p. 33)
(Dec. 26) Dating back to 1932, the highly popular radio series, "The Shadow" airs its final episode, entitled "Murder by the Sea."

1955
The last stage musical of Cole Porter (1892-1964), *Silk Stockings*, is premiered. Between 1955 and the time of his death, he writes or arranges music for four movies.

1956
Released less than a year before his death at age fifty-seven, *The Harder They Fall* is Humphrey Bogart's last film. In it, he plays a press agent who decides to expose the ruthless side of boxing.
(July) Ending a long tradition, Ringling Brothers and Barnum and Bailey Circus performs its last show under a canvas tent.

1957
(October) London's St. James Theatre, which is 122 years old and was the scene of plays by Charles Dickens, presents its last production and closes. (see p. 37)
Once a theatrical sensation, the Ziegfeld Follies appears one last time — a pale imitation of its former glory. (see p. 37)

1959
Appearing only briefly because of his death after shooting begins, horror master Bela Lugosi's last movie, *Plan Nine From Outer Space*, features a wealth of cheap sets, a stand-in for Lugosi hiding behind a cape, and a few laughs at the film's overall ineptness. (see p. 35)

1960
(March 29) The Roxy Theatre in New York, the nation's most famous picture and stage show palace, closes after more than three decades. (see p. 39)
(Jan. 28) The last "Goon Show" of the highly successful British Broadcasting Company radio series, which dates from 28 May 1951, is entitled "The Last Smoking Seagoon."

Pepe, a soporific 195-minute Cinemascope extravaganza, proves to be the last movie for both actress Billie Burke (1885-1970) and actor Charles Coburn (1877-1961).

1961
The Misfits, a melodrama about cowboys and a divorcee roping wild mustangs in Nevada, is the last movie for actress Marilyn Monroe (1926-1962), leading man Clark Gable (1901-1960), and veteran character actor James Barton (1902-1962).

1964
(Feb. 2) After nearly a century as a famous tryout house for new plays, Baltimore's

Ford's Theatre closes with *A Funny Thing Happened on the Way to the Forum*. (see p. 41)

1965
The Pawnbroker is the last major movie "condemned" by the Legion of Decency, largely because it contains a brief shot of a woman's breasts. (see p. 40)
(June 2) The last show is run at New York's nineteen-year-old Paramount Theatre before the showplace is closed and demolished.

1966
(April 16) After eighty-three years, the old Metropolitan Opera House in New York City closes. (see p. 41)
(Aug. 29) The sensational British rock group, the Beatles, make their last appearance at Candlestick Park, San Francisco. (see p. 42)

1967
The movie *Guess Who's Coming to Dinner?* proves to be the last time Katharine Hepburn and Spencer Tracy appear together on screen, Tracy dying shortly after the film's completion at the age of sixty-seven.

1969
(Aug. 18) The last act at the Woodstock weekend rock festival is Jimi Hendrix who, with his group, plays a searing rendition of the "National Anthem".
Called "the best film of

1944" by one critic, *Airport* proves to be the last feature made by talented, often wasted actor Van Heflin (1910-1971).
(Dec. 21) Old-time burlesque, the striptease variety, comes to an end in Baltimore when the venerable Gayety Theatre burns down.

1970
(Sept. 12) After an eighteen-year run on television, "The Jackie Gleason Show" flickers out.

1973
(Jan. 16) After nearly fourteen seasons on television, the popular series "Bonanza" finally airs its last episode.

1974
(Dec. 28) Veteran radio announcer Milton Cross hosts his usual Saturday broadcast, describing the plot and trappings of Puccinis *Turandot*. The composer's last opera also turns out to be the last performance for Cross, who dies on 3 January 1975. (see p. 44)

1975
(Sept. 1) The longest-running TV western, "Gunsmoke," ends after twenty seasons.
(Dec. 31) The famous NBC peacock, logo of the TV network's color presentations, displays her eleven-plumed tail for the last time.

1976
Earning an Academy Award for his part as a crazed television newscaster, actor Peter Finch makes his last film appearance in the black comedy, *Network*.

1977
New Year's Day, 1977, is the last ushered in by Guy Lombardo, ending a tradition begun in 1929. The popular bandleader dies later in the year. (see p. 45)

(Nov. 17) The last strip of popular comic "Li'l Abner," appears as cartoonist Al Capp retires after forty-three years. (see p. 46)

1980
(Feb. 1) The final episode of long-running television soap opera, *Love of Life*, is broadcast, ending a run that began in September of 1951. (April 20) Broadway's longest-running show, *Grease*, finally closes after 3,388 performances.

1981
(March 6) After nineteen years on "The CBS Evening News," beloved anchorman Walter Cronkite steps down. (see p. 47)

The Last Play of Moliere

The greatest writer of comedies (Shakespeare definitely included) of all time, Jean Baptiste Poquelin, who took the name Moliere, was born in 1622 and spent part of his early acting career in debtor's prison.

He began writing comparatively late in life — not until his early 30s — but once he took pen in hand quickly turned out a succession of masterpieces. Most deal with flaws of human character, deriving their humor from universal frailties rather than puns or mistaken identity, as Shakespeare habitually relied upon in his comiedies.

The best of Moliere's comedies include *Le Tartuffe* (1664), which dealt with religious hypocrisy; *Le Misanthrope* (1666), on the antisocial man; *L'Avare* (The Miser) (1668), concerning greed; *Le Bourgeois Gentilhomme* (1670), on the *parvenu*; and *Les Femmes Savantes* (1672), which dealt with affected intellectuals.

By a stroke of fate which Moliere must have considered ironic if not amusing, his last comedy, *Le Malade Imaginaire (The Imaginary Invalid)* was actually the history of his death. For some time, the playwright's health had caused his friends intense anxiety and he began paying more and more attention to the medical symptoms he was experiencing. All the while, he was writing a play about hypochondria, which was produced at the Palais Royal on 10 February 1673, with the playwright in the title role.

One week later, Moliere was feeling worse and was urged not to go to the theatre. He disregarded the advice and performed with difficulty. During the performance, he was seized with a convulsion which he managed to disguise. After the play was over he complained of being cold and had to be carried home. Several hours later, the victim of symptoms of tuberculosis which were not imaginary, he died at the age of fifty-one.

Edmund Kean's Last Performance

One of England's greatest tragedians, Edmund Kean was born in 1787, the son of actress Ann Carey and an unknown father, possibly George Savile, the Marquis of Halifax. At the age of four, he made his first appearance onstage as Cupid in Noverre's ballet, *Cymon.*Three years later he was sent to school but ran away to sea as a cabin boy. Not long afterward, finding discipline on board ship even worse than at school, he feigned deafness and lameness so well he convinced even the physicians at Madeira, where he was examined. By the age of fourteen, he was back on the stage, playing Hamlet and other major roles. He also joined the circus for a while, breaking both legs while performing with horses in the process.

Kean's first great performance took place on 26 January 1814, at London's Drury Lane Theatre. As Shylock in *The Merchant of Venice*, he aroused the audience to almost uncontrollable enthusiasm. He himself was so immersed in the tragic parts he played that on one occasion he said, "I could not feel the stage under me." On 29 November 1820, Kean appeared for the first time in New York as Richard III, scoring a great success. "Seeing him act," Samuel Coleridge said, "was like reading Shakespeare by flashes of lightning."

Kean's private life, however, continually put him in hot water with the public. Named as a co-respondent in a divorce case and deserted by his wife and children, he became despondent, and frequently did not show up for performances. During the height of his marital problems, Kean took to the stage as Richard in a house crowded with men anxious to denounce him . As a result, they made so much noise not a word of the play was heard.

By 1829, though only 42, Kean was nearly worn out. This resulted in at least one tragi-comic experience which was related by G. W. Baynham in *The Glasgow Stage*. "The Iago to his Othello was an old actor called Willie Johnstone," Baynham wrote. "Johnstone was very rheumatic. Kean was also weak in the knees. In the business of the third act, both actors knelt in front of the stage, and neither of them found it possible to get up again. On Iago saying to his general, 'Do not rise yet,' Kean was heard to mutter, 'D————d if I think I shall ever rise again!' Both gentlemen remained, unable to move, until Kean managed to raise himself by clinging to his ancient friend, in which endeavor both nearly rolled over together, the gallery boys meanwhile applauding vociferously, and shouting, 'Try it again, Willie, try the other leg.' At last, Mr. Alexander, who was playing Roderigo, taking pity on poor Willie, came on the stage and placed him safely on his feet, amid a cry from the gods of 'houp-la,' and a round of applause for his humanity."

At first intensely jealous of the early theatrical successes of his son, Charles, Kean came to be proud of the young man's success and in 1833 agreed to appear with him at Covent Garden. On 25 March 1833, he was playing the part of Othello to Charles' Iago when suddenly, in the third act, at the words, "Villain, be sure," Kean collapsed, falling on his son's shoulder then whispering, "O God, I am dying. Speak to them for me."

Two months later, on 13 May 1833, he suddenly leapt from the bed he had taken to, and with the old fire upon him, cried, "A horse, a horse, my kingdom for a horse!" His last words were from the dying speech of Octavia in *The Foundling of the Forest*: "Farewell, Flo — Floranthe."

Donizetti's Last Opera

Although he lived a relatively brief life (dying at the age of fifty), Gaetano Donizetti composed about seventy operas during the span of a quarter-century, including the perenially popular tragedy, *Lucia di Lammermoor* and the sparkling comedy, *Don Pasquale*. During the first half of the twentieth century, however, his works were considered old-fashioned, chiefly by some music critics who seldom bothered to study the scores but found it easier to repeat the opinions of others. After 1950, the situation changed, when a new generation of singers (and the advent of long-playing records) introduced opera audiences to the tuneful subtlety of Donizetti's music.

Had he lived longer, Donizetti might have composed even greater masterpieces than *Lucia* or *L'Elisir d'Amore* (another comic gem). In the year 1830, when he was thirty-two, Donizetti contracted syphilis, which was never diagnosed (and, in any event, could not have been effectively treated during his lifetime). Gradually, his mental capacities began to deteriorate. During the rehearsals of the last opera he was to compose, *Dom Sebastien*, his appearance and manner made people think there was something seriously wrong with him. Sometimes he would forget what he was saying in mid-sentence and stare at those around him in such a queer, fixed way that he made them uncomfortable. Other times, he would fly into violent rages that left him incoherent and shaking all over. Nor did the singers help his condition. During the *Dom Sebastien* rehearsals, the prima donna, who was the director's mistress, insisted that half a baritone aria be deleted because she objected to standing on stage while it was being sung. Donizetti argued briefly, then had a seizure so violent he had to be carried home.

To make matters worse, *Dom Sebastien*, produced at the Paris Opera on 13 November 1843, was not as successful as Donizetti felt it should be. Two months later, on 18 January 1844, *Catarino Cornaro*, which was composed before *Dom Sebastien*, also failed in a production in Naples.

The double fiasco undoubtedly hastened Donizetti's decline. Unable to concentrate or sleep, his condition was only exacerbated by doctors who tried nearly every form of remedy in the hope that something would work. Late in 1844, the anguished composer wrote to a friend, "I fell out of bed at night and beat my head on the floor to escape...tell the doctors that night is the saddest thing for someone with blood rushing to his head and with sensitive nerves, besides the strictness in diet, in drink, in hours set for waking and sleeping. Light, light! Either that of God, or that of oil and wax! Twelve hours of convulsions — twenty-four leeches, bathing, medicine for vomiting. Hot poultices on my thighs...nothing. Nothing."

Eventually committed to a mental institution, Donizetti wrote no more operas and died in 1848. His early demise, according to his biographer, William Ashbrook, "can only arouse sincere regret that his declining health did not permit him to pursue his career further. The majesty and range of *Dom Sebastien*, with its rich variety and moving eloquence, are clear indication that he had arrived at a maturity of style that, had his health not failed, held great promise for the future..."

The Last Composing Bach

One of the world's greatest and most prolific composers, Johann Sebastian Bach (1685-1750) was also one of the world's all-time great fathers, siring twenty children during the course of two marriages.

Many of his offspring turned out to be musicians and composers, they in turn producing other musicians and composers, but none had the original Bach's talents. Of his own children, Johann Christian (1735-1782) and Carl Philipp Emmanuel (1714-1788) were the most gifted.

Another son, Johann Christoph Friedrich Bach, was also a musician and taught the skill to his son, William Friedrich Ernst, who was born at Buckeburg in 1759. His main gift seemed that of being unobtrusive, for he managed to earn a living for himself and his family in France, Holland, and Westphalia while remaining virtually anonymous. In fact, when he turned up at the unveiling of a monument to Johann Sebastian Bach at Leipzig on 23 April 1843, his presence came as a surprise to Hermann Hirschbahn, who described William (and got his age wrong) in *Neue Zeitschrift fur Musik* as the "only surviving grandson, an old — but still active — man of eighty-one, with snow-white hair and expressive features.

He had come to the ceremony with his wife and two daughters from Berlin. No one — not even Mendelssohn himself, who had long lived in Berlin — knew anything about him."

A composer of chamber music, as well as a ceremonial cantatas, arias, and other works, William Friedrich Ernst remained an unknown, largely because his music was quite undistinguished. He died in 1845, the last link to the great Bach, whose music was just then being revived by Felix Mendelssohn for nineteenth century audiences.

Barnum's Last Big Show

America's greatest showman could piously say, "I would rather be called the children's friend than the world's king" one moment and cynically smile that, "Every crowd has a silver lining" the next. Even more to his credit as a successful packager of mass entertainment, Phineas Taylor Barnum sincerely believed both aphorisms. He loved children, trusted their judgment, and by putting on shows that appealed to them rather than their elders, he became fabulously wealthy.

Barnum was not always completely honest, but he knew how to capture the public's attention. During his long career — from 1835 when he was only twenty-five until his death fifty-six years later — he introduced America to the likes of Jo-Jo the Dog-faced Boy, the Fiji Mermaid (which was really a monkey stitched to the bottom half of a fish), the original bearded lady, the midget General Tom Thumb, the woolly horse, Siamese Twins, and other assorted freaks almost without end. But he also enticed "the Swedish Nightingale," Jenny Lind, to the United States and was pleased to see his country-men pay huge sums for the privilege of hearing the soprano sing good music. Later in his career, after suffering disastrous financial losses as the result of two fires, Barnum bounced back, and, with James Anthony Bailey, put together "the greatest show on earth." During the latter part of the nineteenth century, it was truly that.

Barnum's last show, at the end of a 100-day run in England, was his most expensive and opulent. The trip across the Atlantic cost $350,000, to which Barnum added $12,000 a day rental for London's Olympia, where the show would be given. Once in England, the showman was relieved to find the British effusive in their praise for him. At a banquet held in his honor at the Hotel Victoria, more than 200 guests toasted him. The editor of the *Pall Mall Gazette*, G. A. Sala, even managed to compare Barnum to the world's greatest conquerors. "Mr. Barnum was not by any means the first showman," he said. "What was Julius Caesar's action on the Lupercal but a show? What were Alexander the Great's progresses but shows? And in modern times Napoleon the Great was even a still more splendid showman. But the exhibitions of these men were associated with bloodshed, desolation and ruin, and the misery of widows and orphans. But Mr. Barnum, on the contrary, while he had more elephants than Alexander the Great when he went to India, instead of making people miserable, amused and instructed them. His show was thoroughly wholesome, useful and pleasing, and that was why he was supported..."

The show that opened several days later drew nothing but praise. More than 15,000 attended the first performance, including the Prince of Wales' son (later King George V). When Barnum asked the young man if he was going to stay until the end, he replied, "Mr. Barnum, I shall remain here until they sing 'God Save Grandmother.' " The *London Mirror* called the circus, especially the dramatic pageant entitled "Nero, or the Destruction of Rome," a "grand show...It surpasses anything of this kind ever attempted in this or any other country." Obviously a crowd-pleaser, the Roman epic as conceived by Barnum, featured everything from triumphal processions to orgies, gladiatorial combats and chariot races.

In February of 1890, tired but happy, P.T. Barnum came home to Bridgeport for the last time. On 7 April 1891, he died in the city which he had served as mayor for four terms, leaving a sizable estate even after the deduction of generous bequests to colleges and children's societies.

Seven weeks later, just as the flood of tributes to him began to diminish, Barnum's grave was nearly robbed by a trio of men who were driven off by gun-firing guards at the cemetery, causing the master showman's name to grab the headlines once again.

No doubt Barnum, if he did not actually plan that midnight raid, would have appreciated the final bit of excitement given the public in his name.

Van Gogh's Last Painting

The epitome of the artist who was not "discovered" until after his death, Vincent Van Gogh sold only one picture during his life and — with some justification — considered himself a monumental failure. In 1890, he wrote to his brother, Theo, "...The prospect is getting darker, I see no happy prospect at all."

By July of that year, Vincent was not only unhappy but suicidal. On the twenty-third, he wrote, "I would perhaps like to write to you about many things but in the first place the desire to do so has completely left me, and then I feel how useless it is." Four days later, on a Sunday afternoon, he went into a nearby field with a revolver, worked a bit on his last painting, *Wheatfield with Crows*, and then shot himself in the chest.

The wound was not immediately fatal. Van Gogh made his way back to his room that evening and concealed his condition until a friend became suspicious and sent for the doctor. When Theo arrived the next day, he found Vincent sitting up in bed, calmly smoking a pipe. The two brothers talked through the night until Vincent said, "I want to be going," and died shortly afterward, at 1:30 a.m. 29 July 1890.

Studying *Wheatfield with Crows* from the vantage point of time, the mental specialist Dr. G. Kraus said it was the only one of Van Gogh's paintings to display visible signs of disintegration and incipient delerium.

Edwin Booth's Last Performance

Born into a family of actors in 1833, Edwin Booth was the older brother of John Wilkes Booth and younger brother of Junius Brutus Booth, Junior, and son of Junius Brutus Booth, Senior.

A native of Belair, Maryland, Edwin became manager of the Winter Garden Theatre, New York, in 1862. There, the three brothers played together in a memorable production of *Julius Caesar* — a play featuring the assassination of a great political leader, Edwin was to recall after John Wilkes murdered President Abraham Lincoln on 14 April 1865.

Revulsion at his younger brother's deed sent Edwin into retirement for nearly a year, but he returned in 1868, with his own theatre built at the corner of 23rd Street and Sixth Avenue in New York City. The playhouse opened on 3 February 1869 with a production of *Romeo and Juliet*.

Despite artistic successes, Booth went bankrupt in 1873, which caused him to embark on national and international tours which further enhanced his reputation. He was, however, a moody and unhappy man, prone to melancholia and much affected by the insanity of his father, younger brother, and second wife. By the late 1880s, his health began to fail and he experienced occasional attacks of paralysis. One, in Rochester, New York, on 3 April 1889, was so severe that fellow actor Lawrence Barrett went before the curtain to inform the audience that "the end has come" for Booth. He survived that attack but never fully recovered his strength.

Booth's final performance took place on 4 April 1891 at the Brooklyn Academy of Music before a standing room only audience of 2,000. Playing Hamlet, his most famous role, Booth displayed obvious symptoms of weariness, cutting several speeches and scenes in a drastic manner. "Few New Yorkers have ever known him to cut the text so much," one reviewer commented. "...His movements on the stage were easy and graceful, but his lack of physical strength was plainly apparent. Excepting those lucky persons who had choice seats in front, nobody heard all he said. His voice was husky, and there was scarcely a trace of his old fire in his speech and action..."

Nevertheless, the end of the play brought long and spontaneous applause for the famous actor, who returned to the stage and said, "Ladies and gentlemen, I hardly know what to say to you. I have said all I can say. I thank you for your kindness and I hope this will not be the last time I shall appear before you. I intend to rest next year and care for my health, but hope to appear again in the near future."

Booth never returned to the stage, dying on 7 June 1893 at the age of 59.

The "Waltz King's" Last Waltz

A composer whose music has never gone out of style and who was called the most musical of all composers by Richard Wagner, Johann Strauss, Jr.'s waltzes are nearly synonymous with nineteenth century elegance and the joy of living. A superb craftsman who never seemed at a loss for melody, Strauss often jotted musical notations on bills, shirt cuffs, even a bedsheet that was nearly sent to the laundry before its tune was rescued.

Of Strauss' 479 works with listed opus numbers (the famous "Blue Danube" waltz is number 314), only 167 are waltzes. The rest are marches, quadrilles, and polkas. He also composed 17 operettas and operas, unfortunately having been smitten by the success of Jacques Offenbach during the late 1860s and early 1870s.

Strauss's last numbered work, Opus 479, is entitled "Klange aus der Raimundszeit," and in the tradition of the waltz, is in three-quarter time. It is not really a typical Strauss waltz, but more a potpourri of "melodies from the age of Raimund" — that is, Ferdinand Raimund, an Austrian actor who was popular in Vienna from 1817 to 1836. In this eight-minute nostalgia piece, Strauss quotes from the works of his father and Josef Lanner, another early waltz composer who lived from 1801 to 1843.

Strauss's last real waltz in the style that made him famous was opus 477, "An der Elbe," a less famous companion-piece to the "Blue Danube," in that it was dedicated to a river. There the similarity ends for while "An der Elbe" has several pleasant melodies, it is in no way comparable to Strauss's earlier masterpiece. Shortly after composing it, and while at work on his ballet *Aschenbrodel* (Cinderella), Strauss died in 1899 at the age of 73.

Caruso's Last Performance

Still the most famous of all operatic tenors, Enrico (christened Errico) Caruso was the seventeenth of twenty-one children produced by his mother, Anna. When she heard her son sing solo in the church choir, Anna kept him from the street crime life that had destroyed so many young Neapolitans by encouraging him to sing and study music.

THE LAST TIME WHEN

After captivating Europe, the thirty-year-old Caruso made his American operatic debut at the Metropolitan on 23 November 1903, as the Duke of Mantua in Verdi's *Rigoletto*. He was obviously nervous, cracking on the high notes, but before season's end he was a New York favorite.

During the next 18 years at the Met, Caruso appeared in 36 roles in 4 languages. He made a great deal of money — about $300,000 a year — but he also spent a lot, often nearly $10,000 a season just for tickets which he gave to those who could not afford them.

A great trencherman and toper as well as a spender, Caruso loved a good joke. Once when Lillian Nordica was about to lift her voice in a love duet with him, he put a hot potato in her hand. His idea of great fun was to fill a fellow singer's hat with water or flour and watch what happened during the performance. In *Tosca*, when Antonio Scotti stooped to pick up the paint brush beneath Caravadossi's easel, he had to yank at it for several minutes because Caruso had nailed it to the floor. On another occasion, Caruso sewed up the sleeves of Vittorio Arimondi's coat and nearly collapsed with joy when the singer fell for the joke during a live performance.

Every once in a while, Caruso shared jokes with his audience. In August of 1920 his home was burglarized of $500,000 worth of jewels, a fact which was well known among opera fans. That same month, during a performance of *La Boheme,* Caruso sang the words, "Your lovely eyes have robbed me of my jewels"...at which point he turned to the audience and gave an impressive Italian shrug that brought down the house.

Caruso could also be childish in addition to being childlike. When he was hissed in Naples, he refused to sing there again, and kept his promise, even when friends begged him to sing a World War I benefit for the San Carlo Opera House. (Instead, he wrote a check for $50,000.) Once, having gotten a bad review, he quit the Metropolitan but was enticed to return. Intensely superstitious, he never started trips on Tuesdays or Fridays.

In December of 1920, while singing in Donitzetti's *L'Elisir d'Amore* at the Brooklyn Academy, a blood vessel burst in Caruso's throat. Instead of stopping, he insisted on singing the rest of the act while stagehands stood in the wings, passing handkerchiefs and towels to the bleeding singer. Only when the audience demanded that he stop did Caruso do so. Later, apparently recovered, he sang four more times, the last as Eleazar in Halevy's *La Juive* on Christmas Eve of 1920.

The next day he collapsed, doctors diagnosing his condition as acute pleurisy. After several operations for the removal of lung abcesses, Caruso returned to Naples. There, in a waterfront hotel where he could look at Mount Vesuvius, he died on 2 August 1921.

Pavlova's Last Dance

Most famous for a two-and-a-half minute dance called "The Dying Swan," choreographed by Michel Fokine, the beloved ballerina Anna Pavlova begain her dancing career in 1892. After seven years of rigid discipline at the St. Petersburg Imperial Theatre School, she joined the Russian Imperial Ballet, becoming prima ballerina at twenty-four.

In 1908, Pavlova began a life of touring, taking ballet to the most remote corners of the world, in many cases giving people their first contact with the art. During the 1920s she continued to dance despite a painful knee injury, but had prepared for the future by forming her own company and studying choreography. In 1930, she was planning to design a ballet to an orchestral version of Bach's well-known *Toccata and Fugue*.

Late that year, she made a British tour, which ended at Golders Green on 13 December. Pavlova then went to Cannes in the south of France to relax, but seemed unable to do so.

At a New Year's Eve party, she entered a Cannes restaurant to great applause but not long afterward, a pigeon flew in through an open window and landed on her shoulder. Pavlova was upset at the incident, mostly because of a Russian superstition which said that a bird flying into a room was an omen of death. Five minutes after midnight, the famous ballerina left.

A few days later, she left for Holland and another tour, but as soon as she arrived in The Hague, on Saturday, 17 January 1931, she collapsed from what the local physician diagnosed as pleurisy of the left lung. By Thursday the inflammation had spread to her right lung, at which point she lost consciousness. At midnight on 23 January, she opened her eyes, tried to cross herself, and whispered to her maid, "Get my swan costume ready."

Half an hour later, Pavlova died, one week before her forty-ninth birthday. She left an estate of nearly $500,000 but no will. The Soviet government ended up with most of her British assets.

Sousa's Last March

Although known during his day as a composer of operettas, suites, and songs, John Philip Sousa was most famous for his marches, of which he wrote 136. His most beloved march, of course, was "The Stars and Stripes Forever," which he composed during an ocean crossing in 1897. (Subsequently, "The Stars and Stripes Forever" was used by circus bands as a distress signal. Its most urgent rendition came on 6 July 1944 at Hartford, Connecticut, when the Ringling Brothers tent caught fire, killing 168 people.)

Living and working to the ripe age of seventy-seven, Sousa's final composition, appropriately, was a march. Now rarely performed,

"The Circumnavigator's Club March" was first played on 10 December 1931 at the exclusive New York club whose members had all traveled around the world. It was warmly applauded.

On the manuscript of the march, dated 29 October 1931, Sousa listed his credentials as a world-traveler and finished with the lines, "God forgive my mistakes. I hope the copyist will."

In that same year, after a final brief tour, the internationally famous Sousa Band fell victim to the Depression, losing money for the first time. Sousa continued traveling and performing, however, and after rehearsing for a guest appearance with the Ringgold Band of Reading, Pennsylvania, died of a heart attack in his hotel room on 6 March 1932. Fittingly, the last piece he had run through during the rehearsal was "The Stars and Stripes Forever."

Last Performances of John Barrymore

"The Great Profile" died on 29 May 1942, of myocarditis with chronic nephritis, cirrhosis of the liver, and gastric ulcers as contributing factors, leaving behind some household furniture, a car, less than $10,000 in cash, and a wealth of classic anecdotes about the fabulously talented actor corrupted by, and bored with, success.

Requesting that he be "left on the money-making side of my face" (his left), John Blythe Barrymore lived and died a legend. The son of actors Maurice Barrymore and Georgianna Drew, he was born into the theatre. He tried desperately to resist his heritage, however, fancying himself a cartoonist and artist and even worked briefly during his youth for the *New York Telegram* (for twenty minutes) and the Hearst organization (one day) before turning to the theatre. The only consolation of this period was the sale of a gruesome picture entitled "The Hangman" to Andrew Carnegie for $10.

His theatrical debut, in October of 1903, when he was twenty-one, produced only one notice from the Chicago press — a pan by Amy Wright. More than a decade passed before he took his career seriously, but once he did so, John Barrymore became the talk of the theatre world. During the 1920s he starred in *Hamlet*, *Richard III*, and *Peter Ibbetson*, then went to Hollywood, where he was supposed to appear in filmed versions of Shakespeare's plays but never did.

Drinking, yachting, marrying (four times), and spending money furiously, he aged neither wisely nor well, seemingly content to mock his own career in a succession of less-than-memorable movies during the 1930s.

He was finally enticed back to the theatre in 1939, partly to help the budding career of his fourth wife, a young woman just barely out of her teens named Elaine Jacobs. Taking the stage name Elaine Barrie, she and John agreed to appear in a comedy by Catherine Turney and Jerry Horwin entitled *My Dear Children*. Predictably, it dealt with a once-great matinee idol who went to a Tyrolean castle for a weekend with an adventuress only to run into his three daughters. Barrymore considered the play inconsequential but amusing.

The problem was that he had great difficulty remembering the lines as well as suppressing his profanity onstage. And as a result, audiences flocked to the theatre to see what would happen next.

Barrymore seldom disappointed those looking for an impromptu laugh. One night he completely halted the play in order to talk with actor Ned Sparks, who was seated in the second row, then turned back to the cast and said: "Well, now, if somebody will give me a cue, we'll get along with the play." On other occasions, when he failed to hear his prompter from the wings, he would yell offstage; "Give those cues louder, we can't hear 'em!" When he dropped a cigarette on the floor, he delighted the audience by swearing loudly and naturally. One night in the midst of a love scene which ended with the line. "I will take you to Lake Como," he drew a mental block. "I'll take you to..." he began. Pawing his brow as he thought for the location, he tried again and again. "I'll take you to...."

Finally a spectator in the silent house sneezed.

"That's it! Thanks!" Barrymore shouted over his lady's shoulder, bringing down the house.

A success largely because of his ad-libbing, *My Dear Children* had 117 performances, ending its Broadway run and Barrymore's stage career on 18 May 1940. Barrymore then returned to Hollywood, appearing in *The Great Profile*, *World Premiere*, and his last film, *Playmates* (1941) with Lupe Velez and Kay Kyser.

As Barrymore was dying at sixty in Hollywood Presbyterian Hospital, his last visitor was his brother Lionel, who reported that the only word he uttered was a weak, "Hello." The great actor no doubt would have preferred biographer Gene Fowler's version of his last words: "Is it true you're the illegitimate son of Buffalo Bill?"

Last Jeanette MacDonald-Nelson Eddy Picture

One of the most famous movie teams, and certainly the best of the singing ones, Nelson Eddy and Jeanette MacDonald first got together in 1935 with *Naughty Marietta*. The picture was the twenty-eight-year-old MacDonald's twelfth and thirty-four-year-old Eddy's second. During the next seven years they were together in *Rose Marie*, *Maytime*, *Girl of the Golden West*, *Sweethearts*, *New Moon*, *Bitter Sweet*, and *I Married an Angel*. They also appeared separately in four pictures each.

Released in July of 1942 with music and lyrics by Richard Rodgers and Lorenz Hart, *I Married an Angel* dealt with a Budapest banker who fell asleep during his birthday party, had a dream in which he courted and married an angel, then awakened to discover that the woman was real and among his guests. "A more painful and clumsy desecration of a lovely fiction has not been perpetrated in years," wrote Bosley Crowther, describing the film as "a very ponderous posturing of what is meant to be a coy, innocent dream."

Part of the trouble was that MacDonald and Eddy had lost a bit of the bloom of youth, at least in the eyes of Crowther, who added that the stars "are not exactly a pair of sylphs and no one should willingly embarrass them by asking that they pretend that they are. So Metro, which did so, is responsible quite as much as they for the botch that has been made..." From the vantage point of several decades, the *New Yorker* in 1978 called the movie "as bland as operetta but without its energy."

Perhaps sensing that the magic was gone from the collaboration, MacDonald and Eddy went their own ways. She appeared in *Follow the Boys* (1944), *Three Daring Daughters* (1948), and *The Sun Comes Up* (1949), co-starring with Lassie for her swan song.

Eddy continued alone in *Phantom of the Opera* (1943), *Knickerbocker Holiday* (1944), in which Charles Coburn sang "September Song," and *Northwest Outpost* (1947). He also sang the part of Willie the Whale in Walt Disney's 1946 animated feature *Make Mine Music*.

Eddy died in 1967, MacDonald in 1965.

The Last March of Time

Although it was around for only sixteen years, *The March of Time* exerted an enormous influence on Americans, partly because it was the only regular series offering a lengthy look at the news during the Depression and World War II era.

The driving force behind the series was Louis de Rochemont, whose interest in filmmaking dated back to his childhood. While attending public schools in Winchester, Massachusetts, he photographed "newsreels" in the streets of neighboring towns and sold them to local neighborhood movie houses. In 1922, the twenty-three-year-old de Rochemont was present with his camera when Kemal Ataturk seized Smyrna and when the tomb of Tutankhamen was opened.

Convinced that the moviegoing public was ready for a regular documentary series, de Rochemont and Roy Larsen, circulation editor of *Time* magazine, originated the *March of Time* series.

First presented on 1 February 1935, sandwich boards advertised the new series as a "Dramatization of the World's Greatest News Events." The premiere showing took place at the Capitol Theatre in New York City and almost simultaneously in seventy first-run movie houses across the country. Volume one, number one was entitled "Metroplitan Opera," but was in fact made up of six parts for a total length of twenty-two minutes.

The first sequence described the role of Prince Saionji in Japan's struggle between democracy and militarism; this was followed by a report of how the "21 Club" had frustrated Prohibition agents; next came a piece on British traffic lights and the native opposition to them; then a look at an American in France who refused to pay a traffic fine unless France repaid part of its war debt to the U.S.; a fifth section investigated the accomplishments of the National Recovery Administration; finally, there were the first sound pictures ever taken at the Metropolitan Opera, featuring the formal resignation of General Manager Giulio Gatti-Casazza.

The March of Time was generally well received, although by 1939 it had dispensed with its multi-subject format and usually dealt with a single topic. Some of these were "Labor and Defense" (December, 1940), "When Air Raids Strike" (January, 1942), "America's Food Crisis" (March, 1943), and "The Returning Veteran" (April, 1945). Narrated by Westbrook Von Voorhis, the series occasionally broke new ground, as in the 1942 episode, "We Are the Marines," which contained the words "damn" and "hell" to illustrate how tough the Marines were. Such rampant profanity, of course, had never been heard in American movie houses previously.

But if the series had its high points, it also had its lapses of good sense. In a 1946 episode entitled "Atomic Power," for example, one participant was scientist Albert Einstein. With perhaps the greatest mind of the century in front of its cameras, *The March of Time* restricted his entire contribution to just two words — "I agree."

The series occasionally resorted to faked recreations which were depicted as actual events. In the same "Atomic Power" sequence, Dr. James Conant and Dr. Vannevar Bush, ostensibly stretched out on the sands of New Mexico after the Alamogordo A-bomb blast, were actually lying on the floor of a garage in Boston.

The March of Time was one of the first victims of television news, exhibitors showing an increasing reluctance to pay for the series after World War II. The final installment, Volume 17, Number 6, entitled "Formosa — Island of Promise," appeared in August of 1951.

By that time, de Rochemont had moved on to produce his own full-length pictures, including the highly praised *House on Ninety-Second Street*. He died on 24 December 1978, just a few days short of his eighty-ninth birthday.

Toscanini's Last Concert

The death of Arturo Toscanini on 10 January 1957 closed not only a career but an era, for Toscanini was the last living link with the great Italian romantic composers. As a twenty-year-old cellist, he was in the orchestra pit at La Scala in Milan on the night Verdi's

Otello had its world premiere in 1887; as a conductor, he had learned Verdi's last great works from the composer himself.

The son of a poor Parma tailor, Toscanini rose to become the highest paid classical conductor in history, receiving up to $9,000 for a single broadcast. A notorious womanizer and musical tyrant, he also liked to watch children's programs on television and would collapse with laughter watching a dinner guest trying to cut meat with a folding knife. And although he was the most famous conductor of the mid-20th century, he shrank from personal publicity, not once in his entire career granting a formal interview.

An Italian who loved Wagner and Beethoven, Toscanini was a genius who could not be intimidated into performing cerebral musical exercises. Most compositions by modernists he dismissed simply as "not music for me." Passionate about his art, he could make musicians redden with shame, burn with rage, or soften with sympathy. When a rehearsal went poorly, he frequently stormed offstage, ripped up scores, upset furniture, or cried out that the players were "beasts." Yet performers were often amazed at the beauty he wrung from them. Once, listening to a recording she had made with Toscanini, soprano Herva Nelli exclaimed, "How did I do it? He must have hypnotized me."

After conducting the Metropolitan Opera orchestra from 1908 to 1915, the New York Philharmonic (1928-1936), and at Salzburg and Bayreuth, Toscanini gave his first radio broadcast with the NBC Symphony Orchestra on 25 December 1937. The weekly concerts became standard fare for music lovers for the next seventeen years, a period during which Toscanini made the orchestra a synonym for excellence, via countless recordings.

In 1954, Toscanini and David Sarnoff of NBC disagreed on artistic issues, which led to Toscanini's decision to quit. The final concert, on 5 April, was marred by a temporary mental lapse on the maestro's part. No doubt upset and saddened by recent events — and eighty-seven years old besides — Toscanini suddenly paused during the Bacchanale from Wagner's *Tannhauser*. The beat of his right arm became frail, he failed to give cues, and at one point he pinched his eyes with the fingers of his left hand as if searching desperately for an illusive thought.

The well-trained orchestra continued playing, knowing the piece well, but then Toscanini did the incredible — he stopped conducting. As the performance fell apart, first cellist Frank Miller got up and tried to conduct.

Meanwhile, in the NBC control booth, a production executive, fearing that Toscanini was incapacitated, ordered the concert cut off, and had announcer Ben Grauer say it was because of "technical difficulties," A recording of Brahms' First Symphony went out to the radio audience just as the man realized that Toscanini had recovered. The Brahms was taken off and sound switched back to the live concert. Altogether, the interruption had consumed only twenty-eight seconds, but Toscanini was furious. As soon as the concert was over, he dropped his baton to the floor, stepped from the podium, left the platform, and never returned to the stage.

"Should this have been his permanent farewell to any kind of a public appearance," Olin Downes wrote, "his name will remain supreme and his achievement imortally revered."

It was Toscanini's last public concert. In June of 1954, he led a recording session of excerpts from Verdi's *Masked Ball* and *Aida*. Two-and-a-half years later, when newsboys in Milan shouted, "Il maestro e morto!" no one needed to ask to whom they were referring.

Bela Lugosi's Last Picture

The most famous and sinister of all screen villains, Bela Lugosi first appeared in the role of Dracula with which he was synonymous in 1930. The story of a Transylvanian vampire count who finally gets his comeuppance in Yorkshire, *Dracula* launched both Universal Studios and other filmmakers on a seemingly endless parade of horror sequels, not the least of which was *Abbott and Costello Meet Frankenstein* (1948). Lugosi was in that one, too, although not featured in the title.

By 1956, the year of his death, Bela Lugosi was into his seventies but still active as the screen's practitioner par excellence of evil. The last movie he completed was *The Black Sleep*, which concerned a Victorian brain surgeon who experimented on human beings, producing freaks who eventually turned on him. Leslie Halliwell described the film as a "gruesome and humorless horror film notable only for its gallery of wasted talent." The other stars included Basil Rathbone, Lon Chaney, Jr., John Carradine, and Akim Tamiroff.

After *The Black Sleep*, Lugosi began work on *Grave Robbers from Outer Space*, but died on 16 August 1956. A double was used to complete the movie, which was released in 1959 as *Plan Nine From Outer Space*. Obviously still considering the possiblility of doing slightly more "artistic" pictures, Lugosi died clutching the script of Ed Wood's *The Final Curtain*, the story of a vaudeville actor who dies on stage but does not realize it.

According to his biographer, Lugosi's last request, which was granted, was that he be buried in Dracula's cape.

The Marx Brothers' Last Movie

During the 1930s, the release of a new Marx Brothers movie was an occasion for celebration, the team of Harpo, Chico, and Groucho (with occasional help from Zeppo and Gummo) having delighted audiences with *The Coconuts, Animal Crackers, Duck Soup, A*

Night at the Opera, Monkey Business, The Big Store, and a half-dozen other hilarious films.

After Groucho appeared solo with Carmen Miranda in *Copacabana* (1947), the team got together again in *Love Happy* (1950). "The last dismaying Marx Brothers film, " wrote Leslie Halliwell, "with Harpo taking the limelight and Groucho loping in for a couple of brief, tired appearances. A roof chase works, but Harpo tries too hard for sentiment, and the production looks shoddy."

Featuring the exploits of a private detective named Sam Grunion (Groucho), *Love Happy* included Chico and Harpo as a couple of zanies trying to help some struggling thespians get their show on Broadway. Marilyn Monroe made a brief appearance as Grunion's client, Illona Massey was stunning as the evil but seductive Madame Egilichi, and Vera-Ellen danced. "Incidentally, does anyone have any idea whatever became of the Marx Brothers?" wrote Bosley Crowther of the *New York Times* on 23 April 1950. "The weary and uninspired comedians who pull themselves painfully through this film...are certainly not the Marxes we used to know. Could they be imposters? Or are their writers imposters? We'd like to know."

The last movie in which the three Marx Brothers appeared (although not as a team) was *The Story of Mankind*, a 1957 fantasy-comedy in which, having learned the secret of the H-bomb, mankind is put on trial to determine if the human race should be allowed to continue. Stars of the film were Sir Cedric Hardwicke as the head of an outer space high tribunal (the script writers were careful to point out that he was not God), Ronald Colman (his last feature) as mankind's defense attorney, and Vincent Price as Mr. Scratch, the devil.

In addition to many other stars (including Peter Lorre as Nero, Virginia Mayo as Cleopatra, and Hedy Lamarr as Joan of Arc), Chico Marx turned up as a monk listening to Christopher Columbus explain his theory of reaching the east by heading west. A bit later, Groucho appeared as Peter Minuit of the Dutch East India Company, bargaining for the island of Manhattan with dialogue such as:

Indian: "How!"

Groucho: "Three minutes and leave them in the shell.".

Finally, Harpo made the scene as a red-wigged Sir Isaac Newton, discovering gravity while playing a harp conveniently placed in the meadow. (As a grand finale, he pressed an apple through the strings of his harp and happily shuffled the slices.)

The Story of Mankind was a sorry way for the talented brothers to end their movie careers, even if the picture achieved a certain camp appeal as a result of its blatant use of stock footage, cheap sets, and hilariously corny narration.

The Last Ziegfeld Follies

The epitome of lavish musical theatre and gaucherie in America, *The Ziegfeld Follies* appeared regularly for almost a quarter of a century, offering titillation, comedy, and music. The product of Florenz Ziegfeld, who was the enterprising son of a serious musician, the annual shows were apparently just what America wanted — a cleaned up, slicker version of the famed *Folies Bergere of Paris.*

First appearing in 1907, *The Ziegfeld Follies* (not called by that title until the 1911 edition) had a number of highlights — and lowlights. In the very first edition, the chorines marched up and down the aisles beating on snare drums; a year later, in a number based on a taxicab motif, they wore flimsy costumes, headlights, red tin flags, and signs reading "for hire"; the 1909 version featured a chorus line of women wearing battleship-shaped hats which lit up when the stage was darkened; one scene in the 1915 *Follies* took place under water and called for elephants to spout on cue; the patriotic finale of the 1917 edition, with music by Victor Herbert, started out with Paul Revere's ride and ended with a parade of U.S. forces before President Wilson (enacted by Walter Catlett); former heavyweight boxing champion James Corbett acted in the 1923 version, quite terribly; and in 1927 Claire Boothe Luce rode a live ostrich decorated with a rhinestone collar.

Despite these less-than-subtle touches, the shows did have their moments, providing a vehicle for such stars as W. C. Fields, Leon Errol, Eddie Cantor, Ed Wynn, Fanny Brice, Marion Davies, Will Rogers, Gallagher and Shean, Olsen and Johnson, and countless others.

Produced annually (except in 1926, 1928, and 1929) until 1931 under the supervision of showman Ziegfeld, the series continued after his death with versions in 1934, 1936-7, and 1943 (which was dominated by Milton Berle).

Finally, in 1957, a fiftieth anniversary edition was produced, but it was a pale and shoddy show with a chorus line of just six women, which must have made Ziegfeld turn in his grave. "The spirit had all but vanished," critic Louis Kronenberger remarked, "the songs had no tunefulness, the lyrics no bounce, the sketches no crackle, and though the dances had moments of color, they quite lacked distinction."

The End of the St. James Theatre, London

Constructed on a site occupied by an old hostelry dating back to the time of Charles II, the St. James Theatre, London, opened on 14 December 1835 with *Agnes Sorel*, a "burlesque with music."

The following year, young Charles Dickens produced a series of plays but none was successful. He also wrote his only opera libretto, the two-act *Village Coquettes*, with music by John Pyke Hullah. The work was presented on 6 December 1836 at the St. James, and forgotten until 5 September 1862 when it was revived in Danish at Copenhagen, apparently without music. Hullah, who, like Dickens, was born in 1812, went on to write *The Barbers of Bassora* in 1837, *The Outpost* in 1838, and then gave up opera composition and became a music teacher.

In any event, the first years of the St. James Theatre's operation were not very successful, the only money-making entertainments during the mid-1830s being a wild beast show and a German acting company. Later, the theatre gained a measure of renown with the production of *Lady Audley's Secret* and *The Belle's Stratagem* with Sir Henry Irving appearing as Doricourt.

In May of 1893, Mrs. Patrick Campbell caused a sensation at the St. James when she appeared as Paula in *The Second Mrs. Tanqueray*. Other well-received productions followed — *The Importance of being Earnest*; *The Prisoner of Zenda*; *Old Heidelberg*; and *His House in Order*. So successful was actor-impresario George Alexander during the 1890s that the entire auditorium was renovated in 1900 and Alexander himself was knighted in 1911. Among the other great actors to appear at the St. James early in the century were George Arliss and Gladys Cooper.

The St. James suffered some bomb damage during both World Wars but emerged in serviceable condition. Since it had been around for more than a century, the theatre seemed safe enough, until early 1957 when plans were revealed to demolish the landmark and replace it with an office building.

Cries of "It's a disgrace!" were heard, the most impressive voice that of actress Vivien Leigh, star of *Gone With the Wind* and then-wife of Sir Laurence Olivier. So upset was she by the plan to tear down the St. James that on 11 July 1957 she stood up in the British House of Lords and shouted, "My Lords, I wish to protest against the St. James Theatre being demolished!"

The actress probably never delivered a line that had less effect on her audience. "They did not move a muscle," she later remarked.

A few seconds after the brief speech was delivered, Sir Brian Harrocks, Gentleman Usher of the Black Rod (sergeant-at-arms) escorted Miss Leigh out.

Miss Leigh formed a committee to save the St. James Theatre, and led marches and demonstrations during the rest of the month. One highlight: a response and pledge of 500 pounds from Sir Winston Churchill. "I hope you succeed in your defense of St. James Theatre," he wrote, "although, as a parliamentarian, I cannot approve of your methods."

Early in August, the theatre owners announced that they had deferred demolition in order to find out if the St. James could be preserved. Upon hearing this news, the American philanthropist Huntington Hartford immediately pledged $100,000 toward the fund.

As it turned out, that the was the highwater mark of the save-the-St. James campaign. Much talk followed, but it soon became obvious that the necessary money could not be raised.

Accordingly, in October of 1957, the St. James Theatre, aged 122, was torn down. Its last production, starring John Gregson, was a now-forgotten play entitled *It's the Geography that Counts*.

Roxy Theatre

"What's playing at the Roxy? I'll tell you what's playing at the Roxy. A picture about a Minnesota man so in love with a Mississippi girl that he sacrifices everything and moves all the way to Biloxi — that's what's playing at the Roxy." — Guys and Dolls

Billed as "the cathedral of motion pictures," the Roxy in New York was in fact the largest theatre built since the fall of Rome. It had its own hospital, 6 box offices, a radio studio, an apartment for the owner, an orchestra of 110, 5 organists, and a corps of ushers, all reported to be ex-Marines. At its opening in 1927, 125 special policement held back the crowd which included among its 6,000, Mayor Jimmy Walker of New York, Harold Lloyd, Charles Chaplin, and Gloria Swanson, star of the gigantic theatre's first movie attraction, *The Love of Sunya*.

The creation of Samuel "Roxy" Rothafel, a free-spending impresario, the Roxy Theatre cost $11 million to build, but like a yacht, upkeep was the real problem. Sandwiched between the Scylla of the older Capitol Theatre and the Charybdis of the new Radio City Music Hall, the Roxy was never able to top its premiere as far as success was concerned.

To its credit, the management tried just about everything to make the mammoth theatre successful, including spending lots of money. Its stage shows featured everything from dog acts to the New York Philharmonic; its chorus of Roxyettes and three pipe organs kept things jumping. But, except for the war years, when the movie industry was booming everywhere, the Roxy had trouble paying its bills.

In 1956, the twenty-nine-year-old house was purchased by Rockefeller Center, Inc. A major renovation followed and the Roxy reopened in April of 1958. It was impossible, however, to keep the 5,717-seat auditorium even close to filled, especially with *The*

Gazebo, the Glenn Ford-Debbie Reynolds vehicle which was the Roxy first-run feature in February of 1960, when the management made the final decision to throw in the towel. (The stage show accompanying the film, by the way, included such household names as Dick Roman, Maria Neglia, Harrison and Kossi, Les Marthys, and the Bizarro Brothers.)

After the stage show-movie format was discontinued on 23 February, the Roxy ran double-feature revival films, finally closing on 29 March 1960. The last night's feature was a two-year old British romance entitled *The Wind Cannot Read*, starring Dirk Bogarde.

By midsummer, the Roxy was demolished to make room for a 900-room and 600-car garage addition to the Taft Hotel.

The Last of The Legion of Decency

Founded in 1934 by a committee of U. S. bishops, the Roman Catholic censorship board known as the Legion of Decency had the announced purpose of arousing public opinion against "objectionable" motion pictures. The term "objectionable," of course, pertained not only to violence and sexuality, but to any anti-religious sentiments which might be expressed or inferred in the picture.

Publishing its reports in Catholic newspapers across the nation, the Legion of Decency exerted enormous pressure on the motion picture industry for a quarter of a century. Its rating system classified films into categories ranging from A-1 ("morally unobjectionable for general patronage") to C ("condemned"). No reference was made to the film's artistic value, the avoidance of pre-marital sex, divorce, and irreverence being more important to the group's members. Periodically the legion elicited annual pledges from church-goers across the nation or threatened to boycott a film, which was usually enough to panic most producers and studios.

Under its rating system, the Legion condemned films such as Roman Polanski's *Knife in the Water* (1961) because of "nudity in the treatment," and Ingmar Bergman's *The Silence* (1963) because the director's "selection of images is sometimes vulgar, insulting to a mature audience and dangerously close to pornography." In an indirect manner, the legion was also responsible for elimination of homosexual references from *Cat on a Hot Tin Roof* (1958) and *Spartacus* (1960), probably the last Hollywood productions to perform such obeisance.

By the early 1960s, the twentieth century had started to catch up with the Legion of Decency, which began to face pressure to bring itself in line with changing public taste and a liberal interpetation of obscenity by the U.S. Supreme Court. Nevertheless, the legion gave a C rating to the sincere and socially important motion picture *The Pawnbroker*, in 1965, merely for showing a woman's breasts.

That was the last major film to feel the Legion's impact. A reorganization in 1966 changed the organization's official name to the National Catholic Office for Motion Pictures. In line with Pope John XXIII's policy of updating Catholic thought, the new organization was a pale, de-fanged shadow of its former self.

The Last of Ford's Theatre, Baltimore

Six years after Abraham Lincoln was assassinated in Washington and the U. S. government ordered Ford's Theatre there closed, owner John T. Ford came to Baltimore and opened another theatre. Its first production, in 1871, was Shakespeare's *As You Like It* with James W. Wallack.

Not long afterward, Gilbert and Sullivan's smash musical hit, *H.M.S. Pinafore*, had its American debut at the Baltimore Ford's Theatre, and a tradition was started. Ford's was considered a good place to try out a show. In fact, producer David Belasco considered it unlucky to open his plays anywhere else. Over the years, most of the truly important plays — and many stiffs — were seen at Ford's. In 1930, Alfred Lunt played opposite Lynn Fontanne in *Elizabeth the Queen*. It was there that Tallulah Bankhead did *The Skin of Our Teeth*, and Humphrey Bogart and Judith Anderson performed *Saturday's Children*.

As more and more Baltimoreans moved to the suburbs and public transportation declined, however, it became a chore getting to what was called the "Temple of the Drama," much less finding a parking space. And so, the theatre was torn down to make room for a parking lot.

The last performance took place on 2 February 1964, the curtain going up on *A Funny Thing Happened on the Way to the Forum*, starring Jerry Lester, Arnold Stang, Paul Hartman, and Edward Everett Horton. When the curtain came down, the audience stood and sang "Auld Lang Syne."

Among the crowd on hand for the occasion was a gentleman who collected doorknobs from landmarks. Seeing him standing outside with a screwdriver, the police chased him away.

The Last Performance at the "Old Met"

It is no easy matter to save a landmark in New York City. Lovers of the old Metropolitan Opera House at Broadway and 39th Street discovered that fact during the early months of 1966. Although plans had been made to demolish the superb auditorium which opened on 22 October 1883 and replace it with a showroom for the fashion industry, it was hoped that somehow the old structure could be saved. A strong preservation campaign caused nearly everyone in the area — and much of the nation — to take sides, a phenomenon that inspired cartoonist Whitney Darrow, Jr. to caption a *New*

Yorker cartoon of a wife visiting her husband in prison,"Tell me, Harry, what's the consensus in your cell block on saving the old Met?"

On Saturday afternoon, 16 April 1966, the last scheduled opera at the old Met was followed by a gala farewell performance in the evening. The matinee featured the Met's 444th rendering of Puccini's *La Boheme*, with Richard Tucker, Gabriella Tucci, Jerome Hines, and Fernando Corena the principals. Later, an audience of 4,000 began to arrive in Rolls-Royces, Mercedes, Cadillacs, limousines — patrons of the opera who had paid up to $200 a ticket for the opportunity of hearing the last notes die away at the old Met. (One estimate placed the total value of the crowd's furs at $10 million.) Among the assembled was former heavyweight boxing champion Gene Tunney, a longtime fan of opera.

The gala performance began at 8:10 with Leopold Stokowski conducting Wagner's "Entrance of the Guests" from *Tannhauser*, and ended at 1:30 the next morning with the singing of the final trio from Gounod's *Faust*, the opera which had opened the old Met 83 years before. The singers were Hines, Tucci, and Nicolai Gedda, with George Pretre conducting the orchestra.

After the audience sang "Auld Lang Syne," the auditorium that a rival impresario of the 1880s called "that new yellow brewery on Broadway" began to empty for the last time. A few guests lingered to look for souvenirs, but most of the metal seat numbers were already gone. One man was observed stealing a light bulb while a well-known singer got away with a chair. Ouside, the posters proclaiming the gala performance were also taken.

Nine months later, the final act of the old Metropolitan Opera House was accompanied by an anvil chorus of wreckers, all final attempts to save the building having failed. As the stage was being torn up, Huntington Hartford, perennial patron of lost preservation causes, warned dolefully, "This is going to give America a black eye for years to come."

The Beatles' Last Performance

When the Beatles — John Lennon, Paul McCartney, George Harrison and Ringo Starr — arrived in the United States for their fourth American concert tour, there was little indication that the singing group was about to retire — or become focus of a very serious controversy.

Making their last English public appearance at Wembley on 1 May 1965, the Beatles came to the United States in early August of 1966, only to discover that their music was being banned on many American radio stations.

Sparked by a statement made in an interview with Maureen Cleave of the *London Evening Standard*, dozens of stations in the

Bible Belt had stripped their libraries of Beatles' music. In answer to a question dealing with the importance of religion and Christianity, Lennon had said, "Christianity will go. It will vanish and shrink. I needn't argue about that. I'm right, and I will be proved right. We're more popular than Jesus right now. I don't know which will go first — rock n' roll or Christianity. Jesus was all right, but his disciples were thick and ordinary."

Horrified by the comments, Tommy Charles, manager of a Birmingham, Alabama, radio station, said, "We just felt it was so absurd and sacriligious that something ought to be done to show them they cannot get away with this sort of thing." A public announcement was made that henceforth the Beatles' records would be banned.

Other stations followed suit, even scheduling bonfires for the burning of Beatles records and pictures. In Reno, Nevada, station KCBN broadcast an anti-Beatle editorial every hour and announced a rally to burn Beatles albums. Boycotts of music by the offending quartet were announced by radio stations in Ashland, and Hopkinsville, Kentucky; Dayton, Bryan, and Akron, Ohio; Dublin, Georgia; Jackson, Mississippi; Barnwell, South Carolina; and Corning, New York. On the other hand, station WSAC in Fort Knox, Kentucky, began playing Beatles music for the first time "to show our contempt for hypocrisy personified."

The controversy soon took on global perspectives. On 10 August 1966, shares in the Beatles' Apple Music Company took a slide on the London stock market, dropping from $1.64 to $1.26. In Pamplona, Spain, and in Johannesburg, South Africa, radio stations added their votes to the display of anti-Beatlemania.

Meanwhile, the Beatles landed at O'Hare International Airport in Chicago, disembarking at a maintenance hangar in order to avoid a crowd waiting for them at the main terminal. Speaking before television cameras at a North Side hotel, John Lennon issued a sort of apology. "I'm not anti-God, anti-Christ, or anti-religion," he said. "I was not knocking it. I was not saying we are greater or better. I suppose if I had said television was more popular than Jesus, I would have got away with it. I am sorry I opened my mouth."

Referring to the record-burning threats, he then added, "I think its a bit silly. If they don't like us, why don't they just not buy the records?"

Two days later, although Lennon had not asked, the Vatican City newspaper *L'Osservatore Romano* accepted his apology. "It cannot be denied that there is some foundation to the latest observation of John Lennon about atheism or the distraction of many people," the editor noted. In London, the *Catholic Herald* added that Lennon's

43

remarks were "arrogant," but "if a worldwide opinion poll could be taken, we would probably find that John Lennon was speaking the bare truth."

Finally left in peace to do what they did best, the Beatles toured the United States, giving their final concert at Candlestick Park, San Francisco, on 29 August. There were no tears, since only Brian Epstein, the Beatles' manager, fully realized it was the end of the road for the group.

Any lingering hope that the quartet would be reunited died on 9 December 1980, when John Lennon was murdered by a demented fan.

Milton Cross' Last Opera Broadcast

"Good afternoon, opera lovers from coast to coast," the mellifluous voice intoned every Saturday afternoon, as between 12 and 15 million radio listeners sat back to enjoy the Texaco Metropolitan Opera broadcasts. More than 800 times during the course of 43 years, announcer Milton Cross invited Americans to share his enthusiasm for grand opera, describing the scenery and costumes, explaining often convoluted plots, anything to bring closer to his audience the unseen visual aspects of the musical drama they were about to share with him.

He never approached his job as the spokesman for an elite group. "The majority of our listeners by far are plain, average American folks who have never attended an operatic performance," he once observed, "but who have made acquaintance with it and come to love it entirely through radio. That the number of such listeners extends into the millions is the richest and most encouraging word possible."

Never speaking down to his listeners, Cross spent many hours in the New York Public Library perusing scores, comparing lyrics, and studying the lives of composers and singers. He frequently went to rehearsals of new productions and even studied the sets beforehand to be absolutely accurate in his descriptions.

One of the last vestiges of the golden age of radio, he had a voice that brought him instant recognition. During a trip one summer to the Bayreuth Festival in Germany, a woman seated in front of him suddenly swiveled in her chair and exclaimed: "Why, Mister Cross!"

Born in 1897, Cross studied singing at the Damrosch Institute (later to become the Julliard School of Music), then took a job as a ballad singer with WJZ, the Westinghouse station in Newark, in 1922. That led to announcing and then to describing opera broadcasts with the Chicago Civic Opera. His first opera with the Metropolitan was on Christmas Day of 1931, a performance of Humperdinck's *Hansel and Gretel*.

The then-innovative idea of having a between-the-scenes narrator generated thousands of letters from grateful listeners. One person in Indianapolis wrote: "We all agreed it was the best program we have ever been privileged to hear over the air." A Pennsylvania housewife added: "We voted to set aside a small sum each week to devote to a trip to New York to see and hear opera in the Metropolitan Opera House."

From then on, Cross was an institution every Saturday from December to April. He died on 3 January 1975 of an apparent heart attack at his home in New York City, while preparing for the next day's broadcast of Rossini's *L'Italiana in Algeri*. The week before, on 28 December 1974, Cross had hosted Puccini's *Turandot*, his last broadcast.

Toward the end of his career, Cross' meticulous intonations lost some of their precision and he even made occasional flubs. His army of listeners only loved him more for it. His most-rembered on-the-air spoonerism occurred when, intending to remind his listeners to stay tuned for the news, he said, "Now stay stewed for the nudes."

Guy Lombardo's Last New Year

Scoffed at by critics as the "king of corn," band leader Guy Lombardo played and replayed his "sweetest music" until he became a national institution. The more popular he became, the angrier grew his detractors. "The reason why Guy Lombardo is so popular is because the world has so many dumb people," one churlish critic declared.

Lombardo's response was typically mellow. "We're giving the public what they want," he said. "We don't force bad songs on them. We play music people like to hum while they're dancing." Thus as jazz and popular music underwent numerous vogues, Lombardo was able to add: "We lost 'em in the teens sometimes, but we catch 'em again later on."

Born Gaetano Albert Lombardo, the eldest son of musically trained parents, Lombardo played in or led a band for sixty-three of his seventy-five years, starting out in the women's clubs of London, Ontario, his birthplace. With brothers Carmen, Victor, and Lebert, he moved the band to Cleveland in 1925 where he played on a local radio station without pay. Two years later, he made his first network broadcast from Chicago.

Moving to the Roosevelt Grill in New York in 1929, he made his first New Year's Eve broadcast there, playing :"Auld Lang Syne" on the stroke of midnight. After the grill closed in the 1960s, the traditional Lombardo New Year's celebrations moved to the grand ballroom of the Waldorf-Astoria. It was there that he gave his forty-eighth and last performance, welcoming in the new year of 1977.

He died on 5 November 1977. For the preceding 40 years, he had never earned less than $1 million annually, selling a grand total of 400 million records.

Li'l Abner's Last Comic Strip

First appearing in 1934, the "Li'l Abner" comic strip outlived seven U.S. Presidents, at its height was syndicated in 900 newspapers around the world, was made into a 1956 Broadway musical, and earned creator Al Capp $500,000 a year at the peak of his fame.

"In his prime, he was one of the two or three greatest cartoonists this country has ever produced," said David Manning White, a Virginia Commonwealth University Professor specializing in the comics.

Born Alfred Gerald Capp in 1909, the man who was often mentioned as a new Swift, Rabelais, or Mark Twain, felt uncomfortable at the comparison. "As soon as you think of yourself as a satirist, you're sunk," he once said. "You're pompous. You think your words have great and enduring meaning. I was a cartoonist."

Despite his protestations, of course, there was never any denying Capp's satirical bent. His outrageous satire of politicians, such as the baby-kissing blowhard, Senator Jack S. Phogbound, and the greedy General Bullmoose ("what's good for General Bullmoose is good for the nation") made him the darling of political liberals during the 1950s.

But during the 1960s he changed from darling to demon by creating Joanie Phoanie, a Joan Baez-type folk singer who ate caviar while warbling about poverty and protest. He also created the organization known as S.W.I.N.E.--Students Wildly Indignant about Nearly Everything, further incurring liberal wrath.

Capp's explanation for the switch was a simple one "When conservatives were fraudulent, I attacked them," he said. "The liberals loved me. The conservatives maintained an icy silence. Then liberals became too suffocatingly smug. I attacked them."

On a less political level, Capp peopled his strip with lovable types such as Li'l Abner himself, the bigfooted, painfully shy, impoverished hillbilly; Daisy Mae, his enamored pursuer, and later his wife; pipe-smoking Mammy Yokum, and Joe Btfsplk, the unhappy charcter who moved beneath a perennial black cloud. "He's created some characters that will go down in the history of our times," said cartoonist Charles Addams. " The names and general connotations have become part of the language."

Suffering from emphysema, Capp finally gave up the comic strip at the age of sixty-eight, deciding to kill it completely rather than sell it to another artist. "I think I stayed on longer than I should have," he said. "There's no goodbye strip...it seems to me cheap to say something maudlin. Whatever you say is a strip too much, so I

just broke off. There's a story and it cuts without any farewell, without any goodbye. Now I'm going to see if I can get breathing again."

The final Li'l Abner strip appeared on 13 November 1977. Almost two years later, on 5 November 1979, Al Capp died.

Walter Cronkite's Last Newscast

After nineteen years as the anchorman of "The CBS Evening News," a period during which he projected a warm father image and became one of the most trusted public figures in America, Walter Cronkite ended his own era on Friday, 6 March 1981.

"This is my last broadcast as the anchorman of the CBS Evening News," he said at the end of the show. "For me, it's a moment for which I have long planned but which nevertheless comes with some sadness. For almost two decades, after all, we've been meeting like this in the evenings. And I'll miss that."

His voice steady and eyes dry, Cronkite assured the television audience that, "Old anchormen, you see, don't fade away, they just keep coming back for more," alluding to the fact that he would reappear in future specials.

As a tribute to Cronkite's stature, even the rival television networks took note of his departure. John Chancellor, NBC anchorman for nearly a decade said, "He brought such distinction to his work as a network anchorman that he made the rest of us look better."

Cynics observed that some of the rival networks' approbation may have come from relief. For thirteen years, with Cronkite at the helm, "The CBS Evening News" was number one in audience ratings.

1519
Leonardo da Vinci: "I have offended God and mankind because my work didn't reach the quality it should have."
1628
Francois de Malherbe (Official poet of Henry IV and Louis XIII, stopping a priest's description of Heaven): "Hold your tongue! Your wretched style disgusts me!"

1635
Spanish dramatist, **Lope de Vega:** "Ah, I would willingly give all the applause I have received to have performed one good action more."

1668
William Davenport (after being unable to finish poem): "I shall ask leave to desist, when I am interrupted by so great an experiment as dying."

1719
Joseph Addison: "See in what peace a Christian can die."

1731
Daniel Defoe: "I do not know which is more difficult in a Christian life, to live well or to die well."

1757
French writer **Bernard de Fontenelle:** "I feel nothing except a certain difficulty in continuing to exist."

1774
Oliver Goldsmith (asked if his mind was at ease): "No, it is not."

1778
Voltaire (as bedside lamp flared up): "The flames already?"

1779
David Garrick: "Oh, dear!"

1784
Samuel Johnson (to a Miss Morris, daughter of a friend): "God bless you, my dear."

1788
Thomas Gainsborough: "We are all going to heaven and Van Dyke is of the company."

1791
Wolfgang Amadeus Mozart (commenting on the *Requiem*, his last work): "Did I not tell you that I was writing this for myself?"

1796
Robert Burns (referring to a bill collector): "That damned rascal, Matthew Penn!"

1809
Franz Josef Haydn: "Cheer up, chidren, I'm all right."

1815
John Singleton Copley (asked how he felt): "Happy, happy, supremely happy."

1816
Richard Brinsley Sheridan: "I am absolutely undone."

1817
Jane Austen (asked if she wanted anything): "Nothing but death."

1824
George Gordon, Lord Byron: "I want to sleep now."

1827
Charles Willson Peale (after his wife reported she could not feel his pulse): "I thought not."
1830
William Hazlitt: "Well, I have had a happy life."
1832
Johann Wolfgang von Goethe: "More light!"
1835
Charles Lamb: "My bedfellows are cramp and cough — we three all in one bed."
1835
Scottish poet, **James Hogg** (after severe hiccoughs): "It is a reproach to the faculty that they cannot cure the hiccough."
1845
English writer **Sydney Smith** (on being told he had swallowed ink instead of medicine by mistake): "Then bring me all the blotting paper there is in the house."
1847
Felix Mendelssohn (asked how he felt): "Weary, very weary."
1848
Emily Bronte: "If you will send for a doctor, I will see him now."
1849
Anne Bronte: "Take courage, Charlotte, take courage."
1850
Honore de Balzac (referring to a fictional doctor in his works): "If Bianchon were here, he would save me."
1855
Charlotte Bronte: "Oh, I am going to die, am I? He will not separate us. We have been so happy."
1856
Heinrich Heine: "God will pardon me. It's this profession." Then: " Write...write...paper!...pencil!...."
1861
Elizabeth Barrett Browning (asked how she felt): "Beautiful."
1862
Henry Thoreau: "One world at a time..." Then: "Moose...Indian..."
1862
John Drew: "This is but another act and I am playing my part."
1867
American poet **Fitz-Greene Halleck:** "Maria, hand me my pantaloons, if you please."
1875
Georges Bizet: "How are you going to tell my father?"
1875
Jean Baptiste Corot: "I hope with all my heart there will be painting in heaven."

1878
Author **Bayard Taylor:** "I want - I want - oh, you know what I mean, that stuff of life."
1880
George Eliot: "Tell them I have great pain in the left side."
1881
Modeste Mussorgsky: "It's the end. Woe is me."
1881
Thomas Carlyle: "So this is death...well..."
1882
Henry Wadsworth Longfellow (to sister): "Now I know that I must be very ill since you have been sent for."
1883
Richard Wagner: "I am fond of them, of the inferior beings of the abyss, of those who are full of longing."
1886
Franz Liszt: "Tristan!"
1886
Emily Dickinson: "I must go in for the fog is rising."
1888
Louisa May Alcott: "Is it not meningitis?"
1889
Robert Browning (informed of a favorable reception of his latest work): "How gratifying!"

1891
Phineas T. Barnum: "How were the circus receipts today at Madison Square Garden?"
1893
Edwin Booth (asked how he felt by grandson): "How are you yourself, old fellow?"
1897
Johannes Brahms (after some wine): "Ah, that tastes nice, thank you."

1898
Lewis Carroll: "Take away those pillows — I shall need them no more."
1899
Johann Strauss, Jr. (advised to sleep): "I will, whatever happens."
1900
Stephen Crane: "It isn't so bad. You feel sleepy...and you don't care. Just a little dreamy anxiety — which world you're in — that's all."

1900
Oscar Wilde (drinking champagne): "I am dying beyond my means."

1902
Samuel Butler: "Have you brought the checkbook, Alfred?"
1904
Anton Chekhov (given champagne): "I haven't drunk champagne for a long time."
1906
Henrik Ibsen (after his wife said he would get better): "On the contrary."
1907
Edvard Grieg: "Well, if it must be so."
1908
Joel Chandler Harris (asked how he felt): "I am about the extent of a gnat's eyebrow better."
1909
J. M. Synge: "It is no use fighting death any longer."
1909
George Meredith (referring to his physician): "I'm afraid Sir Thomas thinks very badly of my case."
1910
Gustav Mahler: "Mozart!"
1910
Leo Tolstoy: "I don't understand what I'm supposed to do."
1910
William Sydney Porter (O. Henry), to friend: "Charlie, I'm afraid to go home in the dark."
1911
William S. Gilbert (who saved a yong woman from drowning, then had heart attack): "Put your hands on my shoulders and don't struggle."
1913
Poet Joaquin Miller: "Take me away! Take me away!"
1915
Charles Frohman: "Why fear death? Death is only a beautiful adventure."
1921
Enrico Caruso: "Doro, I can't get my breath!"
1924
Franz Kafka (after ordering his works burned): "There will be no proof that I ever was a writer."
1924
Eleanora Duse: "We must stir ourselves. Move on! Work! Work! Cover me! Must move on! Must work! Cover me!"
1924
Anatole France: "Maman!"
1924
Giacomo Puccini: "My poor Elvira! My poor wife."

1926
Harry Houdini (to brother): "I'm tired of fighting, Dash. I guess this thing is going to get me."

1926
E.W. Scripps: "Too many cigars this evening, I guess."
1927
Isadora Duncan: "Adieu, my friends. I go on to glory."
1929
Sir Henry Arthur Jones (asked whether he would like either his niece or the nurse to spend the night at his bedside): "The prettier. Now fight for it."

1931
Anna Pavlova: "Get my swan costume ready."
1932
Hart Crane (just before he jumped overboard): "Goodbye, everybody."

1936
G. K. Chesterton: "The issue is now clear. It is between light and darkness and everyone must choose his side."
1936
Alban Berg (urged by his wife to stop working): "But I have so little time."

1937
James M. Barrie: "I can't sleep."
1937
Maurice Ravel: "Tell me not everything I wrote was bad."
1939
Douglas Fairbanks: "Never felt better."
1940
F. Scott Fitzgerald (asked by Sheilah Graham if he wanted some Hershey bars): "Good enough. They'll be fine."

1942
George M. Cohan (referring to his wife): "Look after Agnes."
1943
Alexander Woollcott (stricken during radio broadcast, speaking to cast member): "Go back in there. Never mind me. Go back in there."

1946
Gertrude Stein: "What is the answer? What was the question?"
1950
George Bernard Shaw: "Sister, you're trying to keep me alive as an old curiosity, but I'm done, I'm finished, I'm going to die."
1951
Andre Gide: "Before you quote me, be sure I'm conscious."

1952
Gertrude Lawrence (appearing in *The King and I*): "See that Yul gets star billing. He has earned it."

1956
Alexander Korda (after doctor gave him injection): "If I say good-night to you now, my friend, will you promise me that I won't wake up again?"

1959
Ethel Barrymore: "Is everybody happy?"

1965
Jeanette MacDonald (to husband, Gene Raymond): "I love you."

1972
George Sanders (suicide note): "I am leaving because I am bored."

1977
Joan Crawford (To housekeeper praying at her bedside): "Damn it ... Don't you dare ask God to help me."

Chapter Two

Sporting Lasts

Chronology

392 A.D.
Following a series of riots, the 293rd edition of the ancient Olympic Games proves to be the last, ending a sports tradition more than 1,100 years old. (see p. 64)

1791
(Jan. 17) British boxing champion Tom Jackling (real name Tom Johnson), a 4-1 favorite, loses the title in eighteen rounds to Big Ben Brian and never fights again.

1829
(Nov. 13) Sam Patch, a daredevil whose last stunt is fatal, dives from a 125-foot tower into the Genesee River near Rochester, New York. His body is not seen again until the spring of 1830. Patch is probably America's first professional sports casualty.

1875
America's most famous balloonist, Washington Donaldson, makes his last flight, which ends with his death in a crash.

1877
Champion trotting horse Goldsmith Maid runs her last race, wins it, and retires at the age of twenty.

1882
(June) Hindoo, one of the greatest racehorses of the nineteenth century, wins his last race at Gravesend racetrack, Sheepshead Bay, easily defeating Eole for the Coney Island Cup. Experts say Hindoo never races again because the two-and-a-quarter mile distance ruined him.

1889
(July 8) Boxing without gloves becomes a thing of the past as Jake Kilrain and John L. Sullivan fight the last bareknuckle championship fight. (see p. 65)

1892
(Oct. 15) The last no-hitter pitched from a distance of fifty feet is hurled by Charles Leander "Bumpus" Jones of Cincinnatti, his team winning over Pittsburgh, 7-1. In 1893, the distance between the pitcher's mound and homeplate is increased to sixty feet, six inches.

1896
Internationally-famous tightrope walker Blondin (Jean Francois Gravelet) makes his final appearance, at the age of 72 in Belfast, Ireland.

1897
Adrian Constantine "Cap"
Anson plays his twenty-second and final baseball
season, all with Chicago of
the National League. During
his last season he bats .302
in 114 games and at the age
of 46, is the oldest man to hit
a home run in the major
leagues.

1897
Baltimore beats Boston, four
games to one, in professional baseball's fourth and last
Temple Cup Series, the pale
attempt to generate post-
season interest by matching
the first- and second-place
clubs in a best-of-seven.

1903
(Aug. 14) "Gentleman Jim"
Corbett, aged thirty-seven,
goes into the ring for the last
time, losing a ten-round
decision to Jim Jeffries at
San Francisco.

1908
William G. Grace, champion
British cricket player since
1864, plays in his final
contest.

1909
Dan Patch, one of the greatest harness racing horses in
America, retires undefeated.
He is so famous that chewing
tobacco, cigars, pillows,
washing machines, and a
two-step dance are named
after him.

1910
"Wee Willie" Keeler ends a
nineteen-year career in
baseball, batting .300 in
nineteen games with the New
York Giants.
(July 4) Former heavyweight
boxing champion Jim Jef-
fries comes out of retirement
for his last fight, losing to
Jack Johnson on a fifteen-
round knockout.

1911
(Sept. 22) Although old for a
baseball player (44) and fat,
veteran pitcher Cy Young
manages to win the 511th
and last pitching victory of
his career. (see p. 66)

1915
(March 14) Stunt flier Lincoln
Beachey, who delights
crowds with his death-defying dives and loops, makes
his last flight, and crashes
into San Francisco Bay.

1916
(Sept. 4) In a unique double-
last, pitchers Christy
Mathewson and Mordecai
"Three-Finger" Brown pitch
the final games of their
careers, against each other.
(see p. 67)

1917
Honus Wagner plays his last
season with the Pittsburgh
Pirates, hitting .265 in seventy-four games.

1919
Ty Cobb hits .384 for the
season to win his last batting
title (his twelfth since 1907).

Ironically, in 1922 he bats .401 but loses the title to George Sisler's .420.

1920

(May 16) Spanish bullfighter Joselito, born 1895, is fatally gored fighting his last bull.

(Oct. 2) The Cincinnatti Reds and the Pittsburgh Pirates play major league baseball's last triple-header. (see p. 68)

(Oct. 12) In his final start, Man O'War, winner of nineteen out of twenty races, easily defeats Sir Barton at Kenilworth Park in Windsor, Ontario.

1922

J. Frank "Homerun" Baker plays his last major league season, appearing in sixty-nine games with the New York Yankees and batting .278. Despite his nickname, Baker hit only ninety-four homeruns in his thirteen-year career.

1924

(June 7) Veteran mountain-climber George Leigh-Mallory scales his last peak; he disappears only 775 feet from the summit of Mt. Everest.

1925

(Jan. 1) Notre Dame's "Four Horsemen" play together for the last time, leading the Irish to a victory in the Rose Bowl. (see p. 69)

1927

"The Big Train," Walter Johnson, plays his twenty-first and final season with the Washington Senators, winning just five games and losing six before retiring from the mound at age forty.

1928

(April 7) At the age of forty-four, Lester Patrick, manager-coach of the New York Rangers, plays the last game of his career — and his first as goalie, filling in for injured Lorne Chabot. The Rangers win the game, 2-1 in overtime, and Patrick retires once again.

(July 21) Heavyweight boxing champion Gene Tunney, thirty, scores a twelve-round TKO over Tom Heeney of Australia and retires undefeated.

Veteran outfielder Tris Speaker plays his twenty-second and last season, appearing in sixty-four games with the Philadelphia Athletics and hitting .267, seventy-seven points below his lifetime average.

1929

William Tatum Tilden II wins his seventh and last U.S. National Lawn Tennis Championship before turning professional.

1930

The last attempt by Sir Thomas Lipton to win the America's Cup yacht race ends in failure for the British tea tycoon, who began his quest in 1899 and spent $10 million dollars on losing efforts. He dies in 1931 at the age of eighty-one.

Pitcher Grover Cleveland Alexander fails to win a game in his last season, giving up forty hits in twenty-one and two-thirds innings for the Philadelphia Phillies.

1931

Fans of the Indianapolis 500 witness the last race in which the winner averages less than 100 miles per hour (Lou Schneider: 96.629 mph).

1932

(March 20) The pride of Australia, thoroughbred racehorse Phar Lap wins the $50,000-added Agua Caliente Handicap in Tijuana, later dying of arsenic poisoning when a nurseryman accidentally sprays his grazing area.

Levi Burlingame, an active jockey for sixty years, rides his last race in Stafford, Kansas, at the age of eighty. He falls from the horse, breaks his leg, and retires thereafter.

(Aug. 15) At the age of thirty-seven, former heavyweight boxing champion Jack Dempsey, attempting a comeback, fights for the last time, being outpointed by King Levinsky.

1933

In the last game of the season, Babe Ruth enter-

tains New York Yankee fans by pitching one last time.

It is the last year the leading thoroughbred racehorse earns less than $100,000 (Singing Wood: $88,050).

1934

The 1934 season is the last in which all baseball games are played in the daytime.

Pitcher Burleigh Grimes throws the last legal spitball. (The pitch was outlawed in 1920, but those already throwing it were allowed to continue.)

1935

(May 25) Babe Ruth hits the last three home runs of his career, the blasts coming just five days before the final game of his career.

(Sept. 22) In Madrid, Juan Belmonte kills the 1,650th and last bull of his career, then retires.

1936

The year is the last during which the Professional Golfers' Association leader earns less that $10,000 (Horton Smith: $7,682).

1937

Rogers Hornsby ends an active baseball career of twenty-three seasons, hitting .321 in twenty games for the St. Louis Browns.

1938

The last James Bennett Gordon international balloon race (an annual event since

1906) is won by a Polish balloon team.

(Nov. 5) The last survivor of the players in college football's first game, William Preston Lane, dies at age eighty-seven. The game, played on 13 November 1869, saw Rutgers defeat Princeton, 6-4. Lane played for Princeton.

1939

(April 30) First baseman Lou Gehrig plays the final game of his career and ends his 2,130 game consecutive streak for the New York Yankees. (see p. 70)

(Aug. 7) The last auto races are run at Brooklands, one of England's earliest tracks.

1941

Jess Pritchett, a bowler who competed in every American Bowling Congress Championship except two since 1902, appears in his last tournament.

Despite a mediocre (7-6) year in 1940, forty-one-year-old Robert Moses "Lefty" Grove manages to win seven games with the Boston Red Sox in 1941. The seventh and last victory is the 300th of his career.

1942

(March 27) Heavyweight boxing champion Joe Louis meets his twenty-first and last "Bum of the Month" (since winning the title on 22 June 1936), knocking out Abe Simon in the sixth round. (see p. 71)

(Oct. 24) Practically extinct as a means of scoring in football, the dropkick comes to life one last time to help decide a close contest.

1945

Don Hutson, star receiver for the Green Bay Packers, plays his final season, catching forty-seven passes, scoring ten touchdowns and kicking thirty-one of thirty-five points-after touchdowns.

1947

Six years after retiring from baseball, Jay Hanna "Dizzy" Dean, returns to the mound for one final fling with the St. Louis Browns. He lasts four innings, giving up one base on balls, three hits and no earned runs. He does not receive credit for the victory, however.

(Aug. 27) Called the greatest bullfighter in the world, Manolete fights his last bull, dying at the age of thirty from wounds suffered in the contest. (see p. 72)

Mel Ott winds up his twenty-two year baseball career with the New York Giants, failing to get a hit in four at-bats as a pinch-hitter.

1948

At the age of eighty-two, Professor Ivy Baldwin, a tightrope walker, takes his final stroll, across a Colorado canyon. (see p. 73)

1950

(April 26) After nearly four decades, thoroughbred horse racing comes to an end at Havre de Grace Track in Maryland.

(Oct. 1) After exactly a half-century at the helm, Connie Mack manages his last game for the Philadelphia Athletics. (see p. 74)

The last National Football League championship game is played for which any player receives less that $1,000. (Winning Cleveland players get $1,113, losing Los Angeles players get $686.)

1951

Joe DiMaggio plays his final year with the New York Yankees, appearing in 116 games and batting .263.

1952

(March 23) Sixty-four-year-old Willie Hoppe wins his fifty-first and last billiards title, by defeating Japanese star Kinrey Matsuyama, 50-37, in sixty tense rounds.

(Sept. 21) Before a meager crowd of 8,822, the last major league baseball game at Boston's Braves Field is played. (see p. 75)

(Sept. 29) Powerboat racer John Cobb rides his last mile, his craft disintegrating on the smooth waters of Loch Ness, Scotland, while it is going more than 200 miles per hour during a race against time to set a record.

(Dec. 14) One of the most durable and versatile of National Football League players, Sam Baugh of the Washington Redskins plays his last game at the age of thirty-seven. (see p. 76)

1954

Mildred Ella "Babe" Didrikson Zaharias wins her fifty-sixth and last major golf tournament despite being ill with cancer since 1953. She dies in 1956 at the age of forty-two.

(April 19) Clarence Demar of Boston, winner of seven Boston Marathons (the first in 1911 and last in 1930), competes in the event for the last time at the age of sixty-five. He finishes seventy-eighth, going the distance in 3:58:34.

Roger Bannister, first man to run an official sub-four minute mile, retires from racing.

1955

(May 31) Racing driver "Wild Bill" Vukovich rides his last race, dying in an accident during the "Indianapolis 500."

(Sept. 21) Heavyweight boxing champion Rocky Marciano knocks out Archie Moore in the ninth round of their title fight in New York City, then retires undefeated.

Bruising fullback Marion Motley plays his last season of pro football, gaining only eight yards in two carries for the Pittsburgh Steelers.

1956

The eighteenth and last season of pitcher Bob Feller is a poor one. Appearing in nineteen games, the once "Rapid Robert" gives up sixty-three hits in fifty-eight innings for an 0-4 mark with the Cleveland Indians.

Jackie Robinson plays his tenth and final year with the Brooklyn Dodgers, hitting .275 in 117 games.

1957

(Sept. 24) After nearly a half-century, the last major league baseball game at Brooklyn's famous Ebbets Field is played. (see p. 77)

At Nurburgring, auto racing driver Juan Manuel Fangio wins his last championship race, then retires from Grand Prix competition a five-time champion.

(Sept. 29) In use since 1889, the Polo Grounds are used for the last time by the New York Giants baseball team. (see p. 80)

The Philadelphia Phillies become the last team in the National League to break the color barrier on signing black third baseman John Kennedy. (see p. 79)

1959

The Boston Red Sox, last team in the American League to have an all-white team, break the color barrier with the signing of Pumpsie Green. (see p. 79)

1960

(Sept.28) Ted Williams, 42, ends his playing career by hitting a 420-foot home run off the Baltimore Orioles' Jack Fisher. It is his 29th home run of the year and 521st of his 19-season career.

1961

Robert Garrett, last survivor of America's first Olympic team, dies at the age of eighty-five.

(Sept.) Count Wolfgang von Trips, one of the world's fastest auto racing drivers, is killed along with eleven spectators in a horrendous accident at the Grand Prix of Italy at Monza.

1962

(April 3) Jockey Eddie Arcaro, retires after 31 years, riding in 24,092 races and earning $30,039,543 in purses.

(April 23) British auto racing driver Stirling Moss drives his Lotus into an embankment at Greenwood, England, breaking nearly every bone in the left side of his body. He survives, but races no more.

The Washington Redskins, last team in the National Football League to have an all-white lineup, finally break the color barrier by drafting running back Ernie Davis and trading him to Cleveland for black receiver Bobby Mitchell. (see p. 80)

1963
(May 25) Great Britain officially ends its traditional amateur-professional class distinction in cricket.

Stan Musial plays his last game with the St. Louis Cardinals, batting .255 in 124 games.

Fullback Joe Perry plays his sixteenth and last season of pro football, carrying the ball twenty-four times for a total of ninety-eight yards with the San Francisco Forty-Niners.

Like Lefty Grove, pitcher Early Wynn stays around past his prime in order to win his 300th career victory. It's his final season, with the Cleveland Indians, producing a mark of one victory and two losses.

(Nov. 11) Alex Delvecchio of the Detroit Red Wings plays the last of 548 consecutive hockey games, ending a streak that began on December 13, 1956.

1964
Boris Shakhlin, winner of ten world gymnastics championships for the Soviet Union, retires.

Dick "Night Train" Lane makes the last of his sixty-eight career interceptions with the Detroit Lions, returning the ball eleven yards. He retires from professional football after an unproductive 1965 season.

1965
(April 28) Sir Stanley Matthews, British soccer star, ends his career at the age of fifty in an all-star game played at Stoke-on-Trent.

Warren Spahn closes out his twenty-one season baseball career by winning seven games and losing sixteen, playing for both the New York Mets and the San Francisco Giants.

After falling and fracturing his hip on 29 July, Casey Stengel retires the following month as manager of the New York Mets, ending a fifty-four year baseball career.

(Nov. 4) Johnny Kerr of the NBA Syracuse team, the most durable of professional basketballers, plays the last of his 844 consecutive games, ending a streak that began on 31 October 1954.

1966
(Oct.6) Sandy Koufax pitches the last game of his baseball career in the second game of the World Series against the Baltimore Orioles. Sabotaged by Willie Davis' 3 successive errors in the fifth inning, Koufax takes the loss and retires from baseball with an overall record of 169 wins and 90 losses, counting 4 World Series with the Dodgers.

Jim Brown, star running back of the Cleveland Browns. retires after nine years of pro football.

Durable jockey Johnny Longden rides his 32,407th race, last in a career dating back to 1926.

Star receiver-rusher Ollie Matson plays his fifteenth and final year in the NFL, carrying the ball 29 times for 101 yards for the Philadelphia Eagles. He also returns 26 kickoffs for a total of 544 yards.

1967

Edward Charles "Whitey" Ford's sixteenth and final year with the New York Yankees produces only two wins and four losses. Ford retires with a lifetime mark of 236-106.

Playing in his twenty-first and final season for the Cleveland Browns, Lou Groza kicks the last of his 234 career field goals.

1968

(April 7) Auto racing driver Jim Clark, winner of 19 out of 30 contests, rides his last race at Hockheim, West Germany, his car crashing while moving 175 miles per hour.

Mickey Mantle plays his last season with the New York Yankees, batting .237 in 144 games.

1969

(Dec. 21) Having moved from Green Bay to Washington, celebrated football coach Vince Lombardi finishes his career with a loss. (see p. 82)

1970

(June 21) In the ninth and last World Cup soccer championship to be played under the official title of the Jules Rimet Trophy, Brazil is victorious over Germany.

(Sept. 2) Chicago Cubs outfielder Billy Williams plays the final contest of his 1,117 game streak, tops for durability in the National League.

(Dec. 3) After five years in the American League, Emmett Ashford, first black umpire, retires at the age of fifty-six.

1971

(July 18) Internationally-famous soccer star Pele plays his last game for Brazil, retiring from world competition. (see p. 82)

1972

(Sept. 30) Roberto Clemente of the Pittsburgh Pirates doubles, for the 3,000th and last hit of his major league career. Shortly afterward, he dies in a plane crash.

(Nov. 2) Freddie Parent, last survivor of the first modern World Series in 1903, dies at ninety-six. (see p. 84)

1973

(May 8) Ralph Darwin Miller, America's last nineteenth-century baseball player, dies at the age of 100.

1974

(July 24) After gaining more than 40,00 yards during a

professional football career going back to 1965, master quarterback John Unitas announces his retirement.

1975
(July 6) Champion filly Ruffian breaks her leg in her last race, a match with Foolish Pleasure, and has to be destroyed. (see p. 84)

1976
(July 20) Two years after blasting record-breaking home run number 715, Henry Aaron hits the last home run of his long and illustrious career. (see p. 85)

The last college All-Star-Professional football championship game is held at Chicago, ending the series that started in 1934. As usual, the Pros win in a thunderstorm-shortened contest.

1978
(March) Karl Wallenda, septuagenarian tightrope-walker, is killed in a 123-foot fall while walking between two hotels in San Juan, Puerto Rico. (see p. 86)

1979
Establishing an iron-man record for the National Football League, 41-year old defensive end Jim Marshall of the Minnesota Vikings plays the 302nd consecutive and last game of his career. Dallas Cowboy quarterback Roger Staubach throws the last pass of his pro career in a 21-19 playoff loss to Los Angeles, an incompletion intended for Drew Pearson. His last pass that is caught is done so inadvertently by Dallas offensive lineman Herb Scott.

1980
Hockey immortal Gordie Howe, fifty-two, finally retires, playing his last game for the National Hockey League Hartford Whalers. Howe began his career in 1946 with the Detroit Red Wings.

The Last Ancient Olympics

Dating as far back as the fifteenth century B.C., the ancient Olympic Games were first held in 776 B.C. at Olympia, on the border of Greece and Macedonia. The first recorded winner was Coroebus, representing Elis, a southern district of Greece.

Originally restricted to running contests, the ancient Olympics became longer (from a one-day to a five-day event by 472 B.C., year of the seventy-seventh Olympiad) and more sophisticated, offering a variety of athletic contests as the games became more popular. During the seventh century B.C., wrestling, boxing, horseback riding and chariot racing were added. The year 396 B.C. saw the introduction of a foot race in which the contestants wore armor. Incidentally, the marathon run was never part of the ancient Olympics.

The first Olympians performed wearing loincloths, but in 720 B.C. they were abandoned after an accident. Orsippus of Macedon, lost his cloth after the race began and, "unimpeded," won going away. That started a trend toward nudity which, in turn, attracted more and more women spectators, who were barred from the games. They climbed trees and used other subterfuges in order to watch, despite the threat of being put to death.

One woman named Pherenice disguised herself as a trainer in order to see her son Peisidorus perform in the boxing events. When he won, Pherenice's joy gave away her secret, and she was later brought to trial. When the woman pleaded for mercy on the grounds of love and motherhood, she was released, but the judges ruled that in the future trainers would also have to appear naked at the games. Later, although the date is not known, the Olympic rule against women was relaxed.

In 66 A.D., Roman Emperor Nero presided over the Olympics when he visited Greece on a tour. (He fancied himself a singer, accompanying himself on the lyre, and made a journey to Greece to visit his talents on the populace.)

At first limited to young Greek men, the games were opened to Roman youths after Greece became part of the Roman Empire. Eventually, this led to discord and then scandal when the Greeks charged that the Romans were professionals. The Romans responded by setting fire to the athletes' dormitories and wrecking the stadium. Finally, Emperor Theodosius decided that the Olympics were more trouble than they were worth and cancelled the games after the 293rd Olympiad in 392 A.D.

After an uninterrupted span of more than 1,100 years, the ancient Olympic Games were over. The last recorded victor was a fellow named Varastad, an Armenian.

The Last Bareknuckle Championship Fight

Unlike later boxers who used padded gloves and fought within three-minute round limitations, prizefighters of the bareknuckle era had to be prepared to battle from a few seconds to several hours. Rounds ended when a man was thrown down or knocked to the ground, at which point he had thirty seconds to return to "scratch," the line drawn in the dirt from which each new round started. There was no limit to the number of rounds to a fight, if one boxer did not stay down.

Under these rules, many bareknuckle fights lasted quite a long time. In 1871, for example, Jem Mace and Joe Coburn "fought" a single round which lasted about an hour, not a solid blow being struck as the two men felt each other out. In 1825, Jack Jones and Patsy Tunney fought a 278-round marathon in Cheshire, England, which lasted 4½ hours.

By 1889, professional prizefighting was in the process of adopting the Marquis of Queensberry rules which called for the use of gloves, forbade wrestling or gouging, and limited rounds to three minutes. Thus, when American heavyweight champion John L. Sullivan met Jake Kilrain for the title on 8 July 1889, at Richburg, Mississippi, the bareknuckle style was definitely on its way out.

So, incidentally, were both fighters. Both past their primes, Kilrain and Sullivan exacerbated the aging process by being heavy drinkers and eaters. On the day before the title bout with Kilrain, Sullivan's breakfast consisted of a seven-pound sea bass, five soft-boiled eggs, a half-loaf of bread, a half-dozen tomatoes and a cup of tea. For lunch, he had a small steak, two slices of stale bread and a bottle of ale. Dinner consisted of three chickens with rice, Creole-style, and another half-loaf of bread dunked in chicken broth.

The next afternoon, under a broiling sun and a temperature of 107 degrees, Sullivan's stomach began to complain. He asked for some whiskey but his manager refused to allow him to drink it. In the meantime, Kilrain was busily guzzling shots of bourbon between rounds at the recommendation of one of the timekeepers, William "Bat" Masterson. Although taking a terrible beating, Kilrain's digestive tract seemed to be in better shape when Sullivan began to vomit in the forty-fourth round. After his manager finally permitted him a drink, Sullivan's spirits rose.

"Will you draw the fight?" Kilrain asked at this point.

"No, you son of a bitch," Sullivan replied, heaving furiously in Kilrain's general direction. "Stand up and fight."

Kilrain promptly stepped on Sullivan's foot with his three-eighths-inch spikes and knocked the champ sprawling with a chopping sledgehammer blow to the jugular. But somehow Sullivan managed to recover from the blow and went on to defeat Kilrain in seventy-five rounds.

The next time the champion fought for the title it was with gloves and against a younger and more agile opponent, James J. Corbett.

Kilrain continued to fight for a few years more before returning to Baltimore where he spent his remaining years as a bartender and local celebrity until his death in 1937.

Cy Young's Last Victory

Baseball records are made to be broken, but one of the least assailable seems to be pitcher Cy Young's 511 career victories. For one thing, few pitchers last twenty-two years in the major leagues; those who do are supported by an army of short, long, for-lefties- or righties-only relief hurlers.

Nevertheless, Young's record is remarkable. No other pitcher has even nudged the 500-win mark. Young passed that figure late in the 1910 season, his twenty-first in the major leagues. However, by the spring of 1911, Young was forty-four years old and so fat he could hardly bend down to pick up an immobile ball, much less run to handle a deftly bunted one. On 15 March, a sports flash from Hot Springs, Arkansas, carried the news that Young had quit.

The retirement did not last long. Young returned to the Cleveland Indians, won three games and lost four, then was released on 15 August. The last time he had pitched was 29 July against Washington. He was taken out of the game at the end of three innings after he gave up five runs in a 7-1 loss.

After being notified of his release, Young said he was not yet finished with the game, a statement that turned out to be true. Three days later he signed a contract with Boston of the National League, a team that could afford to take a chance, since it was fourteen-and-a-half games behind seventh place Brooklyn.

Between 22 August, his first day with Boston, and 2 September, Cy appeared in four games and won three of them. A tough loss followed, bringing Young's record with Boston to 3-1.

Then came a contest billed as a pitchers' duel between Young and Christy Mathewson on 12 September, the only time these two faced each other. More than 10,000 fans were on hand expecting to see Cy beat the Giants, but he had a terrible day. He gave up nine runs, including three homers, in less than three innings. The final score was New York 11, Boston 2.

After a tie game against St. Louis that was called because of darkness, Cy Young took the mound on 22 September against Pittsburgh at Forbes Field. Only 1,200 were on hand to see the great pitcher's final career victory, a 1-0 whitewashing of the home team. Young fanned Honus Wagner three times and ended the game by striking out pinch-hitter Tommy Leach with a man on second.

After this, Young lost the next three contests in which he appeared. His last game was a sorry affair, coming on 6 October, against Brooklyn. Cy was left in until the Dodgers had clobbered him for eleven runs, seven of them in one inning.

The next spring Young went south with Boston but finally retired, saying, "My arm will no longer do the work that was so easy."

Cy Young died on 4 November 1955, at the age of eighty-eight.

Baseball's Double Last

Baseball fans experienced the bittersweet emotions of a double last on 4 September 1916. Two great pitchers decided to end their long careers on that day by facing each other one more time.

The participants were Christy Mathewson and Mordecai Brown,

two pitching giants who have since entered the Baseball Hall of Fame.

Mathewson was born in 1880 and began his baseball career in 1900 with the New York Giants. After losing three games that year without a win (he gave up thirty-five hits and twenty-two bases on balls in thirty-four innings), "Matty" found the groove in 1901. From then until 1915, when he slumped to 8-14, he had only one losing season, four times winning thirty or more games. Then, in 1916, after appearing in twelve games with the Giants, Matty went to the Cincinnati Reds as manager. Taking over for Buck Herzog and Ivy Wingo, who together "led" the team to a 35-50 record (an average of .412), Matty won fourteen of the next forty-three games (a .326 average) as the team slipped into last place. Early in September, when the fifth place Chicago Cubs came to town, it was obvious that something needed to be done to heighten fan interest.

Fortunately for this aspect of the game, Mordecai Peter Centennial (born in 1876) Brown, otherwise known as "Three-finger" (for obvious reasons), was also nearing the end of the trail as a pitcher. Brown's best years had paralleled those of Matty, beginning in 1904, but by 1916, "Three-finger" was almost forty and had a 2-2 record for the season, which clearly would be his last.

By mutual agreement, the two pitchers decided to bow out together in the second half of the Sunday doubleheader at Chicago. Before the game, Mathewson and Brown each received a bouquet of American Beauty roses.

The Cubs jumped to a 2-0 lead in the bottom of the first inning but Cincinnati, led at the plate by Mathewson's double and two singles, kept pecking away at Brown until they enjoyed a 10-5 lead going into the bottom of the ninth inning. At that point, Matty nearly fell apart, yielding three runs, but he hung on to gain the 10-8 victory.

For Mathewson, who died in 1925, it was his 373rd career win against 188 losses. For Brown, who died in 1948, the defeat was his 130th against 239 victories.

Baseball's Last Triple-Header

During the nineteenth century, major league baseball teams occasionally played triple-headers, but the practice was discontinued after 1900.

An exception was made on 2 October 1920, largely because Cincinnati and Pittsburgh of the National League were fighting for third place and needed to play all their remaining games against each other to decide which team would prevail.

In order to get all three games in before sundown (there were no night games in those days), the first game began at noon. Visiting Cincinnati won the opener by a score of 13-4. They capitalized on a seven-run seventh inning to take the second contest, 7-3. In the third game, Pittsburgh was ahead, 6-0, when darkness settled over the city and the game was called.

The triple-header may have been wearying to both fans and players, but it was enjoyable to at least one person — 24-year-old "Jugglehandle Johnny" Morrison, who started his first game for Pittsburgh and won a 3-hit shutout. That started a pitching career which lasted until 1930, Morrison accruing a major league mark of 130 wins and 80 losses in 11 seasons.

Without the triple-header, he might never have gotten the chance to prove himself or to go into the record books as the last pitcher to win the third game of a baseball triple-header. There is little likelihood that fans of the present or future could tolerate such a glut of baseball, or that modern owners would ever again consent to provide three games for the price of one.

The Four Horsemen's Last Game

Still the most famous football offensive backfield of all time, the "Four Horsemen" of Notre Dame were so named by sportswriter Grantland Rice, who compared their inexorable quality to the biblical "Four Horsemen of the Apocalypse." The men, who played together for the first time in 1922, were quarterback Harry Stuhldreher, right halfback Don Miller, left halfback Jim Crowley, and fullback Elmer Layden.

While the Four Horsemen were at Notre Dame, the team won 27 games, lost 2 and tied 1, scoring a total of 782 points to 118 for the opposition.

The group's final contest was on 1 January 1925, when Notre Dame met Stanford in the Rose Bowl after an undefeated season. More than 52,000 spectators were on hand to see if Ernie Nevers, Stanford's 200-pound fullback, could match the power and speed of Notre Dame's line and Four Horsemen backfield.

The game started inauspiciously for the Irish, Stanford's line manhandling Notre Dame's second-stringers into position for a field goal. But in the second quarter, Notre Dame put together a long drive, as Layden plunged over from the three-yard line to make the score 6-3. Only minutes later, Layden intercepted a pass by Nevers and sprinted seventy-eight yards for another touchdown. The first half ended with the score Notre Dame 13, Stanford 3.

In the third quarter, Stanford's fate was sealed when its quarterback fumbled a punt on his own twenty-yard line. The Irish converted the error into a touchdown, to lead by 20-3.

Nevers singlehandedly got that TD back by intercepting a pass and working the ball to the eight-yard line. A short pass gave Stanford its first touchdown and brought the count to 20-10. Not long afterward, however, Layden intercepted another pass and carried it thirty-five yards for another score. The final result was Notre Dame 27, Stanford 10. As the game ended, thousands of fans listening to radio or watching at public halls where "gridgraphs" were set up rushed into the snow-covered streets of South Bend to celebrate.

Time dimmed the Four Horsemen's exploits, but only slightly. Notre Dame alumni everywhere mourned when, on 27 January 1965, Stuhldreher became the first of the legendary quartet to pass away. Layden, who played a year of professional football after graduation and then returned to Notre Dame as football coach and athletic director, died on 30 June 1973. Miller retired as a United States Court bankruptcy judge in 1965, and died at age seventy-seven on 29 July 1979.

Crowley is still alive, the last of the famous Four Horsemen.

Lou Gehrig's Last Game

The 1939 baseball season was just eight games old and New York Yankees star Lou Gehrig was just thirty-five when he decided to call it quits. "I went up there four times with men on base," he said, referring to the last game he played in which the Yankees lost to the Washington Senators, 3-2. "Once there were two there. A hit would have won the ball game for the Yankees, but I missed, leaving five stranded as the Yankees lost. Maybe a rest will do me some good. Maybe it won't. Who knows? Who can tell? I'm just hoping."

With that, the man with a lifetime batting average of .340 and 493 home runs ended his string of 2,130 consecutive games. The streak, never approached before or since, began on 2 June 1925, when the 21-year-old Gehrig was sent in to pinch-hit for Pee Wee Wanninger. (Ironically, Wanninger took over the shortstop position in 1925 from Lewis Everett "Deacon" Scott, whose record of 1,307 consecutive games was — and remains — the closest any player ever got to Gehrig's durability streak.)

Gehrig's final game, on 30 April 1939, saw him go 0-for-4 at the plate while making seven putouts and two assists at first base. For the season, he had four hits, all singles, in 28 at-bats for a batting average of .143. The man who led the league in 1931 with 184 RBIs batted in just one run in 1939. He was replaced in the lineup by 'Babe' Dahlgren.

Still unaware that Gehrig was suffering from a crippling disease of the nervous system, the newspapers speculated on his chronic lumbago and gall bladder problems, adding hopefully that Lou would be back once warm weather arrived.

Such was not the case, of course. Having saved a great deal of his salary, Gehrig retired gracefully, but his last days, during which he worked for the New York City Parole Commission, were not happy ones. His strength diminished rapidly and in 1940, when the Yankees collapsed late in the season, one New York newspaper attributed the team's failure to several key players having caught "Gehrig's disease." Gehrig angrily filed a $1 million libel suit against the paper, which quickly apologized, but the mental anguish may have hastened his decline.

He died on 2 June 1941, a couple weeks short of his thirty-eighth birthday. No cure has yet been found for his mysterious affliction, now nicknamed "Lou Gherig's disease."

Joe Louis' Last "Bum of the Month"

A fighting heavyweight champion, Joe Louis successfully defended his title twenty-one times between 30 August 1937 and 27 March 1942, earning $1,506,351 in the process. His opponents, nineteen of whom were knocked out, lasted an average of six rounds, one minute, before succumbing.

Partly because some of the fighters were not exactly household names (although Louis did not avoid any genuine contenders), reporters started referring to each new Louis victim as the "bum of the month." Louis took on all contenders, even after he entered the U.S. Army as a private early in 1942. Louis' earnings from his last two title fights, totaling $83,246, were donated to the Army and Navy Relief Funds.

Louis' last "bum of the month" was 6-foot-4-inch, 255-pound Abe Simon, who had given the heavyweight champion a good battle on 21 March 1941, lasting 13 rounds before being knocked out. The rematch took place on 27 March 1942 at New York's Madison Square Garden before a crowd of 18,200.

The first round was slow, both fighters sparring and searching for an opening, but in the second, Louis exploded a series of shots off the challenger's chin, sending him to the canvas for a count of two at the bell. Simon recovered in the third round and even came close to winning the fourth with some hard body-punching. Louis ended the round with a typical flurry of activity. The fifth round was marred by a low blow by Simon, which caused Louis to attack fiercely, knocking Simon down once again.

The challenger rose at the count of five and was once again saved by the bell. Early in the sixth round, Louis landed a right and left to Simon's jaw, bringing the fight to an end. In the dressing room later, the champion referred genially to Simon's butting and low blow tactics. "He didn't really hurt me," Louis said. "I had more trouble with his head than with his fists. In fact, his hardest punch was the one with which he hit me on the right hip."

For the next four years, Louis toured for the U. S. Army, putting on exhibitions. When he returned to active duty as heavyweight champion in 1946, he was thirty-two years old and a much less explosive fighter than before the war. Nevertheless, he successfully defended his title against Billy Conn, Tami Mauriello, and Jersey Joe Walcott twice, before retiring in 1949.

Unfortunately, Louis did not stay retired and therefore ran into some unhappy bouts himself. His last title fight came on 27 September 1950, when he was defeated on a fifteen-round decision by Ezzard Charles.

Louis continued the comeback trail during 1951 against a string of mediocre fighters. (His last knockout victory, incidentally, came on 15 June 1951, when he dispatched Lee Savold in six rounds.) Then, on 26 October, Louis ran into an up-and-coming fighter named Rocky Marciano. It was the last fight of Louis' career, Marciano wearing down the thirty-seven-year-old ex-champion before knocking him out in the eighth round.

Louis stayed retired after that, spending a great deal of time in Las Vegas where he was "on exhibit" as a handshaker and public relations man. He died in 1981 at the age sixty-six.

Manolete's Last Bull

Matadors and royalty are the only ones who live well.
— Spanish saying

During his brief life, Manolete lived extremely well. The most famous Spanish bullfighter was born Manuel Rodriguez in Cordoba, the great-nephew of a minor league bullfighter and son of a bullfighter who went blind and died in the poorhouse when Manuel was five years old.

In 1929, when he was twelve and working as a plasterer's assistant, Manolete got his first chance to fight a calf, but was knocked down twenty times and decided to remain in plastering.

After serving in the army, Manolete came under the influence of Jose Flores Camara, a 35-year-old matador who instructed him in the art of bullfighting. He began his professional career in 1934 and was a senior matador by 1939. Ten years later, he was recognized as the very best, spectators paying $100 a seat to see him.

In classic fashion, however, the rise to success took its toll. Manolete drank a great deal of American whiskey and his timing began to suffer. Once, in Peru, he took nine thrusts to kill a bull and left the ring with tears streaming down his cheeks. His once-loyal followers were chanting, "Manolete, you couldn't even handle a robust field mouse if confronted by one in the bathroom." Stung by the criticism, Manolete retired at the end of 1946.

He was unable to live in peace during the following months, partly because he still had an itch for combat and partly because he was jealous of the success of Luis Miguel (Dominguin), the new matador who had replaced him in the fans' hearts. In 1947, Manolete came out of retirement and on 27 August appeared on the same program with Dominguin at Linares, Spain. The bulls they were to face were of the dreaded Miura strain, called "bulls of death" because of their ferocious and unpredictable natures.

Matador Gitanillo de Triana led off the card. Manolete followed, killing the second bull but missed his first thrust and thus lost the ear. After Dominguin and Gitanillo killed two more bulls, Manolete went once again into the ring.

His adversary was a Miura bull named Islero, which was immediately recognized as dangerous because it refused to follow the fluttering silks, stopping short on each charge to look at the man behind the cape. "Malo — bad, bad," a friend warned Manolete as they watched the warmup. "It hooks terribly to the right. Stay away from this one, Chico."

However, Manolete refused to play it safe. He performed a half-dozen perfect veronicas, finishing with a half-veronica that brought him so close to the bull that its neck hit and nearly knocked the matador to the ground. After several more passes, Manolete disdained the safer method of stabbing the bull from the side. Instead, he made his thrust from directly above. Just as the sword entered, Islero hooked ferociously, flinging Manolete high into the air. Twice the bull spiked the matador as he lay on the ground, then Islero pitched over dead.

Bleeding profusely from the thigh, Manolete was taken to the operating room and given four blood transfusions. He regained consciousness long enough to ask if the bull had died.

Assured that it had, Manolete then gasped, "Doctor, I can't feel anything in my right leg... Doctor, I can't feel anything in my left leg... I can't see!"

A few moments later, Spain's greatest bullfighter, a legendary figure who had made more than 2 million dollars, was dead at the age of 30.

Ivy Baldwin's Last Walk

For three decades before World War I, "Professor" Ivy Baldwin, a diminutive, mustachioed, fierce-eyed man with a fine sense of balance and a vast contempt for death, was as famous as many a king. Touring the world making balloon ascensions and parachute jumps, diving into nets from incredible heights and walking high wires, he was the supreme daredevil of his era.

Born in Houston, Texas, Baldwin began his death-defying career in 1881 when he was just fifteen. He traveled with circuses until 1892 when he turned his attention to ballooning. During the Spanish-American War he served with the Signal Corps and his balloon was shot down in the battle of Santiago.

His greatest moment came years later in 1907 when he went to Eldorado Springs, Colorado, to walk across a steel cable which resort owner Frank Fowler had strung across South Boulder Canyon. The cable was 635 feet long and more than 500 feet above a raging torrent. As 14,000 people watched, the "Professor" walked the dizzy wire with ease, pausing to stand on his head in the middle.

Taking a liking to Colorado, Baldwin settled there and continued walking across the high wire for a total of eighty-six times. Then, in 1928, he announced his retirement at the age of sixty-two. As the years passed, Baldwin continued to look longingly at the high wire still hanging rustily across the canyon. Finally, old, arthritic, and convinced the world had forgotten him, Baldwin decided to cross the canyon once more.

Resort owner Jack Fowler, son of the original owner and a brother of writer Gene Fowler, was horrified. Knowing that Baldwin had celebrated his eightieth birthday on 31 July 1946, he vehemently refused to allow Baldwin to make the attempt. The "Professor" persisted, until finally, in 1948, Fowler gave in. He strung a new and shorter wire lower in the canyon and reluctantly gave his permission for Baldwin to cross it.

On his eighty-second birthday, the "Professor" put on his tiny camel-hide shoes, picked up his 24-pound balancing pole and once again stepped out into the yawning space. Halfway across, he stooped, knelt creakily until one knee touched the wire, then lurched to an upright position and finished the stunt. Crowds below applauded, sang "Happy Birthday," and donated $425.25 for a present. The panting "Professor" was so invigorated by the response he walked across again the next day.

That was Baldwin's last walk. Five years later, on 9 October 1953, he died at the ripe age of eighty-seven.

Connie Mack's Last Game

"I am not quitting because I'm too old. I am quitting because I think the people want me to quit." Thus spoke eighty-eight-year-old Connie Mack (Cornelius Alexander McGillicuddy), shortly after he announced he was stepping down after a half-century of managing baseball's Philadelphia Athletics. The date was 18 October 1950. Probably one reason Mack remained manager for so long was that he had owned a controlling interest in the team since 1901.

Mack was correct in saying he had worn out his welcome. With the exception of a fourth place finish in 1948, the Athletics had finished in the second division of the American League every season since 1933. The team's last pennant came in 1931; its last World Series victory was in 1930. Wearied by the consistently poor performance of the A's, and intrigued by the improvement of the rival Phillies, Philadelphia fans were deserting the A's by the thousands. In 1949 the team had a paid attendance of 815,514; in 1950 total attendance plunged to 310,085. Still sharp-eyed enough to read the red ink without spectacles, Mack decided to call it quits.

Born in 1862, he broke into organized baseball as a catcher in 1884, making it to the major leagues two years later. After a four-teen-year playing career with Washington, Buffalo, Pittsburgh and Milwaukee (of the Western, later American, League) during which he fielded well and batted .251 including a grand total of two home runs, Mack left the field to manage. He remained with Milwaukee through 1900, then joined the Philadelphia A's.

The glory years for Mack and the team came in two long bursts: from 1901 to 1914, when the A's won six pennants and were out of the first division only twice; and from 1925 to 1933, a period which produced three pennants and no finish lower than third. The 1930 squad was one of baseball's best, winning 102 games during the regular season and defeating the St. Louis Cardinals in the World Series, 4 games to 2.

One of the most respected men connected with sports, the 6-foot-2-inch Mack was awarded the $10,000 Edward W. Bok prize for distinguished service to Philadelphia in 1929. Before then, the award had gone only to artists, scientists, educators, and philanthropists.

After that, however, it was mostly downhill until 1950, a season which began with moderately high hopes and ended in disaster. By the time the Athletics played their last game for Mack on 1 October 1950, they were 5 games out of seventh place and 46 out of first. Only 1,387 fans turned out to see the end of Mack's half-century of managing. On the mound for the A's was 30-year-old rookie pitcher Johnny Kucab, who was in constant trouble during the game but managed to scatter the 12 hits for his first major league victory, defeating the Washington Senators by a score of 5-3. That brought down the curtain on the A's season, the team winning 52 games and losing 102. For Mack the victory was his 3,627th as manager of the A's against 3,891 losses.

Two-and-a-half weeks later, Mack announced that he was retiring. He sold his interest in the Athletics in 1955 and remained on the sidelines until his death on 8 February 1956, just two weeks short of his ninety-fourth birthday.

By then, the Athletics were gone from Philadelphia, having played their last season there in 1954 (51 wins, 103 defeats) before moving to Kansas City. Kucab was also gone, having retired from the major leagues in 1952 after a career total of 5 victories and 5 defeats.

The Last Game at Braves Field

Opened on 18 August 1915, Braves Field in Boston replaced the "South End Grounds," for forty-five years the home of the National League baseball team. Players who made the move said it was like going from a three-room apartment to a brand new mansion. "The Largest Ball Park in the World," postcards of that era rightfully called it. Standing at home plate and staring at the distant walls, Ty Cobb predicted that a ball would never be hit out of the new park. He was very nearly right.

About 42,00 fans jammed Braves Field for the opening game to see the home team defeat the St. Louis Cardinals, 3-1.

As Cobb had predicted, nearly all the home runs hit at Braves Field were inside-the-park jobs. The first homer hit out of the park was by Cardinal outfielder Walton Cruise, who parked a ball in the right field "jury box" on 26 May 1917. He did it again on 16 August 1921, except that having been traded by St. Louis, Cruises's second blast was for hometown Boston.

On 7 July 1936 the annual All-Star Game was played at Braves Field for the first and only time. Because of a foulup concerning the availability of tickets, only 25,556 fans showed up, the smallest crowd in All-Star game history. That was also the year President Bob Quinn, desiring to erase the stigma of a losing nickname for the team, conducted a poll to rename the club. The unhappy choice was Bees. Under that name, the Boston team continued to lose until 1941, when they changed the name back to Braves.

The Braves finally won a pennant in 1948 and also attracted 1,455,439 fans to the park.

After that it was all downhill. The team lost the World Series in six games to Cleveland, and got steadily worse until 1952, when the Braves finished seventh before a grand total of 281,278 paid watchers.

Unbeknownst to the Braves fans that season, the last game their team would play in Boston took place on Sunday, 21 September 1952 before a crowd of 8,822. The visiting Brooklyn Dodgers won, 8-2, to clinch at least a tie for the pennant.

In March of 1953, owner Lou Perini announced that he was moving the Boston franchise to Milwaukee. Braves Field was sold to Boston University and converted to a football-only stadium.

Sam Baugh's Last Game

Certainly one of the most versatile and durable players in National Football League history, Samuel Adrian Baugh of the Washington Redskins came into the ranks of college football with scouting reports that read, "Too lean and fragile... he can't play the kind of football we play in this conference."

At 6-foot-2, and weighing just 175 pounds, he did appear fragile, but managed to become an All-American in 1935 and 1936 while leading Texas Christian University to victories in the 1936 Sugar Bowl and 1937 Cotton Bowl. Although offered a baseball contract as a third baseman for the St. Louis Cardinals, Baugh signed an $8,000 contract with the Washington Redskins.

In his first game as a rookie, Baugh completed eleven of sixteen passes against the New York Giants, leading the Redskins to a 13-3 victory. He also led the team to a division-winning 8-3 record in 1937 and a 28-21 win over the Chicago Bears for the NFL championship.

Baugh was on hand in the 1940 title game, which the Bears won by the unprecedented score of 73-0, but two years later gained a measure of revenge by making one of the game's outstanding defensive plays, stopping a Bear drive on the Washington twelve-yard line by intercepting a pass in the end zone. The Redskins hung on to win, 14-6.

In 1945, Baugh, having made the conversion from single-wing to T-formation, completed 70.3 percent of his passes to set an NFL record. In one game against the Giants, he complete 20 of 24 throws, the misses being "throwaways," as he explained later. The Redskins lost the championship game to Cleveland, 15-14, however, when one of Baugh's passes hit the goal post for a safety.

Finally, at the age of thirty-seven, the man known as the "Redskin Rifle," "Sweetwater Stringbean," or more commonly as "Slinging Sam," reached his final season, 1952. After breaking his hand in a preseason game, he was limited during the season to holding the ball for placekicks, the quarterbacking job going to rookie Eddie LeBaron.

After sixteen years in the NFL, Sam Baugh played his final game on 14 December 1952. About 22,000 Washington fans turned out to watch the hometown Redskins rally to beat the Philadelphia Eagles, 27-21. Baugh started the contest, but after handing off on three unsuccessful running plays, he appeared only to hold the ball for extra points and field goal attempts, one of which was blocked.

As the game ended, hundreds of youngsters crowded around Baugh. Thirty minutes later, he was still on the field busily signing autographs.

The Last Game at Ebbets Field

For nearly a half-century, baseball was played at Ebbets Field in Brooklyn in a manner never before imagined.

It was at Ebbets Field that fly balls bounced off Babe Herman's head; where Leo Durocher snarled, superfan Hilda Chester cheered, and the Dodger "Sym-phony" played out of tune for two decades. At Ebbets one woman always bought two seats, for herself and for her gray tabby cat. It was at Ebbets that a fan once exclaimed, "We got three on base," and his neighbor, no doubt remembering that the Dodgers often had peculiar base-running habits, asked, "Which base?"

Even the park's 1913 opening had a wonderful zaniness about it. The grand march through the portico had to be postponed while a misplaced key was found. Then, just as the marchers reached the flagpole in centerfield, it was discovered that no flag was available. The facility was also missing a press box, which had to be added later.

Named after Charlie Ebbets, one of the owners of the Brooklyn Dodgers (who were known as the "Superbas" until 1910), the field was an institution for families of Dodger fans through the years. History was made in 1947 at Ebbets when Jackie Robinson became the first black in the twentieth century to play major league baseball.

Although always colorful, the Brooklyn Dodgers frequently annoyed their fans, who coined the phrase "wait until next year" as a result of the Dodgers' penchant for fighting, scratching, and clawing their way into the World Series and then becoming pussycats. In 1916, the team lost the series to the Boston Red Sox, then fell to Cleveland in 1920, and to the New York Yankees in 1941, 1947, 1949, 1952, and 1953. (In addition, the fans had to suffer through post-season playoff losses in 1946 and 1951 as well as a final day defeat for the 1950 pennant.) Finally, "next year" came in 1955, the glorious "Bums" taking the Yankees in seven games.

In 1956, however, it was business as usual, the Dodgers winning the pennant and losing the World Series to the Yankees. Meanwhile, plans had been made to move the Brooklyn franchise west to Los Angeles, there being more "gold" in California. At first few believed it was possible — until in 1957, when it became obvious to even the most dedicated optimists that the Dodgers were leaving Brooklyn.

The 1957 season was not a particularly memorable one on the field, the Milwaukee (nee Boston) Braves having supplanted the Dodgers as the reigning dynasty in the National League. Perhaps that — combined with residual hope that somehow the Dodgers would be back — was the main reason only 6,702 fans were on hand to see the final game in Ebbets Field on 24 September 1957.

Playing well, the Dodgers defeated the Pittsburgh Pirates, 2-0, behind 24-year-old rookie pitcher Danny McDevitt (who subsequently went on to a mediocre career with a lifetime mark of 21 wins and 27 losses through 1962). The team mired in third place, Dodger fans were more interested in seeing if catcher Roy Campanella would play and thereby reach consecutive game number 99 to be only 1 contest away from the National League record for catchers playing in 9 straight sessions of 100 consecutive games each. (He reached that figure on 28 September in Philadelphia, but it was Campy's last moment of glory on the playing field. On 28 January 1958 his baseball career came to an end after he was paralyzed in an automobile accident.)

Paying homage to the bittersweet final event at Ebbets Field, pipe organist Gladys Goodding, who first played nineteen years before, dredged up a number of appropriate tunes to play between innings. They included "Que Sera Sera," "Thanks for the Memories," "How Can You Say We're Through?" and "When the Blue of the Night Meets the Gold of the Day."

Finally, after the game ended, she launched into "May the Good Lord Bless and Keep You," but the sound was drowned out when someone in the control booth put on a recording of the song "Follow the Dodgers" at the same time. For Ebbets Field, it was a predictable conclusion.

To make way for apartment houses, the temple of the Dodgers for forty-five seasons was demolished in 1960.

The Last Teams to Break The Color Barrier

Historically, professional sports teams refused to admit black players, although the ban was not as complete as is generally believed. In baseball, for example, the Toledo Club of the 1884 American Association, a major league, had two blacks on the squad. They were the Walker brothers, Moses Fleetwood (1857-1924) and Welday (1860-1937), who had brief careers as catcher and outfielder, respectively.

By the 1890s, however, there were no blacks on any major league baseball team, an unofficial ban that persisted until 1947, when the National League Brooklyn Dodgers signed Jackie Robinson and Dan Bankhead. Other clubs were slow to follow. The color barrier was not completely broken in the National League until 1957 when the Philadelphia Phillies signed their first black player. He was John Kennedy, a third baseman who appeared in just five games that year and came to bat only twice, failing to hit safely both times. He was released after that season and did not catch on with another club.

In the American League, the Cleveland Indians led the way in promoting integration by signing Larry Doby for the 1948 season. Eleven years later, as the last team to break the color barrier in the American League, Boston signed Pumpsie Green, an infielder who played five seasons in the major leagues.

American professional football had no official ban on blacks and even "prided" itself on it on its liberal attitudes. It did have an unofficial quota system, however, which in its own way was just as insidious as baseball's ban.

During the 1920s at least four talented black players made it to the professional National Football League. They were: linebacker-end Paul Robeson (later a famed actor) who played in 1920 with the Hammond Pros, in 1921 with Akron, and in 1922 with the Milwaukee Badgers; Fred "Duke" Slater, tackle, who played from 1922 to 1931 with Milwaukee, Rock Island, and Chicago's Cardinals; halfback John Shelbourne, who played with the Hammond

Pros in 1922; and running back Frederick "Fritz" Pollard, whose career with Akron, Milwaukee, Hammond, and Providence lasted from 1919 to 1925.

Nevertheless, most teams were nearly all-white, a situation that began to be corrected only after World War II. The last team to have a black player was Washington, which was all-white as late as 1961. In the 1962 draft, however, Redskin's owner George Preston Marshall selected Heisman trophy winner Ernie Davis. He then traded Davis to Cleveland for black receiver Bobby Mitchell. At the same time, John Nimsby, Leroy Jackson, and Ron Hatcher joined Mitchell on the Redskin roster as the first black players.

The Last Giants Game at the Polo Grounds

> *Cheer for your favorites*
> *Out at Coogan's Bluff,*
> *Come watch those Polo Grounders*
> *Do their stuff.*

Long after most of the 11,606 fans had drifted away, three musicians sat in the visiting team bullpen, playing that familiar tune one last time. Some of the people still around remarked that it might have been more appropriate to play a funeral march, for it was truly the end of an era. It had arrived at exactly 4:35 p.m. on 29 September 1957. The New York Giants had played their final game at the Polo Grounds at 155th Street and Eighth Avenue, their home since 1889. Few traditions in New York City had lasted one-third as long.

Opened on 8 July 1889 before a standing-room-only crowd of 10,000, the Polo Grounds was the scene of nearly every kind of sports exhibition from automobile racing to Gaelic football. Polo, however, was never played there.

In 1890, the Polo Grounds was the home of both the New York Giants of the National League and the New York Giants of the Players' League, a rival organization the ballplayers had formed when baseball's owners refused to listen to their grievances. The National League Giants became sole occupants of the park the following year and proceeded to celebrate by losing the first four games to Boston. "...They acted like men under the influence of a drug... what's the matter with the Giants?" a sportsman queried on that occasion. The Giants snapped out of that losing streak, of course. After a less than respectable decade during which the team finished second and third a few times but also sank to eighth and ninth on occasion, the Giants' golden era arrived in 1902. That was when John J. McGraw, feisty infielder of the old Baltimore Orioles, took over as manger. For the next thirty years the Polo Grounds, home of the dreaded Giants, was the most famous sports arena in America.

The 1911 season was only a few games old when the Polo Grounds caught fire one night, leaving nothing intact but the left field bleachers and the clubhouse backing on Eighth Avenue. Manager McGraw suggested that the blaze had been caused by great masses of peanut shells which had accumulated beneath the stands and were highly vulnerable to the smallest spark. Whatever the cause, the Giants moved in with the Yankees (then the Highlanders) of the rival American League and not a game was postponed

The 1921 season may have been the greatest season in Giant history. The Polo Grounds had been rebuilt and a new powerhouse risen from baseball's ashes: the New York Yankees.

When the regular season ended with both New York teams victorious, The Big Apple happily prepared for its first intracity series. Led by twenty-six-year-old slugger Babe Ruth, the Yankees built a 3-2 lead but the Giants won the next three games to take the series. Having been forced to endure four consecutive World Series losses since their team won in 1905, Giants fans nearly went crazy with joy.

There were other great Giant years at the Polo Grounds after that — 1923, 1924, 1933, 1936, 1937, 1951, and especially 1954, year of the next World Series win after six previous losses. Nevertheless, during the mid-1950's, some baseball owners began to look greedily to the West Coast. One was Horace Stoneham of the Giants, who used the excuse of declining attendance as an opportunity to move the franchise to San Francisco. Giants fans protested but, of course, it did no good. Sooner than seemed possible, the Giants' last day arrived.

Pittsburgh's Pirates were the "bad guys" for the final contest at the Polo Grounds, and they played the part — to the hilt. When it was over the score stood at Pirates 9, Giants 1. Sixty-six years and five months had passed since the nineteenth century reporter had asked, "What's wrong with the Giants?"

The question still seemed relevant in 1962 when the New York Mets of the National League moved into the Polo Grounds for their first season. When that season ended with the Met's record standing at a disastrous 40 wins and 120 losses, manager Casey Stengel said, "I won with this club what I used to lose."

In 1962 and 1963, of course, the transplanted Giants of San Francisco returned to their old home to play the Mets. Although only five years had passed, nearly all of the 1957 Giant heroes were gone: Don Mueller and Hank Sauer had retired in 1959, Ray Jablonski and Whitey Lockman in 1960; pitcher Ruben Gomez had been traded to Cleveland and pitcher Johnny Antonelli had retired in 1961. Thus, of the old team, only Willie Mays and Stu Miller remained to cheer — or boo.

81

Vince Lombardi's Last Game

Ironically, the football coach who lived by the dictum, "Winning isn't everything — it's the only thing," finished his career with a loss.

Admittedly, miracle worker Vince Lombardi, who won six division championships and two Super Bowls while with the Green Bay Packers in the 1960s, was in his freshman year with a perennially also-ran club. Not since 1955 had the Washington Redskins won more games than they lost. Thus, when it was announced after the 1968 National Football League season (a disappointing one, too, for the Packers, who lost the Western Division championship to the Baltimore Colts) that Lombardi was moving to Washington, Redskin fans went wild with joy.

In many ways, their expectations were justified. Using the same intimidating tactics that worked at Green Bay, Lombardi led the ragtag Redskins to seven victories and two ties in the first thirteen games.

The final game of the 1969 season, played at Dallas on 21 December, saw the Cowboys jump to a 10-0 lead before the Redskins kicked a thirty-two yard field goal. With Dallas leading 13-3 in the final quarter, Chris Hanburger of the Redskins picked up a fumble by Calvin Hill and ran nineteen yards for a touchdown to bring the score to 13-10. It seemed as if Lombardi's Packer heroics were ready for a re-run until Dallas settled down, moving the ball sixty yards in ten plays for a touchdown that decided the issue.

The 20-10 loss gave Lombardi an overall season mark of seven wins, five losses and two ties (the number of wins and losses the Packers earned during Lombardi's first season at Green Bay), which was more than enough for most Washington Redskin fans.

But the miracle of Green Bay was not to be repeated in the nation's capital. Lombardi died of cancer on 3 September 1970 before he could lead the team to further glory.

Pele's Last Game for Brazil

By almost universal acclaim, Edson Arantes do Nascimento of Brazil, better known as "Pele", was the greatest soccer player of his time.

Born in 1941, Pele was the son of a relatively obscure soccer player, Joao Ramos do Nascimento, who played under the nickname Dondinho, and taught the boy the rudiments of the game. At the age of five, the youngster was a familiar figure in the streets of Bauro, Brazil, kicking a "ball" made from a stocking stuffed with rags. His only interest seemed to be soccer, for by the time he was ten, Pele had dropped out of school because of poor grades and rowdy behavior. He was a terror even against soccer players three times his age. "Football was the only career I ever thought of," he once said. "I wanted to follow my father's path. I was convinced he was the best player who ever lived but that he never had a chance to prove it."

Pele soon became a star with the Bauro team but was rejected by the top-ranking Sao Paolo squad. He was only fifteen years old at the time. Pele bounced back immediately to earn a spot on the Santos team. In 1958, he led the Brazilian National team to a World Cup championship, scoring three goals against France in the semifinal game and two more against Sweden, to give Brazil its first international soccer victory. The whole country went mad, acclaiming Pele as a national treasure and calling him the "Black Pearl." During the height of his career, from 1956 to 1971, he earned as much as $500,000 annually, easily making him the highest paid athlete of his day.

The climax of his playing days came in the final game of the 1970 World Cup, played before a sellout crowd of 112,000 in Mexico City's Azteca Stadium. Pele scored a goal in the first half and set up two scores in the second to lead Brazil to a 4-1 victory over Italy. "That was the greatest excitement I ever had as a player," said the man who scored 1,086 goals during his career.

Having reached the age of thirty, Pele retired from international competition on 18 July 1971. The day was one of both acclaim and mourning in Brazil and for the whole world. Officials in Seville, Spain, cancelled the bullfights there so fans could stay home and watch Pele's farewell game, which was played at Rio de Janiero against the Yugoslav team.

Before the contest started, Pele trotted around the field to the accompaniment of the national hit song "Obrigado Pele" ("Thank you, Pele"). A record crowd of 130,000 then watched Pele's 110th appearance with Brazil's national team. During the first half, he attempted four shots but failed to score. He watched the second half from the official box as Brazil rallied from a 1-0 deficit to gain a 2-2 tie.

A self-effacing and generous man as well as a gifted athlete, Pele was asked in January of 1967 to be the guest of honor of a Harlem group as the "most popular man of the Negro race in the world." The entire Santos soccer team happened to be in New York at the time, which prompted Pele to say in a TV interview, "I learned that this has connotations of a racial struggle in the United States, and I made one condition to accept: I would come only if all the white players on the Santos team were also invited."

When the hosts declined, so did Pele. "I just thanked them for the thought," he said.

Last Living Player of the First World Series

On 1 October 1903, Clarence "Ginger" Beaumont, centerfielder for the National League Pittsburgh Pirates, stepped to the plate, faced pitcher Cy Young of the American League Boston Pilgrims, and flied out.

The World Series, America's classic sports confrontation, had begun. Subsequently, Pittsburgh won the game, 5-3, but the Pilgrims took the series, five games to three, and not long afterward became the Boston Red Sox.

Of the twenty-seven men who played in that initial World Series, the first to pass away was Jimmy Sebring, Pirate outfielder, who died on 22 December 1909, at the age of twenty-seven. The others were more fortunate, living an average of 40.9 years after the series.

Beaumont, finishing his playing days in 1910, died on 10 April 1956 at the age of seventy-nine. The two most famous ballplayers in the 1903 confrontation, shortstop Honus Wagner of the Pirates and Young of Boston, died within a month of each other, Young on 4 November and Wagner on 9 December 1955.

The last survivor was shortstop Frederick Alfred Parent of Boston, who played his only World Series games in 1903. Coming to the plate thirty-two times, he safely hit nine times, including three triples, for an average of .281. He finished his career with the Chicago White Sox in 1911, then lived until 2 November 1972 and the ripe old age of ninety-six.

Ruffian's Last Race

Ruffian, one of the fastest fillies in horseracing history, began her competitive career on 22 May 1974, and ended it in death less than fourteen months later. During that brief time, she earned $438,429, while winning by at least six lengths in seven of her first ten races.

Because of her rapid success which captured the public's imagination, it was inevitable in an age that had already pitched Billie Jean King against male rival Bobby Riggs that a match race would be arranged between Ruffian and a top colt. That colt turned out to be Foolish Pleasure, winner of the 1975 Kentucky Derby. While Foolish Pleasure had been preparing for the Derby, Ruffian was recovering from a hairline fracture of a bone in her right hindleg. In the seven-furlong Comely Stakes, the mile Acorn, and the mile-and-a-half Mother Goose, she set records, proving she was still a worthy opponent for any male counterpart.

Promoters of the match race selected New York's Belmont Park as the track for the event and the stake was set at $350,000.

Before the race, Ruffian's jockey, Jacinto Vasquez, made an inspection on foot of the course that would be traveled. He noted two places on the track that smart jockeys tried to avoid. One was a small hump of ground near the railing where the chute crossed the training track about a sixteenth of a mile from the starting gate. The other was the intersection of the chute and the main track a couple of furlongs beyond, where the texture of the track became harder. Vasquez made mental notes to avoid both spots, even if it meant taking Ruffian wide.

After the preliminaries were completed, Ruffian and Foolish Pleasure, with Braulio Baeza up, broke from the gate. Running close together but not bumping, they moved out of the chute and joined the main track, going from a firm base to one resembling concrete. The change at first seemed not to affect either horse; Ruffian, ahead by three-quarters of a length, was moving effortlessly. "Then I decided I'd better save something and tried to hold her back," Vasquez said later. "You can't do a mile-and-a-quarter pumping away. It's too fast, and I took a chance that Baeza would do the same thing. But just after joining the main track, she broke her leg. She just broke her leg. It sounded like a shot."

As Foolish Pleasure raced ahead, Ruffian and Vasquez edged off the track. An examination revealed that both sesamoid bones in the horse's right foreleg were shattered. While still on the track, Ruffian was anesthetized, the bones set, and a cast applied. But when the drug wore off, nothing could be done to hold her down. "Nobody realizes the tremendous strength of a horse coming out of anesthesia," said Dr. Alex Harthill, one of the veterinarians present. "We tried our best, but she just fought so hard she smashed the cast we'd put on her leg. She never got up."

Ruffian was destroyed that very day and lies buried in the Belmont infield, just to the right of the toteboard about a sixteenth of a mile past the finish line.

Hank Aaron's Last Home Run

Henry Aaron is best known for home run number 715, which came on 8 April 1974. The round-tripper, which was struck off pitcher Al Downing of Los Angeles, carried Aaron past Babe Ruth's career mark of 714.

That blow was enough to insure Aaron's inauguration into the Baseball Hall of Fame at the first opportunity. After hitting the historic home run, as a member of the Atlanta Braves, Aaron remained in the major leagues three more years, which were not particularly good ones for the slugger. He finished the 1974 season with twenty home runs, his lowest total since his rookie year of 1954, and a .268 batting average (about thirty points below his lifetime average), then was traded to the Milwaukee Brewers of the American League.

Appearing in 137 games with the Brewers in 1975, mostly as a designated hitter, his average slumped to .234 and his home run output to 12. The following season proved to be the last for Henry Aaron, who was 42 years old. The last of his career home runs came on 20 July 1976. Coming to bat in the seventh inning, following a home run by teammate George Scott, Aaron hit number 755 off of California Angels' pitcher Dick Drago. Milwaukee won the game, 6-2.

Aaron appeared in several games after that, but hit no more homers. In the final game of the season, he got the last of his major league hits, an infield single. Shortly after the season was over, he announced his retirement, holder of a baseball record which may never be broken.

Karl Wallenda's Last Walk

Using only a few tools, tremendous ability, and a deep belief that he would continue his profession "as long as God lets me," aerialist Karl Wallenda held the world's attention for more than half a century. The tools were flexible steel poles twenty to twenty-five feet long, weighing from twenty to forty-two pounds. In addition, he wore a pair of red ballet slippers, especially made with the welt on the inside of the sole so there would be no raised edges to catch on a cable. The ability was balance, augmented by a great deal of courage.

Born in 1905, the son of a catcher in a flying act, Wallenda had his own high-wire act by the time he was seventeen. Three years later, he brought his brother Herman and two other men into the act, creating the first high-wire pyramid with the Zirkus Gleich in Milan, Italy. Then, in 1947, Wallenda created what he regarded as his masterpiece, an act that no team but the "Flying Wallendas" could perform: the seven-person pyramid. It consisted of three tiers of aerialists linked by shoulder bars, at the very top of which stood a woman on a chair, its seat balanced on the bar borne by the middle-tiered men.

From 1947 until 30 January 1962, the pyramid was regularly performed as the climax to the Wallendas' act. Until that day, in fact, four generations of the family had performed on a high wire for eighty-eight years without a fatal injury. Night after night, they defied death from the height of fifty feet, since Wallenda refused to use a safety net because he claimed its presence would invite falls. Then, on that fateful night in Detroit, Dieter Schepp, Wallenda's nephew, who was at the base of the pyramid and who had only the year before escaped from East Germany, felt himself slipping. "I can't hold it," he cried out.

The pyramid collapsed, three men falling to the ground, three others catching the woman and holding her and the wire until an improvised net could be spread out below. Schepp was killed; Wallenda's son, Mario, was paralyzed from the waist down.

A year later, a third member of the Wallenda circus family plunged to her death at Omaha, Nebraska. Henrietta Kreis, the sister of Wallenda's wife Helen, was standing atop a fifty-foot pole on 18 April 1963 and swaying in a wide arc when she suddenly fell backward. Circus colleagues said the woman, known in her act as Miss Reitta, was extremely nervous before going on because her fiberglass pole had broken during her last performance in Florida. She was concerned, they said, because she had to use a temporary pole.

Despite the tragedies, Wallenda continued to walk the high wire. "The rest of life is just time to fill in between doing the act," he said, when asked if he contemplated retiring. "Our life is show business. Without show business, we don't survive, and we have to exist."

Helen Wallenda, meanwhile, refused to watch the act after 1962. "I always sit in a back room and pray," she said.

Following the tragedies, Wallenda walked another 15 years and was 73 years old on 22 March 1978 when he began his last walk. A strong wind was blowing as he stepped onto the 750-foot wire strung 123 feet above the pavement between two hotels in San Juan, Puerto Rico. "When he checked it out this morning," said Bill Carpenter, promotion manager for the Pan American Circus, which employed Wallenda, "I asked if he wanted to go on in such a strong wind. He replied, "Don't worry about it. The wind is stronger on the street than up here."

Midway across the strand, wind gusts caused the wire to dance beneath Wallenda, who shouted "Hold tight!" to members of his troupe holding guidewires to steady the cable.

"Sit, Poppy, sit!" shouted Jane Baird, a reporter for the *San Juan Star* who was covering the stunt.

Wallenda started to squat as if to sit, but at that moment a powerful gust of wind blew him off the wire. He landed on a taxicab, bounced onto the pavement, and was dead before help could arrive.

He was buried on 27 March, some 1,500 people filing by the open coffin above which a 24-foot balance pole hung in tribute.

Some Babe Ruth's Lasts

Nearly as famous a pitcher as a slugger, George Herman "Babe" Ruth hurled his last game on the final day of the 1933 season. Although thirty-eight years old and nearing the end of his career, he went the full nine innings against the Boston Red Sox, yielding twelve hits and three bases on balls. He was tough when he had to be, winning by the score of 6-5. It was his ninety-fourth career victory against forty-six defeats.

The Babe's last game was on 30 May 1935, after he was traded to the National League Boston Braves. In the starting lineup for the Memorial Day double-header at Philadelphia, he struck out in the top of the first inning, then hurt his knee while going after a fly ball in the bottom of the first. He left the game, never to return as an active player.

Less than a week before, on 25 May, Ruth had his last moment of glory. Playing against the Pirates at Pittsburgh, he hit three home runs, including a towering blast that was the first ever hit out of Forbes field, and a single. At the end of the game, the Pittsburgh fans gave him a standing ovation.

Last Words

1920
Joselito (Jose Gomez), Spanish bullfighter gored by small bull with defective vision: "Mother, I'm smothering."
1924
Pat Moran, manager of Cincinnati Reds, to John Evers: "Hello, John. Take me out of here."
1927
Theodore "Tiger" Flowers, thirty-two, middleweight boxing champion operated on for removal of a growth over his left eye: "If I should die before I wake, I pray the Lord my soul to take."
1933
Wilson Mizner, fight manager: "Well, doc, I guess this is the main event."
1959
Max Baer, heavyweight boxer: "Oh, God, here I go!"
1970
Brian Piccolo (to wife): "Can you believe it, Joy? Can you believe this shit?"
1972
Moe Berg, Boston Red Sox catcher: "How did the Mets do today?"

Chapter Three

Literary Lasts

Chronology

1711
(Jan. 2) *The Tatler*, a chatty gossip and literary paper started in 1709 by Joseph Addison, prints its final number.

1712
(Dec. 6) Last issue of the magazine *The Spectator*, which writers Addison and Steele published beginning on 1 March 1711, is printed.

1757
Benjamin Franklin ceases publication of *Poor Richard's Almanac*, which began in 1733.

1776
The Boston News-Letter, the first U.S. newspaper (founded 1704), ceases publication.

1795
The last issue of *Ames' Almanack*, which originated in 1726, is published.

1820
Poor Robin's Almanac, first printed in Great Britain in 1661, ceases publication.

1849
(Sept. 28) Final number appears of the *Register*, a weekly news magazine established almost four dec- ades previously by Hezekiah Niles. (see p. 93)

1861
(June 22) The last issue of *Spirit of the Times*, America's first sports periodical, is published. (see p. 95)

1865
The Liberator, William Lloyd Garrison's anti-slavery magazine first published in 1831, prints its final issue.

1898
(August) The last issue is published of *Godey's Magazine*, a periodical for women first printed in 1830. (see p. 96)

1905
The New York Evening News publishes its last issue.

1914
The last issues of *Health* (first published in 1845) and *The Chautauquan* (from 1880) are printed.

1918
(Sept. 5) The last issue appears of *Puck*, an American humor magazine first published in 1877.

1923
(April) Last issue is published of *Outing*, an early American sports magazine first printed in 1882.

1925
(April) The last issue of *Current Opinion*, a "thought-provoking" magazine first published in 1888, is printed.

1926
(January) First published in 1893, *McClure's* magazine is absorbed by *Smart Set*.

1928
(Oct. 13) *The Independent*, first published in 1848, prints its last issue.

1929
(September) The last issue appears of *The Youth's Companion*, first published in 1827. The magazine printed the "Pledge of Allegiance" to the American flag in its 8 September 1892 issue, the first time the oath was ever printed.

1930
Last issues are published of *Forest and Stream* (first printed in 1873) and the *Herald of Gospel Liberty* (dating from 1808).

1932
(February) The celebrated and gaudy sex-scandal-sports weekly, *National Police Gazette* prints its last issue. (see p. 97)

1932
New York's *Daily Graphic* folds.

1935
In June, the final numbers of *New Outlook* and *Overland Monthly* are published. The magazines began in 1870 and 1868 respectively.

1941
(August) The last issue is published of *The Living Age*, first printed in 1844.

1948
(Jan. 29) The last *Chicago Sun* appears.

1949
The New York Star, formerly *PM*, folds. (see p. 99)

1950
(Jan. 4) The last issue appears of the *New York Sun*, which originated in 1833. (see p. 100)

1952
The *New York Daily Compass* goes out of business.

1952
(Sept. 29) The *Manchester Guardian* ends its practice, in effect since 1821, of printing front-page advertisements.

1953
(June 1) The pocket-sized magazine *Quick* is published for the last time.

1954
(March 17) The sixty-year-old *Washington Times-Herald* goes out of business.

1954
(March 25) *The Recorder*,

London's short-lived conservative newspaper, folds.

1955
(Jan. 29) First published in 1841, the *Brooklyn Eagle* goes under. (see p. 101)

1956
(August) *American* magazine folds after a run of eight decades. (see p. 102)
(October) Twice forced to suspend operations since midsummer, the *Boston Post* goes down for the third and final time.

1957
(January) First published in 1873, *Woman's Home Companion* goes out of business.
(Jan. 4) Once one of America's most popular magazines, *Collier's* prints its final number. (see p. 103)
(June) *Etude*, the delight of music teachers and scourge of pupils, goes out of business. (see p. 104)

1958
(May 24) The *International News Service*, started in 1909 by William Randolph Hearst, expires. (see p. 105)
(July) The *New Orleans Item* folds.

1959
It is a bad year for magazines in Great Britain. Appearing for the last time are *Home Chat* (published since 1895), *Everybody's* (since 1925), *Sketch* (since 1893) and *TV Mirror* (since 1953).

Some American newspapers which expire this year: *The Grand Rapids Herald, Montpelier Evening Argus, Columbus (Ohio) State Journal,* and *Charlotte News.*

1960
Newspapers are dropping like flies in London. Casualties of this year include the *Sunday Graphic, Empire News* (since 1884), *London Star,* and *News Chronicle.*
(September) The *Wichita (Kansas) Beacon* is sold to the *Morning Eagle,* ending an eighty-eight-year-old journalistic rivalry.

1962
(January) The city of Los Angeles experiences a double death, when both the *Examiner* and the *Mirror* cease publication within hours of each other.

1963
(Oct. 16) The *New York Mirror*, aged thirty-nine, prints its last edition. (see p. 106)

1966
(May 2) The last issue in which the *London Times* devotes its entire front page to ads is printed. (see p. 108)
(Aug. 15) The *New York Herald-Tribune* goes out of business; it was founded in 1841. (see p. 107)

1967
(May 22) Germany's leading magazine of political satire,

Simplicissimus, ceases publication after seventy-one years. (see p. 109)
(July 10) The final number is printed of the *Boston Traveler*, which was founded in 1825.

1968
(June 13) *Reporter* Magazine ceases publication. (see p. 110)

1969
(Nov. 2) *This Week*, Sunday supplement to many American newspapers for thirty-five years, publishes its last issue. (see p. 110)

1971
(September) *Al-Hoda*, the last American newspaper published in Arabic, issues its final newspaper, ending an enterprise extant since 1898.

1972
(March) *Auction*, a well-known art magazine, folds.
(Sept. 1) The *Newark News* prints its final afternoon edition after eighty-eight years of publication.

1973
(Jan. 25) The last large-sized issue of *Life* magazine is published. (see p. 111)

1977
(March 25) The *Long Island Press*, in circulation since 1821, prints its final edition.
(July) The final issue of *Coronet* Magazine appears.

1979
(Jan. 8) *New Times* magazine, fails to set the world on fire and departs with a sneer at America. (see p. 114)
(August) *Look* magazine, suspended in 1971 only to reappear later, folds a second time. (see p. 113)

1980
(March 26) *Paris-Hebdo*, a flashy imitation of American "city" magazines, goes out of business after only twelve issues.

The Last Issue of Niles' Register

The *Time* or *Newsweek* of its day, *Niles' Weekly Register* (later the *National Register*) provided valuable information to the public and future historians by reporting just about everything of interest that happened during the first part of the nineteenth century.

It was the creation of Hezekiah Niles, an accident-prone, moralistic, often humorous Philadelphia printer's assistant, who struck out on his own after a business partner took the money and ran. Typically, Niles was philosophical about it. "Bonsal, peace to his soul, was a bad man," he confided to a friend. "I knew it too late."

THE LAST TIME WHEN

On 11 September 1811, Niles wrote and published the first issue of his *Weekly Register* and sent it free to a list of about 1,500 readers, hoping it would catch their fancy. In order to spice up the periodical which had agate type and virtually no illustrations, Niles often spoke to the reader as a personal friend. "Since the last publication," he wrote on 17 November 1813, placing himself in the third person,"(the editor) has been nearly denied the use of his *right* arm by a rheumatic affection, attended with the usual pain, which now appears happily relieved..." Minor misfortunes such as these were duly reported to his readers over the years.

Niles also reported on his experiences as a juror. "A person was brought in for damages in the amount of $1,283," he wrote, "for seducing the wife of another, who had been married eighteen years and was the mother of nine children. That's a good one."

By the time he reached his fiftieth birthday, Niles had been writing and editing the *Register* for more than fifteen years. Nevertheless, he was not a wealthy man. One reason was that he did not allow advertising in the periodical, feeling it might compromise his freedom to write about various topics and issues. Thus, despite its broad appeal and gradually increasing circulation, the *Register* limped along financially, with Niles keeping only a step or two ahead of his creditors. He might have added more subscribers had he been inclined to make the paper more sensational, but he generally adopted a milder tone as he grew older, ignoring personal attacks.

The issues he chose to promote were not always glamorous ones. He favored abolishing postage on all newspapers, for example, reasoning that a free press was vastly more important to a government than any revenue it might engender. He was fiercely nationalistic and was in favor of a national bank. When his views clashed with those of other men, however, he invariably provided huge space for the opposite opinion. In an 1812 instance, he printed long resolutions of those opposing a tax on whiskey, although he personally favored a heavy tax, both from a moral and mercantile point of view.

In 1836, after a quarter-century of publishing the *Register*, Niles had a stroke which left the right side of his body paralyzed. On 6 July, he wrote his will with his left hand and on 3 September said farewell to his readers. "I know my own resources," he wrote, "and the vainness of a hope of relying on any other. The work is my own, whether it be good or bad; and has been persevered in with invincible industry, and oftentimes under distressing circumstances, until, at length, I am, temporarily at least, placed in a condition that compels a retirement from its active duties...I retire from the editorial seat with feelings of gratitude and without hostility to any human being."

Turning the paper over to his son, William Ogden Niles, Hezekiah spent the last years of his life as a semi-invalid, and died on 2 April 1839 at the age of sixty-one. By that time, he was celebrated enough to have two communities named after him — Niles, Ohio, the birthplace of William McKinley and Ring Lardner — and Niles, Michigan.

After his father's death, William Niles moved the publication's office to Washington and changed the periodical's name to *Niles' National Register* in an ambitious move to make the paper into a more imposing publication. But he had neither his father's ability nor energy, publicly admitting as much when he turned the paper over to Jeremiah Hughes, an old friend of Hezekiah's, after a brief tenure as publisher and editor. However, the *Register* was never able to recapture the momentum it had once had and its final number appeared on 28 September 1849.

The Last Spirit of the Times

Generally conceded to have been the first all-around sporting journal in the United States, the initial number of *Spirit of the Times* appeared on 10 December 1831. By 1837, it was a weekly periodical of eight large-sized pages.

Founded by an Englishman, William T. Porter (who because of his six-foot height, was called "York's tall son"), *Spirit of the Times* at first reflected British sporting attitudes and described many events which would not ordinarily have interested Americans except for the dearth of sporting news. A colorful writing style often made articles interesting even for those who had no prior knowledge of the participants, however. For example, the account of an 1837 walking match between British pedestrians Robert Fuller and Ralph Burn contained this purple patch:

"Burn's countenance was thin and pale, but there was a kind of determination in it which combined with his thick frame, sturdily formed legs, and flat feet, made it at once appear that a steady and lasting pace was his principal forte. Fuller, on the other hand, is remarkably good-looking and health was pictured on his smiling countenance, which, with his beautiful symmetry, his points so clearly developed, and the elasticity of his frame, excited no small degree of admiration..."

In addition, the typical *Spirit of the Times* carried advertising ("Elegant timing watches for horsemen," "Imported bulls for sale"), a column entitled "Things Theatrical," as well as features dealing with fashion, field sports, fishing, agriculture, and court proceedings. At first a regular reporter of British cricket matches, the magazine soon became a heavy promoter of the fledgling sport of baseball in the United States.

In 1856, Porter sold the magazine to George Wilkes, original publisher of the *National Police Gazette*, who changed the magazine's title to *Porter's Spirit of the Times*. By this time, Porter's influence on baseball was so strong that writing a century later, baseball historian Harold Seymour asked, "What if Stonewall Jackson had not been accidentally shot by one of his own men before Gettysburg? What if General Howe had not dallied over cakes and Madeira at Mrs. Murray's house, giving Washington's men a chance to make good their escape? And what if the editor of the influential *Porter's Spirit of the Times* had not switched his allegiance from cricket to baseball? Doubtless baseball would have prospered anyway in the pre-Civil War eras, but its development might have been much slower than it was."

Unfortunately for the periodical, it was not destined to benefit from its innovative spirit. The Civil War itself put such a damper on organized sports that *Spirit of the Times* foundered and went out of business on 22 June 1861.

The Last of Godey's Magazine

In print for nearly seven decades, *Godey's Magazine* (which began its existence as *Godey's Lady's Book*) was by far the most popular women's periodical of the day. Just prior to the Civil War, its circulation reached 150,000 — justifiably, for between 1837 and 1850 nearly every popular writer in American appeared in its pages, including Ralph Waldo Emerson, Henry Wadsworth Longfellow, Oliver Wendell Holmes, Nathaniel Hawthorne, Edgar Allan Poe, and Harriet Beecher Stowe.

Begun in 1830 by Louis A. Godey of Philadelphia, the magazine's first issue contained a color picture of a woman's walking dress as the frontispiece (color was rare in periodicals of this period), and a variety of articles, essays, and poems which, taken as a whole, clearly indicated that the woman of 1830 would best serve by being an intelligent — but not too intelligent — adjunct to her man.

A couple of examples: "When we are in the company of sensible men, we ought to be doubly cautious of talking too much lest we lose two good things — their good opinions, and our own improvement; and disclose one thing which had better have been concealed — our self-sufficiency, for what we have to say we know, but what they have to say we know not."

Another: "A furious wife, like a musket, may do a great deal of execution in her house, but then she makes a great deal of noise at the same time. A mild wife, will, like an air-gun, act with as much power without being heard."

In addition to these bits of philosophy, the first issue of *Godey's* contained specious bits of medical advice ("If a patient, suffering from excessive action of the heart, eat asparagus, M. Broussais assures us he will experience considerable relief..."), an article on the niceties of dancing ("the arms should be kept in an easy semi-oval position, so that the bend of the elbows be scarcely perceptible; otherwise, they would present right angles, which would so offend the eye as to destroy all appearance of ease of elegance...the dress should be held between the fore-finger and thumb of each hand; it is a matter of importance to overcome both tremor and rigidity of the fingers, which should be gracefully grouped, so that the palm be partially seen in front..."). There were also several pieces of fiction with intriguing titles — "Jack the Shrimp" by Mrs. S .C. Hall, and "The Leper's Confession," by R. Penn Smith.

From these beginnings, *Godey's* made a success out of sentiment and fashion while studiously avoiding politics or other controversial matters. Godey branched out in 1841, publishing *The Young People's Book or Magazine of Useful or Entertaining Knowledge*, which, if nothing else, must certainly take the all-time prize for having an indecisive title. In 1877, at the age of seventy-three, Godey turned the magazine's editorship over to S. Annie Frost and died a year later.

By the 1880s, *Godey's* was clearly in decline, partly because women were becoming liberated from the notion that their place was always in the home. Large numbers of them had taken up bicycling, which scandalized many persons, because riding such a vehicle forced women to display their ankles or, even more horrifying, separate their legs. In any event, *Godey's Magazine*, a traditional advocate of parlor and kitchen living for women, was well behind the times by the end of the century. A victim of a magazine boom which opened new markets for the more popular writers, *Godey's* literary reputation declined, also. Its last issue was published in August of 1898.

The Last Police Gazette

During the latter part of the nineteenth century, the *National Police Gazette* was *Playboy*, the *National Enquirer*, *True Detective*, and *Sports Illustrated* all wrapped up in one — sixteen pale pink quarto pages of sex scandals, crime, cheesecake, and lurid advertising, profusely illustrated with magnificently detailed wood-cuts. The publication was not offered for sale at most reputable newsstands but was found in practically every barbershop and saloon in America.

First appearing on 13 September 1845, the *National Police Gazette's* ostensible purpose was to expose crime, and during the Mexican War its back pages were filled with pictures and descriptions of deserters. In fact, the *National Police Gazette* sensationalized crime to the extent that its first editor, George Wilkes, was under constant attack by crime bosses on the one hand (for uncover-ing crime scandals) and the police department on the other (for exposing police corruption). In 1850, the magazine's plant was demolished during an assault by unidentified thugs, which resulted in six deaths. The culprits (or their sponsors) were never discovered.

A period of decline followed, although by 1878, the *National Police Gazette* was America's oldest continuous weekly newsmagazine. Its circulation had dropped, however, and it seemed the paper would soon go out of business. At this point, Richard K. Fox entered the picture. Fox, the grandson of an Irish clergyman, was vulgar, prejudiced, narrow-minded, addicted to violence, and a genius in one respect: he knew how to put together a magazine that would sell like hotcakes.

From 1878 to the end of the century was the *National Police Gazette's* golden age. For writers, Fox used moonlighting reporters from New York's dozen daily papers, offering them free booze, food, and ten dollars for a weekend's work at the magazine. Rumor has it that many big-league journalists succumbed to Fox's temptations, although the paper carried no bylines during this period.

Fox's influence was evident in every issue of the *Gazette*. He was a dedicated hater, detesting all foreigners (especially the Chinese), clergymen, society's upper classes, politicians, blacks, college boys, doctors, and even criminals. Thus instead of an article being headlined, "Black man lynched," it carried a banner that read, "Woolyheaded African half-ape stretched from tree by righteous Mississippi gentlemen." In 1889, when a white woman named Rosa Hosier married a black man, Charles Helm, the *National Police Gazette's* caption read: "A pretty white girl of Xenia, Ohio, marries a hunk of charcoal and parades the streets with him." Fox's description of opium-smoking was inevitably titled, "The Mongolian Curse," and an 1883 expose of Chinese opium parlors in New York labeled, "blighting effects of the introduction of a debasing celestial habit among the young girls..." contained woodcuts of leering Orientals enticing overly innocent-looking children into smoke-infested dens.

Crass as he was, Fox occasionally spoke out on the humanitarian side of certain issues. In 1892, for example, while most newspapers took the side of steel mogul Andrew Carnegie following the strike and riot at Homestead, Pennsylvania, the *National Police Gazette* called Carnegie's Pinkerton strikebreakers "hired assassins," and the workers "determined breadwinners," adding,"There was no occasion for such bloodshed...the starving workmen of Homestead...had committed no lawless acts. Mr. Carnegie's property was perfectly safe. Although the workmen were suffering under the great wrong done them by their rich and despotic employer, they were peaceable and inclined to meet the issue in a proper and lawful manner. The act of sending an armed force of irresponsible men to Homestead invited bloodshed, and Mr. Carnegie or his representative is responsible for the result. The murder at Homestead is a matter for the Congress to give serious consideration."

At its zenith at the turn of the century, the *Police Gazette* began to be imitated by daily papers, which — thanks to photographs — were able to out-sensationalize and out-yellow-journalize Fox. Prohibition knocked out the magazine's barroom circulation and the opening of barbershops to women resulted in a loss of subscriptions in that area. Fox died a multimillionaire in 1922, but by that time the *Gazette* was in a period of sad decline. In February of 1932 it was sold, bankrupt, for $545. That was the last issue of the real *National Police Gazette*, even though the title was revived in 1933 as a confessions magazine and a Canadian company issued a version of the old scandal-sports-sex sheet in more recent times.

The Last Issue of PM

When it first hit the streets on 18 June 1940, the New York afternoon newspaper known as *PM* proclaimed that it was "against people who push other people around." The financial baby of publisher Marshall Field and artistic creation of founder-editor Ralph Ingersoll, *PM* was innovative in that it did not accept advertising. This policy was followed, the paper said, so that it would not be swayed from its sense of fairness by financial motivations.

Born in an era and atmosphere of chaos — its first issue was picketed by members of the Newspaper Clerks Delivery Union protesting *PM*'s recognition of the rival Newspaper and Mail Deliverers Union — the periodical remained in the thick of controversy during its entire brief history. Its drama critic, Louis Kronenberger, was barred from the Shubert brothers theaters in 1943 because of "unfair, unjust, and cruel" reviews. That, combined with *PM*'s listing of the Shubert production of *The Student Prince* as a "shoddy revival of the tuneful Romberg operetta," led to Kronenberger's joining Alexander Woollcott of *The New York Times* as an official *persona non grata*, at least as far as the Shuberts were concerned. A month later, Governor Leverett Saltonstall of Massachusetts characterized a *PM* story about anti-Semitic outbreaks in Boston as "a stinking article," and ordered reporter Arnold Beichman to leave his office.

Because of its advertising policy, *PM* lost money until 1944, the same year it was chosen by a poll of 600 City College of New York students as the most popular afternoon paper in the city. In 1945, the newspaper was in the black for the first time in its history.

Then, in one of the strangest about-faces in American business — or perhaps thinking that it was time to capitalize on his long-awaited success — publisher Field decided in 1946 to accept *PM*'s first advertising. Ingersoll promptly resigned. The cost of setting up advertising then led to the paper's dipping once again into the red.

To make matters even worse, it turned out not many advertisers were interested in buying space in the paper.

After struggling on for two more years, *PM* published its last issue on 26 March 1948. It then became the *New York Star*, a short-lived newspaper whose main claim to fame was that it first published the popular comic strip, "Pogo." The *Star* went out of business in 1949.

The Setting of The New York Sun

During its 116 years of publication, the *New York Sun* was more famous for the quality of its hoaxes than it was for its news coverage.

First published on 3 September 1833 by Benjamin H. Day, a twenty-three-year-old printer, the *Sun* rapidly became the first successful penny newspaper in New York. Within a year, its circulation rose from 1,000 to 8,000, but the paper only really caught on after publication of a four-part series in August of 1835 headlined, "Great Astronomical Discoveries Lately Made by Sir John Herschel at the Cape of Good Hope." The series, written by Richard Adams Locke, told how a renowned British astronomer had invented a 7-ton telescope with a 24-inch lens capable of magnifying an object 42,000 times. With this instrument, Herschel had discovered incredible objects on the moon — a blue animal "the size of a goat with a head and beard like him, and a *single* horn," as well as a "strange amphibious creature of a spherical form, which rolled with great velocity across the pebbly beach." The professor also saw creatures about 4 feet tall which both flew and walked upright and had a face that "was a slight improvement upon that of the large orangutan..."

Readers, taken by the detail of the articles, swelled the *Sun*'s circulation to 19,500. Nine years later, many of the same readers who should have known better were taken in by another series, "The Atlantic Crossed in Three Days! Signal Triumph of Mr. Monck Mason's Flying Machine!" This fictitious account, subsequently known as the "balloon hoax," was written by Edgar Allan Poe.

After the Civil War, the *Sun* was purchased by Charles A. Dana, who guided the paper through its glory years until 1897. Under Dana, whose motto was, "I have always felt that whatever the Divine Providence permitted to occur, I was not too proud to report," the *Sun* continued its sprightly ways, using the then-new interview technique to brighten up its stories. During this period, its city editor, John B. Bogart, was credited with coining the phrase, "When a man bites a dog, that is news."

Also, during Dana's tenure, the *Sun* achieved worldwide fame when writer Francis P. Church replied to an eight-year-old's query with the "Yes, Virginia, there is a Santa Claus," editorial in 1897.

After Dana's death, able editors followed but the *Sun* went into a slow decline. A series of mergers during the early years of the twentieth century eventually led to the *Sun*'s setting on 4 January 1950. In that issue, it ran its own obituary, blaming rising printing costs for its demise.

A loser for years, the *Sun* was then eighth in a field of nine Manhattan newspapers, its share of advertising revenue dropping from ten percent of the total market to five percent in a decade. Studies had been made but no one had the slightest idea how to save the venerable newspaper.

It was, after all, an age when fewer and fewer people could be induced to swallow a hoax or believe in Santa Claus.

The Last Issue of Quick Magazine

When it was first published in May of 1949, *Quick* magazine was considered quite innovative. For one thing, it was so small it could fit into the pocket, a selling point publisher Gardner Cowles hoped to exploit.

For awhile, *Quick* was quite successful. Its circulation jumped from 300,000 to 1.3 million over a 4-year period. In 1952, its income was close to $4 million. Starting with an editorial staff of 5, it quickly added another 20 staffers, but when paper and print costs leaped by 25 percent soon afterward, *Quick* was in financial trouble.

The magazine's basic problem was that its abnormally small pages proved to be too great a hurdle for advertisers, who found they had to prepare special ads rather than merely reducing already existing ones. Not enough advertisers took the trouble. With limited revenues from advertisers, each copy of *Quick* cost ten cents more to produce than readers paid for it.

The 1 June 1953 edition of *Quick* was its last in the small format. Shortly after its demise, it was bought by the *Philadelphia Inquirer* for $250,000. It was changed to a biweekly with a larger format but after 9 months that experiment also died.

The Last of The Brooklyn Eagle

First published in 1841, the *Brooklyn Eagle* was known as a crusading and prosperous newspaper for more than a century. During the late 1800s, it fought against political bosses and for the Brooklyn Bridge, against the consolidation of Greater New York and in favor of Long Island highways. In 1922, its peak year for profit, it finished $400,000 in the black.

Part of its success could be traced to the penurious salary policy of the *Eagle*'s management, which made the paper notorious for hard work and low pay. In its early days, the poor pay was offset by the *Eagle*'s reputation as one of the nation's leading papers. Walt Whitman and H. V. Kaltenborn were among its writers; until the turn of

101

the century it had the largest circulation of any afternoon paper in the country. Even as late as 1951, its Pulitzer Prize-winning series on organized crime was influential in helping topple New York City Mayor William O'Dwyer.

Mounting labor troubles combined with the general decline of Brooklyn to topple the *Eagle*. On 29 January 1955, the paper missed its first issue in 114 years, as members of the Newspaper Guild refused to cross a picket line of striking typographers. A month later, the last publisher of the *Brooklyn Eagle*, Frank D. Schroth, closed the paper for good. "On January 28, the paper had 130,000 circulation...and many loyal advertisers. It also had 630 employees. Now it has nothing. No circulation. No advertising. No employees. The consequences of the strike have destroyed the *Eagle*."

The Last Issue of American Magazine

Founded in 1876 as *Frank Leslie's Popular Monthly*, a truly mass-audience publication, *American Magazine* was retitled in 1906 and rapidly became even more popular as a muckraking, youth-oriented journal. Between 1915 and 1923, its most prosperous years, circulation leaped from 500,000 to 2 million. Articles and stories by H. L. Mencken, Edna Ferber and Bruce Barton appeared regularly. *American Magazine* was also the first U. S. publication to run Kipling's highly successful poem, "If."

The generally lowbrow nature of *American Magazine* assured its success well into the 1950s, circulation remaining at about 2.5 million. It specialized in short features, one of the most successful being "It's the Law!" ("In Pasadena, California, it is illegal for a businessman to be alone in his office with his woman secretary." "An ordinance in Zion, Illinois, prohibits teaching pets to smoke cigars.") Another equally pithy feature favorite was entitled "Why Don't They?" and solicited reader participation. ("Why don't they make keys with slots in them so that identification can be written out on a tiny slip of paper and inserted as in luggage tags — Vera-Inez Porter, Minneapolis, Minn.")

Despite holding fast to its 35-cent price and maintaining its circulation, *American Magazine* began losing advertisers soon after World War II. In 1953, the annual deficit was $800,000. Tighter management practices reduced the loss in 1954 to $150,000, and in 1955, the magazine broke even. After dipping into the red again in 1956, Crowell-Collier decided to call it a day. The August 1956 issue was the last for the 80-year old magazine. In addition to the regular short features, it included articles entitled "Let's Take the Mystery out of Cooking," by Rex Stout, "My Best Friends are Monkeys" by Vance Packard, and "A Teenage Dream Come True," (on the budding career of 17-year-old Susan Strasberg).

There was also a notice on page eight calling attention to the fact that *American Magazine* was going out of business — but that its best features would be continued in *Woman's Home Companion* and *Collier*'s.

Neither reader nor publisher, of course, knew then that both of those venerable magazines were also destined to fold — a mere five months later.

The Last Issue of Collier's Magazine

One of the most popular American magazines during its long history, *Collier's* was founded in 1888 as *Once a Week* by immigrant Bible salesman Peter Fenelon Collier.

Freely mixing fiction and news reporting, Collier sent Richard Harding Davis as a special correspondent to the Spanish-American War and the Russo-Japanese War, paying him the unprecedented salary of $1,000 a week at the turn of the century. The crusading editor and publisher also used his magazine to speak in favor of income taxes and women's suffrage and to denounce phony patent medicines and politicians.

Collier's often set the trend in art and literature as well. Henry James' classic short story "The Turn of the Screw" was first published in *Collier*'s. Artist Frederick Remington's paintings appeared in the magazine along with Charles Dana Gibson's voluptuous Gibson Girl drawings, which earned the artist $1,000 apiece.

In 1919, the magazine was sold to Crowell Publishing Company and the emphasis shifted from art and exposes to cartoon and light fiction.

Although the change in format was regretted by some, the magazine was regularly read by Hollywood moguls on the lookout for film material and frequently they purchased *Collier's* stories. (The 10 April 1937 issue, for example, contained two short stories, "Stage of Lordsburg," by Ernest Haycox, which was made into the 1939 John Wayne epic, *Stagecoach*, and "Bringing Up Baby" by Hagar Wilde, which became the 1939 movie of the same title, starring Cary Grant and Katharine Hepburn.)

Collier's golden age was 1925 to 1943, after which circulation began to decline. In 1953, the magazine lost $7.5 million and another $4.5 million in 1954.

The final issue was dated 4 January 1957. Making no mention of its own passing, the magazine featured an upbeat story on "good kids" as opposed to delinquents and urged readers not to miss the following parts of several continuing features.

Its influence lingered, however, so much that in a 1964 survey of several hundred New Yorkers' reading habits, nine percent said they currently read *Collier's*. Seven percent said that if they had to pick out only one magazine on a list to receive, it would be *Collier's*.

The Last Woman's Home Companion

First published in Cleveland in 1873, *Woman's Home Companion* was an early service magazine, loaded with helpful hints to homemakers via departments ranging from "Mother's Corner" to "Flowers — Care and Culture." During the early years of the twentieth century, it published serials by Willa Cather and Edna Ferber. A strong competitor to *McCall's* and *Good Housekeeping*, it began to lose ground after World War II, when changing lifestyles caused many families to cut back magazine subscriptions.

By 1956, *Woman's Home Companion* was losing money, but it clung tenaciously to its traditional format. In fact, the three-part novel starting in the January 1957 issue, "Blue Camellia" by Frances Parkinson Keyes, seemed right out of the nineteenth century: "Lavinia lived in two worlds — the real world in the sacrifices, the rewards of prairie life, and in a dream world which only had room for herself and Fleex. She longed for the magic moment when the two would be one." Other features of the same issue, extremely typical of the fare offered regularly by the magazine, dealt with "How to Take a Day Off," "How to Care for your Sick Child at Home," "Dishtowels are Gay Gift Wraps," and for those with a desire for something meatier, a think-piece by Eric Sevareid on America's mood, circa 1957. There was no mention of the fact that *Woman's Home Companion* was about to fold.

That issue was indeed the surprise ending for some 440 editorial, advertising, business and clerical staffers of the magazine, many of whom had worked at their posts for twenty years or more.

The most concrete early information concerning the magazine's demise came at Christmas, when a note was pinned on the bulletin board that read: "We regret to inform you that there is no Santa Claus."

And those readers who might have cared never did find out if Lavinia and Fleex found that magic moment.

The Last Issue of Etude

Once the most widely read music publication in the world, *Etude* was first issued in October of 1883 at Lynchburg, Virginia. At that time, the editor explained, music teachers who did not live near large cities had "very little, if any, other means of acquiring that necessary information." Publisher Arthur Presser's original investment in the new magazine was a mere $250.

The stake paid off handsomely. *Etude*'s circulation reached 250,000 in the peak year of 1919. From the start, the periodical — which sold for 10 cents — was highly thought of by music teachers, who relied on it for hints on technique as well as its advertisements suggesting graduation gifts ("A very attractive lyre design pin — 10K, solid gold, $1.25") *Etude* was not particularly loved by thousands of students who had to plunk through the monthly exercises or read feature articles such as "The Great Composers' Love of Flowers," "Why are Sharps Harder than Flats?" or "A Thought for the Piano Tuner."

A few months after the first issue's publication, Presser moved the magazine to Philadelphia and began publishing music in it. When he died in 1925, both *Etude* and Presser's Bryn Mawr music publishing company were internationally renowned. Over the years contributors included Maurice Ravel, Walter Damrosch, Artur Rodzinski, Lauritz Melchior, Renata Tebaldi, and Cesare Siepe.

During the 1930s and 1940s, *Etude*'s circulation dropped to 50,000 but it was carried at a loss until 1957, when Arthur A. Hauser, one-time cellist and publisher, officially admitted that it was out of tune with the times. The availability of musical conservatories, he said, provided the advanced teaching service originally supplied by the magazine.

Etude's last issue was in June of that year. Highlights included a cover portrait of Beethoven, an interview with Tebaldi, a biographical sketch of composer Igor Stravinsky, and a lengthy obituary of pianist Joseph Hofmann.

The Last of the International News Service

Started in 1909 by William Randolph Hearst, who wanted a private news service for his own chain of papers, the International News Service (INS) was never a profit-making operation. A proud man, Hearst kept it going long after it became obvious INS was a loser.

To compete with Associated Press' thoroughness and United Press' color, INS soon fell back on sensationalism. "On a coronation story," one critic of INS wrote, "editors could rely on the Associated Press for the dimensions of the cathedral, the U. P. for the mood of the ceremony, and the International News Service (sometimes) for an interview with the barmaid across the way."

Despite its slapdash style, INS did have some well-known columnists, including Bob Considine, Ruth Montgomery and Louella Parsons. According to writer Charles Einstein, the INS headquarters in New York also may have been one of the last great zany newsrooms: "The staff included the only man who ever got a medical discharge from the French Foreign Legion," Einstein wrote, "as well as a one-armed copy boy who, when harassed, would cry out, 'For Chrissakes, I've only got two hands.'"

On another occasion, INS sports editor Lawton Carter dictated his column about the Chicago Cubs to Professor Albert Einstein after he yelled, "Give me Einstein," to the switchboard operator, who promptly referred to her celebrity file rather than transferring Carter to the member of the sports staff he really wanted to speak to.

By the 1950s, INS was costing the Hearst chain $3 million annually. The best solution seemed to be a merger, which INS and U. P. had been exploring since 1927. Finally, after 31 years, the merger was brought about on 24 May 1958, and the two organizations became United Press International.

Fittingly, the traditionally thorough Associated Press beat the new United Press International on its own birthday story. Picking up the news from the Dow Jones wire, AP told the merger story a full nineteen hours before UPI acknowledged is own existence.

The Last New York Mirror

"The *New York Mirror*, 39, a partner in the Hearst Corporation, died yesterday at its home, 235 East 45th Street, after a long illness. It is survived by a sister, the *New York Journal-American*. Funeral services will be held at 11 a. m. today at the *New York Daily News*, 220 East 42nd Street."

Thus wrote a sardonic obituary writer about the *New York Mirror* on the afternoon of 15 October 1963, only hours after the final edition of the newspaper was to hit the streets. For most of the 1,600 employees of the paper, the closing was a surprise. Some, such as Assistant City Editor Mortimer Davis, accepted the news with little more than a shrug. "Second time this has happened to me," said Davis. "On 3 January 1950, the *Sun* folded under me." Others were less philosophical. "Typical Hearst closing," said one rewrite man. "They ring down the curtain in the middle of the third act and don't tell anybody anything."

Founded in 1924 by William Randolph Hearst, the original *Mirror* promised its readers that it would be ninety percent entertainment and ten percent news. It largely held true to that promise, featuring a variety of picture puzzles, yo-yo contests, and other schemes to encourage readers to "play" the paper, even if they wouldn't read it.

It was also not above using sensationalism to sell papers. During the 1920s, for example, the *Mirror* called for the reopening of the lurid Hall-Mills murder case, contending that it could produce new evidence against the wife who allegedly murdered her minister husband. Nothing came of the newspaper's claim, however.

Later, the *Mirror* capitalized on public interest in the Lindbergh kidnapping case, describing how representatives of the newspaper were going to Canada to talk to some gangsters who knew where the baby was. The *Mirror* planned to bring the child back and present him to New York City Mayor James J. Walker on the steps of City Hall. It turned out that the gangsters knew nothing about the kidnapping.

In 1934, veteran newsman Arthur Brisbane took over the *Mirror* and promised to do away with trivia and emphasize news. But, when the paper continued to lose money, Hearst telegraphed Brisbane: "Dear Arthur, you are now getting out the worst paper in the United States."

The death blow to the *Mirror* came in 1963, when a 114-day newspaper strike caused it to lose crucial advertising. Thus, although it had a daily circulation of 800,000 and 1.8 million on Sundays, the *Mirror* could not pull itself out of the downward spiral.

The last issue, No. 99 of Volume 40, dated 16 October 1963, was 56 pages long and did not mention the paper's demise. The page one headline read: "Valachi Sings Here Today."

At 1:25 a.m. on that morning, Mort Ehrman, night editor and a member of the *Mirror* staff since 1925, said before walking out of the office for the last time: "Well, gentlemen, good night, and before you leave be sure to kill the bottles."

New York City, which had sixteen general circulation newspapers at the turn of the century, was down to six.

The Last of the New York Herald-Tribune

Once known as "the Bible of the West," the *New York Tribune* was founded on 10 April 1841 by a balding New England minister of 30 named Horace Greeley. Having borrowed $1,000 to get the enterprise going, Greeley promised his readers that "the immoral and degrading police reports, advertisements, and other matters which have been allowed to disgrace the columns of our leading penny papers will be carefully excluded from this, and no exertion will be spared to render it worthy of the hearty approval of the virtuous and refined, and a welcome visitant at the family fireside."

Greeley's venture staggered along for the first few months, mixing morality and disarming truth ("Congress did nothing yesterday to speak of") with limited advertising, the paper losing money at the rate of $200 to $300 a week. But at the end of one year, circulation stood at 10,000 and was rising rapidly.

Greeley was soon a celebrated man as a result of the paper's success, although he was not universally liked. Sam Houston once remarked, for example, that Greeley was a man "whose hair is white, whose skin is white, whose eyes are white, whose clothes are white and whose liver is, in my opinion, of the same color." Nevertheless, the *Tribune* was known as a crusading paper, taking a firm stance against slavery before such a view was popular.

Greeley ran for President in 1872, and died less than a month after being defeated. The *Tribune* continued to remain influential in the decades that followed (although it often lost money). In 1924, it acquired the venerable *New York Herald* and became the *Herald-Tribune*.

The paper held its own until the troubled 1960s, when so many dailies went out of business. Its final publisher, John Hay Whitney, struggled for eight years, only to lose an estimated $20 million. Then on 21 March 1966, William Randolph Hearst, Jr. and Roy Howard announced the formation of the *World-Journal-Tribune* Corporation which, they hoped, would put out the *Herald-Tribune* in the evening. The plan soon disintegrated, however, and the last edition of the *Herald-Tribune* appeared on 23 April 1966. The Sunday edition and certain elements of the format were merged into the *World Journal Tribune*, which lingered only until 5 May 1967. The big headline on that sad issue proclaimed the paper's demise, beneath which was a smaller headline on the equally ill-fated war in Vietnam: "Marines mop up on Hill 881."

Last Newspaper with Solid Front-page Advertising

"On this...the last day of traditional front-page advertising in this newspaper, H.R. Owen Ltd. are proud to offer at 17 Berkeley Street, London W.L. Tel: May. 9060..." began the classified advertisement for a London car dealer, following with a full-column listing of new and used Bentleys, Daimlers, and Jaguars for sale.

It was 2 May 1966, the last day the *London Times*, as it had daily since 1785, dedicated its front page solidly to advertising rather than news. The next day, Londoners were greeted with news headlines in unaccustomed large type: "London to be new H.Q. for NATO," "Clash between the major fuel industries," "Rebuff to a Rhodesian Minister," along with a poem in the lower righthand corner explaining what had happened. It read:

> Dear Jenks (deceased) of whom is sought the kith,
> Dear QC1, for sale with ancient Rover,
> Dear Skiing Foursome anxious for a fifth,
> Page one no more is yours, so please turn over.
> Dear Charity, inviting your bequest,
> Dear Widow, cheerful, good but simple cook,
> Dear Gentlefolk who welcome paying guest,
> Page One your simple pleas no more will brook.
> Dear SRN, the queen of irrigation,
> Dear Thankers, ever grateful to St. Jude,
> Dear Titled Lady, find a new location,
> Page One on graver issues now must brood.

Frequently in the late eighteenth and early nineteenth centuries, the *Times* carried parliamentary reports alongside the classified advertisements on page one, but only twice during its entire history did it depart from tradition by putting major news stories on the front page. The first departure was on 7 November 1805 when the

Times reported Admiral Nelson was victorious at Trafalgar. The second was on 25 January 1965, following the death of Sir Winston Churchill.

A spokesman for the *Times* called the decision to abandon front-page advertising "a natural development in the progress of the paper."

During the early nineteenth century, all British and most American newspapers used their front pages solely for advertising. After the Civil War, however, most U.S. papers had broken the tradition, although a few retained the front page classified ads until about 1900. In Great Britain, a London newspaper called *The Morning* experimented with news on the front page in 1892, but the change was criticized as "un-English." In September of 1900, however, the *Daily Express* was launched with front page news and the fashion caught on.

Some of the more staid periodicals held out, notably the *Times* and the *Manchester Guardian*, which, founded in 1821, retained front page advertising until 29 September 1952. That left the *Times* as the sole remaining holdout, a situation that was maintained for nearly fourteen years.

The Last Simplicissimus

Established in 1896 by a young publisher named Albert Langen and a talented caricaturist, Thomas Teodor Heine, the satiric German magazine *Simplicissimus* soon won wide recognition for its reckless courage and aggressive liberalism.

Known as *Simpl* to its devotees, *Simplicissimus* used poisonously mocking prose and brutal drawings to attack the pompous and complacent elements of German society, from the debauched morality of the middle class to the thick-headedness of the Prussian officer class to the dim-witted self-satisfaction of the German peasant.

One of the most famous cartoons was a Heine caricature of Kaiser Wilhelm II in 1898. The Kaiser, then on a trip to Palestine, was portrayed in a pilgrim's cape. Enraged, the Kaiser had Heine thrown in jail and Langen was forced to flee to Paris.

Perhaps because of its notoriety, *Simplicissimus* featured articles by many famous authors, including Anton Chekhov, Arthur Schnitzler, and Thomas Mann.

Prevented from publishing at the outset of World War I, the magazine took on new teeth under Franz Schoenberner, who became editor in November of 1929. Schoenberner did not take long displaying his anti-Hitler feelings. In a 1930 issue of the magazine, a cartoon by Heine showed two German policemen lifting the top of Hitler's head to display a void inside. "Isn't it strange that you can make such a lot of trouble with so little stuff?" read the caption.

The final issue of *Simplicissimus* that bore Schoenberner's name as editor was published in March of 1933, two months after Hitler became chancellor. On the first page of the magazine was a drawing of the Reichstag fire with a caption that read: "Out of this fire will a new phoenix rise?"

Eventually, Schoenberner fled Munich, where the magazine was published, and made his way across the border to Switzerland.

After World War II, the magazine was revived, but postwar Germans were largely apathetic and *Simplicissimus'* circulation remained low. Apparently, targets as juicy as Kaiser Wilhelm and Adolf Hitler were lacking and, perhaps as a result, the humor was indistinct. The magazine, a biweekly, appeared for the last time on 22 May 1967.

Last Issue of the Reporter

From the day it started in 1949, the *Reporter*'s standards were high. Its writers stayed close to the facts and the magazine's founder-publisher Max Ascoli cheerfully accepted the postwar United States' role as arbiter and international policeman.

Among the contributors to the *Reporter* were James Thurber, Ray Bradbury, Gore Vidal, Vladimir Nabokov and Dean Acheson, the former U.S. Secretary of State, who wrote a critique of popular songs.

Over the years the number of subscribers to the magazine remained fairly steady at 210,000; the problem according to Ascoli, was that their identity changed from liberal-academic to less literary types, which resulted in publishing houses, the major advertisers, reducing their advertising. Another cause of the *Reporter*'s demise was that its postwar attitude did not change even after United States involvement in Vietnam. Supporting that involvement, Ascoli's magazine inevitably incurred both the moral and financial wrath of American liberals.

The final issue of the *Reporter* appeared on 13 June 1968. Its contents included an article on Hubert Humphrey's chances in the coming election, a piece entitled "Adam Clayton Powell's Last Stand," and a eulogy for Maryland's forward-looking new constitution, which had just been rejected by the voters.

In his editorial farewell to his readers, Ascoli wrote, "The time for an end had to come to this magazine, and the end had better be inflicted by me than by somebody else when I am not in condition to write..."

The Last Issue of This Week

A weekly supplement to Sunday newspapers with a great deal of similarity to *Reader's Digest*, *This Week* was born in the mid-1930s, did well in to the 1950s, then quickly outlived its usefulness.

Not exactly tacky, *This Week* had a somewhat hasty, unplanned look. Occasionally issues attempted to present a theme, as on 1 June 1969, which featured a young married couple on its cover and continued the matrimonial theme inside. Stories included a profile on Priscilla of Boston, "queen of the wedding business," by Joe McCarthy; an historical piece about the nineteenth century penchant for getting married in a soaring balloon, by George A. Gipe; and *This Week*'s food editor Myra Waldo presented "A Toast to the Happy Couple" with several punch recipes. Just sixteen pages long, however, it was clear *This Week* was fatally low on advertising.

Five months later, the supplement came to an end with the 2 November issue. "For 35 years, the editors of *This Week* magazine have been privileged to enter the homes of more than 20 million Americans every week," a closing editorial box noted. "We have entertained, informed, amused, helped — and occasionally irritated — our readers throughout the United States. We have enjoyed being an extra member of the family."

Going out partially in style, Olddens' regular "Last Laugh" cartoon had been retitled "Last Last Laugh," but had nothing to do with the situation at hand. Nor was it particularly funny.

The Last Large-sized Life Magazine

For thirty-six years, *Life* was the biggest magazine in the world and acted that way. The cover picture, on its first issue (dated 23 November 1936) was a gee-whiz shot of the Fort Peck Dam on the Missouri River in Montana, the perspective-compressed concrete supports resembling something out of a science-fiction movie — which of course, was just what *Life* wanted.

During the 1930s, when the Depression had made nearly everyone think small, *Life* reversed the process by presenting a magazine that measured thirteen-and-a-half by twenty-one inches opened flat — a display area larger than many of today's television screens. The daring concept caught on. The first week that *Life* was on the newsstands caused near panic for everyone concerned: dealers telephoned and telegraphed for more copies, presses literally creaked and broke down trying to keep up with the demand, and paper stocks ran low.

The editors of that first *Life* magazine included a startling full-page photograph of an obstetrician holding up a newborn baby with the caption: "*Life* begins." That, of course, was more than just a coy announcement of the magazine's birth. It was a proclamation that *Life* was willing to shock, educate , and explore, for, surprisingly (at least to readers of a later generation), that shot of a baby caused some people to protest that the magazine, in its very first issue, had already gone too far. (One must remember, after all, that practically the only "respectable" magazine of that era which showed anything as daring as female breasts was *National Geographic*.)

Later, during World War II, the same criticism was directed at *Life* when its photographers shot, and its editors published, pictures of dead soldiers that some complained were "too brutal." Staffers were not discouraged, however, recalling the words of John Shaw Billings, *Life*'s managing editor, during the Spanish Civil War, "If free men refuse to look at dead bodies then brave men will have died in vain."

As success came to *Life*, its staff became increasingly bold and innovative, for they not only had to top other magazines but top their own weekly efforts. This led one photographer to ask a general, "Would you please move your army back two steps for a better composition?" Success bred the feeling among staffers that a story on Pius XII was "*Life*'s first pope," (and therefore, the first real press coverage given to *any* pope). Trying to get an edge on the competition, *Life* hired a pair of lip readers with binoculars to report on what Queen Elizabeth and Prince Philip said as they watched their first American football game. ("Why does that man leave the huddle first?" she asked, a perfectly logical question.)

At its height, between 1945 and 1955, *Life* sold 8 million copies a week. In addition to stunning photographic journalism, it presented works by some of the world's finest writers. Ernest Hemingway's novel *The Old Man and the Sea* first appeared in the magazine, complete in one issue. Other contributors included Evelyn Waugh, Graham Greene, Robert Penn Warren, James Michener, Norman Mailer, and John Hersey.

The end of the big magazine came with "sickening suddenness," as one *Life* staffer put it. There had been rumors in 1961 and 1970, as one magazine after another folded. A fairly well-kept secret until early December of 1972, the last issue of the large-sized *Life* magazine was dated 25 January 1973. On its cover was a collage of the year's events and names ("Olympics, Hurricane Agnes, Fischer, Vietnam, Godfather, Berrigans...") at the very bottom right-hand corner of which was the word "Goodbye."

Subsequently, *Life* reappeared as a smaller magazine but for nearly everyone, of course, it was just not the same.

The Last Issue of Coronet Magazine

A family-oriented magazine aping *Reader's Digest* in both physical size and subject matter, *Coronet* was first published in 1936 and boasted a circulation of more than 2 million a quarter-century later.

A mixed bag of short features, *Coronet* attempted to stay current with changing mores during the 1970s. The December 1976 issue, for example, contained a pair of articles which paid deference to shifting attitudes regarding sex and marriage. One was entitled:

"Divorce Etiquette: How to Spare the Kids." The other, addressed to housewives and professional women, was provocatively titled: "When Your Rival is a Man."

The same issue also carried several hoary features which might have appeared in a *Coronet*, circa World War II. One, entitled "Funny Fashion Laws," pointed out that in Minnesota, "...it's illegal for a woman to dress up and try to impersonate Santa Claus on any city street. Violators can get a fine of $25.00 and/or up to thirty days in a local jail."

Another feature, apparently straight out of the seventeenth century, consisted of the magazine's official "witch" responding to questions. One, an answer to "Dear Leonora," began, "For nine days wear rosary beads under your clothing. They should not touch your skin. But before you begin, dip a white round, silky pebble into holy water and carry it with you at all times..." Et cetera.

Partly because of its general lack of distinction and also because of declining readership for most magazines during the postwar eras, *Coronet* became a late casualty, its final issue appearing in July of 1977.

The Last (?) Look Magazine

There is no guarantee that a last *Look* is really that. In 1971, the once-popular competitor of *Life* gave up the ghost after thirty-four years, only to turn up again.

A biweekly which began as a monthly, *Look*'s first issue was dated February 1937, and sold for ten cents. The number featured a profile of Nazi strongman Hermann Goering as well as articles on actress Joan Crawford, Franklin Roosevelt, and the promise of "200 pictures...1001 facts!" Popular (the first issue sold 700,000 copies) and controversial (because of the Goering article, it was banned in Nazi Germany) from the beginning, *Look* had a circulation of 1.7 million in less than a year. Its success continued until 1969, when it reached a circulation peak of 7.5 million. That was three years after its best advertising year, however, when revenues reached $80 million in 1966. By 1970, advertising revenues had dropped to $62.8 million.

Look's best year was also its most controversial. Jacqueline Kennedy unsuccessfully tried to stop publication of William Manchester's *Death of a President*, which was serialized in the magazine before being published in book form.

In 1971, *Look* was planning another potentially controversial series, a 10,000-word extract of former President Lyndon B. Johnson's memoirs. That year, the financial situation of the magazine took a turn for the worse, however, rising mail rates and shrinking advertising bringing a loss that reached $10 million over a

2½ year period. Also citing the influence of television, founder Gardner Cowles announced that the magazine was folding.

After a seven-year hiatus, *Look* appeared again in 1978, but the financial problems quickly proved even more burdensome than in 1971. The publishers called it quits once more after the August, 1979, issue. In the final 96-page issue, there was no mention that the magazine was going out of business. The last item in the book was a picture of actor John Wayne cuddling Marguerite Churchill in the 1930 movie, *The Big Trail*.

The Last of New Times Magazine

Not with a bang or a whimper, but with a sneer and a snarl — *New Times* magazine ended publication on 8 January 1979.

Although it was published for only five years, *New Times* was regarded — especially by itself — as a kind of sophisticated savior of mankind, a literary voice in the wilderness calling to America's better nature. First published during the Watergate scandals, *New Times* specialized in investigative reporting, dealing with subjects such as dangers from aerosol cans, certain cosmetics, microwave ovens, and much of the nation's drinking water. Among *New Times'* most widely read articles were those disclosing racial slurs made by Secretary of Agriculture Earl Butz, who later resigned over the disclosures.

Nevertheless, lack of sustained reader interest in investigative reporting, social issues, and public affairs led to the magazine's demise. Publisher George A. Hirsch cited the attitudes of the "Me Decade" and rising postal rates as the two most crippling factors.

New Times' swan song, the 138th issue, lambasted the nation in an article subtitled "America Shrugged." "Welcome to America," it began. "Our Miss Shields will show you to your table. Such a pretty baby...what'll it be? Have a drink, have a puff, have a snort?...'We do it all for you.' That's the spirit of '79. Proposition 13...Don't think about anything..."

Calling it "the end of a dream," Hirsch did not refer in his editorial to what may have been a contributing factor to the magazine's death. Several months before, after blasting the oil companies in a series of articles, *New Times* accepted advertising from Exxon. Letters poured in, accusing the publishers of gross hypocrisy, readers asking how the magazine that prided itself on being the guardian of the nation's morals could do such a thing.

It was, of course, a good question.

Chapter Four

The Last Time I Saw...

Chronology

224 B. C.
The Colossus of Rhodes, one of the "seven ancient wonders of the world," is destroyed during an earthquake.

262 A. D.
The Temple of Diana at Ephesus, Greece, is destroyed by attacking Goths.

302
The Baths of Diocletian, last of the great Roman public bathing facilities, is constructed.

476
The magnificent statue of Zeus designed by architect Phidias in 435 B.C. is destroyed in a great fire at Constantinople.

1810
A U.S. landmark since 1682, the Penn "treaty tree," located in Philadelphia, is blown down in a storm.

1856
(Aug. 21) The Charter Oak, in Hartford, Connecticut, where the Connecticut colonial charter was hidden in 1687, falls.

1919
Sherry's Restaurant closes in New York City after twenty-one years on Fifth Avenue.

1923
Delmonico's Restaurant in New York City goes out of business after ninety-one years. (see p. 119)
(August) A beloved landmark since Colonial times, the Washington Elm of Cambridge, Massachusetts, has to be removed.

1926
The Cape Henlopen lighthouse, constructed in 1767, is destroyed by a storm, leaving only one Colonial lighthouse intact in all of the U. S. (see p. 118)

1936
(Nov. 30) One of the most amazing structures of its time, the eighty-five-year-old Crystal Palace in London comes to an end in a mass of twisted iron and melted glass after a flash fire. (see p. 121)

1939
(Dec. 14) The Rennert Hotel, Baltimore hangout of local politicians and writer H. L. Mencken, goes out of business. (see p. 120)

1945
(Dec. 31) Fort Niagara, a U.S. military post since 1726, is

deactivated and made a New York State park.

1947
(April 24) Known as the "old lady of Murray Hill," the Murray Hill Hotel, opened in 1884, is closed.

1955
The last alien is processed at Ellis Island, America's premier immigration station since 1892. (see p. 123)

1960
Chicago's last packing house closes as meat packers move west.
In existence as a military facility since 1776, Mitchel Air Force Base at East Meadow, Long Island, is closed.

1961
Despite its landmark status, Chicago's Garrick Theatre Building is torn down. (see p. 124)

1963
The Cavendish Hotel on Jermyn Street, London, famous in Edwardian days as the resort of nobility, is torn down.
(Oct. 28) Demolition begins on Penn Station, a New York landmark since 1910. (see p. 124)

1965
Coney Island's Steeplechase Park, a favorite with amusement park fans, is closed.
(June 30) Two venerable New York hotels, the Savoy Plaza and Park Lane, close on the same day.

1967
(June 30) First opened in 1904, the Astor Hotel, New York, is razed to make room for an office building. (see p. 127)
(Dec. 1) Demolition begins on Tokyo's Imperial Hotel, which was designed by Frank Lloyd Wright and constructed nearly fifty years before. (see p. 126)

1968
(Feb. 13) The final event is held at Madison Square Garden, ending its illustrious forty-three years of history. (see p. 129)
London Bridge, constructed across the Thames River between 1824 and 1831, is torn down and shipped to America. (see p. 127)
(July 15) Willard's Hotel in Washington, D. C., suddenly closes its doors, ending a history dating back to before the Civil War. (see p. 128)

1969
(March 1-2) An 843-year era comes to an end as Les Halles Market in Paris closes. (see p. 130)

1971
(July 24) Garfield's Cafeteria in Brooklyn closes.
(Dec. 5) The Colony Restaurant, famous in New York City for fifty years, closes.

1972
(January) Long an institution, the Smith Brothers cough drop factory leaves Poughkeepsie, New York.
(April 19) The New Yorker Hotel in Manhattan closes after forty-three years. Schrafft's a fifty-year-old institution on 23rd Street, New York City, closes.
(March 18) First activiated in 1663, Fort Wadsworth, Staten Island, is phased out of existence.

1973
(Jan. 15) Demolition begins on the Garden City Hotel, a Long Island landmark since 1874.
(Aug. 23) The University Hotel, New York landmark for nearly a century at 673 Broadway, collapses.

1973
(Oct. 17) The Amberjack, last submarine based at the Key West (Florida) Naval Station, is decommisioned, ending the base's 150-year history as a home for American war vessels.

1974
(July 1) The 174-year old Boston Naval Shipyard, oldest in the nation, closes.

1976
Lucy the Margate Elephant, a beloved architectural oddity since 1881 and last surviving elephant-shaped building by architect James Lafferty, is declared a National Historic Landmark. (see p. 132)

1980
(April 30) Washingtonians bid farewell to Duke's Restaurant, which closes after thirty years. (see p. 133)
(July 3) The Chalfonte Hotel in Atlantic City, first opened in 1904, is demolished.
The Copacabana Palace, a gathering spot for the international set on Rio de Janeiro's ocean-front for fifty-seven years, is razed.

The Last Colonial Lighthouse

From 1716 to 1771, as the American colonies grew from a scattered group of rural communities into a entity cohesive enough to wage war against Great Britain, ten major lighthouses were built along the Atlantic coast.

The first lighthouse — the Boston Light — came about as the result of a petition by local merchants for a "Light House and Lanthorn on some Head Land at the Entrance of the Harbor of Boston..." It was constructed, a tall, graceful tower of stone, and opened on 14 September 1716, its light consisting of either candles or lamps. The first keeper of the Boston Light, George Worthylake, drowned on 3 November 1718, when a boat carrying him and his family capsized. Benjamin Franklin, then a young man, memorialized the event in a poem entitled "Lighthouse Tragedy."

The Boston Light was blown up by the British on 3 June 1776 just before they abandoned the city.

Other lighthouses of the Colonial era included the Tybee Island Light in Georgia (1748), Beavertail Light (1749) in Rhode Island, New London (Connecticut) Light (1760), Sandy Hook (New Jersey) Light (1764), Cape Henlopen Light (1767), Charleston (S.C.) Light (1767), Plymouth (Mass.) Light (1769), Portsmouth (N.H.) Light (1771), and Cape Ann Light (1771). Many of the lighthouses survived for some years after the Revolution, forming the basis for the new nation's lighthouse system, which was created in 1789, one of the first acts of the new government. Eight of the Colonial lighthouses were gone by the time of the Civil War, the two exceptions being the Sandy Hook and Cape Henlopen lights.

The Cape Henlopen structure, which had spent years battling the sand and the wind, finally toppled over during a violent storm in 1926.

The lighthouse at Sandy Hook, which had been financed by two lotteries, was known for a long time as the New York Lighthouse, since it served ocean traffic bound for that port. During the Revolution, American forces tried to destroy the Sandy Hook Light but the tower was too well-built and resisted their efforts. The tower house has survived to the present, the country's oldest and last of the Colonial lighthouses.

The Last of Delmonico's Restaurant

For more than nine decades, the original Delmonico's Restaurant was the standard of excellence for other eating establishments in New York City. It all began in 1827, when a cafe and pastry shop was opened in lower Manhattan by Swiss merchant Giovanni Del Monico and his brother, Pietro.

By 1831, they had opened a complete restaurant at 23-25 William Street and become John and Peter Delmonico. A year later, they were joined by their nineteen-year-old nephew, Lorenzo, who built the business into New York's most celebrated restaurant. In 1836, Delmonico's issued the first printed menus in the United States. Lorenzo, who imported European cooks and recipes, helped popularize green vegetables, salads and ices in this country. Celebrities such as Abraham Lincoln, William Seward, Andrew Johnson, Ulysses S. Grant, Charles Dickens, John Greenleaf Whittier, Henry Wadsworth Longfellow, Bayard Taylor, William Cullen Bryant, Ralph Waldo Emerson, and Samuel F. B. Morse dined there.

In its rooms and banquet halls, foreign nobility were entertained. Louis Napolean, later emperor of France, enjoyed the gaiety and warm hospitality for which Delmonico's was famous. When George M. Pullman constructed the first regularly scheduled dining car in 1868 for his Chicago and Alton Railroad, he named it Delmonico's, in honor of the New York restaurant.

Plots were frequently hatched at Delmonico's. In addition to the political ones undoubtedly conceived by the various U. S. Presidents and their underlings who dined at the restaurant, other schemes were sometimes created as well. In 1889, Delmonico's entertained some 300 people (including Mark Twain and Chauncey M. Depew) who gathered to honor a group of baseball stars just back from a foreign tour. Anxious to prove that baseball was "purely American," and not descended from the British game called "rounders," (which it decidedly was), one of the speakers, Abraham G. Mills, proposed that a committee be appointed to investigate baseball's background and squelch the rumor that it had British ancestry. Subsequently, another group of the same persuasion invented the myth that baseball was created by Abner Doubleday at Cooperstown, New York, an outright lie that was accepted until very recently.

Having come uptown to Fifth Avenue and 14th Street in 1861, Delmonico's moved to Fifth and 44th Street in 1897 and prospered until hard hit by the 18th Amendment. In 1922, it was raided by government agents, who charged that Delmonico's waiters were serving alcoholic beverages to customers. The charge was denied, of course, but not long afterward news leaked out that the famous old restaurant was in dire financial staits.

Early in 1923, Josephine Delmonico became the last of her name to operate the restaurant that her great-great uncle had founded. Joining Stanley's, Murray's, and several other well-known establishments which could not compete with speakeasies, Delmonico's had a gala last night on 21 May 1923, then closed its doors for good.

The Closing of the Rennert Hotel, Baltimore

Late on the afternoon of 14 December 1939, the manager of the Rennert Hotel in Baltimore telephoned H. L. Mencken and said, "Come by for old time's sake and help close down the place." Mencken, who liked good food and drink and also knew history in the making when he saw it, replied immediately: "I'll be there about ten this evening."

He, like many others in Baltimore, knew the old hotel and eating establishment was in financial trouble, but the sudden closing came as something of a shock. Located since 1885 at the southwest corner of Liberty and Saratoga Streets, the Rennert was truly a Baltimore tradition. Robert Rennert, who opened the establishment, was unconventionally successful in that he offered Maryland food while other restaurants specialized in French cuisine. So expert was the kitchen staff that during its heyday the Rennert shipped terrapin and oysters to New York by train in order to satisfy the more fastidious gourmets of Gotham. Tammany Hall leaders, on their way south, invariably stopped at the Rennert for a memorable meal. Called "the palace of the South," the Rennert was thoroughly studied for three weeks by architect George C. Boldt before he constructed the Waldorf-Astoria in New York.

The first U.S. President to dine at the Rennert was Benjamin Harrison, who stopped by in 1885. Later, when the Democratic National Convention of 1912 conducted the business of nominating Woodrow Wilson, the nominee's headquarters was the Rennert. He ate there many times after being elected, as did Baltimore political boss John J. (Sonny) Mahon, who converted the Rennert lobby into Democratic headquarters for the entire state of Maryland.

From 1906 to 1915, Mencken held court in the Rennert dining room every lunch hour. "Terrapin, oyster pie, chicken pie," he reminisced. "There were no 'a la's' on the bill of fare. It was all straight, plain stuff. But when the game laws stopped the Rennert from serving wild duck, that was a hard blow. They kept up the custom of serving seven oysters in a half-dozen, thirteen in a dozen. And good oysters. That was before the Maryland variety began to deteriorate."

Another hard blow — to the hotel as well as its patrons — was Prohibition, which changed the Rennert from one of the more popular gathering places in town to another aging building alive only with memories. Nevertheless, a revival of sorts was held after the nation changed from "dry" to "wet." It was only fitting that at 12:01 a.m., 6 April 1933, Mencken officiated at the Rennert's mahogany bar as Prohibition came to an official end. "Pretty good, not bad at all," he smiled, after tasting the new Repeal beer.

The decline of the hotel continued, however, until by 1939, the owners owed the city $150,000 in back taxes. And so Mencken returned to the old place one last time, had a few beers, reminisced about the old days, and left several minutes before midnight, when the Rennert doors closed for the last time.

The Demise of the Crystal Palace, London

Designed by Sir Joseph Paxton for the International Exhibition of 1851, the Crystal Palace in London was the largest single structure in the world — four times the size of St. Peter's in Rome, seven times the size of St. Paul's in London. A gargantuan structure of cast iron and glass, it had a central corridor one-third of a mile long, was 108 feet high, tall enough to enclose a pair of ninety-foot trees, and was the largest glass-walled building ever built. Because of its size, it used one-third of Great Britain's glass output for an entire year and required 2,000 workers to complete it.

While work was in progress on the Crystal Palace, the huge structure became the focal point of much controversy. Some considered the plans radical, even unsafe, and were certain the first strong wind would shatter the building into trillions of glass slivers or that the summer sun would be magnified enough to roast its occupants. Had it not been for Prince Albert's determination, the new exhibition hall might never have been built.

It was completed in time for the fair, however, and was a tremendous success. In 141 days, 6 million people visited the Crystal Palace to marvel at Colt's new repeating revolver and other technological developments. "The old joke about the gloom, smoke and dirt of London, and the austerity, inhospitality, and semi-lunacy of the British character has been dissipated,"reported the *Illustrated London News*, "and our Parisian friends confess that the 'sombre' city has produced the gayest, most fairy-like, most beautiful and original building in the world..."

When the exhibition was over, the "blazing arch of lucid glass," as Thackeray described it, was threatened with destruction. The government refused to allow it to remain in Hyde Park, so a committee of public-spirited citizens bought it as it stood for 70,000 pounds and a company was formed to have it removed to the then-rural heights of Sydenham.

The great building soon became London's chief place of resort. For years, a fete at the Crystal Palace was essential for entertaining royalty, some of whom included Napoleon III and the Empress Eugenie, the Sultan of Turkey, Shah of Persia, Tsar of Russia, Queen of Greece, Sultan of Zanzibar, and Kaiser Wilhelm of Germany. Displays of fireworks at the Crystal Palace also attracted large crowds, despite the distance from town. Tightrope walker Blondin performed there, not only on the high wire, but playing the part of an ape in a dramatic piece by Henry Coleman entitled *The Child of the Wreck*. While on the high wire, in June of 1861, Blondin turned somersaults, walked on stilts, climbed over the back of a balanced chair, and cooked an omelette, all on a rope 170 feet high which was stretched between the ends of the building.

The Crystal Palace remained intact until 30 November 1936, when it caught fire — through an unknown cause — and crashed to earth, a raging inferno of twisted girders and molten glass. The fire could be seen fifty miles away.

No lives were lost, but had the fire occurred a day later, it might have destroyed hundreds of prize cats from the British Isles and other parts of the world, which were scheduled to arrive on 1 December for the National Cat Club's championship show. As it was, some thoughtful person fleeing the blaze opened the cages of the Crystal Palace aviary, which housed thousands of birds. Most of the birds fluttered through the smoke-filled passageways to the safety of nearby trees.

The Crystal Palace remained a shattered wreck until 1941 when it was discovered that its silhouette was helping guide German planes to their targets. The British government then had it totally demolished.

The End Comes for Ellis Island

New York harbor's Ellis Island, which for decades was the first contact foreigners had with the "great melting pot," became U.S. property in 1808. During the following years, it was the site of a fort and arsenal. Its most famous function began on 1 January 1892, when it became the chief immigration station for the entire nation.

Not long before Ellis Island opened, *Harper's Weekly* described the twenty-seven-acre establishment. The new main building, it said, resembled "a latter-day watering place hotel, presenting to the view a great many-windowed expanse of buff-painted wooden walls of blue slate roofing and of light and picturesque towers." Even more important, the new facility could handle up to 10,000 immigrants in a single day.

The first person to be processed at Ellis Island was Annie Moore, a young woman from County Cork, Ireland. She was presented with a ten-dollar gold piece by Immigration Commissioner John B. Weber.

The first year it was in service, Ellis Island officials processed 445,987 immigrants; in 1903, a total of 857,046 were admitted to America via the New York harbor facility.

Although Ellis Island was hardly an exciting place, there was occasional news from the facility that piqued the nation's curiosity. Shortly after midnight on 14 June 1897, for example, a fire destroyed every building on the island. In 1917, the island drew interest as a holding area for crews of captured enemy ships taken over by the U.S. Government.

Ellis Island served as the chief immigration facility until 1943, and was used thereafter as a detention center for aliens until 1955. That year, the last person to be officially detained was Arne Peterssen, a Norwegian sailor who had jumped ship. The U. S. Government declared Ellis Island surplus property on 4 March 1955.

The ferry boat *Ellis Island*, which took new arrivals to the mainland for more than half a century, made its last run on 29 November 1954, then was left in the slip to rot. Today, some of Ellis Island's buildings are being restored by the U. S. Park Service as an historical museum.

The Demise of the Garrick Theatre Building

Officially designated a National Historic Landmark in 1958, the Garrick Theatre Building at 64 West Randolph Street in Chicago's Loop was considered immune from the wrecker's ball.

The theatre building was designed by Louis Sullivan, a leader of the "Chicago School" of architects which influenced the development of the modern skyscraper. Noted architect Frank Lloyd Wright had served as Sullivan's apprentice from 1887 to 1893.

Erected in 1892, the seventeen-story Garrick Theatre Building featured tall, clean lines, with rich ornamentation. Across its facade were bas-relief medallions of famous persons; the theatre itself had a bold but delicate conical ceiling, the work of Sullivan's talented partner, Dankmar Adler. Acoustics experts called the theatre the equal of Carnegie Hall. Furthermore, the director of the architecture and design department of the Museum of Modern Art in New York, Arthur Drexler, gave his support to the belief that the building should be preserved. More than fifty college and university schools of architecture, as well as many European intellectuals, agreed.

Thus it was that the Garrick Theatre Building, deemed uneconomical, was torn down in 1961.

The End of Pennsylvania Station, New York

Opened in 1910, New York's Pennsylvania Station was so large and solid it must have seemed indestructible. Perched on the ledge of the main entrance were six stone eagles, each weighing 5,700 pounds; 84 magnificent Doric columns, each 90 feet tall, added to the structure's illusion of strength. Covering 9 acres of Manhattan, Pennsylvania Station most nearly resembled, in both size and atmosphere, the Roman baths, featuring rich detail in solid stone, extravagant and weighty grandeur. But when the city fathers of New York decided Pennsylvania Station had to go to make way for the new Madison Square Garden and 33-story skyscraper, it went.

The decision made many unhappy. "If a giant pizza stand were proposed in an area rezoned for such usage," architecture critic Ada Louise Huxtable wrote in the *New York Times*, "and if studies showed acceptable traffic patterns and building densities, the pizza stand would be 'in the public interest' even if the Parthenon itself stood on the chosen site."

Hardly the Parthenon, but definitely a victim of New York City's slavish devotion to expediency, Pennsylvania Station felt the weight of the demolition crew's weapons on 28 October 1963.

The Last Days of the Paramount Theatre

Opening on 19 November 1926, New York's Paramount Theatre was long a favorite for those who liked to see two movies and a stage show on the same bill. A remnant of the silent picture era, the Paramount provided its own music with a four-keyboard Wurlitzer organ constructed at a cost of $75,000. The organ was the most celebrated movie house instrument in the United States for decades, booming forth from a spotlighted position next to the orchestra pit.

Like other movie houses, the 3,660-seat Paramount found the going rough in the television era, several times being considered "dead" during the 1950s and early 1960s. It always managed to survive, at least until 1964, when it went dark after being sold to a company planning to redesign the 33-story Paramount building without a theatre.

In the spring of 1965, the management decided to try another revival of the stage show-movie combination, signing Soupy Sales for a 10-day run as host. A veteran TV comic who claimed to have been hit in the face 10,000 times with pies during his career, Sales was selected because he was supposed to be popular with the younger set.

His Paramount Theatre show proved that his popularity was genuine, a line of 3,000 youngsters stretching from Times Square to Eighth Avenue on West 43rd Street and not ending until it reached the corner of 42nd Street. Pushing through police barricades that had been set up, several youngsters overturned the wooden horses and in turn were thrown to the ground themselves.

No one was seriously hurt and the show was a smash success. After the appearance of Soupy Sales and his associated acts — The Detergents, who started out with a song about laundromats, the Hullaballoos, Little Richard and others ("with names that have become to entertainment what wrestler's titles are to sports," one reporter wrote) — the youngsters filed out and made room for the next audience. It continued that way for the run of the show, the Paramount taking in $146,000.

Subsequent shows, however, fared less satisfactorily. Crowds generally ignored the initial run of the film *Harlow*, as well as a costly music revue that took in only $25,000, and a Glenn Miller stage salute which brought in only $24,000.

On 2 June 1965, the Paramount management gave up the ghost for good. On exhibition at the time was an all-black musical revue and the movie *Black Spurs*. A bit more than a year later, as the building was being converted into an office center, everything in the Paramount Theatre, from seats and chandeliers to marble walls, was auctioned off. A Steinway baby grand piano — minus one leg — brought $1,200, the highest price of the sale.

Those who thought they might be able to purchase the famous organ were disappointed, however. That expensive vestige of the old days had been moved to Los Angeles in March of 1965, after it was sold for a reported $15,000 to the American Association of Theatre Organ Enthusiasts.

The Destruction of the Tokyo Imperial Hotel

In its heyday, Tokyo's Imperial Hotel was the city's most famous landmark, after the Imperial Palace. Over a three-year period, architect Frank Lloyd Wright lived in Japan while supervising its construction. There were 600 Japanese workmen and their families living — "cooking, washing, sleeping," in his words — on the site as the structure rose from plans to completion in 1922.

Constructed in a style that combined the most extravagant features of Mayan and Oriental architecture, the yellow-brick, stone-brimmed building with its rich complexities of unconventional, interpenetrating spaces played host to visiting luminaries such as Babe Ruth, Will Rogers, Albert Einstein, and the honeymooning Marilyn Monroe and Joe DiMaggio.

The building's stability was revolutionary, a triumph of the flexible floating construction that rode out the earth's convulsions — the great earthquake and fire that devastated Tokyo and Yokohama on 1 September 1923, just one year after the Imperial Hotel was completed. In his autobiography, Wright described how the hotel remained undamaged on eight feet of cheese-like soil over sixty to seventy feet of soft mud.

The only hotel ever designed by Wright, the three-story building also survived World War II bombings and was considered one of the architect's masterpieces. The lobby, a large dining hall, a garden in the center, and the hallways connecting the lobby with two flanks won the admiration of both foreign visitors and Japanese. In fact, Wright understood and admired the Japanese — and was admired by them — so well that when he left Tokyo, many of the workmen who had lived on the site, from sweepers to craftsmen, crowded the entrance to the hotel. They wept, laughed, and shook his hand, Western style. Sixty workmen even paid their own way to the Yokohama dock eighteen miles away for a final farewell.

When Frank Lloyd Wright died in 1959 at the age of eighty-nine, it was assumed that the Imperial Hotel would remain as a monument to his genius.

Not long after his death, however, it was noticed that the passage of time had wrought indignities on the building which Wright never foresaw. The cantilevered foundations proved trim enough to see the hotel through the 1923 earthquake, but in the 40 years afterward, as the water level fell, the structure settled three feet, seven inches. Cracks appeared in walls and ceilings. One visitor of the 1960s, novelist Anthony West, called the hotel a "hideous, inconvenient, inadequate, and depressing eyesore."

Even worse, the Imperial Hotel's location was needed to make way for a modern high-rise hotel with 1,000 additional rooms.

Announcement of plans to demolish the building produced an avalanche of protests, editorials and cables from abroad. The influential architect Kiyoshi Niguchi called the old Imperial Hotel "a swan afloat on a lake." Others formed a society to save the building as a "symbol of courage and originality." Mrs. Olgivanna Wright, the architect's widow, flew to Tokyo from Taliesin, Wisconsin in an effort to save the "spiritual presence" of her husband.

Writing in the prestigious *New York Times*, Ada Louise Huxtable protested that "there is no logic to this destruction except dollar logic, a standard that measures art, beauty, history, esthetics, environmental disaster and national pride with a scale of cost and conveniences on which such factors have no worth.... The price of a disposable culture is the right to call ourselves a civilization at all."

In the end, of course, the protests made little difference. Demolition on the historic structure began on 1 December 1967.

The Last of the Astor Hotel, New York

First opened in 1904, the Astor Hotel was a limestone and red brick landmark on the west side of Broadway between 44th and 45th streets for more than six decades. Then, in 1967, it was razed to make room for a new office tower.

At one o'clock on the morning of 30 June 1967, the Astor bar, where George M. Cohan and other show business people were regular customers, served its last round of drinks.

The last party listed on the hotel's "Events of the Day" calendar was in the Versailles Room. It was a birthday party breakfast for Solomon Huber at 9:30 a.m., 29 June.

The last permanent guest of the Astor — former general Omar N. Bradley, then chairman of the Bulova Watch Company — vacated his two-room suite on the eighth floor on Wednesday the 29th, leaving behind a box of facial tissues and a scale.

Also left behind was a tomb-like silence in the 700 rooms spread over ten floors, more than a mile of pale green corridors lined with slate-blue doors and red-figured carpeting, and 18 public rooms with grandiose names such as the Trianon, the Versailles, Regency, Emerald, and l'Orangerie, where Billie Burke accepted Florenz Ziegfeld's marriage proposal.

The End of London Bridge

Usually the last day of a structure such as a bridge comes about because it is demolished. Only rarely is a bridge moved.

Such, however, was the fate of the granite 5-arched, 928-foot-long bridge across the Thames River which was designed by John Rennie and built between 1824 and 1831. Working full time, a crew of

800 men was required to complete the structure, which replaced a stone bridge, several houses and a chapel.

London Bridge had been falling down in nursery rhymes since King Olaf of Norway, an ally of Ethelred the Unready, hitched his Viking ships to an earlier version of the bridge in 1014 and pulled it down. Why he did so is unclear.

At any rate, in April of 1968, London Bridge was sold for $2.46 million to McCulloch Oil Company of California so that the City of London could replace it with a new six-lane crossing. In May, the first bricks of the bridge were removed, put into crates, and sent to Lake Havasu City, Arizona. The community actually had no need for a bridge, but created one in the hope that the 137-year-old structure would attract tourists.

The dismantling of the bridge did not proceed without incident, naturally. In November of 1968, some students from Shoreditch College, Surrey, stole several 56-pound pillars and a 224-pound baluster by disguising themselves as sailors and making their getaway in a minibus. Asking 200 pounds ransom for the pillars and block, the students said they intended to give the money to the Save the Children Fund.

When contractors handling the job refused to give in, the students returned the pieces a day later.

The Demise of Willard's Hotel, Washington

Mid-nineteenth century Washington D. C. was a rough provincial town of muddy streets, rundown boarding houses, and slow transportation — perfect conditions for the enterprising businessman able and willing to invest in establishing a decent hotel close to the White House and houses of Congress.

Two canny Vermonters, Henry and Joseph Willard, filled the vacuum in 1850. Within a decade, their Willard's City Hotel was Washington's social and political clubhouse, partly because there was nothing better and partly because of the Lucullan table Henry Willard set. (One 1859 banquet, for example, offered pheasant, venison, prairie hen, Virginia ham, lobster, partridge, and thirty additional dishes.)

Inevitably, the hotel became a part of American history. In early 1861, with Abraham Lincoln in as President and seven states out, Virginia called for a conference of states to avoid a crisis. Many delegates locked their rooms at Willard's to ensure secrecy. On 23 Fubruary, 1861, Lincoln stopped at the hotel — one day ahead of schedule, to foil plotters — a businessman from New York having to be hastily dislodged from Parlor Number 6 to make room for the President-elect. (Lincoln, by the way, didn't pay for the room until six weeks after the inauguration.)

That same year, after a visit to the battlefront, Julia Ward Howe returned to the Willard and wrote out the lyrics to the *Battle Hymn of the Republic*.

Also during the war, "General" Tom Thumb, P. T. Barnum's famous midget attraction, took his new bride, Lavinia Warren, to Willard's for their honeymoon. Later, in the Willard ballroom, Admiral Robert E. Peary first recounted his adventures in reaching the North Pole at a dinner for members of the Geographical Society.

After the Willard brothers died (Joseph in 1887, Henry in 1909), the hotel was taken over by Joseph's son, Joseph W. Willard, Jr., and, if anything, became even more celebrated. The atmosphere of splendor continued during the twenties when the hotel was used by Calvin Coolidge as the executive mansion for a month while waiting for the late President Harding's widow to move.

With improved methods of transportation making it unnecessary to be within walking distance of the White House, poor public transit along Pennsylvania Avenue and a decline in the neighborhood, the fortunes of Willard's Hotel declined during the 1950s and 1960s.

Between 1965 and 1968, the management lost $1.25 million. Unable to meet its financial obligations, the Willard abruptly closed its doors on 15 July 1968. Hastily mimeographed notices slipped under the doors of each occupied room explained the situation and gave the guest until midnight to make other arrangements.

Goodbye to Madison Square Garden

When it opened in 1925 at Eighth Avenue and 50th Street, New York City, it was the "new" Madison Square Garden, third in a line of Manhattan arenas dating back to 1879. From 1925 until 1968, about 250 million persons attended 144 kinds of events ranging from six-day bicycle races to Communist party rallies. "There was something almost Elizabethan in the raucous knowledgeability of Garden crowds," wrote Murray Schumach. "Politicians who sought to capitalize at times on these captive audiences by taking bows before a sports event were often rocked by an avalanche of boos."

"Raucous knowledgeability" sometimes translated into just plain rowdyism. One memorable occasion in this regard was the night of 7 October 1957, when producer Mike Todd celebrated the first anniversary of his epic movie, *Around the World in Eighty Days*, with a $400,000 party for " a few of my intimate friends." In fact, so many persons crashed the gate that the intimate affair soon became a melee. Motorcycles intended as gifts were stolen and driven out the doors; ushers brazenly stole and peddled bottles of champagne intended for the guests; several inebriates jumped onto the wings of an airplane (another intended gift) and used it as a seesaw until the wings snapped; meanwhile thousands of others started a stampede to snatch up pieces of the birthday cake it had taken 20 days to bake.

According to the engraving on the 50th Street side of the Garden, the facility was "dedicated to athletics, amusements, and the industrial arts," and during its forty-three-year history it surpassed the promise of its dedication. For many, the most memorable night at the Garden was 5 November 1932, when Franklin D. Roosevelt brought his first presidential campaign to a climax before a jam-packed crowd of 22,000. The Garden's political events also included a rally for the German-American Bund in 1939, at which the swastika flew and columnist Dorothy Thompson was ejected for laughing and shouting "Bunk!" The Soviet Union was also represented at the Garden's mass meetings of the American Communist Party.

During its history, the Garden provided spectators a chance to watch Marilyn Monroe riding a circus elephant, see skiers soar from 85-foot jumps into haystacks, hear musicians such as Arturo Toscanini, Jan Peerce, Isaac Stern, Mahalia Jackson, Ignace Jan Paderewski, and listen to Billy Graham struggle to exorcise sin from city and nation.

But it was sports for which Madison Square Garden was most famous. The basic building was 200 feet wide by 375 feet long, large enough for most athletic events, but best suited for boxing. The worst sight lines were those for track and field events, the spectators often not being able to see the winner of some thrilling mile runs. In an effort to improve visibility, Garden officials laid out two tracks with colored, criss-crossed lanes, but the runners became so confused the experiment was abandoned.

The decline of the Garden began in 1959, when businessman Irving Felt purchased a substantial share of stock and soon announced plans to create a new facility. Less than a decade later, on 13 February 1968, the final event at the venerable arena was held — the Westminster Kennel Club's dog show. Just after 11:00 p.m., Ch. Stingray of Derbyabah, a Lakeland Terrier belonging to Mr. and Mrs. James A. Farrell of Darien, Connecticut, was named best dog in the show. As such, he was the last champion crowned at Madison Square Garden.

The Closing of Les Halles Market, Paris

An 834-year tradition came to an end on the weekend of 1-2 March 1969, with the closing of Les Halles Market in Paris.

Founded in 1135 by King Louis VI (better and more appropriately known as Louis the Fat), Les Halles was known as "the belly of Paris," a title given it by Emile Zola.

A food market that also served as the roaring center of Parisian life, Les Halles had streets with colorful names such as Rue du

Lard (Bacon Street), Rue de la Cossonnerie (Game and Poultry Street), Rue de la Boucherie (Meat Street), Quai de la Megisserie (Hides Way), Rue des Orfevres (Goldsmiths' Street), Rue de la Coutellerie (Cutlery Street) and, in deference to the seamier side of life, La Grande Truanderie (Big Racketeering) and La Petite Truanderie, and Vide-Gousset (Purse-snatcher). Along the street were equally colorful restaurants with names such as Quiet Father, Pig's Foot, and Smoking Dog.

The market was filled with history. It was in the Ferronerie (ironwear) area, for example, that King Henry IV was stabbed to death in 1610 while his carriage was caught in a traffic jam. (Henry, by the way, is credited with originating the phrase, "There should be a chicken in every peasant's pot every Sunday.")

Not far away was St. Eustache, the great Renaissance-Gothic church where Louis XIV received his first communion and where Moliere was baptized.

As Paris grew, Les Halles spread, covering what had once been a graveyard for paupers and plague victims. In 1854, the architect Victor Baltard constructed ten iron pavillions that made Les Halles the most modern food depot in the world.

The real beginning of each day at Les Halles was midnight, when the first of 1,000 trucks pulled in with its wares and simultaneously added its share of the 9 tons of garbage created there each day. Because of the wonderful quality and great quantity of garbage generated at Les Halles, the market's rats were a special breed — 200,000 strong, as fat as puppies, and so smart that they sent the oldest of their number to test suspect food, then watched him for hours.

Eventually, Les Halles was deemed too old-fashioned by the French government, which set up a new food market at Rungis, nine miles south of Paris near Orly Airport.

Les Halles' closing was an appropriately picturesque one. A brass band from the Beaux Arts stood on the worn steps of St. Eustache, rendering a shaky version of "It's a Long Way to Tipperary" as students linked arms and shouted anti-Rungis slogans. Young socialites in black gowns strolled through the arched, cast-iron pavilions watching the frantic buying and selling. Prostitutes speculated openly on whether or not they dared take their own product out to Rungis. "Out there," one of them said, "we would be in the open country and always at the mercy of the cops." Rumors flew that Marseilles gangsters had already bought apartments at Rungis and that pimps would turn house trailers into portable brothels.

Amid the uncertainty, only one thing seemed sure: no place would ever have the atmosphere and life of Les Halles. "The belly leaves, but the heart remains," one mourner said.

Lafferty's Last Elephant Building

Admittedly architectural follies, the nineteenth century wood-and-tin elephants constructed by James V. Lafferty of Philadelphia had a certain charm, albeit gross.

In 1881, Lafferty was a promoter with a problem: how to lure potential building lot buyers from Philadelphia and Atlantic City to the relatively desolate, but desirable, beaches of Margate, New Jersey. His solution was a bold one. Enlisting the aid of William Free, he designed and constructed a 65-foot high elephant, complete with a huge, ornate howdah on its back for an observation platform. Divided into rooms which could be entered via stairs leading upward through the legs, the attraction was completed at a cost of $38,000 and advertised in the Philadelphia *Public Ledger* later that year. One advertisement read:

> South Atlantic City. Lots for sale. Improvements are progressing rapidly. Magnificent view can be had from the 'howdah observatory' of the Elephant Hotel of South Atlantic City... being the only hotel in the world in that novel shape, 86 feet long, 29 feet wide, and 65 feet high, 10 feet diameter of legs, 22 feet from platform to floor of hall, 15 feet depth of foundation. Personal attendance will be given to parties who wish to view premises, going and returning the same day.

The "Elephant Hotel" was a great success, visitors flocking to the attraction. Immediately, Lafferty began to visualize a string of similar establishments attracting people all along the Atlantic Coast. He therefore quickly sent plans to the U.S. Patent Office and, on 5 December 1882, was granted U.S. Patent Number 268,503. To discourage imitators, Lafferty included a paragraph which added that, "The building may be of the form of any other animal than an elephant, as that of a fish, fowl, etc...."

As the years passed, Lucy the Margate Elephant became a familiar, yet strange, landmark. Stories circulated telling of seamen who swore off their rum ration after seeing the elephant for the first time without warning.

Three years after completing the Margate structure, Lafferty built two more elephants. The more ambitious was at Coney Island, a growing tourist attraction.

More than 120 feet high, the Brighton Beach "Elephantine Colossus," as it was known, was completed in 1885. C. A. Brandenburgh, the Coney Island manager, promptly threw a press party. After fortifying his guests with a hearty dinner, he led them through the elephant's left hind leg to the "stomach room," which was 60 feet long, 35 feet wide, and roughly triangular in shape. The party then walked through the elephant's diaphragm and along his liver into the left lung where, Brandenburgh explained, a museum would be built. From the "shoulder room" to the "cheek room" they were able to look through the elephant's right eye onto the ocean and peer down the trunk.

In 1884-1885, a third elephant, just 58 feet tall, was constructed at Cape May, New Jersey. Ever the showman, Lafferty named the new wood-and-tin behemoth after a real white elephant, "The Light of Asia," which had died late in 1884 in Philadelphia.

A fan of Lafferty's architectural follies could have visited all three of the elephants during the decade between 1886 and 1896. After that, however, the inevitable began to happen. The structures, highly flammable, were situated in rapidly growing areas whose residents had little desire to maintain anything that was not more than paying its way. Which may explain why the "Elephantine Colossus" at Coney Island , which had not been used for a couple years, suddenly burst into flames on the night of 27 September 1896. That night a passerby spotted a light in the big animal's body. At first he thought it was caused by someone going through the building with a lantern, but a moment later a jet of flame darted from the howdah and an alarm was turned in.

Despite the work of Coney Island's entire fire force, augmented by a bucket brigade, the elephant was completely destroyed.

Four years later, the Cape May elephant, following several seasons of neglect and vandalism, was demolished. By that time, Lafferty had sold Lucy the Margate Elephant and was no longer in the behemoth-construction business.

Incredibly, Lucy survived. She survived a violent storm which swept the Jersey coast on 10 October 1903. She survived the upsetting of oil lamps inside her when she was a tavern in 1904. She survived another storm in 1928. Most miraculously of all, she survived the desire of many area residents to do away with her simply because she was old and impractical. Condemned in 1960, she was saved during the 1970s by a non-profit group headed by Sylvia Carpenter and Josephine Harron, who managed to raise money to have Lucy moved and renovated. The elephant was declared a National Historic Landmark in 1976, thus taking her place as a tribute to American ingenuity alongside such monuments as the Statue of Liberty, the Washington Monument, and Mt. Rushmore.

Last Day at Duke's Restaurant

"I've had nights when I walked out of here feeling ten feet tall," reminisced restaurateur Duke Zeibert on 30 April 1980. "And I've had nights when I wanted to crawl out of here on my belly. Such was the night I dropped a matzo ball on King Peter of Yugoslavia. Hit him on the head. Nice little guy."

THE LAST TIME WHEN

After thirty years, Washington, D. C.'s most famous restaurant was closing to make room for a new shopping mall. Long the hangout of politicians, writers, and other assorted celebrities, the blue and brown restaurant that regulars affectionately described as being decorated "like a bruise" had a "Rest in Peace" wreath near the bar and a Marine playing taps on the trumpet. Nearby, laughing with wet eyes, stood sixty-nine-year-old David George Zeibert, alias "Duke," reminiscing about the good old days.

"We had a writer we called 'Man O'War' Friedman because of his betting habits. He used to ask for his tips up front so he could get down on his daily double. One day Richard Nixon is having lunch. He was Vice President then. Nixon paid with a check and 'Man O'War' brought it to me and asked, 'Is this guy any good?'"

Born in Troy, N. Y., Zeibert, who began his career as a waiter, rose to the top of the heap by dishing out generous portions of acerbic wit along with his restaurant's famous boiled chicken in the pot, beef, and crab cakes. Once he said to Joseph A. Califano, Jr., then secretary of Health, Education and Welfare: "Listen, if you don't smoke, don't come in here."

Not particularly modest, Duke summed up his Washington establishment's success. "There were only two restaurants with soul," he said. "This one and the original Toots Shor. And in this one, the food is good."

"Where else will I be able to get boiled beef in this town?" asked columnist William Safire, who dined on Duke's final day with reporter Daniel Schorr. Also in attendance were House Speaker Thomas P. "Tip" O'Neill, the Reverend Gilbert Hartke of Catholic University, Michael DiSalle, former governor of Ohio, and John Scali, an ABC diplomatic correspondent who reminisced about walking a picket line in front of the network offices. "It was noon," he recalled. "I was startled to see a waiter from Duke's put a small table and chair down on the sidewalk. He pulled a napkin from his pocket, and a tablecloth, set it up, and another waiter appeared with a bottle of wine, a stem glass and a plate of crab cakes. I got halfway through my meal when the cops found a law against it."

As the evening wore on at the famous Connecticut Avenue and L Street establishment, waiters debated who among all the celebrities had been the biggest tipper.

"I think it was a guy named Barney Doyle who owned a print shop," offered Benny Bergman, an ex-Marine who worked for Duke Zeibert for thirty-three years. "He handed out ten dollar bills to everybody who walked by his table — the guy with the napkin, the guy with the water, everyone, even a customer sometimes."

Others thought it might be Jerry Wolman, the Philadelphia sports entrepreneur who tipped fifty percent on every check. A frequent companion of Wolman's, Baltimore attorney, Philip Z.

Altfeld, agreed. "One night we stopped in Duke's after the Redskin-Pittsburgh game," Altfeld said. "And seated at one huge table was the whole Washington coaching staff with their wives or ladies. There must have been at least twenty of them. Anyway, Jerry called over the waiter after a while and said, 'Bring me their check.' The waiter did it, and he paid it. Just for kicks, I guess. When we got outside and the kid drove up with his car, Jerry held a five-dollar bill in one hand and a joint in the other. 'Take your pick,' he said. The kid took the joint. The funny thing was, Jerry didn't smoke the stuff, but he enjoyed giving it away."

Finally, after the last anecdote was told, Duke's began to empty for the last time. As the customers filed out, a middle-aged couple entered the restaurant, obviously looking about for a table.

"We're closed," said Melvin Krupin, the maitre d'. The couple turned to leave, then stopped as a reporter, no doubt hoping to capture a fact of historical importance, asked them their names. "Sorry," said the man. "We're both married to other people."

Last Ancient Wonder of the World

During the second century B.C., a writer named Antipater of Sidon made up a list of "Seven Wonders" — the architectural marvels he regarded as spectacular, something tourists should not miss during their travels in the Mediterranean. (By the time he made up the list, of course, two of the seven wonders were already gone, but that wasn't important. Seven was a magical number and it obviously would not do to delete the marvels just because they were no longer extant.)

At any rate, the Seven Wonders — today known as the Seven Ancient Wonders — were constructed in the following sequence:

First to be built were the pyramids of Egypt, of which the Great Pyramid of Gizeh was largest and most famous. Covering an area of 13 acres and containing 2.3 million blocks of limestone each weighing 2½ tons, the pyramid at Gizeh was constructed by Khufu, or Cheops as the Greeks called him, Fourth Dynasty Pharoah of Egypt, about 2650 B.C. If all the stones of Cheops' pyramid were cut into blocks one foot square and laid end to end, they would form a continuous line nearly 17,000 miles long.

Twenty-five centuries passed before the next Ancient Wonder was constructed. This was the work of King Nebuchadnezzar (died 562 B.C.), whose wife longed for vegetation and flowers in their desert kingdom of Babylon. Being a devoted husband, and having already accomplished his main purpose in life, conquering Judah, Nebuchadnezzar brought in some engineers and built what came to be known as the "Hanging Gardens of Babylon." Actually, the gardens didn't hang from anything, but were terraces of trees, flowers, and other lush vegetation, all irrigated by an especially-designed and very expensive system.

The third Ancient Wonder was built a bit more than a century later at Olympia in southern Greece, home of the Olympic Games. Seeking to appease the gods, the Olympians hired the sculptor Phidias in 435 B.C. to design an ornate statue forty feet high of Zeus seated on a throne atop a twelve-foot pedestal. The statue was constructed of gold and ivory, Zeus' eyes were flashing gems, and it is reported that Phidias worked five years on the project.

Shortly afterward, about 356 B.C. at the Greek town of Ephesus, work began on a magnificent temple dedicated to the goddess Diana. The fourth Ancient Wonder was supported by 127 columns 60 feet high, measured 435-by-225 feet, and took 120 years to complete.

The fifth Ancient Wonder to be built was started in 353 B.C., after the death of King Mausolus of Halicarnassus, a city in Asia Minor. To his memory, his devoted wife, Artemisia, ordered a huge tomb constructed on a hill near the city so that crews of passing ships could see it from a great distance. An oblong 440 feet across, the tomb was 140 feet high. On top of the tomb was a pyramid with 24 steps leading to a statue of Artemisia and Mausolus in a chariot. The structure was so famous that the word mausoleum was coined from the king's name. Reportedly, Artemisia was so grief-stricken she drank Mausolus' ashes in a glass of wine after the funeral.

The sixth Ancient Wonder was the Colossus of Rhodes, on an island kingdom halfway between Athens and Asia Minor, constructed between 292 and 280 B.C. The job was somewhat in the nature of a celebration; Rhodes had been beseiged by Demetrius of Macedon, who finally gave up and left a great deal of war material behind. The Rhodians sold the material for several million dollars and with it constructed a statue 100 feet tall. Legend had it that the Colossus of Rhodes was built with one foot on each side of the harbor and that ships sailed beneath the figure. Even Shakespeare used this mental picture when he had Cassius describe Julius Caesar:

> Why, man, he doth bestride the narrow world
> Like a colossus, and we petty men
> Walk under his huge legs and peep about
> To find ourselves dishonorable graves.

In fact, the Colossus of Rhodes was not built astride the harbor but on a nearby promontory.

Finally, the Pharos peninsula lighthouse at Alexandria, Egypt, was completed in 280 B.C. The work of Ptolemy Philadelphus, the lighthouse was 445 feet high (the equivalent of a 35-story building) and was topped by a circular chamber in which a fire beacon, amplified by mirrors, flashed its light out to sea.

Because the Hanging Gardens were destroyed before the last five ancient wonders were constructed, it was never possible to see all seven. The last year in which it was possible to see six of the seven was 224 B.C.

The fate of the seven architectural marvels was a follows:

After the death of Nebuchadnezzar, the kingdom of Babylon deteriorated rapidly, falling in 538 B.C. to Cyrus the Great of Persia. It is not known definitely that Cyrus actually demolished the gardens, but when the Greek historian Herodotus (484-425 B.C.) visited Babylon and described the city, he made no mention of the gardens, which were obviously gone by that time. In any event, in 275 B.C., most of Babylon's inhabitants were moved to Seleucia, making a ghost town of the once sumptuous city.

The Colossus of Rhodes was next to go, collapsing in an earthquake during the year 224 B.C.

The Temple of Diana at Ephesus, before which Saint Paul preached during the first century A.D., lasted only until 262 A.D., when Goths sacked the city during one of their frequent invasions of the Roman Empire.

The statue of Zeus was the fourth Ancient Wonder to fade away. After the Olympic Games were abolished in 392 A.D., the statue was taken to Constantinople where it was destroyed in the great fire of 476.

The Mausoleum at Halicarnassus remained overlooking the harbor until the early thirteenth century, when the Crusaders, seeking to make the world safe for Christianity, stole the building to use to build a fortress.

Alexandria's lighthouse at Pharos remained intact until Egypt was overrun by the Arabs (639-642), who tore down the upper part. The base was demolished by an earthquake during the fourteenth century.

The last and only remaining certified Ancient Wonder, then, is the Great Pyramid at Gizeh, which has managed to withstand both the ravages of nature and rapacity of mankind (although another dam project in Egypt may threaten even this monument).

Perhaps in disappointment at seeing the Ancient Wonders disappear, some modern writers, scholars, and travelers have created new lists of "wonders." The American Society of Civil Engineers, for example, put together a list on which was included the sewage system of Chicago. In 1937, the magazine *Current History* drew up a list from its readers who nominated the New York subway, and Burton Holmes, writing in a 1946 issue of *This Week*, included the Los Alamos atomic test site.

Chapter Five

Transportation Lasts

Chronology

1869
The *Cutty Sark*, last surviving China Clipper, is launched. (see p. 144)
Donald McKay's last sailing ship is launched. Named *The Glory of the Seas*, she remains in service until 1923.

1897
(Sept. 30) The last cable car runs in Washington, D. C.

1898
(Dec. 24) The last horsecar runs in Boston. (see p. 166)

1899
The Delaware and Hudson canal closes. The facility was constructed between 1825 and 1829.

1900
(May 26) Horsecars run for the last time in Washington, D. C. (see p. 166)

1906
(July 22) Cable cars run for the last time in Chicago.

1911
The last horse-drawn car of the London General Omnibus Company is taken out of service.

1917
(July 26) New York City's last horsecar goes out of service.

1922
The *Regina* is the last ship built for the Dominion Steamship Line of Liverpool. Founded in 1872, the company goes out of business in 1926.

1924
The Chesapeake and Ohio Canal, damaged by floods, is closed to traffic forever.

1925
The last Stanley Steamer automobile is manufactured, ending twenty-eight years of sales. (see p. 159)

1927
The Model T Ford ends its phenomenally successful run, the last one (number 15,007,033) rolling off the assembly line. (see p. 163)

1933
The liner *Caronia*, launched in 1905 for the Atlantic passenger run, is broken up at Osaka.

1934
(Sept. 26) The first liner *Mauritania*, launched in 1907, leaves New York for the last time.
The last Franklin automobiles are manufactured in the United States. (see p. 155)

The *Olympic*, plush sister ship of the *Titanic*, goes out of service at the age of twenty-three. (see p. 144)

1936

A sensational seller during the first years of the Depression the Auburn car is discontinued just five years after its season of record sales. (see p. 155)

The Reo, an early American low-priced car, is manufactured for the last time. (see p. 156)

1937

One of America's early front-wheel drive cars, the last Cord is manufactured.

The fabulous Duesenberg automobile, reputed for speed and luxury, is discontinued. (see p. 158)

1938

(Dec. 3) Trains of the venerable Sixth Avenue El in New York make their last runs.

The last Pierce-Arrow automobile is manufactured.

1940

(June 11) The cars of the Second Avenue El in New York City make their last runs. And, on the same day, the oldest elevated railway service in the city, the Ninth Avenue El, also comes to an end. (see p. 169)

1941

(June 16) The Fulton Street El in Brooklyn is demolished.

(Nov. 14) The last run of the 23rd Street Ferry is made in New York.

(Nov. 30) The 101-year old Nyack Ferry makes its last trip across the Hudson River.

1946

The 52,000-ton liner *Berengaria*, launched in 1921, is sold for scrap after being damaged by fire at New York in March of 1938.

(December) The once-proud liner *Normandie* makes her final trip from New York to Port Newark, New Jersey, and the scrap heap.

1947

It is both the first and last year Americans can buy the revolutionary passsenger car known as the Tucker.

1949

The only commercial liner to carry troops in both World Wars, the thirty-five-year old *Aquitania* is retired from service. (see p. 145)

1950

(Dec. 17) New York's 125th Street Ferry makes its final trip. (see p. 151)

1951

(Jan. 31) The last regularly scheduled run of a narrow-gauge passenger railway in the U.S. takes place in Colorado. (see p. 165)

Opened in 1902, the Rio Grande Southern or "Galloping Goose" Railroad makes its final run.

1952

(July 7) The last tram — or electric streetcar — runs in London. (see p. 167)

(July 30) The Chesapeake Bay Ferry makes its last run, rendered obsolete by the Sandy Point-Matapeake Bridge. (see p. 146)

(Aug. 9) The last cars run on the West Penn Interurban-lines serving Pittsburgh and West Virginia.

(Dec. 26) In continuous use since 1868, Suncock Valley Railroad (New Hampshire) ends service.

(Dec. 31) In operation since 1832 providing passenger service for a penny, Boston's muncipally subsidized ferry makes its final run.

1954

The Henry J, one of the first American compact car, is discontinued.

(Nov. 29) After covering a million miles in 50 years, the Ellis Island Ferry makes its last run. (see p. 151)

1955

(March 30) The last Christopher Street Ferry run is made between New York City and Hoboken, New Jersey, ending 118 years of service. (see p. 151)

(May 12) The last train of the Third Avenue El in New York City rumbles out of Chatham Square Station in Chinatown, ending service going back to 1878.

1956

The Illinois Terminal Railroad, providing electric rail service since 1903, goes out of business.

(June 1) The 146-year-old Shawneetown Ferry makes its final trip across the Ohio River between Illinois and Kentucky.

(Oct. 18) The last streetcar runs in Brooklyn. (see p. 166)

1957

(May) The last steam locomotive of the New York Central Railroad goes out of service.

Manufactured since 1909, the last Hudson automobile is produced.

(April 7) New York City's last electric trolley makes its final run. (see p. 166)

1958

Long a symbol of automotive luxury in the U.S., the last Packard is produced.

(April 26) The "Royal Blue" Baltimore and Ohio Railroad passenger train traveling from New York-Washington, makes its final run.

(July 29) The *San Leandro*, only remaining double-ended San Francisco Bay ferry, makes its final run.

1959

(March 25) The Weehawken, New Jersey, Ferry, in service since 1828, makes its last trip.

(June 30) Passenger service ends on the Old Colony Division of the New York-New Haven and Hartford Railroad.

Having put in thirty-two years at sea, the French liner, *Ile de France* is sold for scrap.

(Oct. 23) In continuous use since 1832, the Camden-Amboy Division of the Pennsylvania Railroad goes out of service.

1960

The third and last Edsel model is sold. (see p. 160)

(Oct. 31) The last Key West-Havana, Cuba ferry runs, service being discontinued because of political difficulties between the two nations.

The 27,778-ton *Britannic* is the last ship to retain the funnel markings and house flag of the White Star Line. She is broken up for scrap in 1961.

First produced in 1928, the Chrysler Corporation's DeSoto is discontinued.

1961

(September) The final Chesapeake Bay trips are made on the ship of the Baltimore Steamship Packet Company, last overnight steamship passenger service in the nation.

(Nov. 10) The *Liberte*, a French Line vessel, in service since 1930, enters New York harbor for the last time.

(Nov. 17) After 127 years of use, Exchange Place Terminal in Jersey City, New Jersey, sees its last trains.

1962

(Jan. 28) Electric streetcars make their final runs in Washington, D.C.

(Sept. 2) The last tram runs in Glasgow, Scotland.

1963

(Jan. 14) One of Great Britain's most celebrated trains, the "Flying Scotsman" makes its final run. (see p. 169)

(Oct. 25) The last steam locomotive regularly used in the eastern U.S. makes its final run.

(Nov. 2) The Newburgh Ferry, N.Y. started in 1743, makes its final crossing.

(Dec. 3) The forty-five-year old *Stavangerfjord*, queen mother of the Atlantic passenger fleet, leaves New York for Norway for the last time.

After more than a century of manufacturing transportation vehicles in America, Studebaker closes its last plant in the U.S.

1964

(Oct. 27) The liner *America* makes her final Atlantic crossing.

(Oct. 30) The venerable Holland-American liner *Westerdam* leaves New York on her final run.

(Nov. 21) Less than a week after the opening of the Verrazzano Narrows Bridge, the Staten Island-Brooklyn Ferry makes its last run.

1965

(June 28) The liner *Washington*, in service since 1933, leaves New York for the last time before being demolished.

(December) Zim Lines of Israel announces its withdrawal from transatlantic service, and sells its three remaining ships.

(Nov. 22) The second liner *Mauritania* logs her last mile before being scrapped.

1967

(Sept. 24) At 12:10 a.m., the westbound *Queen Elizabeth* and eastbound *Queen Mary* pass in the mid-Atlantic for the last time. (see p. 153)

(Dec. 3) After sixty-five years of luxury passenger train service between New York and Chicago, the "Twentieth Century Limited" makes its last run. (see p. 175)

1969

(November) The liner *United States*, holder of the record for the fastest crossing time of Atlantic passenger ships, is taken out of service.

American Export Lines discontinues passenger runs between New York and the Mediterranean, ending a service that began in 1931.

Ten years after the first Chevrolet Corvairs hit the market, production ceases on the rear-engine, air-cooled American car.

1972

(April) Mohawk Airlines, often called "Slowhawk," merges with Allegheny to form US Air.

(May 1) The last trip of the Brighton Belle takes place, ending more than four decades of elegant service between London and the seaside resort. (see p. 178)

1973

(April 28) The last elevated railway in New York City makes its final run prior to demolition. (see p. 169)

1974

(October) The liner *France*, most luxurious and largest of the Atlantic passenger fleet, makes her final Atlantic crossing. (see p. 150)

1977

(May 20) After ninety-four years of service, the "Orient Express" makes its last run. (see p. 177)

1980

(Oct. 31) The London-Paris boat train, in service since 1936, makes its final Channel crossing. (see p. 168)

1981

The Hongqi automobile, a high-priced embarrassment to officials of Communist China, is phased out after more than two decades of production. (see p. 162)

(June 19) After forty-six years, the last truck is built at the General Motors assembly line in Baltimore.

The Last China Clipper

"The ideal of applied art and a sheer delight to the eye" was one description given to the nineteenth-century clipper ships. No one has denied their beauty.

For many years, they were the fastest ships afloat, their secret nothing more than a narrow beam and great sail-carrying capacity. Although constructed before 1812, the first large clipper ship was the 494-ton *Ann McKim*, which was built in Baltimore, Maryland, in 1833. By that time, the term "clipper" was in wide use, although the origin of the word was not certain. (Some attributed it to an outgrowth of the expression "going at a clip." Others traced the word to poets Percy Bysshe Shelley and Robert Burns.)

By the mid-nineteenth century, the old clipper ship was both at its height and on the way out. Falling freight rates and the high cost of oak and other hardwoods necessary to build the ships, combined with the rise of steam to make the clipper ships obsolete as everyday commercial carriers. Nevertheless, they were still produced for special uses, notably those calling for speed. During the California Gold Rush, for example, when fortune hunters were willing to spend extra for a fast passage to the gold fields, 160 new clipper ships transported 90,000 people to California over a four-year period.

The clipper was excellent for the China sea trade, since speed was necessary to prevent the tea from losing its flavor in a ship's hold. The "China Clipper" evolved as a result of this need and races often were held between rival vessels. One of these, the British *Cutty Sark*, built in 1869, covered a record 363 miles in one day.

Taken out of the tea trade in 1879, the *Cutty Sark* carried wool from Australia until 1895, then was sold to the Portuguese. In 1922, she was bought back for sentimental reasons by British Captain Wilfred Dowman.

The last of the China Clippers, the *Cutty Sark* is now preserved alongside the Royal Naval College at Greenwich, England. She was placed there on 25 June 1957 after being restored.

The Last of the Olympic

Whatever happened to the *Titanic*'s sister ship, the one that did not strike an iceberg and become a symbol of life's futility? On a par with the *Titanic* in beauty, size, and speed, the *Olympic* also had her share of troubles during her quarter-century of service.

Put in the water on 20 October 1910, she was handed over to her owners on 31 May 1911, the same day the *Titanic* was launched. Two weeks later, the *Olympic* set out for New York on her maiden cruise. Not long out of Southampton, the Royal Navy warship *Hawke* was spotted four miles away in clear weather and calm water. Incredibly, through a series of bizarre miscalculations, the two vessels continued toward each other in slow motion until they struck. The *Hawke's* nose was battered and the *Olympic* lost about forty feet of plating from her vast quarterdeck. She promptly turned back to Southampton and disembarked her angry passengers, including twenty millionaires worth a total of $500 million.

A year later, heading east when her sister ship sank, the *Olympic* was too far away to be of any help, so she put into Southampton and prepared for the next passage. But no sooner was she in dock than her firemen and trimmers walked off the job. Said one officer in explanation,, "I have no doubt the recent tragedy has been too much for their nerves. Suddenly becoming panic-stricken, they concluded that the best thing for themselves and their frightened families, was to have a voyage off home."

In September of 1915, the *Olympic* was converted to a troopship. Her moment of glory during the war came on 12 May 1918, when she rammed and sank the German submarine U-103.

By July of 1920 she was back on the transatlantic passenger run, at 883-feet long and 46,439 tons still one of the most impressive ships of the commercial fleet. She was also one of the more economical for her size, the first luxury liner to convert from coal to oil, a move that reduced the number of stokers needed to man her engines from 350 to 50.

One last mishap spelled the end of the majestic ship. On 16 May 1934, the *Olympic* struck and sank a lightship off Nantucket in a thick fog. All hands on the lightship were lost. Shortly thereafter, the twenty-three-year-old *Olympic* was withdrawn from service and towed to Inverkeithing, England, where she was demolished in 1937.

The End of the Aquitania

The last of the four-smokestacked liners (one was a fake, installed because pre-World War I passengers judged a ship's reliability by the number of stacks), the *Aquitania* cost $10 million and set out on her maiden voyage in June of 1914 accompanied by a torrent of publicity.

"If the limit of any art exists," said one enthusiast, "it is nearly as possible attained in the *Aquitania*." Designed as a sort of floating art museum, the pride of the Cunard fleet had suites named after painters, as well as a swimming room that resembled a Pompeiian bath.

Its career interrupted by World War I, the *Aquitania* was converted into a troopship, using its twenty-three knot cruising speed to outrun German U-boats. Never fired on, it returned to the commercial Atlantic run and quickly became the ultimate in luxury travel during the 1920s. During this golden age, the *Aquitania* carried many celebrities, such as Zelda and F. Scott Fitzgerald. Cowboy actor Tom Mix led Tony the Wonder Horse down the ship's companionways. One impromptu party featured the Prince of Wales conducting the large orchestra while Prince Louis Mountbatten played drums and the King of Greece watched.

A quarter-century old in 1939, the *Aquitania* once again became a troopship, the only commerical liner to see duty in both wars. Five years later, having carried 384,586 soldiers to and from battle, "Grannie" went into the Halifax Service between Great Britain and Canada.

Her career ended one rainy day in 1949, when, docked at Southampton during a heavy rain, the *Aquitania* had just been given a certificate of seaworthiness by the Board of Trade Surveyors. As they enjoyed their lunch on board ship, the surveyors were suddenly surprised by a loud sound and the rush of water. One of the *Aquitania*'s decks had just been split by the storm and the resulting deluge washed out the lunch of the men who had just inspected her.

In December of 1949, "Grannie" was finally retired at the age of 35. She had crossed the Atlantic 884 times, logged 3 million miles and carried 700,000 peacetime passengers. All trace of her finally disappeared in 1950 when she was broken up at the Faslane, England, shipyards.

The Last Chesapeake Bay Ferry

Long before there was a Chesapeake Bay Bridge, thousands of commuting businessmen, traveling salesmen and vacationing families from Maryland's Western Shore crossed the nation's largest estuary to Maryland's Eastern Shore. "It was quite a trip," recalled one traveler who had made the trip countless times. "Annapolis to Matapeake at ten to twelve miles an hour."

The Chesapeake Bay ferries were generally named after Maryland governors — the *Governor Harrington*, the *Harry W. Nice*, the *Herbert R. O'Conor* — and ran about an hour apart. Patrons with cars often had to wait for two or three ferries before getting aboard. In addition, the trip took forty-five minutes, and in winter was frequently rough and cold. Maryland writer John Hess recalled that one January night the ferry became icebound in mid-bay. "We had plenty of food," he wrote, "but about two in the morning we lost heat. Talk about cold! It was daybreak before the Coast Guard cut us out and we could get through to the other shore."

After World War II, agitation grew for a better and faster way for natives of Baltimore and Washington to get across to the balmy Eastern Shore. Plans were drawn up for the bridge.

Most regular ferry users, upon hearing that the average crossing time would be reduced to about seven-and-a-half minutes, were happy with the news. The completion of the bridge in 1951 led to the end of ferry service, the last run taking place on 30 July 1952.

One bit of consolation for traditionalists came not long afterward. Chesapeake Bay Bridge traffic eventually became so heavy on weekends, it took nearly as long getting across as in the good old ferry days.

The Last of the Ile de France

When she came on the scene in the late 1920s, the 43,000-ton *Ile de France* was given her share of superlatives and meaningless statistics that new steamships always seem to generate. She was, for example, possessed of a main dining room that was "twenty feet wider than the Church of the Madeleine." The bar in her first-class lounge was the "largest afloat." Elsewhere on the ship were other examples of grandeur — a children's playroom with a real carousel, and a complete Parisian sidewalk cafe rather than a mere conventional garden lounge.

But all the gloss nearly came to naught on 27 May 1927, her very first day of sailing anywhere. The *Ile de France* almost had her mizzenmast torn off by a shipyard crane. To avoid hitting the crane, the captain was forced to turn his ship toward a closed drawbridge which opened just barely enough at the last possible moment to allow the ship safe passage.

After that, it was relatively smooth sailing until 1940, when, like so many other luxury liners, the *Ile de France* went to war as a troopship.

Returning to the postwar Atlantic run, the *Ile de France* had a last moment of glory in 1956 when, en route to Le Havre with nearly a thousand passengers, she received a call for help. It was from the *Andrea Doria*, in distress off the New Jersy coast. Pushing her nearly thirty-year-old engines to the limit, the *Ile* reached the sinking liner in time to pick up 758 survivors.

In 1959, having put in thirty-two years at sea, the *Ile* was sold for $1.25 million to a Japanese scrapping firm. As a band played "La Marseillaise" and a few hundred of her faithful friends saw her off, she sailed out of Le Havre for her trip to the graveyard. Only when she was out of sight was the French flag lowered and the Rising Sun run up. She then became the *Furanzu Maru* (which means simply "French ship").

That would have been the end for the *Ile de France*, except that she had been spotted by American movie producer Andrew Stone, who just happened to be looking around for a large ship to sink for a movie he was filming. For four thousand dollars a day he got her, the plan being to sink the vessel in shallow coastal waters, then raise her for scrapping.

When word got out, however, the French government was beseiged with so many cries of outrage, it demanded that the *Ile's* name be removed from every part of the ship. Stone complied, changing her name to *Olympus*, at which point, the Greek Line, which had an *Olympia*, threatened suit. More repainting followed, and finally the *Ile* renamed *Claridon* sailed into Osaka Bay, Japan, to be destroyed.

Stone's movie entitled *The Last Voyage*, featured Robert Stack, Dorothy Malone, George Sanders, and Edmond O'Brien. After using the ship for various exciting scenes, it was sent to the bottom in the film's climax.

Some Last Steam Tugboats

The year 1970 produced at least two interesting survivors for tugboat enthusiasts. One, the *Mathilda*, a seventy-two-foot iron-hulled steam tug built in 1899, was rescued from oblivion in time to be donated to New York's South Street Seaport Museum. It was the last nineteenth century tugboat still operating in 1970. Working out of Montreal, *Mathilda's* greatest moment of glory came in 1961, when she was used to save thirty-five persons from the wrecked freighter *Federal Express*.

The second tugboat discovery was the *Eppleton Hall*, which was found on a mudflat on the Tyne River near Newcastle, England. She was partly burned out and scheduled for destruction but was saved at the last minute by Scott Newhall, executive director of the *San Francisco Chronicle* and founding director of the San Francisco Maritime Museum.

Believed to be the last survivor of her type, the 105-foot *Eppleton Hall* was powered by sidewheel paddles and resembled the vessels used as blockage runners during the Civil War.

After being repaired, the *Eppleton Hall* made her final journey, a trip of about 9,000 miles from Newcastle to San Francisco. Leaving England on 18 September 1969, she arrived in American on 24 March 1970, after being battered by three storms.

The Last of the United States

Constructed during the early 1950s, at the height of the Atlantic crossing boom, the 53,000-ton liner *United States* had a brief but celebrated career. Its designers, thinking partly of the role played by the *Queens* during World War II and partly of obtaining federal subsidies, worked in conjunction with the United States Navy to build a luxury liner that was in reality the world's largest troopship.

As a result, the government paid more than half of the vessel's $79.4 million cost.

Capable of carrying 14,000 troops, the *United States*'s war features included extra large fuel capacity, subdivisions of watertight compartments and distribution of machinery that would allow the ship to operate even if partly demolished. In addition, she was virtually fireproof, more aluminum being built into her than in any other single structure ashore or afloat. Her funnels, lifeboats and deck rails were made of aluminum. Even the ship's bedspreads and draperies were made of non-flammable glass-based materials. The only objects on the *United States* that were capable of burning were the pianos in her lounges (Theodore Steinway had refused to supply aluminum ones) and the butcher's blocks in the galleys.

In addition, the *United States* had sufficient speed to outrun any possible enemy afloat. On her maiden run, she proved capable of forty knots, averaging over thirty-five. At 6:16 a.m., 7 July 1952, just three days, ten hours and forty minutes out of New York, the *United States* arrived at Southampton, breaking the *Queen Mary*'s fourteen-year-old record by an amazing ten hours and two minutes. Not long after Margaret Truman sounded the ship's whistle marking the event, *Punch* observed, "After the loud and fantastic claims made in advance for the liner *United States*, it comes as something of a disappointment to find them all true."

The *United States* was not destined to use her luxurious military might. While 1952 was a year in which fewer than fifteen percent of transatlantic passengers went by air, bouncing along in piston planes that strained to cross the ocean in twelve to fifteen hours, sixteen years later the absolute reverse was true. Only seven percent of the transatlantic traffic was handled by ships. The jet age had arrived, with each single jumbo plane capable of carrying a quarter-million passengers a year — more than three times the passenger capacity of the *United States*.

Losing between $4 and $5 million in 1968 and 1969, the owners of the ship took her out of service in November of 1969, laid her up in Norfolk and took bids to sell her. The following season was the first peacetime year since 1840 that no passenger liner crossed the Atlantic Ocean in winter.

The Last Wooden Whaler

The last survivor of the thousands of wooden whalers that were used to supply Americans with oil for illumination, bone meal, and liver oil during the nineteenth century was launched in 1841, ten years before the publication of Herman Melville's classic whaling novel, *Moby Dick*.

Christened the *Charles W. Morgan*, the ship made thirty-seven lengthy voyages during an eighty-year career, sailing the South Seas and the waters of the Arctic Circle while earning a fortune for her Yankee owners. During the Civil War, the *Morgan* eluded Confederate warships; during World War I, her crew kept a sharp lookout of German submarines. Near the end of her career, the ship was used in two silent films.

In action for nearly a half-century, the *Charles W. Morgan* was restored between 1969 and 1974, then dedicated as a floating exhibit at the Mystic, Connecticut, Maritime Museum.

Last Atlantic Voyage of the Liner France

She was constructed near the very end of the transatlantic steamship era, slipping into the Loire estuary at St. Nazaire as President of the Fifth Republic Charles DeGaulle looked on and Madame DeGaulle christened the ship with a seven-liter bottle of champagne. Billed as the most magnificent of all ocean liners, the *France* was the longest (1,035 feet), one of the fastest (capable of 30 knots), and most luxurious (only two passengers for each crew member).

The last pure express steamer built as a ferry boat between Europe and America, the *France* set out on her maiden voyage in 1962, the year a record number of travelers decided to fly the Atlantic rather than sail. Despite this, the sheer glamour of the *France* as well as the audacity of even thinking of launching her in the jet age, made the ship the most successful liner of the decade.

By the early 1970s, however, it was a different story. Oil prices had increased enormously. Subsidization by the French government soon reached $20 million a year, causing Premier Jacques Chirac to complain that the ship was costing his nation the equivalent of two new hospitals annually. Such agitation eventually led, in 1974, to the decision to retire the still-youthful *France*.

The retirement date was set at 25 October, but several weeks before then, as she lay outside Le Havre, her crew took control of the vessel in an attempt to keep their jobs. For some months, the workers on the *France* had been muttering about the need to do something dramatic. Then, on the morning of 11 September, Marcel Raulin, a cabin steward and former commando, received a message from union officials ashore. "Good morning from Alfred," it read. "Send the oranges." It was a signal that sent Raulin and ten crew members to the bridge, where they informed Captain Christian Pettre that they were taking over.

For the next month, negotiations continued, while the *France* was surrounded by a cordon of coastal patrol boats. After many passengers were sent ashore, French officials took a harder line, refusing to guarantee that the liner would be kept in service. Meanwhile, the crew ran low on fresh vegetables, wine and cigarettes.

It is not known exactly what effect the shortages had on the crew's vote of 10 October. What is known is that the men finally agreed to return the ship to her owners.

Three weeks later, the *France*, most celebrated liner of the French commercial fleet, was taken out of commission. She remained in an inactive status until 1979 when she was purchased by Norwegian Caribbean Lines as a cruise ship.

The Demise of New York's Ferries

Bounded as it is by water on all sides, natives of Manhattan were forced by geography to develop a system of ferries early in their existence. Seventeenth century Dutch ferrymen charged three stuyvers, about six cents, for the half-mile crossing of the East River from Long Island to what later became Fulton Street in lower Manhattan.

Transportation to Staten Island from New York was a precarious and uncertain affair back in 1712 when the first ferryboat charter was granted. Pirogues — broad, flat-bottomed boats propelled by oar and sail — were used in conjunction with sailing sloops at that time; horses traveling on the pirogues and passengers on the sloops. Running time was about three hours.

The advent of steam in the early nineteenth century took much of the dependence on favorable winds and tides out of the ferry operation to Staten Island. It also added an element of danger: in 1871, for example, the ferryboat *Westfield* blew up at the Whitehall Street landing as she was loading 400 passengers, including many children, for a Sunday outing. Sixty-six persons were killed and 200 injured.

By the early 1920s, municipal and privately operated ferries in the New York area accomodated a yearly average of 128 million passengers and 12.5 milllion cars. But even then, during the peak of the ferryboat era, the end was in sight. Bridges and tunnels, added to the American love affair with the car, soon made ferry service in Manhattan an anachronism.

Here's what happened to some of New York City's network of ferries:

The 23rd Street Ferry — One of the first twentieth century ferry systems to go was the 23rd Street line of the Central Railroad, which had been established in 1905. The last run of that line, which connected lower Manattan with the foot of Johnstone Avenue, Jersey City, was made on Friday, 14 November 1941.

The last ticket on the 23rd Street line was sold by Station Master Laroy Clarke to P. Lavender of 1157 Windfield Avenue, Jersey City.

151

On the final trip was Albert A. Smith of Cranford, New Jersey, the line's most overt mourner. A user of the line for 15 years, Smith put up a sign in the ferry house reading: "Goodbye, Twenty-Third Street ferry. We mourn your loss."

The 123rd Street Ferry — With the beginning of World War II and the resultant decline in automobile use, all forms of public transportation benefitted. Even those services that lost money were kept in business, for often the public had no other way to travel from point to point.

One ferry which was about to go out of business before the war but hung on for five years after the cessation of hostilities was the ferry between 125th Street, New York, and Edgewater, New Jersey. After sixty-two years of continuous but gradually declining, service, the ferry's last run was made on 17 December 1950. A crowd of 300 persons was on board to sing "Auld Lang Syne."

Ellis Island Ferry — After covering a million miles in fifty years, the ferryboat *Ellis Island* made her last run on 29 November 1954, to the deserted immigration station in New York harbor.

First put in service on 5 May 1904, the ferry carried 15 million passengers, including 12 million immigrants. While in full-time service, she made eighteen round trips a day, fifty weeks a year, giving employment to thirty-five men.

Seventeen minutes after leaving New York, the *Ellis Island* was tied up at the eastern end of the island and left to rot. A Coast Guard patrol boat conveyed the crew back to the mainland.

Christopher Street Ferry — After 118 years and 8 months, ferry service between Hoboken, New Jersey, and downtown Manhattan on the Christopher Street line ended, when the final ferry to Hoboken ran on 30 March 1955.

On board for the last half-mile trip on the ferryboat *Buffalo* were about 100 passengers, most of them regular commuters. Shortly after 6 p.m. Captain William L. Schopf pulled the 210-foot craft away from the slip and guided it across the river in a matter of minutes.

Established in 1836, the Christopher Street ferry line was one of the most popular in the New York area, with ten new steamboats in operation by the time of the Civil War. So much traffic was handled, in fact, that in 1877, Edwin A. Stevens, then head of the ferry company, bought the New Jersey building that the year before had been used in the Centennial Exposition in Philadelphia. He then moved it piecemeal to Manhattan where it was reconstructed as the Christopher Street Ferry Terminal. Considered an engineering marvel in its day, the building was shaped like a circus tent, the entire roof supported by a single steel girder in the center.

For nearly eight decades, the Christopher Street Ferry Terminal was a national and local landmark, outliving the ferry service it had been puchased to support. Not for long, however, for demolition began on 25 July 1957.

Perth Amboy-Staten Island Ferry — Once a carrier of 12,000 passengers and 3,200 cars a month during peak periods, the Perth Amboy-Staten Island line made its final trip across the Arthur Kill shortly after midnight on Friday, 18 October 1963.

Mayor James J. Flynn, Jr. of Perth Amboy said he saw "no future" for the two ferryboats, the *Irvington* and *Taurus*. In fact, neither he nor anyone connected with the ferry line knew how an unpaid balance of $4,392 owed on insurance premiums would be paid.

Staten Island-Brooklyn Ferry — The long-awaited opening of the Verrazano Narrows Bridge on Saturday, 21 November 1964, sounded the death knell for the Staten Island-Brooklyn ferry run. In fact, the line remained in operation less than a week after the bridge was opened to traffic.

The final run of the ferryboat *Tide* was a festive one. Pulling away from the 69th Street pier at 11:23 p.m., 25 November, her decks were crowded with passengers. Aboard were several hundred singing college students who brought beer and at least one bottle of champagne. Many wore orange lifejackets supplied by the ship; others, notably a group from Wagner College, wore dinner clothes and had arrived in a shiny Packard touring car.

The crowd also included its share of sentimental travelers. One was Blanche McQueeney, seventy-four, who was aboard on 26 July 1913, her birthday, when the regular service started. Also on hand were several steamboat enthusiasts and a smattering of regular commuters.

Up in the wheelhouse was Captain George Sommerville, a boat pilot for almost four decades. "I'm a ferryman," he said sadly. "Where do I go now?"

The Last Voyages of Cunard's Queens

Throughout the history of passenger ships, no sister ships were ever closer than "the Queens," *Elizabeth* and *Mary*, together the culmination of a dream born in 1840 when Samuel Cunard's *Brittania* became the first regularly scheduled Atlantic liner.

When she made her maiden voyage from Southampton to New York in May of 1936, the *Queen Mary* had only the French Line's *Normandie* as a rival for speed and size. Approaching Manhattan, carrier pigeons were released and bands played "Goody, Goody" as she neared her moorings. On her sixth crossing, the *Queen Mary* beat the *Normandie*'s best time for the Atlantic crossing. It went that way for two years, the rival ships regularly beating each other's time by a few minutes or seconds.

Meanwhile, work was proceeding in strictest secrecy on another vessel. That turned out to be the 83,000-ton *Queen Elizabeth*, which made her maiden voyage to New York in June of 1940, canvas shrouds covering her funnels. During World War II, both vessels served as troopships, eluding German submarines while carrying up to 15,000 soldiers on a single voyage.

After the war, the sister ships crossed and recrossed the Atlantic during the glorious 1950s, only gradually losing passengers to the chic liners of the French fleet or airlines. But by 1961 the end was in sight. Losing money on both ships, Cunard put them on winter cruises in an effort to make ends meet.

Then, on 8 May 1967, as the *Queen Elizabeth* steamed toward New York with 711 passengers (capacity: 2,304), a message over the ship's wire instructed Captain Joseph E. Woolfenden to open a sealed envelope he had received prior to sailing. The message contained the news that the two ocean liners were to be retired — the *Queen Elizabeth* within eighteen months, the older *Queen Mary* as early as October of 1967.

Perhaps the most poignant moment for lovers of the Queens came when the two vessels passed each other for the last time. It came at precisely 12:10 a.m., 24 September 1967, when the westbound *Queen Elizabeth*, 27-years old, and the *Queen Mary*, 31, traded horn blasts while closing the gap between them and then opening it again at a combined speed of better than sixty miles an hour.

During 1968, the *Queen Elizabeth* made the Atlantic crossing alone, then was sold to a firm hoping to use her as a Florida convention center. When the firm went broke, the *Queen Elizabeth* was purchased by C. Y. Jung, a Hong Kong shipowner who wanted to refit her as a floating university. On 9 January 1972, after being rechristened *Seawise University* and docked at Hong Kong, the ex-Queen caught fire, rolled over, and ended her life, a probable victim of arson.

The 1,000th Atlantic crossing of the *Queen Mary* turned out to be her last. With a full capacity of 1,450 passengers, the liner pulled away from her 52nd Street pier in New York City on 22 September 1967, as tens of thousands cheered from shore. The trip was marred at the eastern terminus by a strike of dockside crane workers in Southampton which made it necessary for even first-class passengers to carry their luggage ashore. "The voyage was lovely," said actress Lynn Redgrave, who made the trip. "You almost expected Ginger Rogers and Fred Astaire to appear and dance any minute."

On 31 October 1967 the *Queen Mary* made her final journey, one of 13,000 miles. Sold to the city of Long Beach, California, for $3.44 million, where it was to be used as a tourist attraction, the venerable ship was booked with 1,200 passengers willing to pay up to $9,000 for a thirty-nine-day cruise around South America's Cape Horn (the ship was too large to go through the Panama Canal).

Survivor of that grueling , trouble-filled journey, the *Queen Mary* remains at Long Beach today, an 81,000-ton, thousand-foot long reminder of the glorious days when, as the travel agents boasted, "getting there was half the fun."

The Last Franklin

One of the most unusual cars manufactured in the United States, the Franklin, made in Syracuse, New York, offered a range of forty-two models which included twenty non-interchangeable front doors and twenty-five differently shaped rear quarter panels. Also sporting concealed running boards, Franklins were driven by celebrities Amelia Earhart and Charles Lindbergh. The problem was that in 1931 there were only 3,922 other customers across the nation.

The following year, Franklin offered a 6.8 litre V-12 model for $4,000. It It started out as a good car but ended up a monstrosity when Franklin's cost-conscious management insisted on semi-elliptical springs and proprietary axles, which pushed the car's weight from 2 to 3 tons. .

In 1933, an inexpensive model could be bought for $1,385 but the only parts contributed by Franklin were the engine, hood and grille. The rest was shipped in as a package from Reo's Lansing factory. An emblem on the dashboard hid the hole where the Reo's thermometer used to be.

Losing public favor rapidly, the Franklin was last manufactured in 1934, ending an automotive tradition that began in 1902.

The Last Auburn

One of the cheapest cars ever offered to the American public, Auburn advertisements boasted that "they look like $3,000 cars but sell for $695." A Depression sensation, the Auburn leaped in sales from $8 million in 1925 to $37 million four years later. E. L. Cord, the man behind the car, said the Auburn was a sales success because, "There was still a market for a smart, fast model priced under $1,000 among people who had lost their shirts but did not want their neighbors to know it."

The Auburn's best year, 1931, saw sales of the model 8-98 rising from 13,700 to a record 28,103. The company even declared a stock dividend.

Unfortunately, public acceptance did not last long. Faced with declining sales, the Auburn's designers started tinkering with the basic car. The straight-backed sedan of 1935 was an odd-looking vehicle; half of the car consisted of the front hood, the whole thing giving the impression it was leaning over backwards.

In 1936, just seven years after its stock stood at an all-time high of $514 a share, the last Auburn was manufactured.

The Last Reo

During the mid-1930s, Ransom Eli Olds was the only man in the United States with two cars named after him. Founded in 1904, the REO Motor Car Company manufactured the Oldsmobile and Reo, one of the first cars to have a steering wheel instead of a tiller.

In other ways, the Reo was less distinguished. The "Flying Cloud" eight-cylinder models of 1931, for example, had thermometers on one dashboard, were priced from $1,095 to $1,780, and had two-speed gear boxes, and very poor acceleration. With such drawbacks, it is hardly surprising that by 1934, Reo had run up $9 million in deficits. The last model year was 1936.

The Last Cord

The creation of car designer E. L. Cord, the front-wheel drive Cord was well-known for some very good reasons and equally notorious for some very bad ones.

First manufactured in 1929, the Cord was a designer's nightmare. It had, among other things, a counter-clockwise crankshaft which necessitated special gearing so the unit could be cranked in the standard direction; its 4.9 litre engine was underpowered for the car, which weighed 2 tons, was 17 feet long, had a noisy gearbox, averaged 12 miles per gallon of gas, could barely manage 80 miles an hour and cost $2,345. As a result, only 4,400 were sold between 1929 and 1932.

Redesigning followed, and the 1936 Cord got rave notices and even won an award from New York's Museum of Modern Art some years later. Although less expensive and capable of more speed than the 1929 model, the new Cords tended to overheat and jump out of gear. Only 2,300 were sold in the next two selling seasons, and 1937 was the end of the road for the Cord.

The Last Pierce-Arrow

The Pierce-Arrow was supposed to be the car for the discriminating non-conformist. "Until all cars are built alike," read a 1937 brochure, "until all people dress alike, until individuality ceases to be an American trait, Pierce-Arrow will continue to strive for distinction in the motor cars it builds for the select clientele of motordom..."

One of the three P's (with Packard and Peerless) of American cars of the 1930s, the Pierce-Arrow offered synchromesh gearing and free wheeling. Built on a 11'2" wheelbase, the cheapest Pierce-Arrow Model 43 M cost $2,685, the most expensive model 41 S, $6,250. In 1933, the "Silver Arrow," billed as a "dream car" had a twelve-cylinder engine, doors a foot thick, was capable of 110 mph in speed and cost $10,000. Only five were delivered.

In 1935, the Pierce-Arrow offered pile carpeting, pigskin upholstery, concealed blinds for the windows, a cigar lighter, perfume bottles, adjustable rear seats, and upholstered hassocks. But only 787 were sold in 1936 and 166 in 1937.

Faced with such buyer resistance, Pierce-Arrow went out of business in 1938.

The Last DeSoto

One of the Chrysler Corporation's finest products, the DeSoto was first produced in 1928. Through the years it gained a reputation for being exceptionally well engineered. By the late 1950s, however, it was obvious that the car was beginning to appeal to a smaller and smaller segment of the population, deliveries dropping by eighty-three percent from 1957 to 1960. Late that year, Chrysler Corporation officials decided to kill off the DeStoto, only a few 1961 models being offered for sale. Customers who had purchased 1961 DeSotos were offered a $300 rebate if they bought a new 1961 or 1962 Chrysler product before 1 January 1963.

The Last of America's "Popular" Cars

A number of cars, during America's love affair with the automobile, have won the distinction of becoming at least for a time "popular." Whether through design, cost, prestige, these cars have made a mark on the driving public.

Following is a listing of "popular" American cars (extant for fifteen model years or more) and the last year they were produced:

Anderson — 1926	New York — 1928
Brewster — 1937	Oakland — 1932
Case — 1927	Paige — 1927
Chalmers — 1923	Peterson — 1924
Crawford — 1924	Peerless — 1932
Davis — 1928	Pierce-Arrow — 1938
Detroit Electric — 1938	Pilot — 1924
Dorris — 1926	Premier — 1927
Elcar — 1930	Pullman — 1925
Flint — 1927	Star — 1928
Kissel — 1931	Stearns-Knight — 1930
Locomobile — 1929	Stevens-Duryea — 1927
Marmon — 1933	Stutz — 1935
Maxwell — 1925	Velie — 1928
McFarlan — 1927	
Mercer — 1925	Willys-Knight — 1932
Moon — 1930	Winton — 1924
National — 1924	Woods — 1917

The Last Studebaker

For more than a century, Studebaker made transportation for Americans in America.

The business started in March of 1852, when Henry and Clem Studebaker built their first wagon. It had straight sides of heavy oak, iron hinges and was painted green and red with the name "Studebaker" painted in yellow letters.

After that, business went into a slight recession. Henry and Clem made just one more wagon in 1852, then waited until 1857 for their third order. But in 1858 a third brother, John, returned from the California gold fields with $8,000 and that was the real beginning of the business. (No fool, John had made his money not in panning for gold but in selling wheelbarrows he built to the hopefuls who flocked to California to get rich quick.)

By 1867, the Studebaker brothers were worth $223,000. The Civil War had been kind to them—many of General Lee's defeated troops, it was said, retreated from Gettysburg in captured Studebaker wagons originally made for the Union forces.

John Studebaker, who lived until 1917, didn't like the horseless carriage, but allowed the first electrically powered car bearing his name to ride through the streets of South Bend, Indiana, in 1902. Then, on 22 July 1904, the first gasoline Studebaker chugged along as a band played "There'll be a Hot Time in the Old Town Tonight."

By 1928, Studebaker car sales reached $177 million but the Depression brought on such hard times for the company that it went into receivership in 1933. Even the light, low-priced "Rockne Six," named in honor of Notre Dame's legendary football coach, failed to score with the public.

During the pre-war years and immediately afterward, Studebaker's Champion, a medium-priced car, caught on. The company's best year was 1950, when it sold a third of a million cars and trucks and earned a half billion dollars. A slow decline followed, from 1959 the going all downhill for the company. On 9 December 1963, Studebaker announced that it would produce no more cars in America and closed down its venerable South Bend plant. The company continued to produce cars in Canada.

The Last Duesenberg

Last manufactured in 1937, the fabulous Duesenberg was the product of brothers Fred and August Duesenberg, who came to American from Germany in 1885. From their early interest in bicycles and motorcycles, they branched out to boats, tractors, World War I airplanes, and finally in 1919, to automobile racers and passenger cars.

Their special love was for speed, so it was no accident that a Duesenberg was the first American car to win the French Grand Prix at Le Mans. In 1924, the winning car at the Indianapolis 500 was a Duesenberg driven by the team of L.L. Corum and Joe Boyer, who averaged 98.23 miles per hour. The next year, a Duesenberg was the first car at Indianapolis to average better than 100 mph, Pete De Paolo racing the 500 miles at a 101.13 rate. In 1927, George Souders was at the wheel of the third Duesenberg to take the Indy event.

Not very opportunistic, the Duesenberg brothers not only failed to capitalize on their racing success - they sold their business in 1926 to E.L. Cord, who then hired them to create what some still consider the greatest car ever made.

That car was the 1932 Duesenberg Model SJ, which rapidly became popular with European royalty, and U.S. celebrities such as New York Mayor Jimmy Walker, Father Divine, Tyrone Power, Paul Whiteman, Mae West, Clark Gable, Gary Cooper, and numerous gangsters.

Beautiful and luxurious, the Duesenberg could exceed 100 mph in second gear, and go 135 in high gear without the slightest strain. Designed in a variety of materials from pigskin and patent leather to silk, the Duesenbergs often had backseat bars, radios, and even duplicate sets of instrument panels so the passenger could check on the driver's performance. The cars were priced between $19,000 and $50,000.

Unfortunately, E.L. Cord's auto empire began to disintegrate during the Depression and the Duesenberg went with it. So well made was the car, however, that most of the 500 or so Model SJ's that were manufactured are still around today. Their price—assuming an owner can be found who would part with one—probably averages close to a quarter of a million dollars.

The Last Stanley Steamers

First manufactured in 1897, the Stanley Steamer, as perfected by twin brothers Freelan O. and Francis E. Stanley, was a quiet, smooth-running vehicle. It was also capable of extraordinary speed and acceleration compared to other cars of its day. In January of 1906, for example, a Stanley steamer covered a mile in a little over twenty-eight seconds, the equivalent of 127.6 mph.

In addition to being fast, the steamer was basically a very simple machine. "Our present car is composed of but thirty-two moving parts," the Stanleys pointed out in their 1916 catalogue, "which number includes front and rear wheels, steering gear, and everything moving on the car, as well as the power plant. This is about the number of parts contained in a first-class self-starter. We use no clutch, nor gear shifts, nor flywheels, nor carburetors, nor magnetos, nor sparkplugs, nor timers, nor distributors, nor self-starters, nor any of the marvelously ingenious complications that inventors have added in order to overcome the difficulties inherent in the internal explosive engine and adapt it to a use for which it is not normally fitted."

On the other hand, operation of the steamer did cause a certain amount of trouble for many persons, especially before the installation of a condenser that permitted the vehicle to reuse its water supply.

But the biggest problem facing steamer manufacturers was fear itself. Americans at the turn of the century had been through three generations of steam boiler explosions on riverboats and locomotives and were extremely nervous concerning high-pressure boiler systems. The fact that early steam cars trailed a light vapor as they moved along, giving the impression that the vehicle was already on fire or smoldering preparatory to a massive explosion , added little to public confidence. So prevalent was public fear that steamers were not permitted on ferryboats unless the driver extinguished his burner.

Despite these drawbacks, the steamer might have become the car of the future had not a Stanley Steamer hit a gully during speed trials at Ormond Beach, Florida on 25 January 1907. Because the resulting accident gave the impression that the boiler had exploded—it had not—whatever public confidence had been slowly building up, faded away. (The fear was assisted, of course, by rivals who said, "You can't get people to sit over an explosion.")

Because they were strong-willed and more than a bit eccentric, the Stanley brothers continued to fight against their gasoline-engine rivals, but finally gave up in 1925.

The End of the Edsel

"Looks right! Built right! Priced right!" trumpeted the Ford Motor Company as it prepared the American public for the epitome of the push-button era, the 1958 Edsel.

After sifting through 6,000 suggested names for the medium-priced ($2,400 to $3,600) car, it had been named after Henry Ford II's father. Though not the most expensive new car on the market, the Edsel was promoted as the most luxurious. On or near the dashboard were pushbuttons that operated the trunk lid, hood lever, and parking brake. It had a speedometer that emitted a red glow when the drived exceeded his chosen speed. There was a single dial control for both heating and air conditioning, a button to raise or lower the radio antenna, plus an assortment of lights to warn when the engine was too cold or too hot, that the generator was not functioning, the parking brake was on, the oil level low, and gas level low. The control box of the transmission—on top of the steering post in the center of the wheel—had five buttons.

Eighty inches wide, and just 57 inches high, the Edsel was over-powered, with a 345 hp engine. The radiator grille, later to become infamous and almost synonymous with automotive ugliness, was mounted vertically with the letters EDSEL in gleaming aluminum on the middle. Comedians likened it to a toilet seat or horse collar.

In addition to being saddled with this liability, the Edsel did not perform very well. Shortly after the 1957 models hit the market, Tom McCahill of *Mechanix Illustrated* wrote: "On ribbed concrete, every-time I shot the throttle to the floor quickly, the wheels spun like a gone-wild Waring Blender....I couldn't help but wonder what this salami would really do if it had enough road adhesion..."

Added *Consumer Reports*, "Combined with the car's tendency to shake like jelly, Edsel's handling represents retrogression rather than progress...To look at the Edsel buttons pulls the driver's eyes clear down off the road...most gadget-bedecked, more hung with expensive accessories than any car in its price class."

The Edsel purchased by *Consumer Reports* also had the wrong axle ratio, an expansion plug in the cooling system which blew out, a leaky power-steering system, and a heater which emitted blasts of hot air after it was turned off.

But the worst reviews came from the American public, which came, looked, nodded, and left. "The Ford Motor Company has laid an egg," said the manager of New York's franchise.

He was right, In two years, two months and fifteen days, Ford had sold only 109,466 Edsels, losing about $250 million in the process. The death bell tolled in November, 1959.

Because only 2,846 of the 1960 model Edsel were sold, they are as scarce today as the famed and very costly Type 41 Bugatti.

The Last Hudson

Its first advertisements read: "Good looking, big and racy. Note the graceful and harmonious lines. Observe the sweep of the fenders and frame."

The Hudson Motor Company's first car was turned out in 1909. Continuing to sport the "big and racy" look, the Hudson became an automotive success story in a hurry. Its 1927 "Super Six" model was a favorite with liquor smugglers because of its speed. Weathering the Depression, Hudson showed a profit of almost $4 million in 1941.

After World War II, Hudson's Commodore Six dazzled potential car buyers with its wood-grain instrument panel with gold-backed dials, as well as its radio with a volume control that could be operated by foot.

A year later, the ever-innovative Hudson featured its first "step down" model, which placed the floor of the car under rather than over the frame. Thus, despite its overall height of only sixty and three-eighths inches (to sixty-seven inches for the 1947 Buick), the Hudson offered more head room than any competitor. The advertising slogan that year was: "Hudson presents the importance of stepping down."

The step-down model became a favorite with foreigners. Sultan Ahmed I of Turkey bought a 1948 model. In 1949, the company's fortieth anniversary year, 3.25 million Hudsons were sold. The 1950s brought a significant rebellion against large cars, however, and the Hudson was one of the first casualties.

In explaining the decision to drop Hudson from its line of cars at American Motors, corporation president George Romney pointed out that a reduction of just twelve inches in 10,000 cars represented two miles of bumper -to-bumper traffic that was eliminated.

Even more important to American Motors, Hudson sales had begun to dwindle. The once-celebrated car was dropped shortly after the 1957 models appeared.

The Last Hongqi

It cost $70,000, got approximately five kilometers to the gallon, belched smoke, and because of its weight, drove like a tank. In a way, it was miraculous that the Hongqi lasted more than twenty years.

Its longevity may be explained partly by the fact that for drivers in Communist China, the Hongqi was the only game in town. An embarrassment to many in the People's Republic of China, the car was a Chinese version of the Rolls-Royce, a luxury car and status symbol in a nation that prided itself on its non-luxury, non-status-seeking style of living.

Unlike its Western counterparts, the Hongqi, which was first manufactured in 1960, was not turned out by an assembly line. Instead, each of the 400 cars produced annually was made to order of the rank of the official buying it. There was one type for top leaders—with many sophisticated gadgets as well as bullet-proofing; another type for vice premiers and a third, less luxurious style, for ministers and bureau heads.

All styles of the Hongqi had one thing in common—a special, shrill-sounding horn. "It was like a conditioned reflex," said one Chinese worker. "once we heard that sound, we pedestrians automatically stop, other cars stop and the police give the right of way." Unfortunately, the Hongqi horn was used and abused by relatives of the high-ranking officials, who frequently took them on joy rides or shopping trips. Such conduct drew a flood of public criticism, leading the Red Chinese government to phase out the Hongqi in 1981.

The Last Model T Ford

In 1906, automobile designer and manufacturer Henry Ford experimented with a Model N car, which sold for $600, but it wasn't until he had gone a bit deeper into the alphabet that he arrived at the letter T in 1909—and his success was assured.

Priced originally at $850, Ford was able to streamline his production techniques on the Model T, until it cost only $250 in 1925.

Incredibly, the system got even more efficient, a Model T eventually being produced every twenty-four seconds, the 1925 assembly lines completing 9,575 in a single day. The cars netted just $2 apiece profit, but with millions of dollars rolling in from 48,000 spare parts outlets, Ford soon became one of the world's richest men.

The Model T eventually became obsolete, however, having a top speed of 40 mph and few frills (not even a gas gauge). As a result, sales began to decline after 1923, slipping below 1 million annually in 1926.

The next year, having introduced the public to the more sophisticated Model A, Henry Ford allowed the Model T series to end after a 19-year run. On 27 May 1927, the last Model T Ford, number 15,007,033, rolled off the assembly line.

The Last Packard

For years the Packard slogan was, "Ask the man who owns one."

They were indeed a loyal group, America's Packard owners. Ownership of a Packard was accepted as a sure sign of social and financial success. The luxury car's best year was 1928, when 50,000 were sold, one-third of them abroad.

The first of the breed rolled through the streets of Warren, Ohio, in 1899. It was a single-seat buggy type with wire wheels, the brainchild of James Ward Packard who sold the new vehicle for $1,250. Two years later, he produced the very first car to have a steering wheel instead of a tiller handle.

Packard weathered the Depression by entering the medium-priced field and reducing its models' size and horsepower. In 1939, the Packard Six Model 1800 sold for just $975. Following World War II, the company once again went into the "dream car" market, building the first all-steel station wagon in 1948.

In 1953, the Packard dream car known as the "Balboa" was a curiosity with a rear window that was flat with a reverse slope. Two years later, the Request Model was easily one of the ugliest cars on the road. It was followed by the Predictor Series of 1956, an innovative but homely monstrosity on a 122-inch chassis with dual headlights, a grille that predated Edsel's unsightly horsecollar design and a breezeway rear window later copied by Lincoln-Mercury.

Perhaps the Packard car was just too sedate for drivers of the 1950s. Whatever the reason, production stopped in 1958, leaving America with only sixteen automobile nameplates still surviving out of a total of 2,700 manufactured since the industry made a shaky start in 1893.

The Last Horsecars

The horsecar or "omnibus" (from the Latin plural of omnis, meaning "for all") dates back to a line started in Paris in 1827 by Jacques Lafitte, a banker-politician. Lafitte, in turn, seems to have stolen the idea from Blaise Pascal, who in 1662 obtained a patent for a service of public *Carosses a cinque sous* (five-cent coaches). Nothing much came of Pascal's plan.

Lafitte's line made an impression on a certain George Shillabeer, a former British naval officer who was working as a coach builder in Paris at the time. After constructing a few coaches for use in Paris, Shillabeer decided to introduce them into London. On 4 July 1829, he therefore placed the first pair of omnibuses ever seen in Britain on London streets. Each was built to carry twenty-two passengers and was drawn by three bay horses. A great crowd assembled to watch their start, the first trip from the Yorkshire Stingo, a tavern in Paddington, to the Bank of England in downtown London. The fare was one shilling for the full three-mile distance and six-pence halfway.

Pictures of the first omnibuses remind one irresistibly of a hearse—in fact, Shillabeer eventually became an undertaker near the end of his life.

The omnibus proved successful in London, and in 1856 the London General Omnibus Company was established after buying up all its rivals. To celebrate taking over the business, the company put 300 new buses into operation which rapidly became controversial. Outside passengers were arranged in two rows, back to back, facing outward along the side of the bus. To get to their seats, they climbed up a ladder hanging over the rear. When women objected strongly to this aspect of the vehicle, a new one was designed in which a fixed winding staircase was substituted for the gymnastic ladder. In addition, the roof was furnished with "garden seats" arranged across the bus with a center aisle.

The prosperity of the London omnibus reached its zenith in 1905, when 3,484 of them were licensed with 6,169 drivers. That, ironically, was the year the first 241 gasoline buses were registered.

By 1908, the total number of old-style omnibuses had been reduced to 2,115. On 18 October 1911, the last of the London General Omnibus Company's horse-drawn cars was taken off the streets. One horsecar continued its route over Waterloo Bridge until 1916, at which point the era ended.

New York's first horsecar (without tracks) appeared on 18 December 1831 and continued to operate on Fifth Avenue until 1908. The last run on the Sixth and Eighth Avenue lines took place on 20 July 1898.

One horsecar line held out for nearly two decades after that, however. It continued to operate on Bleecker Street until 26 July 1917. During its last year it collected less than thirty cents a day from the passengers it carried.

The last horsecar appearance in Boston was on 24 December 1898. A trolley line replaced it as Boston extended its two-year old subway, the first in America.

Washington , D. C., constructed its first horsecar lines during the Civil War, groundbreaking taking place on 14 June 1862. The first cars arrived on 11 July. There were two of them, one closed and one open. Seven feet wide and fifteen feet long, they seated twenty. The seats were covered with fine silk and velvet; the glass windows were partly stained, furnished with cherry sashes, poplar blinds, and handmade damask curtains.

With the coming of the electric trolley, however, the horsecar rapidly disappeared from the nation's capital. On 26 May 1900, the last run took place, on Belt's LeDroit Park-Wharves Line.

The Last U. S. Narrow Gauge Railroad

The last regularly scheduled run of a narrow-gauge passenger train took place on the night of 31 January 1951. It was snowing, with subzero temperatures, as the westbound San Juan Express puffed into Durango, Colorado. At approximately the same time, 200 miles away, the eastbound train of the Denver and Rio Grande Western Railroad came to a stop in Alamosa.

For seventy years, the Denver and Rio Grande Western Railroad operated in the mountainous region on narrow-gauge tracks only two feet apart. (Because of the terrain, Colorado railroads built tracks a foot narrower than "standard" narrow gauge.) On board the final train were a few hardy railroad buffs, who may have recalled the passing of other narrow gauge lines, notably the Bridgeton and Harrison in 1941.

Although a railroad official explained that the line was losing money and that "you can't run a railroad on sentiment," critics of the Denver and Rio Grande Western Railroad action were plentiful. One, S. Kip Farrington, Jr., wrote later in his book, *Railroading From the Head End,* "It is to our everlasting fame that we have allowed these charming and picturesque lines to be sold down the river."

That, of course, did not alter the fact that the last narrow gauge passenger train was irretrievably gone.

165

The Last of New York's Trolleys

New York City's first street railway system was a line of rails laid along Fourth Avenue between Prince and 14th Street. Ground for the project was broken on 25 February 1832, the ceremony marked with thirteen whistle blasts and appropriate rejoicing in Hinton's Shot Tower Hotel near the East River.

Nine months later, on 26 November 1832, the cars, which looked like ornate stagecoaches, made their historic first run. Two of the omnibuses collided but no one was hurt.

Near the end of the nineteenth century, New York electrified most of its transit lines, but never really committed itself to the trolley, partly because of the early development of its subway system. By the 1930s, most trolley lines were on the way out. (The historic first line of 1832 was converted to buses on 1 February 1935.)

The last electric trolley line in New York City shared the Queensboro Bridge with five lanes of car traffic, running along two outside shelves of the bridge, like running boards on a car. The trolley line would have been abandoned sooner had it not been for the fact that buses were forbidden to stop in the middle of the bridge to discharge passengers bound for Welfare Island. Because of its position outside the cars, trolleys could stop and allow passengers to take elevators to Welfare Island below.

Eventually, of course, the line became too uneconomical to support. Its last run took place on 7 April 1957, the final car leaving Queens Plaza at 12:32 a.m. Most of the 125 passengers were trolley buffs or teenagers. Ten minutes later, having covered the entire 1.6-mile run into Manhattan, the age of the electric trolley in New York was over.

The Last Brooklyn Streetcars

The "golden age" (if it can be called that) of the electric trolley in Brooklyn was during the 1890s. First established in 1832 as horse-car lines, the trolley system spread like wildfire—and some of the drivers drove that way. One waggish poet just before the turn of the century wrote:

> "Blinded visions, ruined dresses,
> broken heads and thoughts of — well,
> are among the mad distresses
> wrought upon the Brooklyn 'L!'
> But we must have rapid transit
> in this town at any cost,
> Take a walk — but if you chance it
> count yourself among the lost."

Apparently, the poem was not all that much of an exaggeration. In 1895, it was estimated that since they were put into operation,

Brooklyn trolleys had killed an average of one person a week. The motormen, who had learned their trade as horsecar drivers, were blamed for the high mortality rate. Not realizing they had the power of fifty horses under their control, they tended to drive recklessly, so much so that as one newspaper put it, "Ere long, the country rang with horror at the holocaust of victims sacrificed to the reign of electricity in Brooklyn."

Brooklyn's trolley system soon became a national joke. A restaurant keeper in Yellowstone Park, for example, used to tell his guests that he had come west from Brooklyn because the trolleys had killed off his family. No less a celebrity than Lieutenant Robert E. Peary said he thought Brooklyn's trolleys as dangerous as an Arctic expedition. One visitor from Providence wrote to the mayor of Brooklyn, urging that, "The people of your city ought to organize and form a vigilance committee and smash every dynamo in Brooklyn...Away with the trolley juggernauts." The Reverend A. W. Mills in all seriousness urged the transit companies to recognize the commandment, "Though shalt not kill." Small wonder that the Brooklyn baseball team eventually took the name "Dodgers."

Few Brooklynites of the 1890s, surrounded by the ubiquitous and lethal trolley, could have foreseen that only six decades later, on 18 October 1956, the last trolley would run in their town.

London's Last Tram

Unlike some cities, which nourished love affairs with various transportation systems, London never cared much for its tram system. Perhaps a certain prejudice lingered from the early days of horsecars, whose raised tracks made driving by coach virtually impossible in Bayswater Road and Victoria Street. Nevertheless, London's tram system, which was electrified in the early part of the twentieth century, became an integral part of the city's public transportation network, carrying some 4 million passengers a year until the 1920s, when motorbuses were introduced.

For three decades afterward, the tram gradually faded until only one section of track remained. Then, on 7 July, 1952, the last tram groaned to a halt outside New Cross depot after a midnight run from Woolwich.

The vehicle selected to make the final journey was No. 1951, a route 40 car. Great crowds gathered along the way, some wearing nostalgic fancy dress, some carrying chalked signs that read, "We want trams!" Becoming ever bolder as the slow-moving car progressed along the five-mile run, passengers stole light bulbs, the trolley's bell, ripped up the seats, took virtually everything that could be torn loose for a souvenir. Meanwhile, travelers placed pennies on the track to be flattened as memorials of the trams's last trip.

Several drivers shared the honor of handling the controls during the run. First Driver Albert Fuller was at the wheel, but at Greenwich he yielded to the mayor of Deptford, F. J. Morris, who piloted the tram through his borough. Later, John Cliff, an official with London Transport who began his career fifty-two years before, drove Number 1951 on its last rattle to New Cross depot.

Shortly before gaining its destination, however, the tram became stuck on a curved section of track and, to the delight of the crowd, another tram had to be brought out to help it over the dead spot.

Many present agreed that the tram era in London could hardly have ended on a more appropriate note.

The Demise of the London-Paris Boat Train

For more than forty years, the most elegant way to travel between London and Paris was on the "Boat Train," one of Europe's last luxury express trains.

Every evening, trains would leave Victoria Station in London and the Gare du Nord in Paris. The next morning, passengers awoke in the other capital city. Service began on 4 October 1936, after plans for a tunnel beneath the English Channel were postponed indefinitely. The Boat Train was made possible by a three-way collaboration between Southern Railway of Britain, Northern Railway of France (Chemin de Fer du Nord), and the Compagnie Internationale des Wagons-Lits, the international sleeping car company which helped form the earlier Orient Express.

In order to make the land-sea-land trip possible for sleeping passengers, several special accomodations had to be made. Sleeping cars were built in France that were narrower than the standard Continental trains. This enabled them to pass through Great Britain's tunnels and bridges, which are not as wide as those on the Continent. Britain's Southern Railway constructed three ferries to transport the sleeping cars across the Channel. Finally, special docking facilities were built at Dover and Dunkirk.

After World War II, its golden age, the Boat Train consisted of nineteen cars including sleepers, railway post office, a buffet and sitting coaches. Until 1959, when the line was electrified, the train was pulled by "Lord Nelson" steam locomotives.

Leaving Victoria Station at 9:25 p.m., the Boat Train bound for Paris arrived at Dover about an hour and a half later. Switch engines pushed the sleeping cars onto tracks aboard the ferry, the coaches were lashed onto the deck, and then jacked up in order to raise the sleepers off their springs. This made the ride more rigid and prevented the coaches from swaying independently.

As soon as the ferry moved away from dockside, the bar and duty-free shops opened for business. Most travelers preferred to stay awake until they could catch a glimpse of the Channel, alive with shipping even at midnight, and have a drink or two. Depending on the weather, the cross-channel crossing took from two to twelve hours.

Arriving at Dunkirk, the coaches were taken off the ferry. Usually the Boat Train arrived in Paris just before 9 a.m.

Because of its unique function, the Boat Train was perhaps the only train in the world equipped with orange life jackets for its passengers as well as bags to be used in case of seasickness. During its heyday, the Boat Train was used by many celebrities and royalty, the train once making an unscheduled stop in the south of England to pick up Winston Churchill. It was said that Adolf Hitler planned to make a triumphal arrival in London aboard the Boat Train following his conquest of England.

A victim of declining revenues, the Boat Train made its final run on Friday , 31 October 1980. "It's a matter of economics," said a British Railway official. "Once it was the only way to go for posh people, and I expect there were certainly some antics on the train in its time. But now it's a bit of an anachronism."

Fare for the trip in 1980 was sixty-six pounds, considerably more than the air fare, but not exorbitant considering the cost of a first-class hotel in London or Paris. For the businessman or traveler with an aversion to flying and need for sleep, of course, the Boat Train had been perfect.

The Last Run of the "Flying Scotsman"

One of Great Britain's most celebrated trains, the "Flying Scotsman" began its London to Edinburgh run in 1862, covering the 393-mile trip in ten-and-a-half hours. Improvements in engineering eventually decreased the time, a century later, to just six hours.

During its history, the "Flying Scotsman" was the first passenger train to officially record a speed of 100 miles per hour.

On 14 January, 1963, however, the train became, as the British put it, "redundant," and it was sold to a forty-two-year-old Nottinghamshire businessman, Alan Pegler. The engine, which was built in 1923, cost just under 8,000 pounds to manufacture; Pegler paid 4,000 pounds for it.

On its final journey as a public carrier, the "Flying Scotsman" pulled the King's Cross-Leeds express as far as Doncaster, slightly less than half the distance from London to Edinburgh.

The Last of New York City's Elevated Railway

The United States city most dependent on the elevated railway as a space-saving means of public transportation, New York made the "el" as much its symbol as San Francisco did its cable cars. Now, however, the elevated trains are all gone, and a whole new generation of New Yorkers has learned to live without the sound of the el clattering past the bedroom window in the middle of the night.

Here's what happened to the four lines in New York City which eventually were demolished because they did not fit into the automobile age, either aesthetically or economically:

The Ninth Avenue El — The oldest elevated railway line in the world, the Ninth Avenue El made its first trial run between Cortlandt Street and Battery Place on 1 July 1868. Its service continued for the following seventy-two years, a boon to many, a bane to some.

Although most residents near the Ninth Avenue El learned to live with the train's noise, the line remained an object of hatred to members of the American Woman's Club at 253 West 57th Street. "The Ninth Avenue trains have made night and day hideous with their noise beneath the club's windows for many years," a spokeswoman for the organization said as the members prepared to celebrate the el's demise.

The happy day for Ninth Avenue El-haters was 11 June 1940, when the last seven-car train, carrying about 500 passengers, left South Ferry at 11:14 p.m. The crowd kept up a continuous cheer from the Battery to the end of the line, 155th Street and Eighth Avenue, which was reached at 12:06 the next morning.

The Second Avenue El — The youngest of New York's elevated lines, had its inaugural run on 1 March 1880. After sixty years of service, it was phased out with a minimum of ceremony, on the same day as the Ninth Avenue cars. The last train left South Ferry at 11:16 p.m. on 11 June 1940, with about 150 passengers going along for the last trip. It arrived at 129th Street and Second Avenue at 11:51 p. m.

The Sixth Avenue El — The first train of the Sixth Avenue elevated line excited crowds of people and panicked horses as it moved north from Eighth Street past the Jefferson Market police court on 29 April 1878. That inaugural run was well covered by all the local newspapers as well as the nationally distributed *Frank Leslie's Illustrated Newspaper*, which described the new line's 14th Street Station as "a modification of the Renaissance and Gothic styles of architecture...somewhat the appearance of a Swiss villa."

In its prime during the 1880s and 1890s, when it was used daily by the best people in New York business and social circles, the Sixth Avenue El had a genteel air about it not attained by other forms of public transit. In fact, James Creelman, nineteenth-century war correspondent and editor, said it was the only elevated railway in the city fit for a gentleman to ride on.

Mark Twain, who lived on lower Fifth Avenue, often rode down to 26 Broadway to visit his old friend Henry Hutchins. Other celebrated users of the Sixth Avenue El included bankers, brokers, and financial giants such as William C. Whitney, the Vanderbilts, Astors, John D. Rockefeller, John W. Gates, J. Pierpont Morgan, and Russell Sage, reported to be the chief owner.

Knowing who was most important along the line's run, the Sixth Avenue El conductors skillfully manipulated the gates so that the end car was reserved for the city's top brass. As for the cars, they were well appointed, with mahogany trim, large silver-plated lamps with acetylene gas lights covered with white China shades. The seats had comfortable cushions in winter and cane upholstering in summer. The cars cost betwen $3,000 and $4,000, quite a figure for the time.

By the late 1930s, however, there was no more luxury on the line. Perhaps because it had degenerated into a noisy vehicle that had outworn its welcome, perhaps because it was the first elevated railway to be phased out, the Sixth Avenue El's last run was a major event in 1938 New York. More than 2,000 people—revelers and sentimentalists, celebrities, vocal groups, and vandals—made the final trips on four "last" trains, each with seven cars.

The event took place on 3 December 1938. As the first southbound train rolled out of the station at 53rd Street, souvenir hunters in the crowd took out knives and cut away the straps, advertising signs, destination plates, and, in a few cases, even lifted up the cane seats and hurled them down the aisles. Soon the sentimental journey had become a rolling bedlam.

The Third Avenue El — The Third Avenue elevated railway, which opened on 26 August 1878, remained in service longest of all the Manhattan lines, serving the city for nearly eighty years.

Its final run started at 6:04 p.m., 12 May 1955, when the last train rumbled out of Chatham Square Station, Chinatown, four minutes late. At the wheel was Motorman William W. Foy, fifty-eight, who described the journey, which should have been a pleasantly nostalgic one, as "the slowest trip in all my years on the el."

The problem was that about 850 persons made the trip for old time's sake and several hundred more tried to. As a result, the packed cars spent an inordinate length of time at each station, departing passengers struggling to get off against the tide of those wishing to board the train.

The last passenger to pass through the gates at Chatham Station before they slammed shut for the last time was Sidney Estcourt, an electrical contractor from Queens.

By the time the train arrived at 14th Street, the cars were so jammed no more passengers could be wedged in. Every station along the line was crowded with well-wishers stopping by to see the last el on its last run. At 14th Street, a large sign was put up which read, "I hate to see you go—but goodbye—Terry and Joe." At 59th Street, two men and a blonde woman brought a pitcher of martinis up to the station platform but couldn't get aboard; also at 59th Street, a middle-aged man in a beret waved a green flag at the train, a tribute to the many Irish workmen who served with the el in its early days. All along Third Avenue, upper story windows were crowded with people who came out of the taverns to raise their glasses in friendly toasts; at 79th Street, an elderly woman on a fire escape even raised her mop in a genial salute.

The train moved slowly but surely toward its destination until it reached 92nd Street, at which point it came to a screeching halt—someone in one of the packed cars had pulled the emergency brake cord. Finally, shortly after 7:30, the train pulled into the 149th Street Station in the Bronx, the last el to run in Manhattan.

A Dramatic Brooklyn Last

Known for years as the "Black Spider" of Brooklyn because it completely obscured the sunlight, the Fulton Street Elevated Railway came to a politically dramatic end. Wearing a helmet and goggles, Mayor Fiorello LaGuardia offically put the torch—a genuine acetylene one—to the outmoded facility at 12:40 p.m., 16 June 1941.

The Last Washington Streetcars

The demise of streetcars in Washington began on 7 September 1958, when Routes 80 and 82, the North Capitol and Maryland lines were converted to bus lines. Three more major routes were abandoned in early 1960.

The last streetcar routes running were the 14th Street and U Street lines, which held out until 28 January 1962. After that date, the nation's capital was an all-bus town. Streetcars from Washington subsequently turned up in Fort Worth, Texas, Barcelona, Spain, and Sarajevo, Yugoslavia.

The Last Horse-Drawn Fire Engines

Surprisingly, horse-drawn fire engines lasted rather long into the age of steam and gasoline engines. This was true partly as a result of sentiment and partly because many early self-propelled fire trucks simply did not work very well.

Generally speaking, the 1920s saw most large cities dispensing with their horse-drawn fire engines. A sampling of last runs:

Baltimore: June 18, 1919

Chicago: February 5, 1923, firehorses "Buck" and "Beauty" making their retirement run.

New York: December 20, 1922, from Fire Company No. 205, Brooklyn.

Philadelphia: New Year's Eve, 1927, the firehorses were a team of white stallions.

Rochester, N.Y.: July 15, 1927. The city honored their animal friends with a firehorse day parade and a bronze tablet that read:

"Our fire horses, glorious in beauty and in service. Faithful friends, we cannot call them dumb, because they spoke in deed every hour of danger. Perpetual remembrance enshrines their loyalty and courage."

The Last Interurbans

As the United States became committed to the electric trolley, there gradually developed a system of interurban cars which by 1908 radiated from many cities like spider webs. Most of the interurban lines—which were nothing more than long-distance electric trolley routes connecting populous areas—were in the Midwest, although the West Coast had considerable routes, as did Pennsylvania and parts of the Northeast.

If one wanted to take the time, it was possible during the early twentieth century to travel extremely long distances by trolley. One could go all the way from Youngstown, Ohio, to Jackson, Michigan, for example, a distance of 440 miles, without changing cars. The trip took 18 hours, 45 minutes.

By taking a succession of trolleys, it was possible to travel from Elkhart Lake, Wisconsin, to Oneonta, New York, a distance of 1,087 miles. It was also possible to go from New York to Chicago, 1,143 miles, with the exception of 187 miles which had to be negotiated by steam. In 1912, a J. S. Moulton actually made such a trip, taking 45 hours, 24 minutes and spending $19.67 in fares.

On the West Coast, early in the century, Henry Huntington, president of the Southern Pacific Railroad, saw the Los Angeles area as a natural interurban territory. He formed Pacific Electric, a series of interurban lines, and for good measure, had a spur constructed to his own house. (His private car had a wood-burning fireplace, kitchen and bath.) At first, Pacific Electric prospered, Los Angelenos using the lines for their seaside vacation trips. The Mount Lowe line, which traveled up Rubio Canyon to the top of Echo Mountain, was a favorite from 1898 to 1948. Then a series of natural disasters struck—fires, rock slides, windstorms and finally a cloudburst that washed out the entire line.

After a wartime boom, Los Angeles fell in love with the automobile and the interurban lines were gradually phased out. The last of them, the Glendale-Burbank Line, started in 1904, was abandoned in 1955.

Back east, the same sort of decline was taking place. One of the last interurban lines to go was West Penn, which operated six different routes in the Pittsburgh-West Virginia area. Its last car ran on 9 August 1952, and more than 5,000 persons gathered to bid farewell to the line.

Only a few years later, passenger service ended on the Illinois Terminal Railroad, which began traveling the Champaign-Danville

173

route in 1903. By 1909, ITR was running more than 100 cars a day over 400 miles of track. The company had the most luxurious cars in the industry, featuring wicker furniture, armchairs with upholstered seats and elegant tulip-shaped lampshades suspended from polished ceilings. ITR was also one of only three interurbans that ran sleeping cars on its night operations between East St. Louis and Decatur. (Fare for the berth was $1.)

The success of ITR was such that in 1948 the company ordered a complete set of new cars. (They were called "electroliners" and on them diners were served "electrosteaks" and "electroburgers." Eventually the ITR electroliners turned out to be the last interurban cars built. Passenger service declined during the early 1950s and the ITR gave up in 1956.

By 1980, only one electric interurban trolley line remained in operation. That was the Chicago, South Shore, and South Bend, which carries passengers ninety miles between Chicago and the Indiana town. When last heard from, it was still making the trip three times a day.

The Last Cable Cars

During the late nineteenth century, many cities in the United States experimented with cable cars. Recognizing the hilly nature of San Francisco, a wire rope manufacturer named Andrew Hallidie used Clay Street hill there to demonstrate the practical nature of cable traction on 1 August 1873.

The idea caught on to the extent that by 1890 there were 500 miles of cable railways in the United States, with some 5,000 cars transporting 400 million passengers annually.

Chicago installed cable lines soon after San Francisco, the first section of line installed in 1882 running from Madison Street to 21st Street. The *Chicago Tribune* reported that, "The [first] cars were covered with flags and banners and in spite of the general prediction that they would jump off the track it was agreed universally that they were the airiest and most graceful vehicles of the sort ever seen in Chicago or anywhere else."

Other cities installing cable traction about this time included Philadelphia, Denver, St. Louis, New York, Oakland, Washington, Kansas City, Cleveland, Providence, Seattle, and Baltimore. The powerhouse at Denver was especially notable because it operated a greater length of cable than any other single powerhouse in the nation. A total of six cables ran from it, one of them seven miles long.

The demise of cable came early, more efficient electrical systems rendering the cable systems obsolete except in the hilliest areas. Philadelphia abandoned her cable cars in 1895, the same year as Providence. Baltimore followed two years later. St. Louis phased out cable about 1900. In Washington, a bad fire completely destroyed the company's main power station on 30 September 1897. While the ruins of the structure were still smoldering, the Board of Directors of the company decided to electrify.

Chicago's last cable system was that of the State Street line, which lasted until 22 July 1906.

By 1940, only San Francisco continued to use Andrew Hallidie's invention for urban mass transit, and there was enormous pressure to do away with the old cars. Controversy raged until 1947, when San Francisco voters, by a 9-1 margin, elected to save the cable cars. One dissenter was Mayor Roger Lapham, who muttered, "Sentimentalists do not have to pay the bills."

Declared U.S. national monuments—the only national monuments that move—the three operating cable car routes in San Franciso are Route 59 (Powell-Mason Line, between Market and the Bay-Taylor turntable), Route 60 (Powell-Hyde Line, between Market and Aquatic Park), and Route 61 (California Line, between Market and Van Ness).

The Demise of the "Twentieth Century Limited"

Service aboard the Twentieth Century Limited, known to railroad buffs for sixty-five years as the world's greatest train, was designed to be comparable with that of the great trans-Atlantic ocean liners.

Traveling between New York and Chicago, the Twentieth Century made its maiden run on 15 June 1902. It consisted then of three Pullman sleepers, a dining car, a car with buffet, barber shop and library, and just twenty-seven passengers—all drawn by a 10-wheeled steam locomotive. The brainchild of George H. Daniels, a former patent medicine salesman, the Twentieth Century was a direct descendant of the Exposition Flyer, a luxury train which ran between New York and Chicago during the Chicago World's Fair of 1893.

Present on the maiden trip of the Twentieth Century was the noted gambler and oil tycoon, "Bet-a-Million" Gates, who made two legendary remarks during the run. At Grand Central terminal in Manhattan, he said that the new train made "Chicago a suburb of New York." Arriving in Chicago, he told reporters there that the train made "New York a suburb of Chicago."

Covering the 961 miles in 20 hours, the Twentieth Century was an immediate success. (Later, the trip time was shortened to 16 hours.) During the first four decades of its existence, the train was believed to be the biggest money-making train in the world. In 1928, a peak year, revenue from its operations was nearly $10 million.

During the golden age of railroading when such trains as the Orient Express and Flying Scotsman were celebrated in song and story, the Twentieth Century Limited more than held its own. Ben

Hecht and Charles MacArthur wrote a play about it in 1932; E.B. White wrote a poem entitled *"The Twentieth Century Gets Through."* Eva Marie Saint and Cary Grant met on the train in the movie *North by Northwest*; numerous authors including Lucius Beebe, wrote books in which the Twentieth Century figured prominently. Regular passengers during its heyday included Theodore Roosevelt, Enrico Caruso, Nellie Melba, "Diamond Jim" Brady, and J. P. Morgan.

After World War II, a series of consolidations precipitated the end of the famous train. The New York Central Railroad had three excellent trains on the New York-Chicago run, each with as many as seven sections—the Twentieth Century Limited, Commodore, and Pacemaker. Seeking to cut back service, management combined the Commodore and Twentieth Century in 1958. As a result, the glamor and identity of the celebrated train began to fade.

Nevertheless, in 1962 a sixtieth birthday affair was held, complete with double-tiered cake with two trains on top. By that year, the Twentieth Century had logged 62 million miles between New York and Chicago.

But the end was near. Patronage dropped off sharply and service declined. At 6 p.m. on 2 December 1967, it pulled out of Grand Central Terminal for the last time, with 104 passengers aboard the half-full train. "You can see looking at the empty seats tonight why we're doing it," a railroad official said.

The final trip was basically without fanfare, although scavengers had been at work, the handsome red and gray curtains that hung over the Century's departure gate having been stolen by souvenir hunters. Police stood by to make sure no one made off with the carpet traditionally rolled out for every trip.

Ironically, the train's last run was marred by the derailment of another train at Conneaut, Ohio. It was the evening rather than the morning of 3 December 1967 when the last Twentieth Century Limited struggled into Chicago's LaSalle Street Station, nine hours late.

The Last Steam Locomotives

The nineteenth century was the age of steam and one of its most sophisticated inventions, the steam locomotive. So refined that many models of the 1890s were capable of speeds of 100 miles per hour, the steam locomotive did not start to be replaced until the mid-1920s. At that time, there were 65,000 locomotives operating, some with twelve wheels, and many faster than their modern diesel counterparts.

Despite the excellent qualities of steam, diesel engines gradually took over, largely because they were cleaner, more efficient, and weighed less. Shortly after World War II, most nations stopped ordering steam locomotives. In 1949, the final thirteen were made for U.S. railroads; seven years later, the Soviet Union built its last steam locomotive. And on 18 March 1960, British Railways gave an appropriate name—Evening Star—to its last steam engine, officially Number 92220, built at Swindon.

Meanwhile, railroads around the world phased out their steam locomotives in favor of diesel. Number 38, the last of the Long Island Railroad's 220 steam locomotives, made its final run in early June, 1960, after traveling more than a million miles. After retirement, it was put on exhibition at the Carriage House Museum in Stony Brook, Long Island. August, 1955, saw the last run of the Wabash Railroad's Number 573 engine,which was constructed in 1899 and had been the only non-diesel on the line for two years.

The last steam engine operated by the New York Central Railroad was Number 1977, which went out of service in May of 1957.

The last steam locomotive regularly used in the Eastern United States was Number 10 operating out of the Brooklyn Eastern District Terminal. Begrimed and clouded in steam from banked-down boiler fires, the old, black, twenty-eight-foot long six-wheeler ended its forty-four year career on 25 October 1963.

"There's no use feeling bad," said engineer Joseph Keane. "The diesel is better in every way, and I can't forget how hot that cab was in the winter, as well as in the sweltering summer."

Another railroad man since 1926, Nicholas G. Cutter, said he would miss the hiss of the old engines. "It was an old-world sound and it was good to hear on a bitter winter day," he remarked a bit sadly. "Actually, I think we might have kept at least one of the steam engines if we could replace parts, but no iron works make them anymore."

He was indeed right. On 19 September 1959, Robert Stephenson and Hawthorns, Ltd., the company that made the first steam locomotive in 1823, announced that it was going out of business.

The Last Ride on the Orient Express

Beginning on 5 June 1883, the luxury train known as the "Orient Express" rolled on its 2,000 mile run for nearly a century as a symbol of railroading's golden age as well as mystery and intrigue. (Actually, there was only one unsolved murder on the Orient Express: it involved an American diplomat who lost his footing and fell off shortly after being stabbed.)

On its maiden voyage from Istanbul (then Constantinople), the French president and a special envoy of the Turkish Sultan were on one platform at Paris' Gare de l'est station. In those days, the trip took six days and six hours (in 1905 the time was shortened to two-and-a-half days), but the passengers considered the luxury worth the slowness.The cars in which they traveled had velvet covered seats trimmed with Brussels lace, lush damask curtains on the windows and fittings of solid oak and mahogany. Hand-cut glass separated the sleeping compartments from the outside aisles. Gourmet meals were commonplace, of course, featuring oysters and pheasant, all served by waiters in morning coats, light blue breeches and buckled shoes.

For decades, the train was featured in many novels and movies, but long before the Orient Express lost its charm for writers of fiction, its glamor was gone for travelers. By the 1920s, the elegant wooden cars had been replaced with cold steel, the porters wore drab brown, and service had deteriorated considerably. With the coming of airline service, traffic on the Orient Express had deteriorated to the point where in 1959, traffic on the old line between Vienna and Bucharest was down to an average one-and-a-half passengers per trip.

Finally, at 12:13 a.m. (seventeen minutes late) on 20 May 1977, the Orient Express began its final run, pulling out of the Gare de Lyon, Paris. Eighteen passengers were in first class for the nostalgic trip. The day coaches were crowded with Greeks, Turks, Yugoslavians, and Bulgarians going home, most unaware of the trip's significance.

Those making the last run had to take their own food and water, for the luxurious dining cars of the once glamourous train were long gone. After sixty hours of partying, the eighteen first class passengers sang "Auld Lang Syne" and gulped the last of their champagne as the Orient Express rumbled into Istanbul's Sirkecci Station on 22 May, ending ninety-four years of service.

The Last of the Brighton Belle

Mile for mile, the Brighton Belle was probably one of the finest trains of the twentieth century. Four times a day it made the fifty mile trip between London and the seaside resort of Brighton, every mile a pleasant one for its passengers.

During its slightly less than an hour's trip, the Brighton Belle offered every traveler restaurant service in his or her seat—complete with damask linen, tablecloths, silver and smiles. The surroundings were elegant, featuring plush carpeting, velvet footstools, oak-paneled walls and shiny brasswork. For more than four decades it had been that way. A particular fan of the Brighton Belle was Sir Laurence Olivier, who once complained when kippers and scrambled eggs were dropped from the menu. They were promptly restored, of course, for that was the way the Brighton Belle was operated.

In the early 1970s, however, it was discovered that the train was beginning to shiver and shake as she got old. And even worse, she wasn't paying her way.

The end came on 1 May 1972, a large crowd gathering to wave goodbye. Some men wore dinner jackets, the women long dresses as they drank champagne, smoked free cigars, listened to the band play "Auld Lang Syne" and chatted about the good old days. After the train pulled out, people came out on the balconies of their homes for a final wave and a shout of approbation.

Not everyone was happy, naturally. Thomas O'Connor, one of the Belle's stewards, said: "It's like the end of a tradition. We shouldn't throw traditions away like that...And where will it go...The trains will probably go to America..."

Chapter Six

Political Lasts

Chronology

633 B.C.
Assurbanipal, last of the great kings of ancient Assyria, dies after building a library and raising level of living to a sumptuous high.

586 B.C.
The house of David, which provided rulers for the Kingdom of Jerusalem for nearly 400 years, comes to an end.

546 B.C.
Legendary for his wealth, Croesus, who rules the ancient Kingdom of Lydia, is the last ruler of his dynasty, defeated by Cyrus the Great of Persia.

538 B.C.
The last Babylonian king, Nabonidus, falls to Cyrus the Great.

332 B.C.
The reign of Pharaoh Nekht-nebf ends the last native dynasty of Egypt as Alexander the Great conquers the ancient nation.

330 B.C.
The Achaemenid dynasty of ancient Persia ends as King Darius III flees from Alexander the Great and is killed.

166 B.C.
Perseus, last king of Macedonia, dies in captivity two years after being defeated by the Romans.

14 A.D.
(May 11) Emperor Augustus Caesar, growing infirm in his last year of life, makes his final public appearance at the Campus Martius, presiding over a census ceremony.

100
The seventh and last king of the family of Herod the Great, Herod Agrippa (27-100), ends the Judean line of rulers at his death.

226
Artabanus IV, last of the Arsacid rulers of Persia, is murdered in a coup d'etat, ending a line of kings almost 500 years old.

407
After four centuries, the last Roman soldiers leave Britain.

476
(Aug. 28) Only fifteen years old, Romulus Augustulus becomes the last Western Roman emperor as the Barbarians take over the once glorious empire. (see p. 189)

507
Visigoth rule in Spain ends with the defeat of Alaric II, eighth king of the Goths.

664
Cadwallader, leader of the Celtic resistance against the Anglo-Saxons, dies, the last Welsh king to wear the crown of Britain.

711
Roderick becomes last Visigothic king of Spain when he is defeated by Moslem forces under Tarik near Medina Sidonia.

751
Childeric III, last Merovingian king of the Franks, is deposed by Pepin the Short.

774
The power of the Lombards comes to an end as their last king, Desiderius, is defeated by the forces of Charlemagne.

987
Louis V, known as "The Sluggard," dies at the age of twenty, the last king of the Carolingian dynasty.

1032
Rudolf III becomes last King of Arles, bequeathing his realm on his death fo Holy Roman Emperor Conrad II.

1171
Adid, the fourteenth and last of the Fatamid Moslem rulers, dies.

1198
Roderick O'Connor, last king of Ireland, dies after being subjugated by the English.

1200
The last ruler of the Chalukya dynasty of India dies. The line was founded by Palukesin I in 543.

1246
The Babenbergs, ruling house of Austria since 976, comes to an end as Frederick II "The Quarrelsome" dies childless.

1258
(Feb. 28) The Abbasid dynasty of the Mohammedan Empire comes to an end.

1268
Conradin, the last crowned Hohenstaufen, is executed, bringing the line of kings to an end.

1282
Killed in a rebellion against the English invaders, Prince Gruffydd ap Llewelyn is the last independent ruler of Wales before that tiny nation is annexed.

1287
Bohemund VII becomes the last Count of Tripoli, dying without issue, ending a line of succession dating back to the First Crusade.

1328
(Jan. 31) The Capetian dynasty of France comes to an end when King Charles IV dies at the age of thirty-four with no heir.

1368
The Yuan dynasty in China, founded in 1271, comes to an end.

1379
The last count of Blois, childless and heavily in debt, sells his title and lands to Louis, Duke of Orleans.

1415
The last independent Prince of Wales, Owen Glendower (1359-1415) leads a revolt against the British until shortly before his death.

1421
The Balsha dynasty of Albania, founded in 1366, comes to an end.

1449
(July 4) After a decade of rule, anti-Pope Felix V abdicates and is made a cardinal. He becomes the last antipope to set up an ecclesiastical government opposing the Vatican. (see p. 190)

1453
(May 29) The Eastern Roman Empire, also known as the Byzantine Empire, falls to the Turks and takes its last emperor, Constantine XI, with it. (see p. 191)

1485
(Aug. 22) Richard III, last Plantagenet king to be crowned, is killed in battle at Bosworth Field.

1492
The rule of the Nasrides, last Mohammedan dynasty in Spain, comes to an end as Catholic sovereigns drive them away after 260 years.

1525
Cuauhtemoc, last emperor of the Aztecs, is murdered by the explorer Cortes as the Spanish subjugate Mexico.

1531
Ferdinand I is the last emperor of the Holy Roman Empire crowned at the city of Aachen, a practice going back to 813 and Louis the Pious.

1533
Atahualpa, last of the Inca kings of Peru, is imprisoned and murdered by the Spanish explorer, Pizarro.

1589
(Aug. 2) Henry III dies, the last Valois king of France.

1603
(March 24) The line of Tudor rulers of England ends with the death of Queen Elizabeth I.

1644
The Ming Dynasty of China, which ruled since 1368, comes to an end.

1700
With the death of King Charles II of Spain, the Hapsburg dynasty in that nation comes to an end.

1708
Ferdinand Charles Gonzaga, becomes last Duke of Mantua, as Austrian forces annex the Italian principality.

1714
In Great Britain, the reign of the Stuarts ends with the death of Queen Anne.

1731
The noble (since 1545) Farnese family of Italy becomes extinct when the last Duke, Antonio, dies.

1737
(July 9) The ancient House of Medici (from 1360) comes to an end with the death of Gian Gastone de'Medici, last male member of the family.

1773
(Sept. 23) Upon the death of Evelyn Pierrepont (1711-1773), who has no children, the title of Duke of Kingston becomes extinct.

1778
William Pitt, Earl of Chatham, makes a dramatic last speech in the House of Lords (for reconciliation with the American colonies), then collapses and dies.

1791
Leopold II (1747-1792) is crowned king of Bohemia, the last ruler to hold that title.

1795
Stanislaus II (1732-1798) is forced to abdicate, becoming last king of Poland.

1796
(Nov. 10) Death of Catherine the Great, last empress of Russia. (see p. 192)

1796
Ercole d'Este III is deposed as Duc d'Este, last in a long line of Lombardy nobility.

1797
(April 18) Ludovico Manin, last doge of Venice, abdicates as the city is besieged by Napoleon. (see p. 194)

1799
(Nov. 7) The First Republic of France comes to an end as Napoleon declares himself emperor. The republic was proclaimed on 21 September 1792.

1806
(July 12) The Holy Roman Empire becomes extinct following the abdication of its last emperor, Francis II.

1814
The French House of Conti (since 1551) becomes extinct.
(July 12) With the death of Sir William Howe (1729-1814), the Irish peerage becomes extinct.

1823
The last emperor of Mexico, Augustine Iturbide, is assassinated, ending his reign which began the year before.

1830
Algiers falls to French after more than three centuries of Turkish rule.

1833
The end of Turkish rule in Greece, which began in 1458. Greece becomes an independent nation.

1843
(July 29) Last Duke of Dorset dies, bringing an end to title held since 1688.

1844
Last Dauphin of France, Louis-Antoine de Bourbon, duc d'Angoleme, dies at age of sixty-nine

1845
With the death of George Francis Wyndham (born 1785), the title of Earl of Egremont, in use since 1749, becomes extinct.

1848
Louis-Philippe, last king of France, escapes to England in disguise as popular revolution ends the monarchy for a second time. (see p. 194)

1848
Henry Clay makes his last attempt to gain the U.S. presidency at the age of seventy-one. As in 1824, 1832, and 1844, he is unsuccessful, losing the nomination to Zachary Taylor.

1850
(June 28) Sir Robert Peel makes his last speech in Parliament, a plea for Great Britain to stay out of the affairs of smaller nations, then is killed in a fall from his horse.

1851
(Dec. 2) The Second Republic of France, proclaimed on 20 December 1848, comes to an end as Louis Napoleon Bonaparte becomes emperor.

1857
Bahadur Shah II, last mogul of India, is deposed by the British. (see p. 195)

1858
In power since 1186, the Moslem Ghor dynasty ends in Afghanistan.

1859
(July 21) Leopold II (1797-1870) the last reigning duke of Tuscany, abdicates in favor of his son, who never rules as Austrians take over principality.

1861
Francis II becomes last king of the Two Sicilies as Italy conquers the tiny kingdom. Francis goes into exile and lives until 1894.

1865
(April 11) President Abraham Lincoln makes his last public speech, urging Americans to join him in binding the nation's wounds.
(April 14) Hopes for a smooth reconciliation of North and South are dashed when Lincoln is assassinated at Ford's Theatre, Washington. (see p. 196)

1866
George V becomes the last king of Hanover, after siding with Austria in its war with Prussia. The victorious Prussians annex the kingdom of Hanover and depose George, who dies in 1878.

1868
(April 11) The shogunate is abolished in Japan, ending the long reign of warlords. (see p. 200)

1880
Pomare V, last king of Tahiti, abdicates as France takes over the largest of the Society Islands.

1885
(Nov. 28) The last King of Burma, Thibaw, is captured and sent into exile by the British, who add the nation to the growing British Empire.

1889
(Nov. 15) Dom Pedro II, last emperor of Brazil, abdicates.

1893
Queen Liliukalani, last monarch of Hawaii, is deposed. (see p. 202)

1896
Queen Ranavalona III becomes the last hereditary monarch of Madagascar as French troops take possession of the island.

1898
Spain loses Cuba, her last colonial possession in the Western Hemisphere.

1901
Britain's last colonial troops leave Canada.

1910
(May 20) For the last time, the monarchs of a score of nations gather in one place. In less than a decade, most will be ousted in revolutions. (see p. 202)
(Oct. 4) Founded in 1143, the Portuguese monarchy comes to an end as King Manoel II flees the country.

1912
(Feb. 12) China's Chi'ng dynasty comes to an end as Emperor Henry Pu-yi is deposed. (see p. 203)

1914
(June 24) King Peter of Serbia abdicates, the last monarch of that nation soon to be eradicated by World War I.
(Dec. 19) Abbas II, last Khedive of Egypt, is deposed.

1917
(March 15) Tsar Nicholas II becomes the last of the Romanoff dynasty of imperial rulers as Russian revolutionaries depose him.

1918
World War I helps hasten the end of monarchies in Bulgaria, Germany, Austria-Hungary, Bavaria, Saxony, and Baden. (see p. 204)

1920
Eugene V. Debs makes his last run for President of the United States, while in prison. (His previous unsuccessful attempts were in 1900, 1904, 1908, and 1912.)

1923
(March 3) Mohammed VI, last Caliph of Turkey, steps down as the new Turkish republic is proclaimed.

1924
After sixteen centuries (since 330 A.D.) the city of Constantinople is no longer the capital of a great empire (Ottoman, previously Byzantine).

1935
The last King of Siam is Prajadhipok, who yields his throne and moves to Surrey, England. (see p. 205)

1940
(June) Albert Lebrun, last president of the Third Republic of France (proclaimed on 2 September 1870), is ousted by Marshal Petain after the Nazi invasion.

1944
(June 23) Although it is summertime and there is no fire in the White House, President Franklin D. Roosevelt makes the last of his famous "fireside chats" to the nation. (see p. 206)

1945
(April 20) Adolf Hitler, only leader of Germany's Third Reich, makes his final decision concerning the strategy of the war he almost single-handedly thrust upon the world.

1946
(Jan. 2) Having fled Albania at the outset of World War II, King Zog is formally deposed in absentia, becoming the last monarch of the nation. (see p. 209)

1946
(June 2) Umberto II rules less than a month as last king of Italy. (see p. 207)

1946
(Sept. 8) Simeon II becomes last king of Bulgaria, abdicating when the monarchy is abolished by the Communists. (see p. 208)

1947
(March 8) King Peter II is deprived of his nationality and his property confiscated as the Yugoslav Assembly

187

abolishes the monarchy and proclaims a republic headed by Marshal Tito. (see p. 210)

1948
(January) King Michael of Rumania becomes the last monarch of that nation. (see p. 212)

1948
America's most persistent campaigner for the Presidency, Socialist Party candidate Norman Thomas, makes his sixth and last run for the office.

1952
(July 3) King Farouk I of Egypt is deposed by a military coup d'etat, becoming the last hereditary monarch of that nation. He retires to Italy for a brief but eventful life of gorging and womanizing. (see p. 214)
(Oct. 3) Baha Alchesay, last hereditary chief of the Apache nation, dies on a reservation. (see p. 214)

1955
Bao Dai and Nam Phuong become the last emperor and empress of Vietnam when a referendum is passed abolishing the monarchy. (see p. 215)

1956
(April 13) Ninety-one years after Abraham Lincoln was assassinated, Samuel J. Seymour, the last eyewitness to the event, dies in Arlington, Virginia. (see p. 197)

1957
With the formation of the Tunisian Republic, Sidi Mohammed el-Amin is deposed as Bey of Tunis, last of this line of rulers.

1958
(July 14) Faisal II, last king of Iraq, is murdered and a republic proclaimed.
(Oct. 4) Rene Jules Gustave Coty, last president of France's Fourth Republic (proclaimed on 7 November 1944), yields to Charles DeGaulle and the establishment of the Fifth Republic.

1964
(July 27) Venerable British statesman Winston Churchill, retired from politics for nearly a decade, makes his last visit to the House of Commons, six months before his death.
(Sept. 13) Premier Nikita Khrushchev, colorful and strong leader of the Soviet Union during the late 1950s an early 1960s, is removed from power.

1966
(Aug. 1) The Colonial Office in London strikes its flag as Botswana, British Guiana, Basutoland, and Barbados gain their independence from the British Empire.
(Sept. 6) The last remaining British territory in Africa, Swaziland, becomes independent.

1969
The last nineteenth century Indian chief, White Cloud, dies at the age of 102. A leader of the Creek nation and friend of Sitting Bull, who saw his oil-rich lands taken over by the U.S. government in 1907, White Cloud became a spiritualist minister and patent medicine salesman during his last days.

1971
(Jan. 2) It is the last day in office for Speaker John McCormack, a member of the House of Representatives for forty-three years.

1973
Constantine II, last king of Greece, abdicates in favor of a republic. (see p. 218)

1974
(Aug. 9) Richard M. Nixon makes his last television appearance as U.S. president, resigning while skirting the issue of his involvement in the Watergate scandal.

The Last Roman Emperor (West)

The last day the Roman Empire was controlled by a single leader was 17 January 395 A.D. On that day, Emperor Theodosius I (The Great) died and, in his wisdom, divided the empire into western and eastern portions.

The eastern half, with its capital at Constantinople, was to be ruled by Theodosius' son, Arcadius; the West, with Rome the capital, was bequeathed to son Honorius.

Rome's great days were long past, of course, and the ruling class had not improved much since the days of Nero and Caligula. In the west, Honorius had troubles keeping the barbarians away from the Eternal City except when Alaric, their leader, was in the mood to accept a bribe. This worked until Easter Sunday, 402, when Alaric and his Visigoths attacked. Fortunately for the Romans, Alaric's family was captured and he agreed to leave Italy in exchange for their safety. A year later, the Roman general Flavius Stilicho defeated Alaric at Verona and chased him through the Brenner Pass. Suffering from hunger and disease, the barbarians were lucky to avoid complete annihilation.

If he had known his Roman history, Stilicho would have realized that he had just done the worst thing possible for his own personal safety. Time after time, jealous Roman emperors had rewarded victorious generals by framing and then killing them, and Stilicho was no exception. Not long after Stilicho had saved the western empire's capital from Alaric, Honorious ordered the general arrested for treason. At first, Stilicho tried to take refuge in a church, but came out the next day when he was told that Honorius had not ordered his execution. Shortly afterward, on 22 August 408, Stilicho was beheaded.

Lacking Stilicho's expertise, Honorius was therefore unable to put up much of a defense when Alaric returned to sack Rome in 410. By that time the whole empire was in a mess, no less than six men claiming the two available crowns. Somehow Honorius muddled through, only to die of dropsy in the year 423, aged thirty-nine

A parade of variously incompetent emperors followed. By midcentury, the Western Roman Empire was under the leadership of the indolent Valentinian III, who was clearly no match for Attila the Hun. The empire probably would have fallen then had it not been for Aetius, another Roman general who had not read his history. After defeating the Germans in Gaul in 451, Aetius commanded Roman and Visigothic legions at Chalons-sur-Marne, routing Attila and the Huns and saving Rome.

Three years later, still stinging with jealousy of Aetius' success, Emperor Valentinian had him murdered. Then in 455, two friends of Aetius, Optila and Thrasustila, joined Valentinian while he was practicing his archery and assassinated him. Maximus, the next western emperor, ruled only from 17 March to 31 May, 455, fleeing when he heard the Imperial City was being attacked. The populace, not appreciating such cowardice, stoned him to death and tore him limb from limb.

If one wonders why anyone wanted to be Roman Emperor, given such conditions, it is best to remember that when he ascended the throne in 475, Romulus Augustulus was only fourteen years old. The real head of government was his father, Orestes, a former secretary of Attila, a fact which should indicate the depths to which the once-glorious Roman Empire had sunk. For a year, Orestes managed well enough, until his soldiers revolted and appointed one of their officers head of the army.

The new Barbarian leader, Odovacar, had Orestes killed on 28 August 476, and forced Romulus Augustulus to abdicate. His life was spared, however, because he was so young, and Odovacar even gave the former boy emperor an annual income of 6,000 solidi (about $30,000) to retire on.

The last Western Roman Emperor did just that, slinking off to Campania to live with relatives. The date of his death is not known.

The Last Anti-Pope

Although it is technically possible for there to be another antipope sometime in the future, it has been more than 500 years since anyone has taken that title. Moreover, the papal succession process

190

has become cut and dried in recent times even as the power of the papacy has declined. It thus seems unlikely that there will ever be a challenger for the papacy serious enough to set up a rival hierarchy.

Another factor inhibiting the appearance of a future contender is that anti-popes of the past have usually found the going difficult. The first was Hippolytus, who ruled from 217 to 235 A.D. against three rival popes who were considered ecclesiastically legitimate — Callistus I, Urban I, and Pontianus. Hippolytus was let off rather easily, abdicating the papacy when he saw the odds were against him, but many of the twenty-five anti-popes who followed him were handled a bit roughly.

Silverius, for example, was banished to the Island of Ponza in the year 537. Constantine II, a layman, proclaimed himself a papal rival in 719 and was murdered. Boniface VII was deposed and murdered in 974. Anti-Pope John XVI was blinded and murdered twenty-four years later. Theodoric was banished to a cave monastery in 1100, as was anti-Pope Innocent III in 1180 (not the Innocent III who served as genuine Pope some years later). In 1102, anti-Pope Albert was banished to the St. Laurentius monastery at Aversa.

There was also an anti-Pope to Pope Gregory XII (from 1410 to 1415), who took the title John XXIII. Much later, of course, the legitimate Pope John XXIII became one of the most beloved figures of the twentieth century.

The last (or most recent) anti-pope was Amadeus VIII (1383-1451), Count and Duke of Savoy. Although a layman, Amadeus was in 1434 a much respected citizen living in retirement at the hermitage of Ripaille on Lake Geneva. At that time, the Council of Basel and Pope Eugene IV, already differing strongly in their views on the power of the papacy, became even more solidified in their opinion. When Eugene declared the council heretical, it retaliated by deposing Eugene, then asking Amadeus if he would accept the Chair of Peter. Thinking he could help bring peace to the church, Amadeus accepted, and in 1439 became anti-Pope Felix V. His authority was not accepted, however, so he quietly abdicated on 4 July 1449. He was subsequently made a cardinal.

The Last Byzantine Emperor

After the fall of the Western Roman Empire, the Eastern Empire continued for nearly a thousand years. Known as the Byzantine Empire because the captial city, Constantinople, was built on the ruins of ancient Byzantium, its first emperor was Arcadius, son of Theodosius I.

Just eighteen when he was crowned, the impressionable Arcadius fell under the influence of Eutropius, a eunuch. This shocked many important people in the empire who felt that eunuchs shouldn't be

191

allowed in government positions. After several years, Eutropius finally fell out of favor and in order to save his life was forced to hide under the altar of St. Sophia's church while the Patriarch of Constantinople delivered a sermon.

Although the Byzantine Empire was never as strong as Rome had been during its heyday, the emperors of Constantinople managed to keep the realm intact by bribery, skillful double-dealing, and occasional displays of bravery and power. One of the strongest Byzantine emperors was Basil II, who ruled from 976 to 1025. Convinced that the empire would collapse if the "Bulgar question" was not solved, Basil headed westward into Thrace and Macedonia in an effort to trap and destroy the hordes of Bulgars threatening Constantinople.

It took him almost forty years, but Basil succeeded. The decisive battle came in 1014 when the Romans fell upon a Bulgarian force in the Struma Valley and began a systematic massacre. When it was over, 14,000 prisoners remained in Roman hands.

Determined not only that these enemies would not fight again but would also be living examples of what happened to those who threatened Constantinople, Basil had the captured Bulgars put in irons and led before his executioners. One by one, every prisoner had his eyes put out, every hundredth man being left with a single eye in order to lead his comrades back home. When the Bulgar chief, Samuel, caught sight of the shuffling gory multitude, he reportedly fell dead on the spot. In any event, the defeat of the Bulgars gave the Byzantine Empire another four centuries of life.

The eventual day of reckoning came in 1453, when the Turks finally closed the ring on Constantinople as the last emperor, Constantine XI, tried vainly to rally his meager forces. As the Turkish soldiers breached the walls of the city, Constantine dismounted, drew his sword, and with three officers, dashed into the swelling flood of the enemy.

His valiant effort failed. The date was 29 May, when the sun rose and shone for the last time on a Byzantine emperor.

The Last Empress of Russia

During the eighteenth century, imperial Russia was perhaps the most advanced nation in the world, with women holding the highest position of governance for much of the century.

The first of these astute women to become empress, or *czarina*, was a nineteen-year-old domestic named Martha who was captured by Russian soldiers. Quickly taking a liking to one of the officers, Alexander Menshikov, Martha met Peter I (The Great) and became his mistress, too. She did so well that Peter married her in

1712. On Peter's death, aided by Menshikov, Martha changed her name to Catherine and ruled from 1725 to 1727.

The twelve-year-old grandson of Peter I took over the throne following Martha-Catherine's death. He ruled for three years, then conveniently died of smallpox on his wedding day.

At that time, his cousin, Anna Ivanovna, managed to have herself chosen Czarina with the help of the supreme privy council. The second daughter of Ivan V, Peter the Great's imbecile brother, Anna had been married at seventeen to Frederick William, Duke of Courland, who died of overeating shortly after the wedding. Anna took up with Count Peter Bestuzev and then Ernst Johann von Biron, a German who was instrumental in helping Anna banish Russians from high positions in the court.

Anna died in 1740, and her son Ivan ascended the throne with Biron as regent. This did not sit well with Elizabeth, the daughter of Peter the Great and Catherine I, who hated Germans. Fortunately for Elizabeth, she was popular with the imperial guards (while still in her teens, she had made a lover of Alexius Shurbin, a sergeant in the Semenovsky Guards, but Empress Anna discovered it and banished everything but his tongue to Siberia). Fearing that Ivan would have her murdered, or even worse, sent to a convent for life, Elizabeth went to the barracks of the Preobrazhensky Guards on the night of 6 December 1741, and somehow enlisted their sympathies. The next morning, Elizabeth was Empress of All Russia.

During her reign, Elizabeth founded the University of Moscow and the Academy of Fine Arts in St. Petersburg. In 1762, she died, and was succeeded by Peter III, grandson of Peter the Great.

Peter's first act was to take Russia out of the Seven Years' War with Prussia, which Elizabeth had brought to a near-successful conclusion. Definitely feeble-minded, Peter was married to a thirty-three-year-old German woman named Sophia Augusta Frederica, who, like Elizabeth before her, was on the friendliest terms with several guardsmen. Almost before he knew it, Peter was writing out his own abdication while the guards looked on.

A few days later, Sophia announced that she was the new Empress Catherine II and that her husband had died of hemorrhoidal colic. Thus began the thirty-four year reign of Russia's last (and most famous) empress.

Catherine the Great divided her time between affairs of state and just plain affairs. Some historians have estimated that Catherine had 300 lovers but that really wasn't so many considering the fact that she lived a long life and was sexually active right up to the end. On 10 November 1796, as a matter of fact, she died of apoplexy at the age of sixty-seven.

The Last Doge of Venice

For centuries Venice was a tiny but influential power in the Mediterranean, its government headed by an administrative officer known as a doge. The first doge was elected in 687 A.D.

Several powerful Venetian families managed to keep the office of doge more or less in the family. The Contarini family, for instance, had eight doges, including Andrea Contarini, who proved his patriotism in 1380 by melting down his gold and silver plate and mortgaging his property to help pay for a war. The 100th doge of Venice, Carlo Contarini (1655-56) was in office during the important Venetian naval victory at the Dardanelles.

Like most long-established offices, the position of doge had its share of good men, bad men, winners, and losers. High points of the Venetian republic included a vistory over the Turks in 1416 and the defeat of another Turkish fleet at Lepanto in 1571. This was achieved by the Doge Sebastian Venier, but shortly afterward the Venetian naval commander, Bragadino, lost Cyprus. Still smarting from the Lepanto fiasco, the Turkish commander had Bragadino's ears, nose, and lips cut off, then ordered him flayed alive, his skin stuffed with straw and carried in triumph to Constantinople.

The most celebrated doge was Marino Faliero (1274-1355), who formed a conspiracy to become dictator, was found out, tried by the Council of Ten, and beheaded. A colorful and tragic figure, he became the subject of literary works by Byron, Swinburne and De la Vigne, a painting by Delacroix, and an opera by Donizetti.

By the late eighteenth century, Venice had declined considerably as a sea power and was ripe for plucking by any of several neighboring states. Thus, in 1789, sixty-three-year-old Ludovico Manin was not particularly eager to take the position of doge when it was offered to him. He accepted finally on 9 March 1789, less than two months before Europe was torn apart by the French Revolution.

Manin managed to keep Venice out of danger until Napoleon came to power, then was forced to choose between siding with Bonaparte or the Austrians. Choosing neither, he managed to alienate both sides, as well as his own countrymen, who declined to defend Venice against Napoleon on the advice of Manin. Later, after Napoleon took the city, Manin was accused of cowardice. He abdicated on 18 April 1797, the last doge of Venice, and died five years later.

The Last King of France

Born in 1773, the eldest son of Louis Philippe Joseph, Duke of Orleans, and Louise Marie Adelaide de Bourbon, France's last king, Louis Philippe, had as godparents King Louis XVI and Marie Antoinette. This was a blessing until the French Revolution, when being associated with royalty was highly dangerous. But, because he early identified himself with liberal elements and attended the debates of the National Assembly, Louis Philippe was well regarded when the trouble started.

In 1794, however, his father was executed, so Louis Philippe fled to the United States, returning to France in 1800 only to find Napoleon firmly in power. Soon he was off to England and another forced vacation.

His position was a tenuous one, largely because the people of France were not sure whether they wanted a king, a republican form of government, or an emperor. Cleverly playing his cards and biding his time, Louis Philippe waited until 1830, when another revolution led to the downfall of King Charles X. Because he had the backing of the popular Marquis de Lafayette, Louis Philippe was thereupon embraced by the chamber and proclaimed "King of the French, by the grace of God and the will of the people."

His reign was largely undistinguished. He became increasingly dynastic and more unpopular as the years went on. Finally, in 1848, yet another revolution led by leftist elements brought about his downfall. After abdicating and fearful that he might be executed, Louis Philippe escaped with Queen Marie Amelie, exiting via a back door of the Tuileries and hiding in a gardener's cottage. The two were then disguised and smuggled out of the country by the British consul on the steamer *Express*, under the names William Smith and Madame LeBrun. Louis Philippe died in England on 26 August 1850.

He was the last king of France. After the 1848 revolution, the French tried democracy until 1852, when the president of the Second Republic, Louis Napoleon Bonaparte, proclaimed himself emperor. The Franco-Prussian War of 1870 brought about his downfall, after which France went back to a republican form of government. Although this form has not exactly worked very well, it seems unlikely the French will ever have another king or queen.

The Last Mogul

Though the apellation is now used to describe anyone with money or power, the original moguls were rulers of the Muslim empire of India from 1526 to 1857. A variant of Mongol, the term is incorrectly derived, since the moguls were mainly Turks rather than descendands of Genghis Khan.

The founder of the mogul empire of India was Babur (full name Zahir ud-Din Muhammad), a descendant of Tamerlane who made raids into India during the early sixteenth century, finally conquering nearly all of northern India. Babur was also a distinguished poet.

Babur's grandson, Akbar (1542-1604), considered the greatest of the moguls, began ruling when he was only twelve years old. Continuing his family's policy of conquest, Akbar enlarged the kingdom to include Afghanistan, Baluchistan, and nearly all of the Indian peninsula north of the Godavari River. Although he himself was illiterate, Akbar was a patron of the arts, letters, and learning, surrounding himself with Muslim divines, Hindu Brahmins, and Jesuits.

Establishing a court at Agra, he constructed magnificent buildings and kept many animals — about 5,000 elephants, 12,000 stable horses, and 1,000 hunting leopards.

Akbar's son Jahangir was a lazy, pleasure-loving man who accomplished very little, but the next mogul, Shah Jahan, was responsible for the construction of India's most beautiful and celebrated building, the Taj Mahal, after the death in 1629 of his favorite wife, Mumtaz Mahal.

Unfortunately for the moguls, the splendor and wealth of their empire soon attracted the imperialistic British, Dutch, French, and Portuguese. From 1746 to 1763 India became a battleground for French and British armies, the brilliant victories of Commander Robert Clive leading to the beginning of the British Indian Empire.

During the late eighteenth and early nineteenth centuries, the moguls were allowed to remain on the throne of India, although they were controlled by the British. The last of the line was Bahadur Shah II, born in 1775, who became mogul in 1837. For twenty years afterward, he served as a figurehead, a man whose gentle nature and considerable talents as a poet made him unexpectedly appropriate to the fall of his great dynasty.

In 1857, Indian soldiers in the Bengal army (known as Sepoys) rebelled against the British. The spark that ignited their anger came when the British issued cartridges coated with grease made from the fat of cows and pigs. Because cows are sacred to Hindus and pigs are anathema to Muslims, the Sepoy soldiers concluded that the British were subtly trying to break down their faith and refused to touch the cartridges. A rebellion followed, the Sepoys proclaiming Bahadur Shah Emperor of all India.

After crushing the mutiny, the British abolished the position of mogul and exiled Bahadur Shah to Burma. He died there in 1862.

Some Lincoln Lasts

On Tuesday, 11 April 1865, two days after the surrender of General Robert E. Lee's army at Appomattox, President Abraham Lincoln appeared at the upper window of the White House and spoke to a cheering crowd of war-weary Americans. Although no one knew it at the time, it was to be the last time Lincoln addressed an audience.

His speech was hardly designed to rouse the rabble. Instead of gloating over the Union's victory, Lincoln discussed the problems of reconstruction: "Let us all join in doing the acts necessary to restore the proper practical relations between these states and the nation." Concerning the new government of Louisiana — which many Northerners found not to their liking — he added, "We shall sooner have the fowl by hatching the egg than by smashing it."

Three days later, having accepted an invitation to attend the final benefit performance of *Our American Cousin* at Ford's Theatre, Lincoln and his wife, Mary, searched for someone to accompany them. In rapid succession, their offer was declined by son Robert, just home from the front and in a state of exhaustion; General U.S. Grant and his wife, who could not abide the First Lady's haughty airs; Speaker of the the House Schuyler Colfax, who was leaving for California the next day; and Major Thomas T. Eckert, head of the military telegraph, who was busy. No less than a dozen potential guests begged off before Major Henry Reed Rathbone and his fiancee, Clara Harris, agreed to go.

In fact, Lincoln himself would have preferred staying home, for his tastes ran more to Shakespeare, and Tom Taylor's cornball 1858 comedy was less than a masterpiece. But the news that the President had accepted the management's invitation produced a near-capacity crowd of 1,675 on a Good Friday evening, traditionally the worst theatre night of the year. Since he had promised to be there, Lincoln kept his word, although the play was already in progress when the presidential party arrived. Action immediately ceased on the stage as actress Laura Keene led the applause and the band struck up "Hail to the Chief."

In the audience that evening was 5-year old Sammy Seymour, who had made the 150-mile journey from Talbot County, Maryland, with his father and a Mr. and Mrs. Goldsboro. When the President entered, Mrs. Goldsboro lifted the boy in her arms to that he could get a good look. Young Seymour thought Lincoln "looked stern because of his whiskers."

The strain of the war had indeed taken its toll on Lincoln. Just fifty-six, he seemed much older to many, his eyes lined with dark circles, the flesh of his face worn-looking and tightly stretched.

Midway through the third act of *Our American Cousin*, the play reached a climax of sorts as the rich American, Asa Trenchard, won a battle of words with his stuffy English hostess, Mrs. Montchessington, who flounced offstage after berating Trenchard for his bad manners. Left alone, Asa watched her go, then delivered the knee-slapping line: "Don't know the manners of good society, eh? Waal, I guess I know enough to turn you inside out, old gal — you sockdologizing old mantrap!"

As the audience laughed at actor Harry Hawk's rendition of the speech, actor John Wilkes Booth, who had sneaked into the President's box, aimed his derringer at Lincoln's head, and squeezed the trigger.

The fateful moment was witnessed by only one person—the assassin, as drapes and flags shielded the presidential party from the audience. Offstage, near the prompt desk, William J. Ferguson, a call boy at the theatre who had been drafted for a small part, heard the shot and looked up at the presidential box. "A puff of white smoke was rising," he said later. "Mr. Lincoln's head sank forward. Then I saw Booth leap to the stage. The excitement was most intense."

Before Booth vaulted over the railing of the box, he was grabbed by Rathbone, but the actor quickly dropped the revolver, pulled a dagger, and slashed Rathbone just above the elbow. "Stop that man!" the major cried as Booth leaped to the stage twelve feet below.

"His spur caught in the flag and he fell to the stage," Ferguson said. "He was up in a second and dashed between Miss Keene and me...He ran swiftly, without any apparent impediment from his shattered leg, hurt when he fell...Booth did not shout 'sic semper tyrannis!' or anything else on the stage. He may have said that in the box to Major Rathbone, but he said nothing on the stage , for I would have heard him."

Concerning the details of Booth's appearance onstage, there is some disagreement. Contrary to Ferguson's account, actor Harry Hawk reported that Booth was brandishing a large knife and calling out the Latin phrase as Booth lurched toward him, causing Hawk to flee up a flight of stairs. A moment later, after cutting the clothes of orchestra leader William Withers with a swing of his blade, Booth disappeared into the night.

Three doctors happened to be in the audience that night, including Dr. Charles A. Gatch, who had served in the war with General Rosecrans, Dr. Africanus F.A. King, twenty-four, so named because of his father's admiration for what was then called the "dark continent," and twenty-three-year-old Charles Augustus Leale, who was, by coincidence, a student of gunshot wounds. Seated only forty feet away from the President, Leale reached the victim first and with a penknife cut Lincoln's collar and coat away from the shoulders and neck. He then removed a blood clot from behind the left ear, pushed his little finger into the wound, and cleared an opening which seemed to facilitate the stricken man's breathing.

As Washington exploded with rumors and panic, twenty-five men carried the paralyzed President across the street into a private home where an all-night vigil began. Before dawn of 15 April, no less than sixteen doctors did their best to save Abraham Lincoln, to no avail. The tragic scene was made even more unbearable by the presence of Mrs. Lincoln,who alternately sobbed and broke into hysterical shrieks, threw herself on her husband's body, and pleaded with anyone with a weapon to kill her, too. Finally, Secretary of War Edward Stanton shouted for some soldiers to "Take that woman out and do not let her in again!" As she was led down the hall, Mrs. Lincoln cried out,"Oh, my God, and have I given my husband to die?" It was the last time she was to see him alive, for at 7:22 a.m. Lincoln breathed his last.

Later, when some of the furor had died down, the First Lady was questioned concerning Lincoln's final words. At first, she recalled she had been resting her hand on Lincoln's knee just before the fatal shot, an act of intimacy that caused her to ask coyly if her husband thought young Miss Harris would take it amiss. The President had replied, "She won't think anything about it." Sometime afterward, however, Mary Lincoln changed her story, stating that just prior to the tragedy the President had whispered to her, "How I should like to visit Jerusalem sometime." Perhaps, having had some time to think about the situation, she had decided that the second line was more apppropriate, although when one considers the slapstick action taking place on stage at the time, such a spiritual sentiment would surely be incongruous.

Even after Lincoln's death, tragedy continued to stalk the family. Mary ended up in an insane asylum while Robert pursued a career in government that produced none of the brilliance associated with his father. Unlike the President, Robert was short and rather plump and had a dour disposition. No doubt his entire life was influenced by the trauma of his father's assassination, a nightmare that repeated itself in 1881 when, as a member of President James Garfield's cabinet, he was in the Washington train station when Garfield was shot by Charles Guiteau. Twenty years later, Lincoln was near President William McKinley at the Buffalo Exposition just at the moment Leon Czolgosz fired the two shots that ended McKinley's life eight days later. Having been on or near the scene of all three presidential assassinations to that time in history, Robert Lincoln declined to attend official functions after 1901, telling a friend on one occasion that there was "a certain fatality about presidential functions when I am present."

During his later years, Robert relaxed with algebraic equations and became an amateur astronomer, setting up a well-equipped observatory in his home at Manchester, Vermont. He died in 1926, the last surviving child of the sixteenth president.

As the years of the twentieth century passed, the number of eyewitnesses to the tragedy at Ford's Theatre inevitably decreased. In 1935, Smith Stimmell, the last member of Lincoln's bodyguard during the war, passed away in Fargo, North Dakota, at the age of ninety-two. Three years later, the first physician to reach the stricken President's side, Dr. Charles A. Leale, died at the age of ninety,

Actress Laura Keene, who held Abraham Lincoln's bleeding head in her lap while Leale ministered to him, died in 1873, but Ferguson lived until 1930, becoming the last survivor of the *Our American Cousin* cast of 14 April 1865. During his sixty years on the stage, Ferguson often supported the actor Richard Mansfield and was an original cast member of the long-running play, *Charley's Aunt*. At his death he was known as the "actor who has played enough melodramatic characters to populate a town."

Although no one can say for certain when the last of the 1,675 spectators at Ford's Theatre that night passed away, it seems highly likely that Samuel J. Seymour was the last to have seen Lincoln alive. By 1955, Seymour had reached the ripe age of ninety-five, but still clearly remembered his initial reaction to the excitement of that evening. While others shouted for police and soldiers to stop Booth or hang him on the spot, young Seymour had been more concerned with the man who "seemed to tumble over the rail and land on the stage." Tugging at Mrs. Goldsboro's skirt, he implored her to "hurry, hurry, let's go help the poor man who fell down."

On 13 April 1956, one day short of the assassination's ninety-first anniversary, Seymour died at the home of his daughter in Arlington, Virginia.

Japan's Last Shogun

For nearly seven centuries, Japan was ruled by a series of military dictators known as shoguns. The shogunate started in 1192, when Minamoto Yoritomo received the title.

The last 264 years of shogunate rule was under the Tokugawa family, who came to power in 1603 when Ieyasu Tokugawa crushed a coalition supporting the rival Toyotomi family.

Japan was continually faced with the problem of how to deal with foreigners. During Ieyasu's reign the primary foreign influence existed in the presence of Christian missionaries, who came to Japan during the mid-sixteenth century with the intention of converting the "heathens." At first, Ieyasu had no prejudice against the Christians, but he gradually learned to dislike them and issued many proclamations designed to suppress Christianity in Japan.

Ieyasu's measures were mild compared to those of his son, Hidetada, who became shogun in 1605. Hidetada's edicts made it a capital offense for any Japanese to become Christian, with the penalty confiscation of all property and death by burning. During this anti-Christian campaign, perhaps 200,000 were punished. A Jesuit priest, Cardin, estimated that between 1,400 and 1,500 were actually "martyred," that is, tortured and killed.

Hidetada at first tried to make public examples of the Christians, but when two priests became heroes after he had them decapitated, the shogun had others beheaded in secret. Hidetada's greatest moment of intolerance came in 1622 when at the "great martyrdom of Nagasaki," he had twenty-five Christians burned and thirty beheaded.

Hidetada abdicated the shogunate in 1623, and was succeeded by his son, Iyemitsu, who was, if anything, even more fanatically anti-Christian. One of his first acts was to order the execution of about 300 of them. Then the Shimabara revolt arose in 1638. Made furious and desperate by the repressive measures, some 37,000 Christians took over the castle of Hara, near Nagasaki, fortified it, and fought pitched battles with Ieymitsu's army. The three-month campaign ended with the inevitable capitulation of the Christians, who were massacred by the Japanese (only 105 were taken prisoner). In a remarkably cynical effort to gain Ieymitsu's favor, the Dutch government had ordered its ships to assist by bombarding the castle.

Christianity thus being crushed in Japan, successive shoguns were free to turn their attention to other matters. Tsunayoshi, who was shogun from 1680 to 1709, was known by the populace as the "Shogun of Dogs" because he loved animals so much. (On one occasion he had a page executed because he accidentally killed a bird.) Tsunayoshi was also a great fan of the traditional No drama, frequently appearing on stage himself. Although eccentric, he was a popular shogun until 1705 when his mother died and he went into self-imposed exile.

The Shogun Yoshimune (1716-1745) was one of the better rulers. Concerned about public opinion, Yoshimune set up a "suggestion box" outside the royal court, kept the key himself, and resolutely saw everyone who put forth a rational idea. Yoshimune was also interested in hunting and was called the "Hawk Shogun" as a result. Once, in 1726, he arranged a hunting expedition for 60,000 men.

The nineteenth century brought increasing pressure from foreign powers — first the Russians, who were discouraged in 1804, then the Americans, who made a more determined effort in 1853, when Admiral Matthew Perry showed up in Uraga harbor with 4 ships, 560 men, and a letter from President Millard Fillmore asking for a trade treaty. The shogun at the time responded by ordering prayers said at 7 principal shrines, but it didn't work. The next year, Perry returned with 10 ships and 2,000 men. A treaty was arranged, which only served to attract other foreigners, namely the British and French.

Because the shoguns had allowed the first foreigners to violate Japan's traditional isolationism, they were associated with the problems that inevitably followed. In August of 1863, Kagoshima was bombarded by the British; then Dutch, French, and American vessels were fired on by shore batteries, leading to retaliation by the foreign navies and the demand for $3 millon reparations.

Fed up with the foreigners, Japanese nationalists began shouting "Sonno Joi" — "Revere the sovereign! Expel the Barbarians!" — which really meant, "Revere the emperor! Get rid of the foreigners and the shogun!"

Unfortunately for Yoshinobu Tokugawa, who became shogun in 1866, there was little support for his position. After only desultory fighting, he surrendered his governing power to the emperor, becoming the last of the shoguns in 1867. A year later the shogunate was formally abolished.

Last Monarch of Hawaii

Discovered in 1778 by English explorer Captain James Cook, who named them the Sandwich Islands in honor of the Earl of Sandwich, the Hawaiian Island chain was ruled by warring native kings until 1810, when Kamehameha I became the first sole ruler of all the islands.

The peace of Kamehameha turned out to be a mixed blessing, largely because he was hospitable to Westerners, who exchanged the islands' sandalwood for whiskey, firearms, and missionaries. Eventually, through the missionaries' influence and proximity to the mainland, a significant portion of the Hawaiian population favored American annexation by mid-century.

Born in 1838, Liliuokalani had married an American and served as regent by the time her brother, Kalakaua, died. She succeeded him on 20 January 1891, becoming the first woman and last person to rule Hawaii.

As soon as she ascended the throne, she was faced with a constitutional crisis, there being considerable agitation to abolish the monarchy. Like her brother, Liliuokalani refused to listen to proposals that would reduce her power, adopting instead a reactionary constitution that resulted in her being deposed in 1893. The next year, because of her involvement with a plot to regain the throne, she was convicted of high treason and sentenced to five years in prison, a penalty that wasn't carried out. In 1898 she formally renounced her royal claims in exchange for a $4,000 yearly pension.

Retiring to her estate, she lived in queenly style, writing more than one hundred songs (including the perennial "Aloha Oe") and a history of the Islands, *Hawaii's Story*.

She died on 11 November 1917 at Honolulu.

The Last Gathering of Royalty

May 20, 1910. Only a decade into the century that was to spell the end for so many monarchies, London was the scene of the greatest assemblage of kings, queens, dowagers, and heirs apparent the world had ever seen at one time. They paced by wearing scarlet and blue and green and purple, a total of nine reigning monarchs, on their magnificent horses, a parade of such pomp and splendor the crowd gasped despite the solemnity of the occasion.

Big Ben tolled nine o'clock as the funeral procession for King Edward VII left the palace with the new King, George V, in the center of the front row. On George's right was William II, emperor of Germany and arch-rival of the dead king.

Behind William rode Kings Frederick of Denmark, George of Greece, Haakon of Norway, Alfonso of Spain, Manuel of Portugal, Ferdinand of Bulgaria, and Albert of Belgium.

There followed a veritable flood of lesser royalty: the Archduke Franz Ferdinand of Austria; Prince Yussuf of Turkey; Prince Fushimi, brother of Japan's Emperor; Grand Duke Michael, brother of Czar Nicholas of Russia; the Duke of Aosta, brother of the king of Italy; Prince Carl, brother of the king of Sweden; Prince Henry, consort of the queen of Holland; and the Crown Princes of Serbia, Rumania, and Montenegro.

A regiment of minor German royalty came next, along with princes from Siam, Persia, France, China, and Prussia. Finally there were three civilian-clad gentlemen, including the former President of the United States, Theodore Roosevelt.

Along Whitehall, the Mall, Piccadilly, and the park to Paddington Station the procession moved, the Royal Horse Guards playing the "Dead March" from Handel's *Saul*. The burst of magnificence was the dying gasp of nineteenth century royalty; four years later, World War I would change the lives of everyone in the procession and most of those who watched.

The Last Emperor and Empress of China

The last dynasty of China, the Manchu (Ch'ing), came to power in 1644 and ruled forcibly until the nineteenth century. Then, a relaxation of prejudice against foreigners allowed western nations to intervene in China's affairs. First, Great Britain established the precedent of "extraterritoriality," which gave certain British citizens immunity from Chinese law enforcement. France, Germany, and Russia followed with similar demands. By the end of the century, Chinese resentment of foreigners directed itself against the Manchus. This, combined with a growing desire for a republican form of government, led to open rebellion.

The power behind the Chinese throne during the end of the nineteenth century and beginning of the twentieth was the Dowager Empress Tzu Hsi. The consort of Emperor Hsien Feng, who died in 1861, Tzu Hsi named her four-year-old nephew Kuang Hsu to the throne in 1875 following the death of T'ung Chih, the son of Tzi Hsi and Hsien Feng.

When Kuang Hsu grew up, he rebelled against the influence of Tzu Hsi and in 1898 started the "hundred days of reform" by issuing decrees modernizing the political and social structure of China. Predictably upset, the dowager empress had Kuang Hsu imprisoned and continued to rule China in a conservative manner.

When Kuang Hsu died, Tzu Hsi looked around for another puppet and settled on the infant Hsuan T'ung (later known as Henry Pu Yi), a distant claimant, as the next in line. While he grew up, of course, Tzu Hsi planned to continue running the government.

Shortly after Kuang Hsu's death, however, Tzu Hsi, who was then seventy-four, suddenly fell ill. Her last acts were to install Pu Yi as emperor and prepare her own valedictory message, which concluded with the lines, "Mourning to be worn for twenty-seven days only. Hear and obey!"

The last words of the woman who had ruled China for so long were equally forceful: "Never again allow a woman to hold the supreme power in the state," she said. "It is against the house-law of our dynasty and should be forbidden. Be careful not to allow eunuchs to meddle in government matters. The Ming dynasty was brought to run by eunuchs, and its fate should be a warning to my people."

Ascending the thrown in 1908 at the age of two, Henry Pu Yi cried throughout the ceremony. He "ruled" for only four years, the end of the Manchu dynasty practically coinciding with the death of Tzu Hsi. In October of 1911 Chinese troops mutinied at Wu-Chang, burning the house of the viceroy and murdering the Manchu garrison, including wives and children. From there the revolutionary spirit spread throughout the country. Finally, on 12 February 1912, Henry Pu Yi was forced to abdicate.

Given an annual stipend, Henry Pu Yi was allowed to live in the summer palace near Peking until 1924, when he left under the protective custody of Japan. Eight years later, the Japanese installed him as president of the puppet state of Manchukuo (Japanese-occupied Manchuria), and in 1934 proclaimed him emperor under the name Kang Teh.

Captured by the Russians in 1946, Henry Pu Yi was sent to Siberia but was returned to the Chinese People's Republic in 1950. He was pardoned in 1959 and died on 17 October 1967.

Last Emperor of Austria, Last King of Hungary

During the nineteenth century, rulers frequently held several positions, making it almost mandatory to have a scorecard in order to tell which sovereign was in power at any particular place.

There was, for example, Francis I of Austria (1768-1835) who was also Francis II, last emperor of the Holy Roman Empire until 1806 when the Holy Roman Empire was destroyed by Napoleon. After the death of Francis, he was succeeded by his son Ferdinand (not to be confused with two other rulers of the same period, Ferdinand I and Ferdinand II, consecutive kings of the Two Sicilies from 1816 to 1859), who became Emperor Ferdinand of Austria. Ferdinand in 1848 gave way to his nephew Francis Joseph (or Franz Josef), who became emperor of Austria and, in 1867, king of Hungary.

There matters stood until 28 June 1914, when the heir apparent to both the crowns, Archduke Francis Ferdinand, was murdered at Sarajevo by Serbian nationalists. This meant that the new heir apparent was twenty-seven-year-old Charles, Francis Ferdinand's nephew. Two years later, following the death of Franz Josef, Charles became Charles I, emperor of Austria and Charles IV, King of Hungary. Both positions turned out to be ends of the lines.

An able commander during World War I, Charles tried to save his two titles on 16 October 1918 by proclaiming an Austrian Federation State. But the disastrous defeat of Vittorio Veneto left him with no choice but unconditional surrender. On 11 November 1918, Charles abdicated as Emperor of Austria and as King of Hungary on 13 November.

Early in 1919, he and his family went into exile in Switzerland. Hope seemed to beckon the next year, when the monarchists triumphed in Hungary. Charles immediately left to regain the throne but was unsuccessful, being arrested and exiled to Madeira. He died there of pneumonia in 1922.

The Last King of Siam

Now Thailand, the kingdom of Siam was once famous for the brilliance of its court, especially under King Narai, who ruled from 1657 to 1688.

Unlike many other small nations of southeast Asia, Siam managed to remain free during the nineteenth century by playing off the British against the French. A succession of kings ruled the absolute monarchy. The last to ascend the throne was Prajadhipok, whose brother, Rama VI (better known as Chulalongkorn) died suddenly on 26 November 1925. Small, frail, and just thirty-two, Prajadhipok managed to straighten out Siam's finances and his own as well by taking out several policies from French and British insurance underwriters against the loss of his throne.

The ruler of 11½ million people who knew him as "Brother of the Moon, Half-brother of the Sun, and Possessor of the Four-and-Twenty Umbrellas," Prajadhipok both sensed and sympathized with the growing republican spirit in his country. During this period of agitation, he was obliged to leave Siam early in 1931 to undergo an operation for removal of a cataract in his left eye. Arriving in the United States that April, he quickly became a popular figure, dining with President Herbert Hoover and touring New York City before being successfully operated on by Dr. John M. Wheeler of Presbyterian Hospital.

Not long after he returned home, Prajadhipok lost his throne in favor of a constitutional monarchy. In 1934, the first general elections were held, and in 1935 he abdicated. Moving to Surrey, England, he placidly drew his "unemployment" checks until his death on 30 May 1941, at age 47. His annual income was $15 million at his demise.

FDR's Last "Fireside Chat"

Warren G. Harding was the first American president to address the nation on radio, but it remained for Franklin Delano Roosevelt to turn the new medium to his advantage. While Harding, Calvin Coolidge and Herbert Hoover were reluctant to use radio, FDR was fascinated by its promise, in part because he had a vocal quality that projected an image of strength and warmth. He had, as one critic put it, "an Uncle Sam brogue."

In 1924, FDR nominated Al Smith for the presidency in a speech that was not only delivered over the radio but written expressly for the radio audience. As in all future speeches to the nation, this one was simple and clear, directed to the lowest common denominator in language with no references or allusions to anything out of the ordinary, no built-in "punch phrases" to generate applause. Three-quarters of the words used by FDR were among the 1,000 most common words of everyday English.

As governor of New York, FDR used radio often; as President of the United States, he delivered more than 300 radio speeches. Twenty-six of these were categorized as "Fireside Chats," informal addresses from the White House. The first, which was delivered on 12 March 1933, set the tone. As biographer Frank Friedel put it, it "was unadorned with the flights of rhetoric or patriotic generalities that usually characterized presidential addresses."

The subject of FDR's first Fireside Chat (the title was given the speeches by CBS bureau chief Harry Butcher) was the banking crisis.

About 60 million Americans — half the nation — heard the address. By 1940, the number of FDR's listeners had reached 100 million. Then at the height of his power as a political figure, FDR's voice was considered so persuasive that network radio officials banned comic impressions of him.

Eleven years after taking office, Roosevelt made the last of his Fireside Chats, addressing the nation on 23 June 1944. It was summertime and there was no fire in the White House fireplace, which had been the case for most of the chats. It was also the day before the opening of the Republican National Convention, which for a shrewd political animal like FDR could hardly have been accidental.

As with most other Fireside Chats, FDR's last one was hardly sensational, dealing generally with the progress of the war and need for Americans to continue making a strong financial and physical effort. One almost suspects he made the speech to upstage the Republicans as well as to subtly remind the nation that he was still active and capable of strong leadership.

The Last King of Italy

Umberto II, the last king of Italy, reigned less than two months, then quietly retired at the age of forty-two after the monarchy was abolished on 2 June 1946. Compared to his predecessor-father, Victor Emmanuel III, Umberto was not very interesting.

At the time it produced Victor, who ruled for 46 years, the 900-year-old House of Savoy was wearing a bit thin. Born on 11 November 1869, Victor Emmanuel III was a short man with a fetish for punctuality and cleanliness. In an attempt to improve the breed, his father, King Umberto I, married Victor Emmanuel to a booming, strapping six-footer, Elena, daughter of Montenegro's peasant King Nicholas.

Victor Emmanuel turned out to be short in stature but long on luck. First, his father took out a life insurance policy worth about $5 million shortly before his death in 1900; then Victor Emmanuel was fortunate enough to choose the winning side in World War I. He came out of the conflict a popular figure, known fondly to Italians as *Il Piccolo* — "the little one."

During the decades that followed, his judgment was less sharp. Fearing Benito Mussolini's potential, he turned the nation over to him in exchange for Mussolini's promise to keep him on the throne. Later he went along with Il Duce's decision to invade Ethiopia, declaring that, "if we win I shall be King of Abyssinia; if we lose, I shall be King of Italy."

By this time, many Italians obviously preferred that Victor Emmanuel be king of nothing, there being two attempts to assassinate him. Nor did the Italian people band together behind their king during World War II. If anything, they hated *Il Piccolo* even more, especially when he confined his duties to visiting safe home-front facilities rather than going to the front, as he had done in World War I.

In July of 1943, with the Allied armies close to Rome and the Italian population aflame with social unrest, Victor Emmanuel called in Mussolini and dismissed him on 25 July. He then made contact with the Allies, and surrendered six weeks later.

After the war, when the monarchy seemed in danger of being dissolved, Victor Emmanuel made a last-ditch effort to save his line. Wearily writing out his abdication (with the wrong date at first), he turned the government over to his son Umberto, as Queen Elena cried.

Umberto, a notorious playboy, was dubbed *Il Re di Maggio* — "King of the May" — during the month he reigned before Italian voters rejected the monarchy by a 5-4 margin.

Victor Emmanuel and Elena sailed for Egypt where he died on 28 December 1947, aged seventy-eight. The Italian radio that evening announced his death in just six words: "Victor Emmanuel of Savoy died today."

Umberto II (born 1904), reigned from 9 May to 2 June 1946, and retired to Portugal immediately following the vote to abolish the monarchy.

The Last King of Bulgaria

Bulgaria emerged as an eastern European power during the eighth century, by threatening the Byzantine Empire to the point where a yearly tribute was paid to avoid an invasion by Bulgaria. Under Ivan II, who ruled from 1218 to 1241, Bulgaria conquered the entire Balkan peninsula except for Greece. After that time, however, the Slavic nation led a checkered existence, and was conquered by Turkey and absorbed into the Ottoman Empire in 1396.

In 1876 a revolt led by Stefan Stambulov broke out, giving Russia an excuse to attack Turkey and create an autonomous Bulgarian state within the Ottoman Empire which Russia hoped to dominate. Eleven years later, Stambulov, who was by then anti-Russian as well as anti-Turkish, selected a young prince named Ferdinand Maximilian Karl Leopold Maria to serve under him. Subsequently, a contemporary account recorded, Ferdinand, a "handsome, smiling, slender youth, perfectly corseted, lips and cheeks bravely rouged, leaving in his wake an exotic perfume, rode gallantly into Sofia amid the cheers of his devoted people."

Lusting for total power, Ferdinand made a deal with Russia and soon Stambulov had been hacked to pieces by assassins. Promoting himself to the top of the ladder, Ferdinand became Ferdinand I, first King of modern Bulgaria.

During the decade that followed, Ferdinand proved himself a master of intrigue known throughout the world. Leo Tolstoy captured his Machiavellian spirit in the play *Plody Prosveshcheniya (The Fruits of Enlightenment)* when he had a valet pick up a newspaper and remark, "Well, let us see what our Ferdinand is up

208

to now." Germany's Wilhelm II both detested and respected him, once saying that, "I cannot stand Ferdinand but he beats us all for brains."

Unfortunately for Ferdinand, he suffered a mental lapse when he cast his lot with Germany in World War I. Following the Allied victory over Bulgarian forces at Dobropole in September 1918, Ferdinand abdicated. He lived a quiet life after that, secluded in Coburg among his birds and flowers, until his death in 1948.

His son, Boris, who succeeded Ferdinand as King Boris III, also chose the wrong side in World War II, agreeing in 1940 to allow German troops to pass through his country, and in March of 1941 signed a pact which made Bulgaria a member of the Axis. He ruled until 28 August 1943, when he died suddenly and mysteriously, of either a heart attack or poisoning.

Six-year old Simeon, his son, succeeded as King Simeon II under a regency, but abdicated on 8 September 1946 when the monarchy was abolished by the Communists.

Years later, as a twenty-one-year-old cadet at Valley Forge Military Academy, he said, "Communists cannot rule forever. Despotisms have always fallen. Why should this one be an exception? I can wait, for I am young." Thus spoke Simeon Rylski, the last king of Bulgaria, as he awaited his chance to rule once again. That was in 1959 — and Simeon is still waiting, no longer so young and hopeful.

The Last King of Albania

The man who was destined to be both the first and last king of Albania was born Ahmed Bey Zogu, on 8 October 1895. His father was Xehemal Pasha Zogu, head of one of the four ruling families in the Albanian province of Mati. At the time, Albania was under Turkish rule.

Young Zog studied at a Turkish military academy until 1912, when he supported William of Wied, a luckless German princeling who accepted an invitation from a revolutionary faction to become king and free Albania from Turkish rule. A short while later, William was forced to flee before the invading Austro-Hungarian armies but Zog finished out World War I as an Austrian officer.

He became active politically following the war when the nation was occupied by Italy in 1921. He was elected president of the Albanian republic on 1 February 1925 and proclaimed King Zog I on 1 September 1928.

Because Albania was a small nation with only one million people, Zog was constantly at the mercy of nearby large powers, especially Italy and Yugoslavia. He sided with Italy and signed a treaty in 1926.

A bachelor when he came to the throne, Zog retained a marriage broker to find a woman with the necessary background, beauty and money. It took a decade to locate the beautiful Hungarian-American Countess Geraldine Apponyi, but she was obviously worth it. Zog married her on 26 April 1938. By doing so, he violated several of the rules he had set up, for Geraldine had no money at all. (At the time Zog met her she was selling postcards in a Budapest art museum.) In addition, Geraldine was a Roman Catholic and Zog a Moslem. Very much in love, Zog married her anyway and prepared to have a son and live happily ever after in his tiny but pleasant kingdom.

He could hardly have been happier on 5 April 1939, the day Geraldine presented him with an heir. The news was accompanied by a 101-gun salute in Tirana, the nation's capital, but only 48 hours later, another noise — that of airplanes — was heard. King Zog and the rest of the nation knew immediately that the planes couldn't be Albanian, largely because there were only two planes in the nation's entire air force. Leaflets fluttering down explained to the populace that "friendly" Italian troops were arriving to take over the country "and reestablish order, peace and justice."

Albania's army of 13,000 was promptly mobilized, the troops armed with ancient rifles and curved daggers. Queen Geraldine and her son were bundled into a car and sent over a 160-mile stretch of rough woods into neighboring Greece where they made contact with British officials who arranged to have them taken to London.

War followed, but it lasted less than two days, the Italians occupying all of Albania while losing only twenty-one men. Zog, meanwhile, had followed his family to London, where he remained throughout the war.

On 2 January 1946, Zog was formally deposed in absentia, and General Enver Hoxha became the new head of the communist-dominated Albanian government.

Invited to Egypt by King Farouk, Zog remained there until 1955, when a tax dispute with Egypt's new revolutionary government sent him to an almost empty villa on the French Riviera. The rest of his days were melancholy. Forced to live without servants (Queen Geraldine did the housework) and writing without sufficient notes (many of the papers he planned to use in his four-volume life story were destroyed in a London bombing raid), Zog talked of moving to the United States for a while. That dream disappeared after he bought a sixty-room mansion on Long Island but was forced to sell it in 1955 after a tax dispute with Nassau county officials.

Six years later, on 9 April 1961, King Zog died in the Foch Hospital in Suresnes, a suburb of Paris.

The Last King of Yugoslavia

The only king ever to die in the United States, Peter Karageor-gevich was just eleven years old in 1934 when he ascended the throne of Yugoslavia under the regency of his uncle, Prince Paul.

A charming youth, who perhaps was incapable of dealing with the Machiavellian politics of pre-World War II days, Peter II was caught in the crossfire between Adolf Hitler and Winston Churchill — and was used by both. "He was too straight," Peter's son, Alexander, wrote later. "He could not believe that his allies — the mighty American democracy, and his relatives and friends in London — could do him in. But that's precisely what happened."

Trying to protect the Yugoslav people from Nazi invasion, Prince Paul advised Peter to appease Hitler by giving in to some of his lesser demands. Peter agreed, which led the British to the assumption that his government was pro-German. Churchill then ordered British intelligence to engineer a military coup to topple Peter, not because doing so would save Yugoslavia from Hitler, but because it would "prove" the existence of anti-German sentiment on the European subcontinent. A month after the coup, in April of 1941, Germany invaded, and King Peter was forced to flee to London. While there, Churchill publicly expressed warmth and affection for the young king-in-exile, calling him, "my boy." Privately, however, Churchill disdained the entire coterie of exiled leaders assembled in London awaiting the war's end. On one occasion, he referred to them as the "Beggar's Opera."

Later, the Allies ignored Peter's request that the Yugoslav guerilla movement be headed by his man Draza Mihailovitch, turning the assignment over to Moscow's favorite, Tito. This practically guaranteed that after the war, Peter would have no monarchy to return to. True to form, the communists abolished the monarchy, and on 8 March 1947, deprived Peter of his nationality and property.

Emigrating to the United States, he worked as a public relations man in New York City during the early 1950s while writing the story of his life, entitled *A King's Heritage* (1955). He aged rapidly in exile, his boyish charm changing to an aimless dispostion that caused friends to wonder if he would die of alcoholism or a broken heart. In the mid-1960s, he separated from his wife and suffered a string of business failures in real estate, plastics, and shipping. Since he was known as a loser, people were reluctant to rent him an apartment or extend him credit.

Finally, in 1971, he died at the age of forty-seven of complications resulting from a liver transplant. Although he was a descendant of Queen Victoria and King George VI had been his godfather, Peter left orders that under no circumstance was he to buried in Westminster Abbey. His will stated that, "Notwithstanding any other desires of my family, it is my desire that I be buried in the United States of America at Liberty Eastern Serbian Orthodox Monastery, in Liberty, Illinois."

The Last King of Rumania

"It's hard for a king to find a job."
— Michael, ex-king of Rumania

The man who was destined to become the last king of Rumania was born in 1921, the son of King Carol II, Rumania's third modern monarch.

In some ways, Carol was more interesting than his son. At the time of his birth in 1893, a 101-gun salute was fired, for he was the first son of a reigning king to be born on Rumanian soil. Carol soon began behaving in a very unkingly fashion, eloping with a commoner named Zizi Lambrino. A Rumanian high court declared the marriage null and void, but Carol and Zizi continued living together until his money ran out. He returned home to marry Princess Helen of Greece, but then met Magda Lupescu, the divorced wife of a Rumanian army officer. A fiery woman who allegedly had the ability to satisfy Carol's reportedly ravenous sexual appetite, Magda so upset Carol's father, King Ferdinand, that he ordered his son to give up the woman or leave the country.

Carol promptly took Magda to Paris. In 1927, when King Ferdinand died, Carol's six-year-old son Michael (by Helen) was declared king. But in 1930, Prime Minister Iuliu Maniu interpreted national sentiment as favoring Carol's return and offered the title to him. Carol returned — followed three weeks later by Magda — to become King Carol II. Queen Helen, mortified, took to wearing a veil and seldom appeared in public.

During the next decade, Carol ran the government in a generally poor manner, rigging elections to his advantage, and spending money wildly on Magda, who, it turned out, had a Jewish father. This revelation sparked several anti-Semitic riots in Rumania, which had fallen more and more under the influence of Nazi Germany. Finally, in 1940 a mob surrounded the Royal Palace and demanded that King Carol hand over his mistress. Carol asked for asylum in Germany. Hitler said, "All right, but I won't take the woman."

Once again, Carol showed his devotion to Magda, taking the royal train for Switzerland and turning the country over to Michael. At the Transylvanian town of Timisaora, the train was boarded by an inspection team, but Magda hid in the bathtub while Carol gallantly sat on the wooden cover above her.

Michael, then nineteen, was over six feet tall and such a handsome man that Rumanian women regularly tore his picture from magazines in stores and carried them off in their handbags. Despite his good looks, however, he was considered a puppet by the Germans, who appropriated most of the Rumanian army for service on the Russian front.

On 23 August 1944, Michael proved that he had more strength and nerve than anyone imagined. On that date, he summoned Marshal Ion Antonescu, Rumania's Nazi strongman, to the palace and ordered him to negotiate a treaty with the Allies. Antonescu laughed, whereupon, following a pre-arranged signal from Michael, four soldiers entered the room and arrested Antonescu. Four hours later, King Michael addressed the nation on radio; at the same time, Rumanian troops on the Russian front ceased fire. It was Michael's finest hour as crowds danced in the streets of Bucharest and shouted "Long live the King!"

After the war, Carol, who had hoped to return and run the country, gave up his claim to the crown but never spoke to Michael again. He died in 1953, in Estoril, Portugal.

Meanwhile, Michael found the Communists a good deal tougher to deal with than the Nazis. He particularly disliked the Communist-backed Premier, Petru Groza. "When I told Groza to resign, he refused," Michael said. "Then I refused to have anything to do with the government thus rendered illegal. I went on strike. I didn't sign decrees. Nothing..."

In January of 1948, Michael received a telephone call from officials of the Rumanian Communist Party. Would he come to Bucharest to discuss "important matters?"

The important matters turned out to be Michael's abdication and a Communist takeover. "If I refuse to sign," the young man said, referring to the paper the Communists handed him, "you cannot force me."

"In that case," Groza warned, "thousands will be arrested. Rumania will be steeped in blood. I am sure Your Majesty does not want such a thing."

Realizing that the Royal Palace was surrounded by Communist troops and that his telephone lines had been cut, Michael gave in to the inevitable. He signed the paper, then went on radio to tell his people that the new Rumanian People's Republic had been declared. Four months later, he was formally dispossessed of 159 castles, 400,000 acres of land, several yachts, and 4,991,502 shares of stock.

Currently unemployed and living in the Swiss township of Versoix, six miles from the old League of Nations headquarters at Geneva, ex-King Michael worked for a time as a stockbroker but prefers working with his hands. He is hardly destitute but not completely happy. "I was born in Rumania," he explains. "I am a Rumanian. Nothing else matters. And now I am a Rumanian refugee living in Switzerland. I get pushed around just like any other refugee."

Michael's financial situation, at least, would be better if he could obtain funds left by his father in a Zurich bank. According to reports, the money is considerable but cannot be obtained even by a rightful heir without knowledge of a specific codeword. Michael, therefore, appears at the bank several times a year, each time trying a different word. So far he has had no luck.

Meanwhile, he waits, hopeful that some development will allow him to reclaim the Rumanian throne. "We live near the airport, just in case," he says.

The Last Apache Chief

Once a powerful Indian tribe of the American Southwest, the Apaches were ruled during most of their history by hereditary chiefs, whose word was law.

After the U.S. government forced the Indians onto a pair of Arizona reservations, it introduced "democracy" to the Apaches by insisting that tribal decisions be made by an elected council rather than by the chief.

Despite government pressure, the 3,700 Indians remained true to the the word of their last hereditary chief, Baha Alchesay, who had been apppointed leader by his father in the 1890s. He continued to rule until he died at the age of 87 on 3 October 1952.

Wisely — perhaps realizing that he was the last of a dying breed — Baha Alchesay appointed no one to succeed himself as chief.

The Last King of Egypt

Farouk I, the last king of Egypt, as well as the last of the 142-year-old Mehemet Ali dynasty, was born on 11 February 1920, the son of King Fuad I and Queen Nazli. He succeeded his father to the throne on 28 April 1936, dissolved the Egyptian Parliament two years later, and proceeded to live an extravagant life of gambling and womanizing.

As a ruler, Farouk was probably shrewder than many realized, severing relations with Germany, Italy, and Japan early in World War II, but not declaring war until 24 February 1945. During the later years of his reign, however, his prestige declined, especially after Egyptian forces suffered a military fiasco during the first Arab-Israeli war. (The Egyptian officers charged that Farouk's unsavory courtiers lined their own pockets by supplying the army with shells that wouldn't fire and grenades that went off as soon as the pin was pulled.) Farouk denied that the defeat was his fault, but not long afterward, a group called the Free Officers organized a conspiracy against the King and on 3 July 1952 brought about a coup d'etat.

Abdicating, Farouk and his family went to Italy, where Farouk renamed himself Prince Farouk Fuad of Egypt. Though much of his wealth had been confiscated by the state, Farouk still had plenty of money and spent it liberally. In 1959, the curator of Egypt's National Musuem, carrying out the first inventory in thirty years, discovered that a jeweled sceptre of King Tut valued at $3 million was missing. He accused Farouk of stealing it, calling him the "most dangerous thief of Egyptian antiquities."

In exile, Farouk was more famous than during his reign as king. He was the subject of several lawsuits. In 1957, for example, he forced Elsa Maxwell to pay $840 damages for saying, while declining to see him, that she did not associate "with clowns, monkeys, depraved people, or malefactors."

Fearful for his life, Farouk wore dark glasses in public and was never without two bodyguards. His knowledge of available women was such that he reportedly knew every call girl in Rome by her first name. When a young starlet appeared on the Via Veneto with a new piece of expensive jewelry, her friends invariably would ask as they examined it, "Farouk?"

Living the high life, Farouk died in style. On 17 March 1965, he had spent the evening gorging himself at Rome's Ile de France restaurant with twenty-eight-year old Anna Maria Gatti, putting away liberal quantities of oysters, roast lamb, cake and fruit, followed shortly after midnight by his usual post-prandial cigar. Suddenly he clutched his throat and fell forward onto the table.

Farouk, last king of Egypt, was dead at 45. On his body were a gold wedding ring, cigarette lighter, watch, pill box, pair of dark glasses, loaded Baretta automatic pistol, identification papers, and a billfold containing $115 in Italian lire and $2,500 in U. S. bills.

The Last Emperor and Empress of Vietnam

During the nineteenth century, Vietnam was divided into three parts: the north, which was known as Tonkin; the territory of Annam in the center and Cochin China in the south. Eventually, France subjugated the entire region, changed the country's name to Indochina, and established a French protectorate in the 1880s governed by the Vietnamese emperor.

Born Prince Nguyen Vinh Thuy in 1913, Bao Dai succeeded his father, Emperor Khai Din, in 1926. In 1934, he married nineteen-year-old Nam Phuong, who gave up life in a Roman Catholic convent to become his empress.

Their joint reign was not a pleasant one. The French rule was succeeded by the Vichy government, the Japanese, and finally, the Communists. Following the Vietnam partition in 1954, Bao Dai accepted Ngo Dinh Diem as prime minister, who promptly engineered a referendum abolishing the monarchy in 1955. Bao Dai subsequently lived in exile, primarily in France.

The empress, who had fled to Paris in 1948 to save her children from being kidnapped by the Viet Minh, bought an estate in Chabrignac at the end of the Indochinese war, living virtually separated from Bao Dai from that time until her death in 1963.

The Last King of Iraq

Long under Turkish domination, Iraq became independent following World War I, its first modern king virtually selected by Winston Churchill, then secretary of state for British Colonies, and Gertrude Bell, a veteran Middle Eastern traveler, author, and Oriental secretary for Baghdad.

Their selection was thirty-six-year old Amir Faisal, who was installed as first modern King of Iraq on 11 July 1921. Faisal I reigned until 8 September 1933, when he died suddenly in Berne, Switzerland. He was succeeded by his twenty-one-year old son, Ghazi Ibn, who served as King Ghazi I only until 4 April 1939, dying in an automobile accident.

Ghazi's four-year old son ascended the throne as Faisal II with the former king's uncle, Abdul Illah, as regent. When Iraq was torn by rebellion in April of 1941, the young king was smuggled out of the country by Queen Mother Aliyah and taken to England. He remained there (and was educated at Harrow) until 2 May 1952, when he attained his majority.

Returning to Iraq, he was reinstalled as king but was almost immediately embroiled in conflict with his cousin Hussein of Jordan. That issue was decided in February 1958, when the union of Egypt and Syria led Hussein and Faisal to form the Arab Federation uniting Iraq and Jordan.

Regarded by many as too pro-Western, King Faisal was getting ready to fly to Istanbul with Crown Prince Abdul Illah on 14 July 1958, when revolting officers led by General Abdul Kareem el-Kassim suddenly burst into the palace. Shots were fired by both the palace guards and officers. Faisal and Abdul Illah were killed, along with Illah's mother, two nurses, and two soldiers.

Fearing public revulsion against Faisal's murder, the killers kept his death a secret, wrapped him in a carpet and smuggled the body away to be buried. The widely disliked Crown Prince Illah was another matter. His body was thrown out the window and dragged through the streets by an angry mob.

It was all over by 6 a.m. The government radio station had been secured by the assassins before they entered the palace. "Citizens of Baghdad!" the announcer proclaimed, "the monarchy is dead! The republic is here!"

The Last Day of the British Empire

By all the standards of logic, the British Empire had no reason for evolving or continuing in existence. At its height, it comprised nearly a quarter of the earth's surface from Australia to Canada. In India, the greatest of the empire's possessions, there were 308 million people in 1897. Hardly any of them had any real say in the government

216

of their nation, which was run by some 1,300 British officials in the Indian branch of the colonial service.

In much the same way, nearly every other facet of the British Empire was unnatural. The vast territories were ruled by a small island nation with few natural resources, a nation run by a government whose policies fluctuated wildly from one session of Parliament to the next, which had a large percentage of citizens challenging the empire's need for existence even during its infancy. With so few armed forces and and little national willingness to force British rule on other people, it is remarkable that the empire ever came into existence, much less last as long as it did.

When the dissolution came, it was rapid. At the conclusion of World War II, the empire was intact, but the British people themselves were worn out by war, taxes, and — to their credit — smart enough to see the handwriting on the wall., Since the beginning of the twentieth century, scores of monarchies had given way to revolutionary governments and the sprit of independence was truly in the air. So the British yielded to and even encouraged, the inevitable. Within a twenty-five-year period after the war, independence was granted to a long list of possessions comprising hundreds of millions of people — Burma, India, Egypt, Bangladesh, Bhutan, Ghana, Kuwait, Jamaica, Malawi, Sierra Leone, Singapore, Uganda, Trinidad and Tobago, Zimbabwe, Somalia, Tonga, to name just a few.

Finally, by 1966 — the year which saw independence granted to Botswana, British Guiana, Basutoland, and the Barbados — it was clear that the sun had finally set on the once-glorious British Empire. At midnight, 1 August 1966, the British Colonial office in London struck its flag. A terse statement from Number 10 Downing Street said, "The Commonwealth Relations Office and the Colonial Office will be merged into a new Commonwealth Office on August 1, 1966. The Secretary of State for Commonwealth Relations will thereafter be known as the Secretary of State for Commonwealth Affairs..."

For those, such as Sir Charles Jeffries, who had served for decades in the Colonial Office, it was a sad moment. " When I joined the office in 1917," he said," I scarcely imagined that I should live to write its obituary notice. In those days it seemed to be about the most permanent institution in the world, dealing with an empire on which the sun never set and was not likely to set in any foreseeable future. It was a compact and cozy office then, more like a club than a government department."

A year-and-a-half after the closing of the Colonial Office, on the afternoon of 19 January 1968, Prime Minister Harold Wilson announced the final homecoming of the British legions. So far as the end of the British Empire can be set at a definite point of time, that was it.

217

Dissolution of the empire continued as Swaziland, last British possession in Africa, gained its independence on 6 September 1968. If some British people were depressed, they could take heart from historian James Morris, who wrote, "In its great days, the British Empire revived many a stagnant alien culture, prodded many dormant people into activity, distributed the ideas and techniques of the modern world on a scale that dwarfs today's world banks and developement agencies....From the United States to New Zealand, from Malaya to Zambia, proud states the world over must acknowledge imperial Britain as their begetter. Britain really was Mother Country to half the earth, and this has made her status in history altogether unique, and her decline an elegiac chapter in the story of all the nations..."

The Last King of Greece

Following the glorious days of its pre-Christian city-states, Greece was a battlegound for forces of the Roman Empire, Byzantine Empire, the Crusades, and Ottoman Turks. Not until 1832 was the nation's independence recognized, when a Bavarian prince was selected to reign as Otto I, but he proved so unpopular he was later forced to abdicate.

Otto was followed by a Danish prince who reigned as George I until he was assassinated in 1913. Constantine I succeeded him, but when he decided to remain neutral during World War I rather than cast Greece's lot with the Allies, he was forced to abdicate in favor of his youngest son, Alexander.

Alexander remained in power just three years, dying in 1920 of an infection after being bitten by his pet monkey. His father was restored to the throne but lasted only two years. Then, after a one year reign by George II, the Greeks voted for a republic in 1924.

A decade of unsettled economic conditions and violent political strife, including coups and counter-coups, finally convinced the Greeks that something drastic had to be done. King George II was therefore returned to the throne in 1935. Once again, he lasted only a year, allowing Premier John Metaxas to proclaim himself dictator in order to avert a communist takeover.

Following the outbreak of World War II, Greece was invaded by the Axis and the government, or whatever passed for it, fled to Cairo, Egypt.

In September 1946, George II was back, obviously one of the most patient and persistent of monarchs. But for the third and last time, he reigned only a year, dying in 1947.

George was succeeded by his brother Paul, who with aid from the United States was able to defeat Communist rebels and rule until his death in 1964. His son, Constantine (born 1940) ascended the throne, but fled into exile on 13 December 1967, after a coup in which the military took over the government.

In June of 1973 the monarchy was abolished and Greece became a presidential republic.

109 B.C.
Marcus Livius Drusus, Tribune of Rome: "When will the Republic find again a citizen like me?"
46
Roman statesman **Marcius Porcius Cato the Younger,** just before he stabbed himself: "Now I am master of myself."
68 A.D.
Nero (Lusius Domitius Ahenobarbus), Roman Emperor: "What an artist the world is losing in me."
69
Aulus Vitellius, Roman Emperor, one of the greatest eaters and drinkers in history, as he was struck down by revolting troops: "Yet I was once your emperor."
79
Titus Flavius Vespasianus, Roman Emperor 69-70 A.D.: "I suppose I am now becoming a god."
180
Marcus Aelius Aurelius Antoninus, Roman Emperor from 161-180 A.D., when asked what the watchword for the day was: "Go to the rising sun, for I am setting."
193
Marcus Didius Salvius Julianus, Roman Emperor, just before being assassinated: "What harm have I done? Have I put anybody to death?"
961
Abd-El-Rahman, Caliph of Cordoba: "I have now reigned above fifty years in victory or peace, beloved by my subjects, dreaded by my enemies, and respected by my allies. Riches and honors, power and pleasure, have waited on my call, nor does any earthly blessing appear to have been wanting to my felicity. In this situation I have diligently numbered the days of pure and genuine hap-

219

piness which have fallen to my lot: they mount to fourteen. O man, place not thy confidence in this present world.''

1405

Tamerlane (Timur), Mongol conqueror: "Never yet has death been frightened away by screaming.''

1542

James V, King of Scotland since 1513, alluding to the fact that his wife had just delivered a daughter and that the crown had come into his family by the daughter of King Robert Bruce: "It came with a lass and it will go with one.''

1603

Queen Elizabeth I, Queen of England since 1558: "All my possessions for one moment of time!''

1658

Oliver Cromwell, Lord Protector of England, who was offered food on his deathbed: "It is not my design to drink or sleep; but my design is to make what haste I can to be gone.''

1702

William III, King of England since 1689, to his physician: "Can this last long?''

1715

Louis XIV, King of France since 1643: "Did you think I should live forever? I thought dying was harder.''

1740

Frederick William I, who was King of Prussia from 1713, replying to priest who said, "Naked came I out of my mother's womb and naked shall I return thither'', replied "No, not quite naked, I shall have my uniform on.''

1789

Ethan Allen, American Revolutionary leader, on being told by his minister that the angels were waiting for him: "Waiting, are they? Well, goddamn 'em, let 'em wait!''

1790

Benjamin Franklin, American Revolutionary leader, to his daughter who had advised him to change his position in bed so that he might breathe more easily: "A dying man can do nothing easy.''

1799

George Washington, first U.S. President: "Let me go quietly. I cannot last long...'' Then: "It is well.''

1806

William Pitt the Younger, British statesman: "I could do with one of Bellamy's meat pies.''

Edward Thurlow, Lord Chancellor of England: "I'm shot if I don't believe I'm dying.''

1821

Napoleon I, Emperor of France: "Josephine!''

1825
Alexander I, Tsar of Russia since 1801: "What a beautiful day..."
1826
John Adams, second U.S. President: "Thomas Jefferson still survives." (But Jefferson died the same day, July 4th, exactly fifty years after both men signed the Declaration of Independence.)
Thomas Jefferson, third U.S. President: "Is it the Fourth?" Then: "I resign my spirit to God, my daughter, and my country."
1830
George IV, King of Great Britain since 1820, to his page, Sir Wathen Waller, who was assisting him to a chair: "Watty, what is this? It is death, my boy — they have deceived me."
Simon Bolivar, South American revolutionary leader, in a state of delirium: "Take my luggage on board the frigate."
Red Jacket, a Seneca Indian leader: "Bury me among my people... I do not wish to rise among pale faces."

1836
Stephen F. Austin, Texas leader, happy that his state was about to be recognized: "Did you see it in the papers?"
1836
James Madison, fourth U.S. President: "I always talk better lying down."
1838
John Scott Eldon, British statesman and jurist, to someone who remarked that it was a cold day: "It matters not to me where I am going whether the weather be cold or hot."
1841
William Henry Harrison, ninth U.S. President, speaking to Vice President John Tyler: "Sir, I wish you to understand the three principles of government. I wish them carried out. I ask nothing more."
1845
Andrew Jackson, seventh U.S. President: "I hope to meet each of you in heaven. Be good children, all of you and strive to be ready when the change comes."
1848
John Quincy Adams, sixth U.S. President: "This is the last of earth. I am content."
1849
James K. Polk, eleventh U.S. President, to his wife: "I love you, Sarah, for all eternity, I love you."
1850
John C. Calhoun, American statesman: "The poor South! God knows what will become of her."
Zachary Taylor, twelfth U.S. President: "I am about to die. I expect the summons very soon. I have tried to discharge all my

duties faithfully. I regret nothing, but I am sorry that I am about to leave my friends.''

1852

Daniel Webster, American statesman, to those at his bedside: "Have I, on this occasion, said anything unworthy of Daniel Webster?"

Thomas Hart Benton, American statesman, called black servant to his bedside, laid her head on his chest, and said: "Kitty, that is the death rattle."

1861

Albert, Prince Consort of Queen Victoria of Great Britain: "Good little woman!"

1862

John Tyler, tenth U.S. President: "There is but one reliance."

1865

Third Viscount Palmerston, British statesman: "Die, my dear doctor? That's the last thing I shall do."

1868

James Buchanan, fifteenth U.S. President: "O Lord God Almighty, as thou wilt."

1874

Millard Fillmore, thirteenth U.S. President, after taking food: "The nourishment is palatable."

1875

Andrew Johnson, seventeenth U.S. President: "Oh, do not cry. Be good children and we shall all meet in heaven."

1878

Victor Emmanuel II, since 1861 the first king of United Italy, to his doctor: "How much longer will it last? I had some important things to attend to."

1881

James Garfield, twentieth U.S. President, after being shot, to Gaskill Swaim, his chief-of-staff: "Oh, Swaim, there is a pain here...oh, oh, Swaim..."

1882

Benjamin H. Hill, American statesman from Georgia: "Almost home!"

Leon Gambetta, French Republican leader, seeing a friend faint when he heard of Gambetta's fatal illness: "Good heavens! Has he hurt himself?"

1885

Ulysses S. Grant, eighteenth U.S. President: "water!"

1893

Rutherford B. Hayes, nineteenth U.S. President, referring to his departed wife: "I know that I am going where Lucy is."

1901

William McKinley, twenty-fifth U.S. President, after being shot: "It is God's way. His will be done, not ours... We are all going, we are all going, we are all going...Oh, dear..."

Benjamin Harrison, twenty-third U.S. President: "Are the doctors here?...Doctor, my lungs..."

1908

Grover Cleveland, twenty-second and twenty-fourth U.S. President: "I have tried so hard to do right."

1910

Edward VII, King of Great Britain since 1901: "I shall go on. I shall work to the end."

1914

Archduke Francis Ferdinand of Austria-Hungary, after being shot at Sarajevo: "It is nothing."

1919

Theodore Roosevelt, twenty-sixth U.S. President: "Please put out the light."

1923

Warren G. Harding, twenty-eighth U.S. President, to his wife who was reading: "That's good. Go on, read some more."

1924

Woodrow Wilson, twenty-ninth U.S. President: "I'm a broken machine, but I'm ready"

1933

Calvin Coolidge, thirtieth U.S. President, to his handyman moments before he was found dead on bathroom floor: "Good morning, Robert."

1935

Huey P. Long, Governor of Louisiana, shot by Dr. Carl A. Weiss: "I wonder why he shot me?"

1945

Franklin D. Roosevelt, thirty-second U.S. President: "I have a terrific headache."

1948

Count Folke Bernadotte, United Nations mediator, was shot just after he acknowledged well-wishers saying "good luck": "I'll need it."

1953

Robert A. Taft, American statesman, to his wife: "Well, Martha, glad to see you looking so well."

1963

John F. Kennedy, thirty-fifth U.S. President, after being shot: "My God, I've been hit!"

Chapter Seven

Lasts of Crime and Punishment

Chronology

1215
The Fourth Lateran Council of the Roman Catholic Church ends "trial by ordeal" as a method of determining a person's guilt or innocence.

1547
The act permitting persons to be boiled to death for certain crimes in England is repealed.

1558
The last victims of "Bloody Mary," Queen of England, are put to death shortly before her death. (see p. 229)

1561
(March 4) Cardinal Carlo Carafa is the last Roman Catholic prelate sentenced and executed by a pope.

1681
Oliver Plunket, Irish Roman Catholic churchman, is the last Catholic to be executed at Tyburn on political-religious grounds. In 1920, he is beatified as a martyr.

1682
(Sept. 5) Three women are executed for witchcraft in England, the last to suffer the penalty in that country.

1692
(Sept. 19) Giles Cory is the last person in the United States to suffer being pressed to death (*peine forte et dure*), his execution taking place at Salem, Massachusetts.
(Sept. 22) Eight women executed at Salem, Massachusetts, are the last victims of the American witchhunt.

1696
An eighteen-year-old student of medicine named Aikenhead is hanged for heresy at Edinburgh, the last person to suffer capital punishment on religious grounds in Scotland.

1708
Torture as an official part of criminal procedure is abolished in Scotland. This means the end of such devices as the boot (in which the foot is inserted and wedges driven between the limb and boot), the rack, the thumbikins (a sort of thumbscrew), the caschielaws (an instrument drawing the body and limbs together, heat sometimes being added as well), the lang irnis (heavy weights, often more than 700 pounds), the harrow bore (perforations through which the teeth of harrows were

225

inserted), the pyne bankis (a form of rack), and artifical prevention of sleep.

1711
(March) Seven women tried and convicted of conspiring with the devil are the last witches punished for that crime in Ireland.

1713
Branding of persons convicted of vagrancy is abolished in England.

1718
A man found guilty and executed for witchcraft is the last victim of such penalties in France.

1722
(June) A woman is burned to death, the last person to be executed as a witch in Scotland.

1726
The last person in England is subjected to being pressed to death, before the torture is abolished.

1736
Britain repeals statutes allowing severe punishment for witchcraft.

1740
Torture is officially abolished in Prussia by King Frederick the Great.

1747
(April 9) Simon Fraser, Lord Lovat, is last British peer to be beheaded. (see p. 230)

1760
(May 5) The Fourth Earl Ferrers is hanged, the last British nobleman to suffer a felon's death.

1772
The "Cave of Roses" where reptiles were kept for the purpose of torturing criminals, is abolished by Denmark's King Gustavus III.

1775
(April 11) Germany's last trial and execution for witchcraft takes place.

1783
The last execution takes place at London's infamous Tyburn gallows.

1789
(March 18) Christian Bowman is the last woman burned to death in Britain. The following year, the penalty is abolished. (see p. 232)

1789
(Oct. 9) Torture of all kinds is officially abolished in France.

1798
(June 4) Lord Edward Fitzgerald becomes the last British subject to be sentenced under the Bill of Attainder Act.

1801
After a formal study during the reign of Catherine the Great, which declared that

all punishments in which the body is maimed ought to be abolished, Tsar Alexander I decrees torture a thing of the past in Imperial Russia.

1803
Edward Despard and his accomplices in a plot to kill George III become the last persons drawn and quartered. (see p. 233)

1827
Laws are repealed which allow "hue and cry," the process whereby persons can be pursued and arrested by anyone within earshot of an alleged criminal. (Hue and cry victims were not allowed to say anything in their defense, being caught while "fleeing" deemed proof of guilt.)

1830
(June 22) The last person legally sentenced to the pillory in Great Britain, Peter James Bossy, stands for an hour. The punishment is abolished in 1837.

1834
Spain formally abolishes the Inquisition, in existence since the thirteenth century.

1844
(April 2) An act of Parliament formally calls for the abolition of England's Fleet Prison, one of that nation's worst jails. (see p. 234)

1849
Marshalsea Prison, founded in England during the reign of King Edward III, is abolished.

1850
Flogging as a form of punishment is abolished in the U. S. Navy.

1862
(March 8) Captain Nathaniel Gordon becomes the last American pirate to be hanged, meeting his fate at the Tombs prison in New York City.

1863
Bridewell's House of Correction is demolished in Great Britain.

1869
Great Britain abolishes debtors' prisons.

1870
The medieval punishment of drawing and quartering is abolished in Great Britain.

1880
Ned Kelly, last of the Australian "bushrangers" or desperados of the bush country, is caught and hanged. (see p. 234)

1881
Deputy Robert Ollinger becomes the twenty-first and last victim of gunslinger Billy the Kid. (see p. 235)

1881
(Sept. 7) Jesse James and

his gang hold up their last train, the westbound Chicago and Alton, at Blue Cut, Missouri.

1881
The last man is flogged in Britain's armed forces, that punishment being abolished by Parliament.

1888
(Nov.3) The mysterious killer calling himself "Jack the Ripper" claims his last victim before vanishing. (see p. 236)

1892
(Oct. 5) The notorious Dalton gang pulls its last job, holding up two banks in Coffeyville, Kansas, before being riddled by lawmen's bullets.

1898
The last American stagecoach robbery is pulled off by a 27-year-old woman, Pearl Hart and a male companion, the two taking $431.

1902
Newgate Prison in London, long famous for its poor conditions, is finally torn down.

1916
The notorious Ilchester Almshouses in Somersetshire, England, established in 1426 to hold and punish debtors, are abolished.

1936
At Owensboro, Kentucky, the last public execution in the U. S. takes place before 20,000 witnesses. The victim is Rainey Bethea, a twenty-two-year-old black man convicted of slaying an elderly white woman. (see p. 238)

1937
Emmett Dalton, last of the notorious gang of bank robbers, dies. (see p. 239)

1939
(June 17) The last man to be guillotined publicly in France, convicted murderer Eugene Weidmann, is executed in front of the Palais de Justice in Versailles. (see p. 240)

1947
The state of Georgia abolishes its last "convict highway camp" (road gang).

1952
(June 16) John F. Barbieri, 30, becomes the last man in the United States to be whipped as a punishment for crime. (see p. 246)

1953
The last prisoners of France's notorious penal colony, "Devil's Island," are freed. (see p. 241)

1955
(June 16) Juan Peron of Argentina is the last head of state to be excommunicated by the pope. (see p. 242)

1963
(March) The famous maximum-security prison, Alca-

traz, is closed down and its last inmates moved to other facilities. (see p. 243)

1964
(Jan. 4) The last victim of the "Boston Strangler" is found dead in her apartment near Beacon Hill. (see p. 245)

1970
(April 18) The last prisoners at Pennsylvania's Eastern State Penitentiary are moved from that facility.

1972
(July 9) After 316 years of having flogging on the books as a legal punishment — and using it — the state of Delaware becomes the last state in the nation to abandon the practice. (see p. 246)

1979
(Aug. 26) Alvin Karpis, once Public Enemy Number One, and the last surviving member of the dreaded Ma Barker Gang, dies at the age of seventy-one. (see p. 248)

The Last Victims of "Bloody Mary"

The daughter of King Henry VIII of England and Catherine of Aragon, Mary was a precocious child who could play the virginal at four and speak fluent Latin at nine. Unfortunately, Henry soon tired of Catherine and, in order to install Anne Boleyn as queen, had to declare his first marriage illegal. This made young Mary a bastard, which no doubt colored the rest of her life. Being brought up a good Catholic, she also objected to her father's squabbling with the pope just so he could change wives now and then.

Biding her time through the reigns of her father and sickly brother, Edward, Mary was rewarded with his early death on 6 July 1553. Mary was proclaimed queen at the age of 37, which delighted her, for there was still time to square things with the church. Above all, Mary wanted to be declared legitimate again, especially in the minds of her countrymen, and that could only happen if the Catholic church gave its blessing to her reign. Marrying Philip of Spain, Europe's most Catholic country, helped, but Mary didn't stop at that. She immediately revived the anti-heresy laws which had been passed in 1400 (and repealed in 1533 during her father's reign) and ordered Cardinal Reginald Pole to round up as many heretics as possible.

It took her a while to act, but once she executed her first non-Catholic, Mary worked with furious abandon.

The Reverend John Rogers of St. Sepulchre's Church, Snow Hill, London, was the first to go. Rogers' crime was exhorting the people to remain faithful to the Protestant religion. Brought to trial,

229

Rogers admitted that he thought the pope was anti-Christ, which led to his being sentenced to death at Smithfield. Rogers' wife and eleven children bade farewell to him at Newgate Prison as he was led to the place of execution on 4 February 1555.

About 300 others followed during the brief reign of "Bloody Mary," as she subsequently became known. In the executions, Mary was partial to high-ranking clergymen, such as Dr. John Hooper, the bishop of Gloucester, Dr. Robert Ferrar, bishop of St. David's, or the Reverend John Lawrence, who was carried to his execution in a chair, his legs having been mutilated by irons. But Mary also permitted the execution of common people, such as Rawlins White, a south Wales fisherman, who was burned at the stake on 30 March 1555.

Nor did Mary confine her spirit of reforming zeal to men. In fact, she created the first female martyr in England, one Margaret Polley, who was accused of expressing the belief that the sacramental bread and wine were merely symbols, rather than actually the body and blood of Christ. Calling her a "silly woman," the prelate before whom she was brought ordered her returned to jail for a month to think it over. When she did not recant, Margaret Polley was burned at the stake.

After that, Mary turned her attention to doing away with Hugh Latimer, bishop of Worcester, Nicholas Ridley, bishop of London, and Thomas Cranmer, Archbishop of Canterbury. The execution of the seventy-nine-year-old Ridley was particularly satisfying to those sadists in the crowd, his pyre being made of green wood which wouldn't burn very well, causing only excruciating pain rather than death. "Let the fire come unto me," Ridley cried out. "I cannot burn!" At that point, a bystander gave the wood a kick, causing it to flare up, igniting some gunpowder that had been laid with the fire, and the flames finally consumed the aged cleric.

And so it went for the next three years. The last victims, convicted of not believing in the doctrine of transubstantiation and of confessing that they did not pray to saints, were John Cornefield, Christopher Browne, John Herst, Alice Snoth, and Catherine Knight, alias Tinley. Two others awaitng execution, John Hunt and Richard White, were released following the death of Queen Mary at the age of 42 on 17 November 1558. The very next day, Cardinal Pole died and the executions were halted.

The Last Beheading in Great Britain

Beheading has never been a prevalent means of punishment for crime in the United States, but was common in France and Great Britain until comparatively recently.

Used by the Greeks and Romans (who called it *decollatio* or *capitis amputatio*), beheading was considered an honorable means of death. Cicero chose it as the way to go on 7 December 43 B.C., after incurring the wrath of Octavian (later Augustus Caesar).

William the Conqueror brought the means of punishment to England, first using it in 1076 on Waltheof, Earl of Northumberland. Thereafter, beheading with an axe or sword was more or less reserved for persons of high rank.

Some notable persons who were beheaded during the years following included Sir Thomas More, Sir Walter Raleigh, Anne Boleyn, Lady Jane Grey, Catherine Howard, the Duke of Monmouth, and Thomas D'Arcy. One of the more spectacular executions took place on 12 May 1641, when a huge crowd assembled on Tower Hill to witness the execution of the Earl of Strafford. Surrounded by his friends, he behaved with great composure, refusing to have his eyes bandaged.

In the eighteenth century, the Earl of Derwentwater and William Bordon, 6th Viscount of Kenmure, both involved with the Jacobite rebellion to restore the descendants of Scottish kings to the English throne, were beheaded on the same day, 24 February 1716.

The last nobleman to be beheaded was Simon Fraser, Lord Lovat, an elderly Highland chieftain who was also involved in the Jacobite plotting. Tried with two fellow Scots, Lord Kilmarnock and Arthur, sixth Lord Balmerino, all three were found guilty in 1746 and sentenced to be beheaded.

Balmerino and Kilmarnock were executed in 1746. Both behaved with stiff-upper-lip bravado. "My Lord, I am heartily sorry to have your company in this expedition," Kilmarnock said. To which Balmerino replied, "My Lord Kilmarnock, I am only sorry I cannot pay this reckoning alone."

The following year, on 19 April 1747, the seventy-nine-year-old Fraser also behaved in character. As he viewed the crowd gathering prior to the "taking off of an old grey head," he said, "Look, how they are all piled up like rotten oranges." He then put on his spectacles to make sure the inscription on his coffin was correct, drank a toast to King James, and said to a companion, "Cheer up thy heart, man. I am not afraid. Why should you be?"

Thirteen years later, the fourth Earl Ferrers, last British nobleman to suffer a felon's death, was tried and convicted for the murder of an old family steward named Johnson. Sentenced to be hanged, Ferrers asked to be beheaded instead. His petition was denied.

On 5 May 1760, he was taken in his own carriage to the Tower of London and hanged. Out of deference to his rank, King George III allowed him to use a rope made of silk.

The Last Person Executed for Sacrilege

France was especially tough on persons who violated ecclesiastical objects, although it was rare that anyone was executed for such offenses. King Louis XIV, after enjoying a sinful youth, became crusty in his middle age and in 1682 passed a series of new anti-sacrilege laws. In 1724, the Duke of Bourbon cracked down on men guilty of stealing from the church by sentencing them to long term (or lifetime) galley slavery. Women were ordered branded or imprisoned.

Even so, 19-year-old Jean Francois le Fevre Barre was hardly prepared for the consequences that followed his mild burst of anti-church sentiment in 1766. First, he refused to take off his hat while a religious procession passed. Then, he mutilated a crucifix.

Brought to trial at Abbeville, the young man was convicted of both "crimes" and sentenced to have his tongue cut out, then to be beheaded and burned. To nearly everyone's surprise and horror, King Louis XV confirmed the court's decision.

Just before the sentence was carried out, Barre broke down. "I did not think they would put a young gentleman to death for such a trifle," he said.

After the downfall of the monarchy, laws were passed abolishing such ferocious punishments for sacrilege.

The Last Woman Burned to Death

Once a common means of execution, especially for religious "heretics" such as Joan of Arc, death by burning was a legal form of capital punishment until the late eighteenth century — particularly for women.

One British account, for example, described the execution of Ann Whale, who murdered her husband by flavoring his gruel with more than a dash of white mercury. Taken to Broadridge Heath Common near Horsham in August of 1752, Ann was "led to the stake, her back chained thereto and then strangled and in about five minutes the fire was kindled and her body consumed to ashes."

In 1776, a woman of eighty who had cut her husband's throat was sentenced to be "drawn on a hurdle to the place of execution on Thursday next and there burnt with fire until she be dead." The order was carried out on 8 August. Seven years later, another woman was burned at Ipswich, and in 1784, Mary Bayley was similarly executed at Portsmouth.

The last woman legally burned to death in England was a certain Christian Bowman, whose career was described in a contemporary pamphlet entitled *The Life and Death of Christian Bowman, alias Murphy, who was burnt at the stake in the Old Bailey, on Wednesday the 18th of March 1789 for High Treason, in feloniously and traitorously counterfeiting the silver coin of the realm. Containing her Birth and Parentage, Youthful Adventures, Love Amours, Fatal Marriage, Unhappy Connections, and Untimely Death.*

232

A year after Christian Bowman's demise, British law was changed, providing that after 5 June 1790, women under sentence of death should be hanged, burning probably being thought to be too cruel and inhuman a punishment — even for hardened criminals.

The Last Persons Drawn and Quartered

Until it was officially abolished as a legal means of punishment in Great Britain, the ferocious act known as drawing and quartering had a very specific set of rules. The victim was dragged on a hurdle to the place of execution, hanged by the neck but not until dead, disemboweled, the entrails burned before the victim's eyes, with decapitation and division of the body into four parts following.

This extreme form of punishment was first inflicted on David III, the last native prince of Wales, who in 1282 made a desperate final effort to establish Welsh independence by attacking English garrisons. In June of 1283, he was betrayed, and after a gallant fight, taken captive. Convicted of treason, he was drawn and quartered at Shrewsbury in October of that year.

In more recent times, the penalty befell an Irish conspirator named Edward Marcus Despard who was arrested along with six others on a charge of plotting to assassinate King George III. In December of 1802, all of the men were found guilty and sentenced to be hanged, drawn and quartered.

The executions took place on 21 February 1803, on Horsemonger Lane, London, near the prison gate. By six o'clock that morning, every possible inch of space affording a view of the scaffold was filled by a teeming mass of humanity. Two troops of cavalry were stationed by the Obelisk to prevent trouble; other soldiers patrolled the roads from the Obelisk to the Elephant and Castle. Despard, fifty-one, took his fate in a firm, almost nonchalant manner, according to those who accompanied him on his last journey. As he and McNamara, another of the doomed men, were being led to the platform, McNamara said: "I am afraid, Colonel, we have got into a bad situation."

Despard, who had served in Great Britain's army, smiled. "There are many better, and some worse," he said evenly. Then, looking at the throngs of people and the gray sky, he added, "What an amazing crowd! Tis very cold. I think we shall have some rain."

A few minutes later, the penalty was carried out.

Seventeen years later, another group of anti-establishment plotters who planned to assassinate British cabinet members were discovered and brought to trial. These men, known as the Cato Street Conspirators, were also tried, found guilty, and sentenced to death. Because the plotters' scheme was so ruthless, some urged that they be drawn and quartered, but the penalty was not carried out.

In 1867, two members of the Irish revolutionary group known as the Fenian Brotherhood, William Smith O'Brien and Richard Burke, were arrested for conspiracy and sentenced to drawing and quartering, but likewise escaped with their lives. Three years later, an act of Parliament abolished drawing and quartering as a penalty for crimes against the state.

The Last of Fleet Prison in London

Notorious for centuries as one of London's worst jails, Fleet Prison, London, was destroyed during the Peasant's Revolt of 1381, the Great Fire of 1666, and the Gordon riots of 1780, but always seemed to rise from the ashes. In the eighteenth century, the artist Hogarth drew pictures of the devices of torture common at Fleet, notably metal clamps which were applied to prisoners' hands and necks.

During its dark history, Fleet Prison became known for the ceremony known as the "Fleet marriage." Under British common law, a marriage was valid if conducted by any person in holy orders, even without banns or license. Few such marriages were performed, however, largely because an act of 1696 imposed a penalty of 100 pounds on any clergyman performing a ceremony unaccompanied by banns or license.

Since clergymen imprisoned for debt had no fear of such a penalty, a brisk clandestine marriage business grew up in Fleet Prison. Tavern-keepers in the area employed touts to solicit young couples who might desire a quick wedding. Not until 1840 were the "Fleet Registers" deemed inadmissable as evidence to prove a marriage.

In the early nineteenth century, continuous public outcry against the facility finally led to an act of 2 April 1844, calling for Fleet Prison's abolition. It was demolished in 1845-1846.

The Last Bushranger

During the mid-nineteenth century, Australia was terrorized by groups of bandits called "bushrangers," most of whom were escaped convicts who had organized themselves into gangs. A series of bushranging acts enabled law enforcement officers to capture most of the desperados but a few continued to plague the authorities.

Born in 1854 at Wallan Wallan, Victoria, Edward "Ned" Kelly was known as the "last of the bushrangers" during the 1870s. The son of a transported Belfast convict, Ned and his brother, Daniel, got into trouble with the law early, stealing horses while still in their early teens. Ned was caught and served three years in jail but remained unrehabilitated. As soon as he was released, he and Daniel started earning their living by robbing banks.

In April of 1878, law officers went to the Kelly home with a warrant for the brothers' arrest. A general melee followed in which the entire family, Mrs. Kelly included, resisted. Ned wounded one of the constables and he and Daniel fled to the hills where they were joined by another couple of desperados named Hart and Byrne. For two years, despite a reward of 8,000 pounds offered by the provinces of Victoria and New South Wales, the gang eluded arrest.

On 28 June 1880, word reached police at Benalla that the Kelly gang had captured the entire village of Glenrowan and were in the hotel there with about forty hostages. A special trainload of deputies was sent out but had to pull up short of the town because Kelly's men had torn up the track. Eventually the police surrounded the hotel and fired sixty shots through the weatherboards before the screams of women and children inside forced them to stop. While this was going on, Ned Kelly managed to sneak out of the building — but not to escape.

The next morning at eight o'clock, a tall figure approached the rear of the police picket line. It was Kelly, wearing a huge greatcoat, walking coolly and slowly toward the police. His head, chest, sides and back were covered with heavy plates of quarter-inch iron. When he was within shooting distance of the police, he paused, his arm and pistol protruded from the layers of metal, and shots rang out.

"The contest became one which, from its remarkable nature, almost baffles description," a reporter wrote. "Nine policemen joined in the conflict and fired point blank at Kelly, but although it was apparent that many of the shots struck him, in consequence of the way in which he staggered, yet he always recovered himself, and, tapping his breast, laughed derisively at his opponents as he coolly returned their fire, fighting only with a revolver. It appeared as if he was a fiend with a charmed life. For half an hour the strange combat was carried on. Then Sgt. Steele rapidly closed in on him, and when within only about 10 yards of him, he fired two shots into his legs, and this brought the outlaw down..."

Thus ended the career of Australia's last bushranger. Several months later, Kelly was hanged and the case, which had cost the government 115,000 pounds, was finally closed.

The Last Man Shot by Billy the Kid

During his brief life (1859-1881), William H. Bonney, better known as "Billy the Kid," reportedly shot and killed at least twenty-one men, which earned him national notoriety, some easy money, and an early grave.

He was hardly a fearless gunman, however, not being above shooting a man in the back if necessary.

Born in New York City, Billy went west with his parents at the age of three, first to Coffeyville, Kansas, then to Colorado. He reportedly stayed out of trouble until he was fourteen, killing his first man (name unknown) at that time. He then left home and went to Arizona, where he killed three Apache braves.

His next victim was a Negro blacksmith who was unfortunate enough to call the young man a "billy goat" when confronted with the charge he had cheated at cards. Bonny dispatched the blacksmith, and, supposedly, the appellation stuck. (As Bonney's name was William or Billy anyway, the story is probably apocryphal.) A trio of card dealers in Mexico and two more in Indiana were next on Billy's list, followed in 1876 by cowboys Billy Morton, Frank Baker, and Andrew L. "Buckshot" Roberts.

By this time, a price was on Billy's head and he was feeling the pressure of being a national celebrity. He waited in ambush for Sheriff William Brady near Lincoln, New Mexico, and shot him in the back on April Fool's Day, 1878. When Deputy George Hindman tried to help out, he became the fifteenth notch on Billy's gun handle.

By now, Billy had a fourteen-man gang and was being pursued by the United States Cavalry all over New Mexico Territory. After Billy killed four more men who stood in his way — cattleman Robert W. Beckwith, gunmen Joe Grant and Jimmy Carlyle, and Indian agent Joseph Bernstein — a posse finally cornered the gunslinger on 21 December 1880.

Billy was taken prisoner, tried for the shooting of Andrew Roberts, and found guilty. Judge Warren Bristol sentenced him to hang until, as he put it, "you are dead, dead, dead!"

Billy replied: "And you can go to hell, hell, hell!"

While awaiting execution, Billy got hold of a pistol, shot Warden J. W. Bell, and broke out of the cell. Before leaving town, however, he settled a score with Deputy Robert Ollinger, who, during the trial kept poking Billy with a shotgun. Waiting calmly for Ollinger to return to the courthouse where he had been drinking, Billy dispatched him with a shotgun blast, then left quietly.

An old drinking buddy of Billy's, Pat Garrett, tracked the Kid to a ranch where he was hiding out and on 14 July 1881, did the only thing possible to make sure Ollinger was the last victim of Billy the Kid — he shot first and asked questions later.

Garrett lived until 1908, when he was shot by an angry tenant who had been working on his land.

Jack the Ripper's Last Victim

While as many as fourteen murders have been attributed to the killer who stalked the Whitechapel section of London during the fall of 1888, it is generally agreed that the man who dubbed himself "Jack the Ripper" probably committed only five of them.

The first took place on 31 August 1888, the victim a prostitute named Mary Ann Nicols. On 8 September, "Dark" Annie Chapman became the second, Elizabeth Stride the third on 30 September, and Catherine Eddowes the fourth on the same night. Panicked, residents formed the Whitechapel Vigilance Committee and began to clamor for the murderer's arrest. Thought to be a butcher because he disemboweled his victims, the killer was given the nickname "Leather Apron" by a nervous public. Feeding the panic, the killer sent notes to the newspapers and George Lusk, head of the Vigilance Committee. On one occasion, the note was accompanied by a piece of Catherine Eddowes' kidney. It read:

> From Hell, Mr. Lusk, sir, I send you half the kidney
> I took from one woman, prasarved it for you, tother
> piece I fried and ate it; it was very nice. I may send you
> the bloody knif that took it out if you only wate while
> longer. Catch me when you can, Mr. Lusk.

The month of October passed with no further killings that could be traced to Jack the Ripper. Then, on 9 November, a landlord named John McCarthy sent his man to apartment No. 13 at 26 Dorset Street to "try and get some rent" from Mary Kelly, who was more than two months behind.

Unable to enter the locked apartment door, John Bowyer peeked through the glass and saw the bloody body of Mary Kelly on the bed.

When police, reporters, and photographers arrived later, they saw the result of one of the most savage mutilation murders in the history of crime. "The poor woman lay on her back on the bed, entirely naked," reported the *London Times*. "Her throat was cut from ear to ear, right down to the spinal column. The ears and nose had been cut clean off. The breasts had also been cleanly cut off and placed on a table which was by the side of the bed. The stomach and abdomen had been ripped open, while her face was slashed about, so that the features of the poor creature were beyond all recognition. The kidneys and heart had also been removed from the body, and placed on the table by the side of the breasts. The liver had likewise been removed and laid on the right thigh. The lower portion of the body and the uterus had been cut out, and these appeared to be missing. The thighs had been cut. A more horrible or sickening sight could not be imagined..."

Perhaps not, but the *Times* was right in there trying.

Despite maximum police coverage, no one could provide a clue or description of the killer. Some residents living next to Mary Kelly reported hearing her singing "Sweet Violets" about one o'clock in the morning before she was murdered but no man was heard or seen with her.

Speculation concerning the Ripper's identity has continued to this day.

Interestingly, those who today blame rising crime rates on the prevalence of television violence had a counterpart in 1888 London. "Is it not within the bounds of probability," wrote the magazine *Punch* during the height of the Ripper panic, "that to the highly colored pictorial advertisements to be seen on almost all the boardings in London, vividly representing sensational scenes of murder, exhibited as 'the great attractions' of certain dramas, the public may be to a certain extent indebted for the horrible crimes in Whitechapel? We say it most seriously: imagine the effect of these gigantic pictures of violence and assassination by knife and pistol on the morbid imagination of unbalanced minds. These hideous picture-posters are a blot on our civilisation and a disgrace to the drama."

The Last Public Execution in the U. S.

"Ten thousand White persons, some jeering and others festive, saw a prayerful Black man put to death today on Daviess County's pit and gallows," a reporter wrote on 14 August 1936.

The place was Owensboro, Kentucky, the victim twenty-two-year-old Rainey Bethea, who had been convicted of assaulting and murdering a seventy-year-old white woman on the night of 10 June. When the state of Kentucky adopted the electric chair as punishment for capital offenses, the legislature retained hanging as the penalty for criminal assault, leaving it optional with county officials whether the execution would be public or private. In this case, Mrs. Florence Thompson, the county sheriff, organized the event to be as public as possible. Under her guidance, a scaffold was erected in a field so that it would be possible for thousands to witness the execution.

Attendance, predictably, was so good that many blacks in the area fled for their lives. And having arranged everything, Mrs. Thompson then stayed away, turning the dirty work of springing the trap over to Arthur L. Hash, a former Louisville policeman.

By sunrise, the three-acre lot was jammed with people, many drunkenly shouting, "Take him up!", "Up on the scaffold where we can see him!", and "Let's go!" Accompanied by the Reverend Herman Lammers, a Catholic priest and G. Phil Hanna, an expert on hanging criminals "without inflicting strangulation," young Bethea knelt at the base of the scaffold and mumbled an inaudible prayer.

When the hangman sprung the trap there was a loud cheer from the crowd. Then, despite the presence of armed guards around the scaffold, many persons rushed forward, attempting to grab the hood from Bethea's dangling form, tear off bits of his clothing, even cut pieces of flesh from his body as souvenirs. Others sat on the roof of the hearse waiting to take Bethea away or crowded around the two doctors who examined the body for signs of life. At 5:45 a.m, a quarter-hour after the trap was sprung, the young man was pronouced dead.

The event produced a furor of indignation throughout the nation, editorials and letters denouncing the "carnival of sadism" and attacking what was Kentucky's third recent public hanging as barbaric. "It was obvious to the reporters covering the Owensboro affair that many in the crowd had been imbibing, perhaps all night, in order to be prepared for the spectacle at dawn.," wrote Malcom Bayley. "Hospitable Owensboro folk entertained visitors from out of town, thus possibly establishing the precedent for a new form of Kentucky's venerable type of entertainment. Hanging house-parties, it is suggested, with a jolly night of fun and a hanging breakfast, may supercede fox hunts and the Kentucky Derby itself as occasions for entertainment."

Five days after Bethea went to his death, officials at Covington, Kentucky, faced with the responsibility of executing yet another black man, John "Pete" Montjoy, carried out the execution in the courtyard of the Covington City Building, barring both press and public.

The Last of the Dalton Gang

The successors to the James Gang — the Daltons, who were cousins of the Younger Brothers — were the last celebrated border bandits of the Old West. In fairness to Ma Dalton and the state of Missouri (often called "the mother of bandits"), it should be pointed out that only four of the fifteen Dalton children went bad. One, Frank, even became a lawman and was killed in the line of duty.

Robert (born 1867), Gratton (born 1862), Emmett (born 1871), and William (born 1873) tried their hands at honest work only briefly before getting in trouble. Itching to break into the criminal big time, Bob stuck up a faro game with Emmett in 1890, then branched out into train robbery.

Selecting the Southern Pacific's Train No. 17 near Los Angeles as their target, Bob, Bill, and Grat bought tickets as passengers, waited until a prearranged time, then pulled kerchiefs over their faces and climbed into the locomotive cab. They shot a fireman but couldn't get into the railway express car and were driven off by the armed guard without getting a cent.

Convinced by the experience that they needed a larger gang, the Daltons rounded up the likes of George "Bitter Creek" Newcomb and "Black Face" Charlie Bryant and proceeded to terrorize the Oklahoma Cherokee Strip for eighteen months. One train netted them $14,000 and another $17,000, thanks largely to Bob Dalton's fiancee, Eugenia, who posed as a nervous rich woman who would ship her money only on the best-protected trains. (Surprisingly, most stationmasters gave her all the information the gang needed to plan its raids.)

By late 1892, however, Eugenia had died of cancer, and Bob was filled with thoughts of grandeur. Recalling how the James brothers had tried to rob a pair of banks near Northfield, Minnesota, Bob selected the Condon Bank and First National Bank in Coffeyville, Kansas, as the gang's twin targets. On 5 October 1892, they rode into town but were recognized despite Bob and Emmett wearing false beards. Having lost the element of surpise, they decided to continue the job anyway, but ran into more bad luck when one of the safes turned out to be a time-locked box with more than ten minutes left on it. By the time the Daltons got it open, the townspeople were firing at them through the bank's windows.

Finally cornered in an alley, Bob and Grat were shot to death and Emmett, hit more than twenty times, was severely wounded. Bill escaped, but was killed the following year by lawmen.

Sent to prison for life, Emmett was pardoned in 1907 and led an exemplary life for the next three decades. In the meantime, on 30 March 1936, the next-to-last Dalton, Charles Ben (one of the honest ones) died in an Oklahoma insane asylum. Emmett, the last of the notorious outlaws, died in 1937, the author of a film scenario entitled *When the Daltons Rode*.

The Last Public Guillotining in France

Some thought Eugene Weidmann was charming. Obviously many women did, for, on brief acquaintance, he was able to lure several of them into lonely situations and murder them in the hope of stealing their money. One was a beautiful young American dancer, Jean deKoven, who was last seen on 23 July 1937. Shortly after her disappearance, a series of bodies turned up, hers among them. The clues eventually led to Weidmann, a smooth-talking German who had served sixteen years in prison for theft.

The trial was a sensation in Paris, concluding with the conviction of Weidmann and his three accomplices, one of whom was a squeamish little Frenchman named Roger Million. As the tribunal returned with its verdict on 31 March 1939, Million shouted, "Don't convict me! I am innocent. I was an instrument in Weidmann's hands." Nevertheless, Weidmann was found guilty of mudering deKoven and five others; Million was found guilty of being an accomplice to murder.

Between April and June, when plans for Weidmann's public execution were finalized, Million's sentence was changed to life imprisonment. Mercy was not granted to Weidmann, who had to listen to the mob gathered outside the jail in eager anticipation of his execution. In the Rue Georges Clemenceau, in front of the Palais de Justice at Versailles, every room, balcony, and window overlooking the guillotine site was rented at fantastic prices. Even a constant drizzle failed to dampen the holiday spirit of the crowd.

At 3:00 a.m., "Uncle Leopold" Desfourneaux, the black-garbed executioner, set up the machine and waited until 4:33, when Weidmann was rushed to the guillotine beneath a cloudy sky. At 4:50 Weidmann was dispatched with such efficiency that only those with a keen eye could see the actual decapitation. Newspaper photographs released soon afterward, however, so outraged the public that a week later, a new law was passed forbidding further public executions.

The Last Devil's Island Prisoner

Founded in 1854, the French penal colony at Cayenne known as "Devil's Island" was actually three separate islands, the "Islands of Salvation." The first, named "Royale" by early French settlers in honor of the king, had a facility called the "Crimson Barracks." It was so named because of the large number of murders which occurred after the guards locked the doors at 6 p.m.

The second island, "St. Joseph" (named after the patron saint of voyagers) contained underground cells for the "incos," or incorrigibles, with openings on the top for guards to peer through.

Finally, there was "Devil's Island" (so named because of the angry sea around it) which contained lonely huts for political prisoners. This island's most famous inhabitant was Alfred Dreyfus, the French army officer who was in all probability framed on a charge of espionage during the 1890s.

Other interesting prisoners included one who managed to get himself the job of executioner. But not long afterward, he got in a fight, killed another inmate and ended up on his own guillotine. He was duly executed — after being good enough to set the blade himself.

Another Cayenne penal colony prisoner who made his mark was Paul Roussenq, an ex-soldier serving twenty years for attempted arson. Perhaps the most unrepentant inhabitant of the penal colony, Roussenq frequently wrote obscene letters to the prison governor, tried to give himself tuberculosis, practiced acrobatics on the grate of his cell, and as a result, earned ten years in extra penalties. Finally, taken to the mainland, he escaped and was never heard from again.

During its 99-year existence, some 70,000 men were sent to the penal colony but only 2,000 returned. The facility was officially abolished by decree on 17 June 1938, but World War II intervened, and hundreds of prisoners remained and died while awaiting their release.

The final band of eighty-eight prisoners left the islands in 1953. A shrimp processing plant eventually replaced the former prison camp.

The Last Head of State
Excommunicated by a Pope

Although it is theoretically possible that a future pope may excommunicate some future national leader, the declining political power of the church has rendered the age-old weapon relatively ineffectual. Thus, it seems unlikely it will ever be used again.

In the past, of course, excommunication was often used and was feared by kings, queens, and even nations. One of the most dramatic examples of excommunication occurred in 1208, when King John of England and Pope Innocent III argued about the appointment of a new Archbishop of Canterbury. Refusing to yield to papal pressure, John said that if the church continued to interfere, he would confiscate its property and send the clergy to Rome with their eyes torn out and noses split "that they might be known there from other people."

Pope Innocent responded by excommunicating the entire nation. On Easter Monday, the bishops of Ely, London, and Winchester ordered the churches closed and refused to perform marriages or say prayers for the dead. King John retaliated by seizing church property and locking up the clergy's corn. As a final indignity, he released a man convicted of robbing and murdering a priest.

Many natives were upset by the papal interdiction but England survived until 1214 when the ban was lifted.

Pope Innocent III was one of the most excommunicating pontiffs in the history of the church. In addition to having trouble with King John, he excommunicated King Philip II in 1198 (for divorcing Ingeborg of Denmark), laid a curse on the whole of Germany in 1208, and excommunicated Otto of Brunswick in 1210 because he murdered Philip of Swabia.

The most excommunicated national leader was Holy Roman Emperor Frederick II, who received the papal punishment first in 1227. The reason was that Pope Gregory IX was convinced Frederick was malingering instead of leading the crusade then in progress. A dozen years later, Frederick's pugnacity led to his being excommunicated a second time by Gregory, who called him a rake, heretic, and anti-Christ in the bargain. Frederick responded by invading Italy and ravaging the papal lands. This probably helped hasten the death of Gregory, who died in 1241 at age 94. In 1245, Frederick was excommunicated once again by Pope Innocent IV, who charged that the Holy Roman Emperor was persecuting the clergy in addition to stealing papal property.

Some other national leaders who felt the papal wrath over the years included King Boleslav II (The Bold) of Poland (for murder-

242

ing the Bishop of Cracow while he said mass in a cathedral); Henry VIII of England (for having his marriage to Catherine of Aragon annulled); and Queen Elizabeth I (as a "usurper"). In 1624, Pope Urban III threatened to excommunicate all snuff-users, so widespread was the filthy habit, but nothing came of it.

By the twentieth century, the weapon of excommunication was seldom used except against communists, notably those leaders in Yugoslavia, Hungary, Czechoslovakia, Poland, Rumania, Bulgaria and China who persecuted church officials. Despite numerous acts of villainy, neither Benito Mussolini nor Adolf Hitler was excommunicated by the pope.

Not until the rise of Juan Peron of Argentina did a non-communist leader inspire a pope with sufficient ire to be excommunicated. Once he started his campaign against the church, Peron became a holy terror. Early in 1955, as if deliberately setting out to taunt the church, he legalized divorce and bordellos. In April, he followed by eliminating five feast days — Epiphany, Corpus Christi, Assumption, All-Saints, and Immaculate Conception — from the list of national holidays (while retaining wife Eva's birth and death days, as well as 17 October, the official Day of Loyalty to Peron).

In May of 1955, Peron passed a bill ending tax exemptions on church property, abolished religious instruction in schools and began to have protesting clergymen rounded up and thrown in jail.

Finally, on 16 June 1955, Pope Pius XII acted by excommunicating Peron, charging that, "the rights of the church have been trampled upon in various ways and violence has been used against ecclesiastical persons...."

Partly because of the papal action and no doubt greatly because he had overstepped the bounds of reason in many areas, Peron was overthrown soon after and went into exile.

The ban of excommunication against him was lifted in 1963.

The Last Days of Alcatraz

The tiny island in San Francisco Bay got its name from the way it was misspelled on an 1826 map. Originally known as "Isla de los Alcatraces," Spanish for "Island of Pelicans," Alcatraz lived up to its description if not its spelling, only pelicans being able to come and go freely during much of the island's history.

At one time, Alcatraz held Civil War prisoners of war, then political prisoners. Later, it became the home of notorious criminals such as Alfonso "Scarface" Capone, George "Machine Gun" Kelly, and Robert "Birdman" Stroud, who spent forty-two years of his life in solitary confinement, seventeen of them in Alcatraz.

The ultimate in maximum security penitentiaries, Alcatraz had a way of reducing even the most confident criminals to smaller-than-life size. Capone, who ruled the roost and even continued his old rackets while in federal prison in Atlanta, became, in the words of one inmate, "a weak little old man with a mop and pail" after being transferred to "the Rock." Other prisoners called him "greaseball" and Capone cringed in his cell for fear of being knifed to death.

The American equivalent of Devil's Island came into being in 1934, a year when many American citizens sincerely believed that hard core criminals were capable of taking over the entire country. In response to this feeling, U.S. Attorney General Homer Cummings proposed establishing "a special institution of maximum security and minimum privileges."

The concept was turned into reality with a vengeance. At Alcatraz, a no-talking rule was strictly enforced, guards were ordered to open fire at the least indication of trouble, shakedowns for weapons hidden in the five-by-nine cells were frequent, and little attempt was made at rehabilitation, only the best prisoners being allowed to work in the clothing factory or laundry as a means of easing their boredom.

During its 29-year history, at least 35 of the 1,576 inmates confined to Alcatraz tried to break out of the supposedly escape-proof structure. Seven men were shot or killed, 22 recaptured, and the rest presumably drowned in the bay's vicious ocean-bound currents.

The most sensational escape attempt was in 1946, when seven convicts stole weapons from a guard's gun cage and were hoping to take the launch to the mainland. But a guard taken hostage managed to hide his keys, leaving the convicts with no way out of the cell block. Rather than surrender, the prisoners chose to shoot it out.

A 3-day battle followed, with 100 combat Marines and a like number of San Francisco policemen being added to the Alcatraz guard staff before it was over.

By the early 1960s, the public was less concerned about putting criminals away forever and the federal government was most concerned about "the rock" falling to pieces. Conspiring with the Pacific Ocean's ravaging salt air, time had corroded the watch towers until it was unsafe for guards to remain in them during a high wind. The concrete walls of the prison had softened to the point where in 1962, three prisoners were able to "spoon" their way as far as the water's edge. One supporting pillar constructed in the early 1800s was cracked from floor to ceiling.

In addition to the looming $5 million repair bill, the federal government was saddled with a maintenance cost of $13 a day per prisoner (but counting everything spent on Alcatraz, including staff salaries and cost of hauling fresh water from the mainland, and dividing the total by the number of prisoners made the per-inmate annual cost just under $50,000). Deciding the price tag was simply too high, Prison Director James V. Bennet set a 1 July 1963 deadline for shutting down the facility.

Early that year, authorities began to move the population of Alcatraz to a new $10 million maximum security prison in Marion, Illinois. Handcuffed and bound in leg irons, the convicts were moved in stages onto the launch for the nine-minute ride to San Francisco. Mickey Cohen, the Los Angeles racketeer serving fifteen years for income tax evasion was transferred from the island on 27 February, reducing the prison population to 64.

The remaining convicts were moved in March of 1963. As it turned out, the very last man to be admitted to Alcatraz was also the last to leave. He was Number 1576, Frank C. Weatherman, 29, who had been convicted of robbery and sent to Alcatraz in December 1962. Some old time cons may have felt a twinge of nostalgia at leaving the old joint, but not Weatherman. "It's mighty good to get up and leave," said the last prisoner of Alcatraz as he departed.

Today, the island is a popular tourist attraction for San Francisco visitors, who tour the crumbling cell blocks where some of America's toughest hoods spent the worst years of their lives.

The Last Victim of the Boston Strangler

Although it may never be known for certain who killed all of the thirteen Boston area women — most of whom were strangled with stockings — the series of murders between 1962 and early 1964 ended after Albert H. DeSalvo was captured and brought to trial.

The stranglings began on 14 June 1962, when the body of Mrs. Anna Slesers, fifty-five, a seamstress, was found in her Back Bay apartment at 77 Gainsborough Street, where she lived alone. During the next year and a half, similar murders occurred at regular intervals, causing panic in the area and making the "Boston Strangler" a part of the folklore of crime.

On 4 January 1964, the thirteenth victim was discovered — Mary Ellen Sullivan, nineteen, a recent graduate of Barnstable High School who had found employment in Boston as a clerk in a finance company. Dr. Michael A. Luongo, Medical Examiner for the Police Department, said an autopsy showed she had been sexually molested before being strangled with a nylon stocking and two scarves.

Miss Sullivan turned out to be the last "Strangler" victim. Arrested late in 1964, was thirty-two-year-old Albert DeSalvo. A onetime handyman and boxer, DeSalvo was a husky man who wore his black hair slicked back in a pompadour and dressed neatly, usually in a freshly laundered white shirt.

DeSalvo was never brought to trial for the thirteen murders because the Commonwealth felt he would plead "insanity" (as a former mental patient), and thus get out of doing any time for the

245

crimes. Instead, he was tried and convicted in January of 1967, for a separate series of crimes, including burglary, assault, and sex offenses against four other women., Although defended by attorney F. Lee Bailey, who argued that his client should be found "not guilty by reason of insanity," DeSalvo was sentenced to life imprisonment.

A month after the sentencing, DeSalvo and two other convicts escaped from the Bridgewater State Hospital, where they were undergoing psychiatric tests. Recaptured soon after, DeSalvo became an inmate at Walpole State Prison. During his stay, police officials continued to debate whether or not he had killed all thirteen of the women. One story that persistently circulated said DeSalvo, rather than being the "Strangler" himself, had been tutored by another convict, for whom he was taking the blame. To other convicts, however, DeSalvo bragged that he had killed the women and went into details concerning the murders.

A drug dealer while at Walpole, DeSalvo was found in his cell on the morning of 27 November 1973, dead of multiple stab wounds. Like the women he probably murdered, he died a statistic: it was the eleventh slaying at Walpole State Prison in the previous two years.

The Last Whipping Post in America

A pre-Revolutionary War punishment used frequently until the early nineteenth century, when imprisonment was gradually substituted, flogging seemed to be on the way out by 1850. On 28 September of that year, the "cat o' nine tails" penalty was officially outlawed in the U.S. Navy and Merchant Marine.

After the Civil War, however, there was a revival of interest in the theory that severe punishment was the only way to deal with certain offenses. In particular, advocates of corporal punishment pointed to the growing number of wife-beating cases in America.

At least one state took drastic action. That was Maryland, where, in 1882 a law was passed which stated that husbands found guilty of punishing their wives with physical force "shall be subjected to whipping, not to exceed forty lashes, imprisonment in jail for a term not to exceed a year, or both."

Following passage of the law, many persons said it would never be carried out.

Then, on 1 December 1882, a man named Charles Foote was given seven lashes under the new law, but many shrugged their shoulders and said he didn't count. Foote was, after all, a black man.

Nearly three years later, the scoffers were still scoffing when twenty-five-year-old Henry A. Meyers, a bona fide white man, was arrested and charged with wife-beating. After returning home in a drunken state on the night of 9 June 1885, Meyers had attacked both his in-laws and wife, Sophia, beating her so badly that, according to a doctor who testified at the trial, "her most intimate friends would have recognized her with difficulty."

"A year in jail and twenty lashes," the judge intoned. Horrified, Meyers promptly appealed the case to the state Supreme Court.

In the meantime, a second candidate emerged in the person of forty-year old Frank Pyers, a Baltimore and Ohio brakeman and former Confederate soldier. On the night of 30 January 1885, Pyers, also returning home in a drunken state, had knocked his wife, Lillie, to the floor and kicked her. At the trial, Pyers protested that he had given the woman "a playful push" but on 18 June the judge sentenced him to six months in jail and fifteen lashes, the whipping to be carried out the very next day.

During the next twenty-four hours, preparations were made for the whipping premiere. Sheriff William Airey, who was selected to administer the punishment, held an informal press conference early the next morning. To the newspapermen, he displayed a trio of cowhide whips, two of which were comparatively light, the third about three feet long and considerably heavier.

Whether Pyers became a model husband after his punishment is not known. Flogging remained legal in Maryland until 1953, when it was finally repealed. In the meantime, other states which had reinstated the penalty also abolished it.

The exception was Delaware, which had an active flogging law on the books since 1656, when the first recorded public whipping was staged in Wilmington. Not only was the law on the books — it was used. In 1952, for example, thirty-year-old John F. Barbieri was found guilty of beating a woman and sentenced to receive twenty lashes and six months in jail.

Both sentences were carried out, the lashes being delivered on 16 June 1952 by Warden Edward H. Wilson of the New Castle County Workhouse. Barbieri, the third man in six years to receive the penalty in Delaware, remained silent, his hands tied atop a pole, during the forty-one seconds it took to administer the blows.

More than a decade passed before the law — once again declared legal by the Delaware Supreme Court in 1963 — was tested. That year an appropriately named Judge — Stewart Lynch — imposed the sentence on a man found guilty of robbery. (In ordering Talmadge R. Basler whipped, Lynch also sentenced him to twenty-five years in prison and fined him $500.) Basler appealed, however, and after the flogging penalty was reduced to 10 lashes, it was finally dropped. Eight years later, on 9 July 1972, Governor Russell W. Peterson signed a bill making the whipping post a thing of the past.

Even in Delaware.

The Last of the Barker Gang

The scourge of law enforcement officers during the 1930s, "Ma" Barker (nee Arizona Donnie Clark) and her four sons — Herman, Lloyd, Fred and Arthur — robbed with no apparent pattern from Texas to Illinois to Nebraska. Like her hero, Jesse James (whom she had once seen ride through Carthage, Missouri, with the Younger Brothers at his side), Ma Barker also showed a willingness to murder if it suited her.

She was vastly more successful than James, stealing at least $3 million during her long career, which might have been longer and more successful if her sons had not shown a penchant for getting caught. Herman, for example, was jailed in 1910 for petty theft and in 1915 for highway robbery. Ma got him off both times, but the family had to move to Oklahoma. In 1922, Lloyd was captured when trying to hold up a post office and was sentenced to twenty-five years in Leavenworth. About the same time, Fred was sent to the Kansas State Penitentiary, and Arthur to the Oklahoma State Prison for life, after killing a night watchman at a hospital he was burglarizing. To make matters even more depressing for Ma, Herman had a shoot-out with police offices while holding up a Missouri bank, and, rather than be caught, committed suicide.

The string of unhappy events did not break Ma Barker but changed her into a "veritable beast of prey," as J. Edgar Hoover so succinctly put it. At fifty-five, she was alone but not defeated. She left her husband, George, to open a hideout for escaped convicts and wanted criminals.

Fred was released in 1931 after Ma hounded his parole board, bringing along friend Alvin Karpis (known as "Old Creepy" because of his somber disposition and sinister smile), who was, if anything, even more crime-prone than the Barker clan itself.

Having a gang at her command, Ma immediately started a new campaign of robbing and killing. Heists followed in Fort Scott, Kansas, in May of 1932 (for $47,000), Concordia, Kansas ($250,000) in December of that year, and concluded in April of 1933 at Fairbury, Nebraska, where the bank there handed over $150,000.

Ma and Karpis then branched out to kidnapping, capturing and ransoming William A. Hamm, Jr., son of the wealthy St. Paul brewer, for $100,000. Edward G. Bremer, a Minneapolis banker, brought twice as much, but during the job Arthur left a fingerprint behind.

Hunted by the police after their pictures graced every post office in the Midwest (as well as the pages of *Liberty* and *True Detective* magazines), Karpis and Fred Barker decided to remove their fingerprints surgically. Joseph P. "Doc" Moran, the attending physician who caused the two lots of pain while leaving their prints intact, was taken for a ride and the gang scattered.

Ma and Fred, tracked down in Florida, were shot and killed by FBI agents on 16 January 1935. That same month, Arthur was arrested in Chicago and sent to Alcatraz. He was killed on 19 June 1939 while trying to escape. Lloyd, the last of the Barker family, was released from prison in 1947 and employed as assistant manager of a snack shop in rural Colorado until 1949, when he was killed by his wife.

Alvin Karpis, last of the gang, was finally caught by the police in 1936 in New Orleans. After thirty-two years in prison — twenty-five of them at Alcatraz — he was paroled in 1969 at the age of sixty-one. For the next decade, he lived in Canada and Spain, dying at Torremolinos, Spain, on 26 August 1979, of an overdose of sleeping pills.

The Last Use of The Pillory

Known in France as the *pillori* or *carcan* and in Germany as the *Pranger*, the pillory — or "stocks" — existed in England before the Norman Conquest, when it was known as the "stretch-neck." It usually consisted of a wooden frame erected on a stool with holes and folding boards for the admission of the head and hands. Devised for the special punishment of quacks and frauds, the pillory caused embarrassment and inconvenience rather than pain.

In 1287, Robert Basset, mayor of London, promoted the pillory's use for bakers who made bread of light weight, but the punishment was soon extended to those who engaged in other vices, such as playing with loaded dice, begging under false pretences, or "decoying children for the purpose of begging and practicing soothsaying and magic." In 1563, the pillory was used to punish a London woman who had meat in her tavern during the Lenten season.

Having been used for religious purposes, it was a simple matter for the pillory to become a political weapon. In 1637, a decree of the Star Chamber prohibited the printing of any book or pamphlet without a proper license from local officials. One of the first violators of that ordinance was Alexander Leighton, who for printing a pamphlet entitled *Zion's Pleas Against Prelacy*, was fined 10,000 pounds, then degraded from the ministry, pilloried, branded, whipped, had an ear cropped and a nostril slit.

A religious zealot, John Bastwick, was sentenced to the pillory and had his ears chopped off after distributing a pamphlet in which he called England's bishops "the tail of the beast." The palace yard was filled with people witnessing the punishment, but according to a contemporary account, "Dr. Bastwick was very merry. His wife, Dr. Poe's daughter, got on a stool and kissed him. His ears being cut off, she called for them, put them in a clean handkerchief, and carried them away with her."

THE LAST TIME WHEN

The most famous person to suffer the indignity of being pilloried was writer Daniel Defoe, who gave himself up in 1703 for having written an anti-establishment pamphlet entitled *The Shortest Way with the Dissenters*. From 29 to 31 July, Defoe daily stood in the pillory, but a sympathetic crowd threw garlands of flowers instead of rotten eggs and garbage at him. Meanwhile, Defoe's *Hymn to the Pillory* was passed around, the spectators laughing and repeating the lines:

> Tell them the men that placed him here
> Are scandals to the times;
> Are at a loss to find his guilt,
> And can't commit his crimes.

It was not always so pleasant being pilloried. Several people died during their punishments. And one man sentenced to the pillory during the time of Queen Elizabeth I was nearly hanged by accident when a rotten board broke beneath him, causing him to dangle precariously for several minutes before he could be extricated. On being freed, he brought suit against the authorities for having a dangerous pillory. Surprisingly, he recovered damages.

By the nineteenth century, use of the pillory was infrequent, its penalty being meted out only to those convicted of perjury. The last person actually committed to the device was Peter James Bossy, who was found guilty of "wilful and corrupt perjury" on 22 April 1830 and sentenced to seven years deportation. As Bossy was about to leave the court, however, Mr. Alley, the counsel for the prosecution, whispered something to the judge. Bossy was thereupon called back and informed that he was also sentenced to six months' imprisonment at Newgate, during which time he would be forced to stand for an hour in the pillory.

"Upwards of twelve years having elapsed since the punishment of the pillory has been inflicted in the metropolis," the *Times* of London felt obliged to report on 5 June of that year, "It is probable many of our readers are unaware of its precise nature; and the following description of the machine, therefore (the old one being no where to be found) which has been constructed for the purpose of carrying that part of the sentence into effect on the person of Bossy...may be interesting..." There followed a detailed description of the pillory's appearance and function, concluding that, "after being fixed in the machine, the culprit will be kept walking round the table...thus exhibiting himself in succession to the persons assembled in every direction."

Bossy's sentence was carried out on 22 June, 1830. In 1837, the pillory was abolished in Great Britain.

France did away with the pillory in 1832. Provisions for its use were eliminated in most of the U.S. by 1839, except for Delaware (1905).

250

258
St. Lawrence, while being burned on a gridiron: "My flesh is well-cooked on one side. Turn the other and eat."
295
St. Maximilian: "Give the new uniform you intended for me to the soldier who strikes me."
1431
Joan of Arc, burned at the stake: "Ah, Rouen! I have great fear that you are going to suffer by my death. Jesus! Jesus!"
1535
St. Thomas More, asked that blindfold be removed on the scaffol: "Let me safely to the gibbet, sir! On the downward voyage let me shift for myself."
1536
Anne Boleyn, to nervous companion: "Take courage. The executioner is an expert of many years' training...and my neck is very slender."
1553
John Dudley, Duke of Northumberland, convicted of conspiracy: "I have deserved a thousand deaths."
1555
Bishop Ferrar of St. David's, on being chained to the stake: "If I stir through the pains of my burning, believe not the doctrine I have taught."
1618
Sir Walter Raleigh, feeling the edge of the axe, said: "This is sharp medicine, but a sure remedy for all evils."
1626
Henri de Talleyrand de Chalais (to executioner): "Do not keep me in suspense!"
1685
James, Duke of Monmouth, about to be beheaded: "Let me feel the axe. I fear it is not sharp enough."

1701

Captain William Kidd, promised pardon but hanged by English: "This is a very fickle and faithless generation."

1780

John Andre, British spy in the American Revolution: "It will be but a momentary pang. I pray you bear witness that I met my fate like a brave man."

1793

Jean Francois Ducas, on the steps of the guillotine platform: "The convention has forgotten one decree...A decree on the indivisibility of heads and bodies."

Marie Antoinette, after stepping on toe of executioner: "Monsieur, I beg your pardon."

Louis Philippe Joseph, Duc d'Orleans, to his executioner, who wanted to remove his boots: "You can do that more easily to my dead body. Come — be quick!"

Marie Charlotte Corday, examining guillotine: "I have a right to be curious. I have never seen one before."

Countess DuBarry, to executioner: "You are going to hurt me. Oh, please don't hurt me."

1794

Georges Jacques Danton, about to be guillotined: "Show my head to the people. It is worth it."

1826

Michael Bestuzhev-Ryumin, Russian revolutionary, after the first rope broke: "Nothing succeeds with me. Even here I meet with disappointment."

1856

William Palmer, about to be hanged, as he stepped onto trapdoor: "Are you sure it's safe?"

1859

John Brown, American abolitionist, who was asked if he was tired: "No, but don't keep me waiting longer than necessary."

1865

John Wilkes Booth, after being shot by Union soldiers: "Tell my mother I died for my country...I thought I did for the best...Useless! Useless!"

Mary Surratt, convicted and sentenced to hanging for her part in the murder of Abraham Lincoln: "Please don't let me fall!"

1875

Daniel Evans, hanged with five others for murder, as he looked over the crowd: "There are worse men here than me."

Boudinet "Bood" Crumpton, western outlaw who committed murder while drunk: "Men, the next time you lift a glass of whiskey, I want you to look into the bottom of the glass and see if there isn't a hangman's noose in it, like the one here."

1878

Sam Bass, shot by Texas Rangers as he tried to rob a bank: "The world is bobbing around."

1879

Charles Peace, English criminal about to be hanged; "What is the scaffold? A short cut to heaven!"

1880

Charlie Bowdre, member of Billy the Kid's gang, just after being shot and falling on his face in front of a posse: "I wish...I wish...I wish..."

1882

Jesse James, putting up pictures on the wall, removed his guns just before he was shot by Bob Ford: "If anybody passes, they'll see me."

Charles Julius Guiteau, killer of President Garfield: "I am going to the Lordy."

1885

John H. (Doc) Holliday, after gunfight at O.K. Corral, dying of tuberculosis, said to nurse who removed his boots: "Damn it, put 'em back on!"

1886

Adolf Fischer, executed for instigation of Haymarket Riot: "Long live anarchy...This is the happiest moment of my life."

1895

John Wesley Hardin, shot from the back in saloon as he was rolling dice: "Four sixes to beat!"

1896

Cherokee Bill (Crawford Goldsby), hanged for murder: "The quicker this thing's over, the better."

1901

Leon Czolgosz, who assassinated President William McKinley: "I am not sorry."

1928

Arnold Rothstein, racketeer who was asked who had shot him: "Me mudder did it."

1930

Carl Pangram, murderer, to hangman: "Hurry it up, you Hoosier bastard. I could hang a dozen men while you're fooling around."

1931

Francis "Two-gun" Crowley, murderer-bank robber, sentenced to electric chair just before his twentieth birthday: "Give my love to mother."

1935

"Dutch" Schultz, gangster shot by Charlie "The Bug" Workman, became incoherent, saying: "Look out, Mama, look out for her. You can't beat him. Police, Mama, Mother, please take me out. I will settle the indictment. Shut up, you got a big mouth! Please help me up. Henry, Max, come over here. French-Canadian bean soup. I want to pay. Let them leave me alone.''

1936

Richard A. Loeb, murderer-kidnapper, after being slashed fifty-six times by fellow convict: "I think I'm going to make it."

1945

Benito Mussolini, as he faced firing squad: "No...No!"

Pierre Laval, Nazi conspirator, to fellow prisoner: "It lasts only a few seconds. It's like being killed in a bus accident on the Place de l'Opera." He then took poison but his stomach was pumped out so he could be shot. Faced with the need for a second group of last words, he said simply: "Vive la France!"

1946

Fritz Sauckel, war criminal hanged: "I pay my respects to American officers and American soldiers but not to American justice."

Julius Streicher, executed for war crimes: "Heil Hitler!"

1951

Hans Schmidt, adjutant of Buchenwald, executed as war criminal, to hangman: "Like me, you are obeying orders. I am dying innocent."

1954

Edward Scott ("Death Valley Scotty") a well-known fraud: "Got four things to live by: Don't say nothing that will hurt anybody. Don't give advice — nobody will take it anyway. Don't complain. Don't explain."

1955

Barbara Graham, asking if she could have a blindfold in the gas chamber: "I don't want to have to look at people."

1960

James W. Rodgers, facing a Utah firing squad, asked if he wanted anything as a last request: "Why, yes — a bulletproof vest."

1963

Frederick Charles Wood, murderer, strapped in the electric chair: "Gents, this is an educational project. You are about to witness the damaging effect electricity has on wood."

1977

Gary Gilmore, facing a Utah firing squad: "Let's do it..." Then: "Dominus vobiscum."

Chapter Eight

Lasts From Wars

Chronology

331 B.C.
The Persian Empire comes to an end with the defeat of Darius III at Arbela

202 B.C.
Zama is the final battle for the kingdom of Carthage, which is destroyed by the Romans.

146 B.C.
The Achaean League, a federation of Greek towns organized for mutual protection, is dissolved after Roman troops rout the league's soldiers near Corinth.

105 B.C.
At Arausio, in France, the Romans are defeated by Cimbri and Teutones. The disaster signals the end of Rome's citizen army. Henceforth the legions will be manned by full-time professional soldiers.

312 A.D.
The Praetorian Guard, select bodyguard of Roman emperors, is disbanded by Constantine I after more than three centuries of service.

378
Supreme for six centuries, the Roman legion is used, for the last time, the Romans being routed by Visigothic heavy cavalry at Adrianople.

451
(Sept. 20) Under General Aetius, the Romans win their last great battle, defeating Attila the Hun at Chalons-sur-Marne.

1066
(Oct. 14) Saxon rule in Britain comes to an end as William of Normandy successfully invades England.

1071
The last Saxon stronghold, the Isle of Ely, finally falls to William the Conqueror.

1291
(August) The ninth and last Crusade, proclaimed in 1267, comes to an end with the fall of the last Christian fortresses on the African mainland. (see p. 261)

1453
(July 17) At Castillon-le-Bataille, the French win the final battle of the Hundred Years War. (see p. 263)

1571
(Sept. 16) At Lepanto, the last sea battle is fought using vessels propelled by oars. (see p. 264)

1648
(Aug. 5) Under Louis II de Conde, the French defeat Spanish forces at Lens, concluding the Thirty Years War.

1685
(July 6) The last formal battle on English soil takes place at Sedgemoor as troops of King James II defeat and capture the Duke of Monmouth.

1743
(June 27) King George II is the last British monarch to personally lead his army into battle, his forces directing at Dettingen. (see p. 265)

1760
At Torgau, a town in the Prussian province of Saxony, Germany, Frederick the Great wins his last victory.

1781
(Sept. 8) At Eutaw Springs, S.C., the last battle in the Southern states of the American Revolution is fought.

1782
(Nov. 10) At Chillicothe, the last battle of the American Revolution takes place more than a year after the British defeat at Yorktown.

1783
(April 11) The official end to the American Revolution is declared. (see p. 266)

1805
(Dec. 2) At the battle of Austerlitz, the forces of the Holy Roman Empire are defeated by Napoleon, bringing the empire to an end.

1813
(Aug. 26-27) Napoleon's last significant victory is fought at Dresden, the French army of 97,000 routing a force of 200,000 Russians, Prussians, and Austrians.

1815
(Jan. 8) The last land battle of the War of 1812 is fought at New Orleans. (see p. 267)

1826
The island of Chiloe, off the coast of Chile, first settled by the Spanish in 1567, finally falls to South American revolutionaries.

1827
(Oct. 20) The last naval battle in which ships all have sails is fought in the Bay of Navarino near Greece. (see p. 269)

1833
The "Battle Axe Guard of Ireland," a military unit formed in 1520, is disbanded.

1842
The last armed resistance against the U. S. Army by Seminole Indians in Florida occurs.

1860
(Dec. 26) Ralph Farnum, last survivor of those who fought

at Bunker Hill, dies at the age of 104.

1861

(June 8) Tennessee becomes the eleventh and last state to secede from the Union.

1864

(Dec. 3) The last two corps are organized in the United States Army for service in the Civil War. They are the 24th Corps and 25th Corps (Colored).

1865

(March 18) The Congress of the Confederate States of America holds its last meeting.
(May 13) The last engagement of the American Civil War is fought near Brownsville, Texas. (see p. 270)
(May 26) The last Confederate general surrenders. He is General Edmund Kirby-Smith, who turns over his army to Major-General E.S. Canby at New Orleans.

1866

(April 2) It is the official last day of the Civil War in South Carolina, Virginia, North Carolina, Tennessee, Alabama, Mississippi, Louisiana, Arkansas and Florida. In Texas, the last day is 2 August. (see p. 270)

1869

(April 5) Daniel T. Blakeman, last survivor of the American Revolutionary Army, dies at the age of 109.

1871

Prussian General Adalbert von Bredow leads the last successful massed boot-to-boot cavalry charge, against French forces.

1905

(May 5) Hiram Cronk, the last survivor of the War of 1812, dies at the age of 105.

1918

(April 21) Baron Manfred von Richthofen, Germany's top ace of World War I, makes his last flight. (see p. 278)
(Aug. 5) The last air raid of World War I is carried out by German zeppelins.
(Aug. 9) After 140 days of continuous shelling by "Big Bertha," the last 42-centimeter howitzer round lands on Paris.
(September) British Field Marshal Edmund Henry Hyman Allenby leads the last successful charge of lancers, routing the Turks.
(Nov. 10) The last capital ship sunk during World War I, the *Britannia*, is torpedoed off Cape Trafalgar.
(Nov. 11) At 11:01 a.m., Private Henry Gunther of Company A, 313th Regiment, 79th Infantry Regiment, becomes the last Allied casualty of World War I. (see pp. 276-82)

1926

(Jan. 15) John Harling, last of the Light Brigade members who charged the Russians at

Balaklava, dies at the age of ninety-three. (see p. 274)
(July 20) Henry Thompson Douglas, the last surviving Confederate general, dies at eighty-eight.

1929
(Sept. 3) Owen Thomas Edgar, the last survivor of the Mexican War 1846-1848, dies at the age of ninety-eight.

1933
(April 13) Adelbert Ames, last surviving Union general, dies at the age of ninety-seven.

1937
(June 14) Mocker, last pigeon who served with the Allied armies during World war I, dies at the age of twenty-one. (see p. 279)

1941
(May) For the last time, biplanes are used in warfare.

1944
(Sept. 16) Having gained total air supremacy, the British order an end to the five-year blackout of London.
(Oct. 17) At the Battle of Surigao Strait, the naval maneuver called "crossing the T" is performed for the last time. (see p. 283)

1945
(March 29) The last V-rockets fall on London.
(May 7) On the next-to-last day of actual fighting in Europe, RAF coastal command aircraft sink their last U-boat of World War II.
(Aug. 15) The last Japanese plane destroyed in World War II is shot down just five minutes before the war is declared over. (see p. 282-85)

1946
(March) Estelle Ann Morgan, the daughter of a soldier who had fought in the battle of New Orleans, receives her final pension check, the last installment paid on the War of 1812.
(April 18) The League of Nations has its twenty-first and last session. (see p. 286)

1947
(Sept. 18) Kenneth C. Royall becomes the last United States Secretary of War as the new Department of Defense consolidates the Navy, Army, and Air Force into a single administrative unit.

1949
Clothes rationing, instituted at the start of World War II, finally ends in Great Britian.
(Aug. 28-31) The last encampment is held by the Grand Army of the Republic (Union) survivors of the Civil War.
(September) The Berlin Airlift, begun in June 1948 when the USSR tried to seal off the city, comes to an end. During the fifteen-month

airlift, 277,000 flights were made at three-minute intervals to supply Berliners with food and fuel.

1951
(Sept. 22) Jacob Horner, last member of George Custer's Seventh Cavalry, dies at the age of ninety-six. (see p. 274)

1952
(Dec. 1) The last surviving Allied leader of World War I, Vittorio Emanuele Orlando of Italy, dies at the age of ninety-two. (see p. 280)

1953
(January) The last propeller-driven fighter plane to be made in the United States, the F4U Corsair, is finally discontinued. (see p. 288)

1956
(Aug. 2) Albert Woolson, the last Union soldier of the Civil War, dies at the age of 109.

1959
(Sept. 1) Formed in 1897 during the last years of Queen Victoria's reign, the Third Battalion of Great Britain's Coldstream Guards is disbanded.
(Dec. 11) Walter Williams, a former Southern soldier, becomes the last survivor of the American Civil War, dying at the age of 117.

1960
Great Britain ends its peacetime military draft system.

1961
(June 15) The United States Navy officially abandons any further use of balloons as war craft.

1962
The U.S. Sixth Cavalry, formed in 1861 and once commanded by General John J. Pershing, is disbanded.

1968
(May 3) Edwin C. Parsons, last ace of the famous Lafayette Escadrille of World War I, dies at the age of seventy-five. (see p. 281)

1969
After serving in the Vietnamese War, the *New Jersey*, last U.S. battleship to see battle, is deactivated.

1971
Josiah Red Wolf, last Indian survivor of the Nez Perces War of 1877, dies at the age of ninety-eight. (see p. 275)

1971
(Nov. 18) The celebrated and very-vulnerable French Maginot Line of World War II comes to an end as parts of the fortress are auctioned to the highest bidders.

1973
(June 18) Fredrak Fraske, last white veteran of the Indian Wars, dies at the age of 101. (see p. 275)
(Aug. 14) The last U. S. bombs fall on Indochina,

ending the war which officially ended on January 27.

1975
The last twelve surviving vessels of San Diego's mothball
fleet, including the cruisers
Galveston and *Los Angeles*,
are either sold at auction or
towed out to sea and sunk.

1979
(Oct. 12) With the death of

Rene Gagnon, John Bradley
becomes the last survivor of
the Iwo Jima flag raising.
(see p. 287)

1980
(January) The last B-29
bomber of the United States
Air force is flown to England
to be put in a British air
museum.

The Last Crusade

Most Christians prefer to think about the First Crusade (from the
Spanish *cruzada*, "marked with the cross") because it brought a
certain amount of glory and success to the forces of Christendom in
their battle to capture the holy city of Jerusalem from the Muslims.
After the first Crusade, however, it was generally a downhill series
of battles and ignominities for the Christian armies. Altogether, during the period 1095 A.D. to 1291, there were eight Crusades, some
highlights of which include:

The First Crusade began in November 1095 when Pope Urban II
called for a papal army to go to Jerusalem and recover the Holy
Sepulchre. Volunteer soldiers turned up from everywhere in the
Western world, led by dukes of France and Italy as well as local
military heroes. These first crusaders reached Jerusalem on 7 June
1099, captured the city on 15 July and promptly massacred countless Muslims and Jews.

The Second Crusade was brought about after 1144, when the city
of Odessa was recaptured by Muslim forces. A new band of crusaders left for the Holy Land in the spring of 1147, but was ambushed
by the Turks near Dorylaeum on 25 October 1147, decimating the
force, made up largely of the armies of King Conrad III of Germany. When the Christian forces finally recovered a year later, they
laid siege to Damascus but gave up after four days, on 28 July,
1148, having run out of water.

The Third Crusade was called for after Jerusalem itself was
recaptured by the Muslims on 2 October 1187. The leaders were
Richard I of England and Holy Roman Emperor Frederick I
Barbarossa. In May 1189, however, Frederick was drowned in the
Saleph or Calycadnus River near Seleucia and most of his army
returned home without fighting a battle. King Richard, who loved

261

nothing better than killing Muslims, fought on by himself, recovering some of the territory lost, thereby making sure more men could be lost in future crusades.

The Fourth Crusade was the brainchild of Thibaut III, count of Champagne, who was blessed by Pope Innocent II as he set out for the Holy Land. Thibaut ran into trouble in Venice, however, when the doge there, Enrico Dandolo, insisted that the crusaders pay their transportation fees in advance. As a result, the army spent the winter stranded at Zara, a town Dandolo wanted conquered in exchange for the money owed him. Later, for reasons which are unclear at best, the crusaders went to Constantinople and sacked the city, despite the fact that it was allied with Christian forces.

The Fifth Crusade followed inevitably, since the fourth was such a disaster. The expedition set off in 1218, its purpose to capture the Egyptian city of Damietta and exchange it later for Jerusalem. After seventeen months, Cardinal Pelagius of Albano, the Papal legate, finally took the city, but when he managed to get his army trapped by a Nile flood, he had to exchange the safety of his men for Damietta.

The Sixth Crusade was led by Holy Roman Emperor Frederick II, who set out with great pomp in September of 1227 but soon turned back after becoming seasick. The pope excommunicated him, Frederick attempted to redeem himself by continuing the Crusade even though disgraced. Using diplomacy brilliantly, he managed to negotiate a treaty with the Egyptian sultan in which he regained Jerusalem, Bethlehem, and Nazareth plus a guaranteed peace of ten years. Pope Gregory IX was not impressed, contending that Muslims should be fought, not negotiated with. He refused to lift the ecclesiastical ban on Frederick.

The Seventh Crusade might never have happened had not King Louis IX of France fallen ill and promised to recover the Holy Land if he got well. As luck would have it, he survived and set out for Egypt, his plan — not exactly original — being to capture Damietta and exchange it for Jerusalem. He was careful to avoid Nile River floods but was captured in April of 1250 and was forced to exchange himself for Damietta a month later.

The Eighth and last Crusade was proclaimed in 1267 by none other than Louis IX, who died three years later. The Muslim forces then proceeded to recapture all the territory taken by the Christians, the last fortresses on the African mainland falling in August, 1291. After that, several popes attempted to stir up interest in more crusades, but in general no one was buying. There were additional expeditions in the years after final crusade, in 1344 and 1345, which ended in defeat. The last major attempt by Christian forces to stem the Ottoman tide came in 1444, when Ladislaus II, king of Poland, was defeated and killed by the Turks at Varna.

The Last Battle of the Hundred Years War

Not long after the last crusaders dragged their spears and lances back from the Holy Land, a major protracted conflict between France and England began. Called the "Hundred Years War" because it lasted 116 years (with two intermissions), the struggle began in 1337 when Edward II of England assumed the title "King of France," claiming that certain parts of that nation belonged to his country as a result of prior claims and agreements. Philip VI of France, predictably, was not impressed. Several years of haggling followed until 1346, when Edward invaded Normandy and beseiged Calais.

The first major battle of the war was on 26 August 1346 at Crecy, where rows of coordinated English archers were attacked by the cream of Philip's army, all wearing heavy coat armor. The longbow-versus-feudal-knight confrontation was a disaster for the French, with more than 1,500 of their soldiers dying before nightfall. In 1347, Edward took Calais and might have reaped even greater rewards had not the Black Plague intervened.

With one-fifth to one-third of the two nations' populations in the throes of the Plague, no major battles were fought until 1354. The English managed to consolidate their position in France until August of 1415, when Henry V set sail for France with an army of 12,000. The most daring of the English leaders, Henry promptly engaged the French at Agincourt, which turned out to be the last and most decisive battle of English archery.

Fortunately for France, Henry V died in 1422, and young Joan of Arc started hearing voices shortly afterward. In 1429, she led sorties that caused the siege of Orleans to be lifted and won another victory at Patay. But she failed in a surprise attack on Paris, fell into disfavor, was tried and convicted for heresy and burned at the stake on 29 May 1431. She had aroused a spirit of French nationalism, however, which together with the logistics of carrying on a war far removed from England, caused the tide to change. As a result, most of the British forces had been expelled by 1451. Bordeaux fell to the French on 30 June of that year, Bayonne on 20 August.

Some French noblemen, especially those of the province of Gascon, remained loyal to the British, however, and they journeyed to London in order to urge continued support. The result was the creation of a new expeditionary force headed by Talbot, earl of Shrewsbury, the last surviving general of King Henry V.

In October of 1452, Talbot came ashore in the Gironde River with a force of about 3,000 men. Most of the population in nearby towns promptly joined the British side, overthrowing the French garrisons. But during the winter and spring, France was able to pour every available soldier southward. In beseiging the town of

Castillon-le-Bataille, the French worked out sophisticated trench systems and gun emplacements in order to offset Britain's superior archers, who were of limited use against heavily-fortified, dug-in troops. At first Talbot tried to outwait or outflank the French; then, realizing time was not on his side, he ordered a frontal assault. The head of his main column was quickly torn to pieces by French artillery and Talbot himself, overthrown by a roundshot, went down outside the trench. The British line broke then and was overwhelmed by counter-attacking troops. Thus the last battle of the Hundred Years War ended on 17 July 1453. The last English outpost on the continent, however, Le Cateau, was not retaken by the French until 1559.

The Last Battle of the Thirty Years' War

Called the Thirty Years' War for obvious reasons, the conflict that broke out in 1618 was actually the first general European war. Involving religious, dynastic, and territorial problems, the struggle began in May of that year when two Catholic officers were thrown from a window by Protestant members of the Bohemian parliament in Prague. This brazen "defenestration of Prague" soon had nearly every country on the continent choosing sides. The French, Swedes, Danes, English and German Protestants joined forces against the Holy Roman Empire, which was made up of Catholics from Germany, Italy, and Spain.

A truly debilitating contest for all concerned, the war ended only after 7 million were dead and most of the leaders had died off or been killed in battle. The war also created such privation that cannibalism became widely practiced. At first only the dead bodies of executed criminals were eaten, but on at least one occasion in Alsace, prisoners were killed and eaten.

Finally, at the French town of Lens, it all came to an end on 5 August 1648, when the forces of Louis II de Conde defeated the Spanish army. Peace negotiations, which had started in 1640, were brought to a successful conclusion known as the Peace of Westphalia. Germany did not recover for two centuries.

The Last Sea Battle of Oar-Propelled Vessels

Nearly three centuries after the last Crusade, the papacy was still locked in combat with Muslim forces. For Christendom, the problem was that by the mid-sixteenth century, the Turkish fleet was in danger of taking over the entire Mediterranean and therefore destroying or severely limiting Western trade. This made the "Muslim problem" not just a matter of mere religious differences; now the Infidel was about to hit the Christian nations where it really hurt — in the pocketbook.

Well aware of the growing Turkish threat on the high seas, Pope Pius V tried several times to form an alliance of Christian powers. At first, he was notably unsuccessful. Spain was broke and distracted by Andalusian revolts; France was simply not interested in fighting the Turks; Venice, formerly the guardian of the West on the Mediterranean but lately gone to seed, distrusted Spain and had a different set of military priorities. As the allies bickered and did nothing, Turkey captured the island of Cyprus and moved its fleet into the Adriatic. Finally, on 25 May 1571, the pope persuaded Venice and Spain to forget their differences and sail against the Muslims.

Assembling at Messina in Sicily, the allied fleet sailed on 16 September for the Gulf of Patras, near Lepanto, Greece, where the Turks awaited them. The Christian fleet was somewhat larger, consisting of 207 oar-propelled galleys, six large Venetian galleasses (slightly larger ships than galleys) and some auxiliary vessels. Led by Don John of Austria, half brother of Spanish King Philip II, and Admiral Andrea Doria, the allied fleet attacked boldly, forcing the Turks to give way in the center and on the right after about four hours' fighting. By day's end, the allies had captured 117 galleys, liberated 15,000 Christian slaves, killed 8,000 Turks and sank or burned 50 galleys. Among the 8,000 allied wounded was Miguel de Cervantes.

Pope Pius V was ecstatic when he heard of the result, holding thanksgiving prayers at St. Peter's and quoting the Fourth Gospel line, "There was a man sent by God, whose name was John."

Soon afterward, the Christian leaders began to argue and lost the territories they had taken in the wake of the great naval victory. The battle of Lepanto remained a symbol of inspiration, however, in that it was the first time a Christian fleet had defeated a Muslim one. It was also the last major engagement of oar-propelled vessels.

The Last British Monarch to Lead an Army

One of the less romantic British kings, George II (1683-1760) was the second Hanoverian import, a man of coarse tastes who used to boast in his German guttural that he "didn't like poetry and didn't like painting." He did love opera, however, especially the works of another German import, George Frederick Handel. He was also a good soldier, distinguishing himself at the battle of Oudenaarde in 1708.

Being of restricted interests and narrow vision, George II found the discipline of military affairs both stimulating and comforting, and ran his own life with the precision of a drill sergeant, committing to memory everything he could learn about the backgrounds of military units throughout Europe. He was particularly addicted to parades, holding and attending them at the least provocation.

It is hardly surprising, then, that George II did not shrink from battle when war broke out with France. Leaving for the Continent as soon as possible, on 19 June 1743 he took personal command of the British army, an outnumbered force of 37,000 weary men short on rations and forage for their horses. Moreover, the British position was not a favorable one near the village of Dettingen.

On 27 June, as the opposing armies groped toward each other, George II rode from the rear guard position directly to the front. Dismounting and drawing his sword he supposedly shouted, "Now, boys, now for the honor of England, fire, and behave bravely, and the French will soon run." Another, less glamorous, report from the battlefield told that after George II had his horse shot from under him, he leaped to his feet and cried out, "Now I know I shall not run away!"

Whatever the exact circumstances, George and the British Army were victorious, successfully driving all French forces from Germany. Returning home, George II was received with an enthusiasm he had never experienced before. Two years later, when the Jacobite invasion threatened, he once again showed his nerve by refusing to leave London for a safer place.

Lasts From the American Revolution

Although Lord Cornwallis surrendered to American forces at Yorktown on 19 October 1781, fighting continued along the eastern seaboard until 27 August 1782, when a skirmish on the banks of the Combahee river in South Carolina between small bands of recalcitrants ended hostilities.

Farther west, an attack on 18 August 1782 by loyalists and Indians against American frontiersmen at Blue Licks, Fayette County, Virginia (now Kentucky), was followed by a retaliatory raid three months later. Collecting a band of riflemen, George Rogers Clark attacked the Shawnee Indian village of Chillicothe on 10 November. That concluded the fighting, Congress proclaiming an official end to the Revolution on 11 April 1783. Two months later, General George Washington's army was disbanded and all soldiers discharged by 3 November. Washington's last day as commander-in-chief of the Continental Army was 19 December 1783, when he resigned his commission at Annapolis, Maryland, then capital of the United States.

As the new nation approached its centennial celebration, a great amount of interest was generated in finding out how many members of the Revolutionary army were still around. The last survivor of those who fought at Bunker Hill, Ralph Farnum, died at the age of 104 in Acton, Maine on 26 December 1860. His passing left about a dozen known ex-soldiers and drummer boys of the Revolution, most of whom were tracked down and interviewed by the history-minded

Reverend E. B. Hillard during the early years of the Civil War — just in time as it turned out, as the years 1863 and 1864 were the last for no less than eight of the centenarians.

Of those who remained, one of the more interesting was listed variously as Alexander Milliner or Maroney, a gentleman of either 100 or 104 in the year 1864 when he was interviewed for the last time. Whatever his real name, he had served in both the Revolution (as a drummer boy in Washington's guard) and the War of 1812 (as a seaman on the frigate *Constitution*). Unfortunately, Hillard lost track of Milliner/Maroney and was unable to report on the date of his death.

Another interesting survivor, Samuel Downing, had enlisted in a regiment of the New Hampshire Line in July, 1780, four months before his sixteenth birthday. He had neglected to tell his parents, who concluded he had fallen off a dock and drowned. Recalling the end of the war and the feelings it inspired in his fellow soldiers, Downing said, "When peace was declared, we burnt thirteen candles in every hut, one for each state." Returning to Saratoga County, New York, Downing became a farmer and remained active until the fall before his 100th birthday, when in one day he pulled, trimmed and loaded fifteen bushels of carrots into his cellar. On his reaching the age of 100 in 1864, he was given a 100-gun salute by his neighbors.

A bit more than two years later, on 19 February 1867, Downing passed away, one of the more celebrated, but not the final survivor of the revolutionary forces. That honor, according to the U. S. Veterans Administration, went to Daniel T. Blakeman of Freedom, Cattaraugus County, New York, who died on 5 April 1869 at age 109. As the final pensioned soldier of the war for independence, he also represented the last direct U.S. Government payment on the conflict which began nearly a century earlier.

The last true daughter of the American revolution was Annie Wright Gregory, whose father had been a drummer boy in Washington's army at Valley Forge. He had sired his last daughter in 1843 when he was in his eighties. Mrs. Gregory survived until the age of 100, dying in December of 1943.

Lasts From the War of 1812

It took the U. S. Government 134 years to pay all the expenses of its second conflict with Great Britain, the War of 1812, which came to an official end on 14 December 1814. On 8 January 1815, the last battle of the war was fought at New Orleans, forces there not yet having received the news of the armistice. Thus, except for those who were killed or wounded in the fierce fighting, the American victory was significant mainly in solidifying the reputation of General Andrew Jackson, who later became President of the U.S.

Not much interest was shown in tracking down or honoring the survivors of the War of 1812. The last warrior, Hiram Cronk, passed away almost unnoticed on 13 May 1905 at the age of 105. The U. S. Government continued to pay pensions to relatives of 1812 veterans, however. One of the most expensive allowances went to Caroline Poulder King, the last surviving widow of an 1812 combatant. In 1869, Mrs. King, who was then 19, married Darius King, then in his early seventies. Following her husband's death eighteen years later, Mrs. King continued to receive benefits until 30 June 1938, when she died at age 89. During the nearly half-decade of widowhood, she received a total of $14,149, or approximately $262 for each of the 54 days her husband served in the army.

But the final pension installment on the War of 1812 was not paid until 1946, to Esther Ann Hill Morgan, eighty-eight, the daughter of a soldier who had fought in the battle of New Orleans. She died in Independence, Oregon, in March.

The Last Frigates

During the final decade of the eighteenth century, in an effort to upgrade its power on the high seas, the United States Navy commissioned the building of six fighting ships of the line, each to be as fast as possible while carrying a great weight of armament. To accomplish this, it was proposed that the new frigates be constructed along the lines of the streamlined Baltimore clipper ships, which were then coming into their own as sleek merchantmen.

Named the *President*, *United States*, *Chesapeake*, *Constellation*, *Constitution*, and *Congress*, the vessels were about 200 feet long and capable of better than 13 knots while carrying 44 guns, a combination that made them formidable. Their launchings were delayed for political and financial reasons, but all were ready by April of 1800, when the *President* finally put to sea. Their presence helped bring about successful campaigns against the Barbary pirates and British during the tempestuous first fifteen years of the nineteenth century.

Not long after the War of 1812, however, the highly-praised frigate fleet began to be broken up. First to go was the *President*, which had fought one of the war's last sea actions, its crew surrendering to the British on 15 February 1815 after a running battle with Royal Navy ships *Endymion*, *Tenedos* and *Majestic*. Taken as a prize of victory, the *President* was scrapped during the winter of 1817-18 at the tender age of eighteen.

Next to go was the *Chesapeake*, whose crew had captured five British merchantmen during the war but had then fallen into enemy hands following a furious battle with the frigate *Shannon*. Taken into the Royal Navy, the *Chesapeake* was broken up in 1820.

Fourteen years later, as the age of pure sailing vessels was coming to an end, the *Congress* was scrapped by the United States government; then, in 1865, the *United States* was demolished, leaving only "Old Ironsides," the *Constitution*, (which survived early destruction largely as a result of Oliver Wendell Holmes' poetic appeal in her behalf) and the *Constellation*. Miraculously, both vessels have been preserved, the *Constitution* at Boston and the *Constellation* at Baltimore. Launched on 7 September, 1797, just six weeks before "Old Ironsides," the *Constellation* is the U. S. Navy's oldest ship.

The last surviving British frigate of the period, the 1,077-ton *Unicorn*, was constructed in 1824, and has been preserved at Dundee, Scotland.

The Last Battle of Sailing Ships

Although steam engines were developed early in the nineteenth century, few navies of the world rushed to adapt them to their uses, military leaders, then as now, preferring to hold onto proven equipment rather than experimenting. As a result, vessels depending wholly on sail for speed and maneuverability continued to dominate the high seas to such an extent that when the combined fleets of five nations fought at the bay of Navarino in 20 October 1827, not one of the ninety-one ships was powered by steam.

The battle pitted the Turkish and Egyptian fleets against a much smaller force of British, French and Russian ships. The Greeks, who were fighting for their independence from Turkey, were only minimally involved in the action, mostly because the battle of Navarino came about accidentally during what was supposed to be a truce.

In September of 1827, the Turkish commander, Ibrahim Pasha, had anchored his fleet in the Bay of Navarino on the west coast of Greece, drawing the ships into a three-lined horseshoe formation in order to provide maximum security while peace talks continued. Leaving two frigates to keep watch on Pasha, British Vice-Admiral Sir Edward Codrington ordered the rest of the Allied fleet withdrawn from the bay.

A settlement might have been reached during this lull had it not been for the arrival of a Greek naval division commanded by a British officer, Lord Cochrane. Pasha reacted angrily to the Greek presence in the bay, dispatching part of his force to chase them away, an action which caused Codrington to order several ships forward. The Turks withdrew but retaliated by bombarding the Greek mainland.

On 20 October Codrington decided to apply pressure by leading a twenty-six vessel force into the harbor of Navarino, his eighty-four gun flagship *Asia* dropping anchor intimidatingly close to the Turkish and Egyptian horseshoe. As the rest of the Allied fleet pulled within pistol shot of Pasha's formation and dropped anchor, an eerie silence settled over the waters.

At this point, a minor incident provided the spark igniting full scale hostilities — Turkish sailors fired on a small British boat from the *Dartmouth* which was moving about on a routine mission, killing and officer and causing the crew of the *Dartmouth* to respond with covering fire. Like an echo of thunder rolling round the bay, one ship after another picked out a target and opened fire, Turkish shore batteries adding to the thick haze of smoke and resultant confusion.

Despite their 1,962-1,294 gun advantage, the Turks and Egyptians were so overwhelmed by the disciplined European fire that in less than two hours they began scuttling their vessels, beaching and burning them even after Admiral Codrington sent envoys to explain that it was not his intention to destroy or capture the enemy fleet.

Ironically, the political situation at the time was so confused that instead of honoring the man who defeated the Turks and Egyptians, the British Government disowned Admiral Codrington and recalled him to London. The Greeks, meanwhile, disregarding the fact that the French and British were fighting for their freedom, sent ships to capture Allied vessels entering the Bay of Navarino.

Thus ended the last battle of sailing ships. Most of the Russian fleet, it should be added, could not even reach the battle area, the wind having suddenly dropped, leaving their ships just beyond firing distance.

Some Civil War Lasts

The "War Between the States," or the American Civil War, of 1861 to 1865, managed to preserve the Union, but only at a frightening cost in lives and future animosity. When the fighting finally wound down, both North and South were drained, although scattered diehard military action continued for some weeks after the informal Southern surrender of 9 April 1865, when General Robert E. Lee and 27,800 Rebel troops laid down their arms at Appomattox Court House, Virginia. Nine days later, General Joseph E. Johnston surrendered 31,200 men to General William Sherman at Durham Station, North Carolina.

The last major engagement of the war took place on 12 May 1865 near Kingston, Georgia, where Confederates surrendered to Union forces. At the same time, a skirmish was in progress at Palmito Hill, near Brownsville, Texas, between 400 Southerners and 500 Union soldiers who were unaware of the truce because of poor communication. The Rebels finally yielded on 13 May.

The last soldiers killed — not counting those who died as a result of lingering wounds — were three rebels who attacked about fifty Union troops near Floyd, Virginia, on 22 May 1865. Two Union soldiers fell, after which the rest of the Northerners chased the rebels six miles to a cemetery where a shootout ensued. Although the Union soldiers tried to get the Southerners to surrender, they would not do so, firing angrily at their pursuers. A burst of more than 300 shots killed the three on the spot, and there they were buried.

Because it involved so many men and touched so many lives, the American Civil War rivaled the Revolutionary conflict as a nostalgia event. Consequently, a great deal of interest was shown in finding out who would be the last survivor of the four million veterans of the war. (Some recalcitrant Southerners maintained that the war's final outcome could be determined only by the allegiance of the last remaining soldier. No one really accepted this, of course, but the challenge added a measure of morbid curiosity concerning which side would have the last survivor.)

By 1950, the first year since 1866 without an encampment of the Grand Army of the Republic, less than a dozen Civil War vets survived, the South having a solid numerical advantage. That year, however, saw the death of John Thomas "Uncle Johnny" Graves, 108, for whose sole benefit the Missouri State Confederate Home was maintained at an annual cost of $25,000. The next year, James W. Moore of Alabama died, followed in 1952 by P. R. Crump, 104, who had enlisted in the 10th Alabama Regiment 99 years before and witnessed Lee's surrender.

By 1953, four Southerners survived along with a pair of Union veterans. Then, on 16 March, James A. Hard III died at Rochester, New York, reducing the Northern force to a single man. Thousands lined the sidewalks to view Hard's funeral procession and school children were given an hour off from classes in order to pay their respects to the city's most celebrated figure. During the funeral services the City Hall bell, which had not sounded since V-J Day eight years previously, tolled thirteen times.

The next Civil War survivor to pass on was Rebel Thomas Evans Riddle, 107, in April of 1954, leaving the South with a three-to-one possibility of "winning" the war by diehard standards.

Two years passed with no further casualties, 109-year old Albert Woolson hanging on for the Union while the Confederacy was represented by John D. Salling (110), William A. Lundy (108), and Walter Williams (114). With the centenary of the Civil War only five years away, Congress in July of 1956 passed a law directing the Secretary of the Treasury to prepare gold medals honoring the remaining veterans of both North and South. That month, when it became obvious that Albert Woolson's lung condition had worsened, putting him on the critical list, Representative John A. Blatnick of Minnesota, Woolson's native state, asked that the process of designing and issuing the medals be accelerated so that Woolson could receive his while still alive.

271

Hastening the bureaucratic process was impossible, however. Woolson, the last Union veteran, died on 2 August 1956, too soon to be honored with the Congressional medals. That day, at the headquarters of the Grand Army of the Republic in Jamestown, New York, Miss Cora E. Gillis closed out the official record book of that venerable organization before leaving for Woolson's funeral in Duluth.

The three Southern soldiers followed soon afterward. Lundy died in September of 1957, followed on 16 March 1959 by John Salling, and on 11 December 1959 by Walter Williams. To commemorate the passing of Williams, President Eisenhower declared a day of national mourning, Fourth Army units led a parade in Franklin, Texas, and more than 5,000 persons filed by to gaze at the 117-year-old lying in state. Said U.S. Senator Ralph Yarborough, "He was the last survivor of a lost cause, the sole remaining soldier of a whole civilization. The combatants are all gone now, but we stand in awe of the bravery on both sides."

The noble sentiments disconcerted some lovers of accuracy, for even as Williams was being eulogized historians and researchers were in the process of showing that the wily old gentleman may have fabricated the entire story, that he was actually only five years old when the Civil War broke out. After a brief furor, however, the apparent subterfuge was soon forgotten. The nation needed a hero, Eisenhower said it was all right, and the evidence against Williams was not concrete. Thus, there was no serious challenge to the authenticity of Williams' claim.

Some Other Lasts From the Civil War —

Last active veteran was Major General John L. Clem, the "drummer boy of Chickamauga," who stowed away at the age of ten so that he could be with the Rebel troops at Covington, Kentucky. He remained in the Army until 1916.

The *last veteran to become a father* was Confederate George Isaac Hughes, who shocked the medical world by siring a son at age ninety-four and a daughter at ninety-six. Hughes died in May of 1937 at the age of ninety-seven. His second wife, aged thirty-nine, was at his bedside. He also had sixteen children by his first wife.

The *last surviving Confederate general* was Henry Thompson Douglas, who built the defenses of Richmond which withstood numerous assaults. After the war, Douglas helped construct the New York City subway system. He fought as an officer in the Spanish-American War and attempted to join up for World War I. He died on 20 July 1926 at age eighty-eight.

The *last surviving Union general* was Adelbert Ames, who died 13 April 1933 at the age of ninety-seven. A member of the 1861 class at West Point, Ames was a twenty-nine-year-old major general when the war ended. He was elected to the U. S. Senate in 1869 and, despite being a Northerner, served as Governor of Mississippi in 1873.

Some Robert E. Lee Lasts

The greatest hero of the Confederacy, General Robert E. Lee led his outnumbered army to many victories during the first two years of the Civil War.

His last great offensive victory took place on 1-2 May 1863 at Chancellorsville, Virginia. With an army of 60,000, Lee was opposed by Union General Joe Hooker, who had 120,000 troops at his command. Keeping only 10,000 entrenched with him opposite Hooker's front, Lee sent General "Stonewall" Jackson, under cover of the woods, around Hooker's right. It was a dangerous plan because it split Lee's forces, but it worked. On the evening of 2 May Hooker's army was surprised and routed. Jackson was killed after the battle, but the Union forces were driven back across the Rappahannock River.

After the war, Lee became president of Washington College (later Washington and Lee) and there spent the remainder of his days teaching the youth of Virginia to be good Americans.

His health failing in 1870, Lee wrote the last letter of his life on the morning of 28 September. It was sent to Samuel Tagart, a Baltimore attorney and railroad man whose family was friendly with Lee's.

"In answer to your question," Lee wrote, "I reply that I am much better. I do not know whether it is owing to having seen you and Dr. Buckler last summer, or to my visit to the Hot Springs. Perhaps both, but my pains are less and my strength greater. In fact, I suppose I am as well as I shall be. I am still following Dr. B's directions and in time I may improve still more...." Later on in the letter, Lee added, "Give my regards to Mrs. Tagart and remember me to all friends, particularly Mr. Sam Smith. Tell Charlie Pitts his brother is well and handsome and I hope that he will study, or his sweethearts in Baltimore will not pine for him long."

While the letter was Lee's last, it was not his last signature. Just minutes after he sealed up the envelope, he autographed a small portrait of himself for Percy Davidson, a Washington College sophomore who requested the signature as a favor for his girlfriend.

Fatally stricken soon afterward, Lee's last words were appropriately military: "Strike the tent."

Lee, who had been deprived of his citizenship because of his decision to join the Confederacy, did not have his citizenship restored until 22 July 1975. He had made his original appeal for restoration 110 years before.

The Last of the Light Brigade

Certainly one of the most overpublicized military actions of all time — thanks largely to Alfred Lord Tennyson's poem — was the 1854 charge of the Light Brigade during the Crimean War.

Led by James Russell Brudenell, Seventh Earl of Cardigan, the British cavalry charge at Balaklava, six miles southeast of Sevastopol, was a brilliant manuever, except that it took place in the wrong direction and was aimed at the wrong enemy units. The original plan was to use the Light Brigade to harass isolated Russian troops who were slowly withdrawing on one flank; but through a mixup in relaying the final orders, the attack took place in the center of the line against well-fortified positions. About forty-percent of the brigade was lost, a figure that might have been considerably higher had it not been for a timely supporting charge by the French Chasseurs d'Afrique. The British display of courage caused General Pierre Bosquet to remark, "It's magnificent but it's not war."

Those Light Brigade chargers who survived Cardigan's folly, however, had much to tell their grandchildren during the decades that followed. The last member of this select group was John Harling, who died on 15 January 1926, aged ninety-three. Queen Victoria herself had pinned the Victoria Cross on Harling's uniform soon after the battle.

The Last Survivors of Custer's Last Stand

Immediately following the Civil War, tremendous pressure was put on American Indian tribes by settlers looking for a new life in the West, by opportunists with rifles out for quick riches and buffalo hides, and by the U. S. Government which was lusting for land and natural resources. Within a quarter-century the Indian was virtually eliminated as a threat to "civilization" from the Mississippi to the Pacific Ocean, but not before putting up a fierce struggle. The number of troops used was small compared to the millions who fought in the Civil War; nevertheless, a generation of American soldiers survived to tell their grandchildren about the battles with the red man.

Certainly the most famous battle of the various Indian wars was the 1876 engagement in which the Sioux Indians wiped out General George A. Custer and 264 Seventh Cavalrymen under his direct command at the Little Big Horn River. The Indians left no white man alive, but there were U. S. troops close to the battle who survived.

The very last white survivor of that shocking day in American history was Jacob Horner, a native New Yorker who joined Custer's Seventh Cavalry Regiment to see the West. Horner lived through the battle of the Little Big Horn only because he was not there at the time. He and a small number of troops were left behind because there were not enough horses. A year after the massacre, Horner fought against the Nez Perces tribe, then left the Army in 1880 "because I met a girl and married her." He later went into the meat business and acted as a technical advisor to film companies on frontier movie scripts. He died at the age of ninety-six on 22 September 1951, three-quarters of a century after the historic battle.

The last Indian survivor of Custer's Last Stand was the multi-named Chief Iron Hail/Dewey Beard/Wa-Sue-Ma-Za of the Oglala Sioux tribe. Settling down in a tarpaper shack on the Pine Ridge Reservation of South Dakota, Iron Hail died there in November of 1955 at age ninety-eight. Apparently, he was the last person at the scene of the battle to pass away.

The Last Survivors of the Indian Wars

In June 1877, just a year after the Custer debacle, another Indian uprising flared in the West, this one involving the formerly peaceful Nez Perces (so-called because they wore pieces of shell in their noses, hence the French description that became their name). Led by gallant Chief Joseph, who was the handsome Indian popularized in American literature, the 200 Nez Perces had lived for generations in the Wallowa Valley of Oregon. His father's refusal to sign a peace treaty in 1863 subjected Joseph's people to pressure that eventually culminated in a 1,300-mile chase by U. S. soldiers across the Northwest.

Four-year-old Josiah Red Wolf was in the Nez Perce camp at Big Hole Basin in Montana on the night of 8 August 1877 when the troops launched a surprise attack. Fording a shallow river, the soldiers swept into the camp, shooting and clubbing women and children and killing Red Wolf's mother and sister. Chief Joseph rallied his warriors, however, soon putting the soldiers on the defensive and capturing an Army howitzer. The battle ended with thirty-five soldiers dead and thirty-eight wounded.

But the Nez Perces had lost between sixty and ninety lives, including some of the tribe's ablest braves. Two months later, on 5 October, the Nez Perces surrendered in the Bear Paw Mountains of Montana. Chief Joseph said: "Hear me, my chiefs. I am tired; my heart is sick and sad. From where the sun now stands, I will fight no more forever."

Josiah Red Wolf survived well into the twentieth century, supporting himself as a cobbler, farmer and country musician. In 1967, he returned to Big Hole Basin and turned the first shovelful of earth for the visitor center at the Battlefield National Monument there. Four years later, ninety-eight-year- old Josiah Red Wolf, last survivor of the Nez Perces War, died in Lewiston, Idaho.

Two white men who fought against the Indians outlived him. One was Simpson Mann, whose U.S. Army service stretched from

1876 to 1891 when he participated in the battle of Wounded Knee, the official final conflict of the long war on the North American continent between Indian and white man. Mann, who joined the U.S. Cavalry for "$12.50 a month, fat meat and six hardtacks a meal," died in 1965 at ninety-eight.

The last official veteran of the Indian wars, Fredrak Fraske, survived until 18 June 1973 and the age of 101. He had seen no action, however. His unit of the 17th Infantry was sent to Idaho in 1894 to quell one of the last scattered uprisings. But when the soldiers arrived, according to Fraske, "there was no shooting, no prisoners taken and no violence. The chief explained to his Indians that they couldn't do much against 400 soldiers so they drifted quietly back to the reservation at Pocatello...."

Last Shot Fired by the Allies in World War I

On the Allied side of the lines, a French Colonial sergeant was nicknamed "Toubib" (Algerian slang for "doctor," because the soldier in question had contracted malaria in Tonkin — later known as Vietnam — and was consequently well-supplied with quinine and opium pills which he dispensed freely to himself and his comrades). For several weeks of static trench warfare, Toubib had carried on a running battle with a clump of bushes in which a German machine-gun crew was hidden. Vowing to demolish the weapon with the last shot of the war, Toubib walked fifteen kilometers on the Sunday night before the Armistice so he could set his watch precisely according to official division headquarters time. Then, just seconds before 11:00 on the morning of 11 November 1918, he pulled the lanyard of his 37-millimeter "canon d'accompagnement" at a point 500 yards behind the lines between Mezieres and Charleville. A second after his round landed on target, Toubib cried out, "This time I can see the effect of my shot immediately!"

He started to dash across no-man's land, but was prevented from doing so on orders from General Ferdinand Foch that troops could not advance without official permission.

Last Allied Soldier Killed in World War I

According to General John Pershing's official order of the day for 11 November 1918, the last American killed was Private Henry Gunther of Baltimore, Maryland. Then with Company A, 313th Infantry, 79th Infantry Regiment, Gunther's platoon was advancing on the Germans near Metz when the men were ambushed. Gunther rushed forward with fixed bayonet. At that very moment, a messenger arrived with notification that the armistice was in effect; Gunther was shot in the left temple and left side and died almost immediately. The official time of his death: 11:01 a.m.

Last Air Raids on Great Britain

Early in World War I — on 31 May 1915 — London was introduced to a new horror in warfare: an attack from the air on defenseless civilians. On that day, the German zeppelin LZ38 dropped 3,000 pounds of bombs on northeast London, killing seven people. Zeppelin air attacks continued sporadically thereafter for the next three years. The air ships carried a variety of small and large bombs. The most devastating weighed 1,000 kilograms and was called *Liebesgaben* (Love token). The zeppelins were slow, although they compensated in the early months of the war by being able to rise above the altitude capabilities of defending airplanes. Until 13 June 1917, the lighter-than-airships exclusively delivered bombs on London, that date marking the first use of massed Gotha bombers which attacked an area around Liverpool Station, London, dropping 72 bombs that killed 162 people and wounded 432.

Eventually, as air protection became more efficient and the Germans were forced to retreat in France and Belgium, the air raids diminished. The last air attacks on London were in May of 1918; the final German air ship raid on London which resulted in death or injury took place on 12 April 1918.

Until the last few months of the war, the zeppelins managed to reach the British coastal towns. The last of these raids was made on 5 August 1918. In the L-70, one of five ships, was Fregattenkapitan Peter Strasser, chief of the German Naval Airship Service, who was an avid champion of the zeppelin as a weapon of war.

That evening, Flight Lieutenant Edgar Cadbury of the Royal Navy Air Station at Great Yarmouth, and his wife, were enjoying a charity concert when an orderly caught Cadbury's eye and told him he was wanted at headquarters. As Cadbury ran toward his D.H.4, the only airplane available, he could see the silhouette of a zeppelin against the northern evening light.

Soon, Cadbury was aloft and in attacking position, abeam of them and about 2,000 feet below. Climbing to within 600 feet of the ship he trained his machine gun on a spot about three-quarters of the way aft. The Pomeroy explosive bullets from Cadbury's plane's gun blew a hole in the fabric, starting a fire which ran along the entire length of the zeppelin. A big fuel tank detached itself from the framework and fell blazing into a heavy cloud layer about 7,000 feet below. Within a minute, the L-70 was a total mass of flames. The other German ships altered course just as Cadbury's engine completely cut out, leaving him thirty or forty miles from land. But after a few sputters and bangs, Cadbury managed to get the engine started again and continued after the remaining zeppelins. Once again he was the victim of bad luck, however — the Lewis gun on his craft jammed from a double feed and could not be cleared in the darkness.

Reluctantly, he returned to the night landing base at Sedgeford, little realizing he was the last pilot to down a zeppelin in World War One.

Altogether, there were 51 zeppelin raids on Great Britain, resulting in a total of 196 tons of explosives dropped, causing 557 deaths.

Richthofen's Last Flight

The greatest flying ace of World War One was undoubtedly Manfred von Richthofen, "The Red Baron," whose first accredited kill took place over Villiers-Ploucich, France, on 17 September 1915, when he destroyed an English two-seater containing 2nd Lieutenant L. B. F. Morris and Lieutenant T. Rees. During the next two-and-a-half years, he averaged a kill every eleven days, reaching a total of eighty by 20 April 1918.

That morning, Richthofen seemed in unusually high spirits, kicking the support out from under a cot on which one of his pilots was napping, as a joke. Then he was off on another mission, one that carried the German airplanes over the British lines where they were exposed to anti-aircraft fire.

Attracted by the smoke, a patrol of Sopwith Camels led by Canadian Captain Arthur Royal Brown approached the German planes. Soon Brown saw that his friend, Lieutenant W. R. May, was in trouble with a red tri-plane on his tail. Diving beneath the two fighters, Brown fired at the German. All three aircraft were close to the floor of the Somme Valley, directly over the guns of an Australian artillery unit which also fired at the tri-plane just as Brown squeezed another blast. Lt. May and another pilot saw the bullets fired by Brown strike the German plane, which moved erratically, sideslipped, then landed.

When the pilot made no attempt to get out, British soldiers moved to the Fokker marked 425/77, which meant nothing to them. But upon examining the papers of the occupant, who had been killed by a single bullet through the chest, they realized they had just witnessed the last flight of the celebrated "Red Baron."

The Last Day of World War I

The Great War ended officially on 2 July 1921, following the lengthy Versailles peace conference. For one nation, however, World War I dragged on for forty years after the last shot was fired.

That nation was Andorra, the 191-square mile Pyrenees republic which declared war on Germany on 4 August 1914, but was subsequently ignored by the Allies who did not invite its leaders to sign the Treaty of Versailles. Not until 18 September 1958 did Andorra forgive the discourtesy by enacting a decree declaring the war officially over.

The Last Carrier Pigeons of World War I

In a way, the thousands of pigeons who carried messages during World War I were just as much combatants as the men in the trenches or pilots dueling in the skies. Perhaps the most celebrated of the Allied birds, Cher Ami, braved gunfire from both sides of the lines to fly twenty-five miles in thirty minutes with a message for Allied gunners while on tour with the Lost Battalion. The bird arrived behind friendly lines with a shredded wing and a broken leg that had to be amputated. Another famous war pigeon named President Wilson also lost a leg while carrying a message in France.

Decorated for bravery like human soldiers, the pigeons also achieved a measure of notoriety once the war was over. The most heroic were "retired" or kept for breeding purposes, and as the years went by, the public was kept informed of the surviving birds' number and welfare.

By 1935, there were only three known World War I pigeons remaining. The first of these to pass away was seventeen-year-old Spike, who had carried fifty-two messages for the American Expeditionary Force (AEF) in France. Hatched in France in 1918, Spike began flying for the 77th Division as soon as he took to the air. Retired after the war, Spike continued to mate until 1934, when he gradually weakened and had to be kept alive with a tonic. He died on 12 April 1935.

Spike's coop companion, Mocker, the last feathered hero of the AEF, also began to weaken early in 1937, but was kept alive on a diet of whiskey and water. Mocker's big moment came during the Allies' final push to break the German Hindenburg line before St. Mihiel. There, a big gun was holding up the American advance so Mocker was given a message with the coordinates of the enemy artillery piece. While flying over the German positions, Mocker was hit by a piece of shrapnel that cost him his right eye and lacerated his skull. He winged his way to headquarters, however, and the big gun was silenced twenty minutes later. As a result, Mocker received the Distinguished Service Cross and the French Croix de Guerre for valiant service under fire. He was just two months shy of being twenty-one years old when he died on 14 June 1937. Like Spike and Cher Ami, he was stuffed and mounted.

The last known carrier pigeon of the war was a German bird named Kaiser, who was captured by an American soldier during the Meuse-Argonne offensive of 1918. Kaiser survived until 4 December 1937.

The Last Biplanes

The standard fighter plane of the "Great War" was the box-like biplane that was given stability by its two wings at the sacrifice of speed and maneuverability. Since the first monoplanes tended to tear apart rather easily, this seemed a fair trade; but as airplane manufacturers learned more about their craft, the biplane gradually became anachronistic.

Nevertheless, most nations clung to the tradtion of double-winged aircraft long after World War I. In Great Britain, for example, the Royal Air Force used a biplane heavy bomber, the Hanley Page Heyford, until May 1941 when it was finally withdrawn from RAF inventory. The Heyford was capable of a top speed of only 142 miles per hour at 13,000 feet while carrying a bomb load of 2,800 pounds. The last biplane fighter of the RAF was the Gloster Gladiator, which entered service in February 1937 and was used during the early years of the Second World War, 444 of them having been delivered to the RAF. Despite its ancient design, the Gladiator achieved a final measure of renown during the defense of Malta when four of their number fought off a large group of Italian aircraft.

The last operational biplane in production for the United States military was the Curtiss SBC Helldiver, which was designed in 1933 as a monoplane, then converted into a biplane. When the Japanese attacked Pearl Harbor on 7 December 1941, the U.S. Navy still had 186 Helldiver biplanes, all of which would have been helpless against the Japanese Zero had they been able to get off the ground in time.

Rather more innovative than the Americans or British, the Japanese dispensed with biplanes well before World War Two. Their last carrier-based biplane fighter was the Nakajima A4N1, which had a maximum speed of about 214 miles per hour. About 300 were built and saw combat from the Japanese carrier *Hosho* during the Sino-Japanese War in 1937. After that they were replaced with faster more maneuverable single-wing fighters.

Last of the World War I "Big Four" Leaders

In both World Wars, five major "Allied" nations joined in fighting three major "Axis" powers. Following the tradition of war which allots glory to the winner and disgrace to the loser regardless of whether it is deserved, the Axis leaders in both wars either went into exile, committed suicide, or had their powers severely reduced. The Allied leaders, meanwhile, went on to become elder statesmen as members of the "Big Three," "Big Four," or "Big Five." (In this regard, it should be noted that for World War I the term "Big Five" is never used, primarily because Tsar Nicholas II of Russia was deposed by the Bolsheviks in 1917 but went on to negotiate a separate — and losing — peace treaty with Germany in March of 1918.)

As elder statemen, the winning leaders of World War I went on to become international figures whose passing away was mourned with appropriate attention to the fact that an era was in the process of ending. The beginning of the end came in 1924 with the death of former U. S. President Woodrow Wilson. Wilson was followed in 1929 by Georges Eugene Benjamin Clemenceau of France and in 1945 by Great Britain's David Lloyd George.

The last surviving member of World War I's winning leaders was the least celebrated of them all, Vittorio Emanuele Orlando of Italy, who started his political career in 1888 at the age of twenty-eight. Although Italy's contribution to the Allied victory was minimal, Orlando walked out of the Versailles discussions contending that his nation was not getting her just rights to Fiume on the Adriatic. During the 1920s, Orlando also walked out on the Fascist regime saying that, for him, "There is no longer a place in public life — there is not even a place in the opposition."

In 1935, however, he mended fences with Benito Mussolini by publicly supporting the Italian invasion of Ethiopia. After World War Two, he flirted with both fascism and communism by urging that Italy withdraw from the North Atlantic Treaty Organization and completely revise its system of alliances, holding that his country had been "abandoned...if not actually treated as an enemy" by the United States and other Western nations.

A controversial rather than significant figure during the latter part of his career, Orlando died at the age of ninety-two on 1 December 1952, the last of World War I's "Big Four."

The Last Lafayette Escadrille Ace

The glamour and importance of the Lafayette Escadrille is perhaps legendary, though it discounts a large number of Americans who flew with distinction in the Lafayette Flying Corps. Only those men of Spa. 124, the original group of volunteers to join up, could call themselves members of the famed Escadrille.

There were only forty-two men on the Lafayette Escadrille roster, and while they received a great deal of publicity, it is a fact that the top ace of the Escadrille, Gervais Raoul Lufbery of Wallingford, Connecticut, had a total of seventeen kills; the top American ace in the Lafayette Flying Corps, Capt. Edward V. Rickenbacker, had twenty-six.

The Escadrille seemed to attract the colorful types — men such as James Norman Hall, author of *Mutiny on the Bounty*, and Edwin C. Parsons, who immediately before the war had trained pilots for Pancho Villa and who was described by writer Arch Whitehouse as a "striking figure aloft or on the ground, for he flew in the dreariest pair of breeches, a ragged mackinaw jacket, and an outmoded crash helmet given him by some amused Britisher. On the ground, he was a fashion plate, a veritable Scarlet Pimpernel, for he sported a smart kepi, an Ascot stock, a neat tunic, breeches, and glossy field boots."

Credited with eight kills and seven possibles, Parsons qualified as an "ace" (more than five verified kills) when the war ended. Still seeking adventure, he became a member of the first class of agents with the Federal Bureau of Investigation from 1920-1923. He then moved to Hollywood, where he became a script writer or technical advisor on such films as *Wings* and *Dawn Patrol*. In 1939, he tried to form another Lafayette Escadrille, but had to settle for serving as a flying instructor as Pensacola, Florida. When he died, on 3 May 1968 at the age of seventy-five, he was the last ace of the famous group of fliers. (Two members of the Escadrille survived him but had less than five kills, and so did not qualify as "aces.")

The Last V-Rockets to Fall on London

On 15 June 1944 the citizens of London, who had already survived nearly five years of steady bombing by the German Luftwaffe, were suddenly exposed to a new "vengeance weapon" of Adolf Hitler. Having seen his once-invincible air force rendered ineffective by the Royal Air Force, Hitler ordered London attacked by V-1 rockets, small, pilotless bombs launched from sites in France and Belgium.

In the first seven weeks they were used, the "buzz-bombs" killed nearly 5,000 people, seriously injured 14,000 more, and damaged 800,000 homes, of which 17,000 were totally destroyed. Deeming that amount of damage insufficient, the German High Command replaced the V-1's with longer-range, more powerful rockets known as V-2's in September. The designer of the new weapon was rocket expert Werner von Braun (later a leader of the U.S. space research efforts in the 1950s and 1960s). In addition to greater destructive force and increased range, another reason for the change to the V-2's was that at least half of the V-1's aimed at London and Allied bases on the continent fell to the ground only miles from their launching sites. The V-2's, much more reliable than the V-1's, weighed thirteen-and-a-half tons and travelled faster than the speed of sound.

Throughout the fall and winter of 1944-1945, Londoners got used to huddling in their basements or air raid shelters as the "second blitz" continued. Although the rockets caused far less damage than the massed bomber attacks, many citizens found them more demoralizing, because the rockets arrived with virtually no warning.

As the Allied armies advanced deeper into France and Belgium, German rocket crews were forced to retreat until their weapons no longer had the range to cross the English Channel. On 29 March 1945, the last V-rocket fell on London.

The Home Office estimated that since the raids began in 1944 8,436 persons had been killed and about 25,000 injured. In comparison, the bomber blitz of London — going back to 1939 — killed 42,000 and injured 50,000. Between the bombers and rockets, nearly one-fourth of the city of London was sufficiently damaged to require total reconstruction.

The Last Crossing of the "T"

The naval maneuver known as "crossing" or "capping the T" came into use during the seventeenth century when warships were first equipped with lines of cannons capable of firing devastating salvos at the enemy. To execute the maneuver, a ship or ships had to be placed in such a position that it would be possible to fire down the line of enemy vessels without being exposed to their guns — in other words, getting a "free shot." A classic example was during the battle of Tsushima Strait of the Russo-Japanese War, in May of 1905, when the Japanese fleet succeeded in destroying the Russians. But as World War II drew to a close, the era of "crossing the T" was also ending, for to "cross the T," one had to see the enemy.

In October of 1944, the greatest battle in the history of naval warfare raged across a half-million square miles of the churned and bloodied South Pacific. The battle for Leyte Gulf pitted the U. S. fleets supporting General Douglas MacArthur's landings on the island of Leyte against virtually the entire remaining Japanese Navy. On 17 October, within minutes after the U. S. cruiser *Denver* fired the first shot of the naval bombardment, the Japanese fleet began converging on Leyte through Palawan Passage toward the Sibuyan Sea. There the Japanese commander, Vice Admiral Takeo Kurita, ran into 259 sorties by planes from the fleet of U.S. Admiral "Bull" Halsey, losing the heavy cruiser *Maya* and his own flagship, *Atago*. Kurita himself had to swim to save his life.

The next day, another portion of the Japanese fleet, under commanders Nishimura and Shima, consisting of two battleships, three heavy cruisers, one light cruiser, and eight destroyers, sailed into the Surigao Strait. There they met a battle line of U.S. ships led by the *West Virginia*, *Louisville*, *Phoenix*, *Tennessee*, *California*, *Mississippi*, *Pennsylvania*, and *Maryland*. Even worse for the Japanese, the tactical position was such that Admiral Oldendorf was able to cap the T, with the *Mississippi* firing a devastating full salvo at 19,700 yards. Before the battle of Surigao Strait was over, the Japanese lost every ship but one in Nishimura's force. Admiral Shima then steamed into the trap and was so confused that he fired torpedoes at an island he thought to be a ship, then fled without coming under fire. Relentlessly pursued by U. S. planes and ships, Shima made it back to Japan with only one heavy cruiser and two destroyers.

In addition to sounding the death knell for the Japanese Navy, the battle was the last time the battle line formation was used in naval warfare. Later, historian Samuel Eliot Morison wrote, "Thus, the *Mississippi* had the honor of firing the major-caliber salvo of this battle; and at the same time, sounding the knell of the old battle line tactics which had been foremost in naval warfare since the seventeenth century... One can imagine the ghosts of all great admirals from Raleigh to Jellicoe standing at attention as the Battle Line went into oblivion."

The Last Night of the London Blackout

Shortly after Hitler's invasion of Poland on 1 September 1939, London and other cities of Great Britain instituted total blackouts as air raid protection. More than five years passed before the lights went on again.

The London blackout did not end when Germany surrendered in May 1945, as one might imagine. Instead, the end of the blackout came nearly eight months earlier, the Luftwaffe having been driven from the skies by the fall of 1944. After the invasion of France, confident that no more bomber attacks would menace the city, the British Government ordered an end to the blackout on 16 September 1944. It was replaced with a dimout similar to that used by United States' coastal cities, but to Londoners it must have seemed very bright indeed.

The Last German U-Boat Destroyed

On 7 May 1945, the last full day of fighting in Europe, an RAF Coastal Command aircraft spotted and sank a German submarine off the English coast. The attacker was a Consolidated Catalina plane of the 210 Squadron, the same type of plane which on 26 May 1941 reestablished contact with the Nazi raider *Bismarck* after surface vessels had lost sight of her.

The Last Japanese Warplane Destroyed

At 5:40 a.m., 15 August 1945, U.S. Navy pilot Lt. Commander Reidy attacked and shot down a C6N1 Japanese reconnaissance plane. It turned out to be the last confirmed aerial victory of the Pacific theatre (and World War II), as five minutes later the war was declared over and all Japanese aircraft grounded.

The Sinking of the Last Japanese Warship

The final Japanese ship sent to the bottom during World War II was a coastal defense vessel struck by a torpedo fired from the U.S. submarine *Torsk* at 9:17 p.m., 14 August 1945, Greenwich Civil Time. The small craft went to the bottom immediately.

A latecomer to the war, the *Torsk* saw action only during the final year. It is now berthed at Baltimore, Maryland, a national monument and tourist attraction.

The Last Kamikaze Mission

One of the more sensational aspects of World War II were the attacks by Japanese "kamikaze" ("divine wind") pilots, whose purpose was to load their planes with explosives and enough fuel for a one-way trip in order to attain a "sure hit" on American ships — and certain death.

In practice, however, getting a sure hit was not so simple a matter, especially during the last few months of the war, when U.S. firepower became so sophisticated that most vessels could throw up a wall of flak that was penetrable by only the most skillful pilots.

A total of 2,257 suicide sorties took place during the war. Of these, 1,321 were "expended," and 936 pilots returned (contrary to the popular belief that no kamikaze pilots survived). A total of forty-five United States ships were sunk and serious damage was done to fifteen battleships and ten aircraft carriers.

Although U. S. records make no mention of it, Japanese records note that the last sortie by suicide aircraft was flown on 15 August 1945 by seven planes of the OITA Detachment, 701st Air Group, Imperial Japanese Navy, led in person by Admiral Matome Ugaki, Commander of the 5th Air Fleet. The results of the raids are not known.

The End of World War II

Back when life was simpler, if it really ever was, two nations at war ended their conflict quite easily by drawing up a treaty some time after one or the other power decided it had had enough. The twentieth century, however, with its truly world wars and multiplicity of national priorities, made many previously simple things complex. Identifying the last day of a war ought to be easy enough. World War II lasted from 1939 to 1945, according to the history books. This statement of fact implies that the official final day of the war would be sometime in the year 1945.

This is certainly true, but not entirely accurate. In Europe, for example, the German Army officially surrendered to General Dwight D. Eisenhower at precisely 1:41 a.m., 17 May 1945. In the Pacific, the Japanese surrendered on 15 August 1945. Despite the seeming exactness of these final days, the U.S.-Japanese phase of the war has at least two "official" endings. The first of these was 31 December 1946, when President Harry Truman declared the official cessation of hostilities. That, however, was still not the end for the U.S. and Japan. Not until ten years, four months, and twenty-one days after the Japanese attack on Pearl Harbor, 28 April 1952, was the treaty signed that was the "real" end. The ceremony coincided with Japanese Emperor Hirohito's fifty-first birthday, May Day, Japan's Memorial Day, and Children's Day. In honor of the occasion, Hirohito composed a poem ("Winter winds have died away/The long-awaited spring is here,") while Japanese Communists yelled "Yankee, go home!" as they tore placards and flags from poles, threw rocks, bags of offal, steel-reinforced bamboo spears, and dumped a pair of U.S. sailors into the 250-year-old imperial moat.

That was only the beginning of the official end for Japan, as it turned out. The Soviet Union did not sign an agreement with the Japanese until October of 1956, and Indonesia waited until sixteen years after the war had broken out to mend fences on 20 January 1958.

In Europe, meanwhile, the fighting may have stopped in 1945 but the sounds of political battling continued until 26 May 1952 when a peace treaty between West Germany, Great Britain, France, and the United States was signed. Guatemala, having declared war on the Axis on 11 December 1941, did not officially end the war with Germany until 23 November 1956, the last country to settle up with the Axis.

The Last Act of the League of Nations

At its peak, the League of Nations was composed of more than sixty countries, but the well-intentioned peace organization never had much power. Meeting for the first time in 1920 without the United States or the Soviet Union, the League did not even have a permanent home until 1936, when it finally moved into its Geneva, Switzerland, headquarters.

By that time, Benito Mussolini had marched on Corfu, Bolivia and Paraguay had fought a three-year war, and Japan had invaded Manchuria. One highlight of 1935 was the League's decision to return the Saar Basin region to Germany after voters there expressed a preference for reunion with the Reich.

Unable to prevent Adolf Hitler's invasion of Poland in 1939, which was followed by declarations of war by France and Great Britain, the League of Nations prepared to disband in defeat. Its last act of an international nature was to expel the Soviet Union on 14 December 1939, for invading Finland.

In May of 1940, Secretary General Joseph Louis Anne Avenol gave the 205 other employees of the League of Nations their choice between resigning at once or hanging on until their contracts expired. All but eight quit. Less than two months later, the League's great white limestone palace was closed and Avenol asked the remaining employees to resign. Avenol himself resigned three weeks later as the League's last employee.

Formal disbandment of the peace organization had to wait for the end of World War II. The twenty-first and last session of the League took place on 18 April 1946. "We have lost many illusions," said President Carl Hambro, "but a better, stronger instrument has been formed."

Left behind were a million-dollar library, the Geneva headquarters building, and $162.28 worth of tea-making equipment.

The Last Iwo Jima Flagraiser

Joe Rosenthal's Pulitzer Prize-winning photograph of six marines raising the American Flag on Mount Suribachi, Iwo Jima, on 23 February 1945, stirred nearly everyone. The picture was made into a postage stamp and served as a model for a seventy-eight foot bronze reproduction by Felix de Weldon overlooking Arlington National Cemetery. Regrettably, participation in that event did not bring good fortune to the six men.

Three of the six men were killed soon afterward in the thirty-five days of fighting for the island. After the battle ended, President Franklin D. Roosevelt ordered the three survivors back to the United States, where they were lionized from coast to coast. Two of the men — Rene Gagnon and John Bradley — took the adulation in stride, but Ira Hayes, a shy and bewildered Pima Indian, found it hard to adjust to the role of celebrity. After playing himself in the 1949 John Wayne movie *Sands of Iwo Jima*, Hayes drifted from job to job and eventually sought escape in drinking. Late in 1953, he was picked up in Chicago, shoeless, shaking, and incoherent, just another of the fifty-one times in thirteen years he had been arrested.

Hayes was on hand for the dedication of the Iwo Jima Memorial in November of 1954, but soon after was forced by his unfortunate circumstances to take a job picking cotton on the Gila River Indian Reservation in Arizona where he was born. He stayed away from alcohol until one night in January of 1955 when some friends enticed him to a party. After drinking with them, becoming ill and leaving, Hayes was found frozen on the sand the next morning. (In 1961, his story was depicted in the Hollywood biopic *The Outsider* in which Tony Curtis played the lead.)

On 12 October 1979, Gagnon, fifty-four, collapsed and died at his caretaker's job at a Manchester, New Hampshire, apartment complex. That left the fifty-five-year-old Bradley, an Antiago, Wisconsin funeral director, as the sole survivor of the Iwo Jima flagraising. According to his son, Steve, he seldom mentions the historic event.

The Last Days of World War II Rationing

The World War II fighting may have stopped in 1945 but many unpleasant results of the conflict lingered on. Not the least of these was rationing, which lasted in some nations for as long as twenty years.

In the United States a major object of homefront wrath was the Office of Price Administration (OPA), an agency established to prevent wartime inflation and ration scarce consumer goods.

The first product to be rationed in the U. S. was gasoline, starting with the Eastern states on 3 August 1941. After the Japanese attack on Pearl Harbor and the declaration of war, widespread rationing followed. Purchase of cars was "frozen" to civilians on 1 January 1942, and tires on 5 January. Coffee, sugar, meat, fuel, oil, bicycles, typewriters, and rubber boots were placed on the list later that year. The ban continued throughout the war — and many additional items, such as shoes, were added — but most restrictions were relaxed soon after V-J Day. The last item continuing to be rationed was sugar, which was regulated until 11 June 1947. That same year, the OPA was abolished.

Rationing in Great Britain was more stringent and of longer duration. Products such as clothes, soap, candy, gasoline and meat were regulated by 1941, and many restrictions, such as that on candy, lasted until 1949. The last item to be rationed in Great Britain was meat, which remained under government control until 4 July 1954.

East Germans, living under rationing since the beginning of World War II, did not see the end of controls on meats, fats, and sugar until 1958.

The Last Propeller Fighter

During the final days of World War II, the German Luftwaffe produced the first jet fighters, but the standard pursuit plane — the piston-engine propeller type — continued to be produced. By the early 1950s, however, the age of the jets had truly arrived.

The last propeller-driven American fighter plane to remain in production was the Vought F4U Corsair, which first flew on 29 May 1940, and was delivered to the U. S. Navy on 3 October 1942. With inverted gull wings, the F4U was the first fighter capable of exceeding 400 mph and was the favorite of hotshot pilots such as "Pappy" Boyington of the Marines and the Navy's "Ike" Kepford. The fastest of the series, the F4U-5N, led the aerial assault on the German battleship *Tirpitz* on 3 April 1944. During World War II, Corsair pilots defeated a total of 2,140 enemy aircraft while losing only 189 of their own planes.

Production of the Corsair ended in January of 1953 when the 12,571st and last plane came rolling off the assembly line at United Aircraft's Chance Vought plant in Dallas.

The Last Battleships

The age of the American battleship began on 3 August 1886 when Congress authorized the construction of the *Texas*. Her keel was laid down in 1889 and she was completed in 1892. Just 300 feet long and weighing 6,315 tons, the *Texas* was considered the last word in fire-power during the 1890s, but subsequent battleships were much larger and more heavily armed.

With her need to protect her far-flung empire, Great Britain relied heavily on battleships, often maintaining as many batterwagons as the world's other top two powers combined. In 1918, before the sun began to set on British power, the Royal Navy boasted fifty battleships. Many remained in service until the end of World War II. Then, suddenly, the end came for the British battleship. In 1948, five of the island nation's men of war were consigned to the scrap heap, causing Viscount Hall, first lord of the admiralty, to remark that, "the first Sea Lord and I feel like two padres conducting a funeral service of a number of old friends."

The doomed British vessels included the thirty-two-year-old *Queen Elizabeth*, which had been the Grand Fleet's flagship in World War I. Aboard her, the Germans surrendered their navy in 1918. During World War II, as she lay moored in the shallows of Alexandria harbor, Italian "human torpedoes" swam beneath her, attached time charges, and blew great holes in her hull. Repaired in the United States, she finished out the war in the East Indies.

Twelve years after the five vessels were scrapped, Great Britain's last battleship followed. Commissioned in 1946, the 44,500 ton *Vanguard* had never fired a shot in anger, but she had inherited a grand old name. Since the first *Vanguard* fought against the Spanish Armada in the sixteenth century, twelve Royal Navy ships had borne the name. As she was towed toward the scrapyard, the last British battleship seemed to have an apprehension about her fate. In Portsmouth harbor she slipped away from four tugs, slewed around sharply and ran bow up on a mudbank where she clung so stubbornly it took an hour to get her off and on her way to the junk heap again.

The United States followed the same melancholy pattern as Great Britain. One by one, the great battleships of World War II were sent to the scrap heap. It was, of course, a necessary move. "We hate to see the end of the trail for this magnificant breed of ship," said Rear Admiral Chester C. Woods in 1958, explaining that the battleship was "the victim of change in military weapons much as the cross-bow had replaced the spear, and mortars and guns took the place of the cross-bow when gunpowder was invented."

At the time Woods spoke, the U. S. battleship *Wisconsin* had been deactivated, leaving the nation without a battleship for the first time since the 1890s.

Not all the great ships were scrapped. Some remained in the mothball fleet. A few, such as the *North Carolina*, *Texas* and *Massachusetts*, were saved from oblivion by citizens of those states who raised sufficient funds to preserve the vessels as monuments and tourist attractions.

Then, in 1968, as the Vietnam War moved into its third year, the United States decided to utilize the fire power of its battleships one last time. The *New Jersey* was returned to duty, leaving Long Beach, California, on 5 September and arriving at her firing station off the North Vietnamese coast on September 30.

On 15 October steaming along the panhandle of North Vietnam, the 56,000-ton vessel attacked the island of Hon Matt. A military spokesman observing the action reported that the *New Jersey*'s fire was so devastating that a "large slice" of the island was knocked into the sea. Even as the ship demonstrated its power, however, there was speculation that it was a sitting duck if North Vietnam decided to employ Soviet guided missiles. After several additional shelling missions, the *New Jersey* was deactiviated in 1969, becoming the last battleship of any navy to see action.

Last Words

1675
Henri de la d'Auvergne, Vicomte de Turenne, French marshal, when told to take cover at the battle of Sasbach: "Then I will come, for I particularly wish not to be killed just now." He was then hit.
1759
James Wolfe, British general, killed at the seige of Quebec: "What, do they run already? Then I die happy."
1820
Stephen Decatur, American soldier, hit in a duel: "I am mortally wounded, I think."
1842
Pierre Cambronne, French general: "Man is thought to be something but he is nothing."
1843
Isaac Hull, American naval officer: "I strike my flag."
1857
Sir Henry Havelock, British general: "Come, my son, and see how a Christian can die."

1861
Sir Howard Douglas, British general: "How little do they know of the undeveloped power of artillery...."
1863
Confederate General **Thomas J. "Stonewall" Jackson:** "Let us cross over the river and sit under the shade of the trees."
Andrew Hull Foote, American naval officer: "We must have charity...charity...charity...."
1864
Union General **John Sedgwick,** who rebuked some of his men who were taking cover from Confederate fire: "Come, come! Why they couldn't hit an elephant at this dist————."
1868
Ramon Maria Narvaez, Spanish general, asked if he forgave his enemies: "I do not forgive my enemies. I have had them all shot."
1872
George G. Meade, American general: "I am crossing a beautiful river and the opposite shore is coming nearer and nearer."
1916
Hector Hugh Munro (Saki), on the battlefield in France: "Put that bloody cigarette out!"
1917
George Dewey, American admiral: "Gentlemen, the battle is done, the victory is ours."

Chapter Nine

A Grab-Bag of Lasts

Chronology

11 B.C.
This year is unique in that it contains a 30 February. It's the last year, however, thanks to Agustus Caesar's calendar reorganization. (see p. 301)

363 A. D.
The Delphic Oracle, respected for a thousand years as a prophet, makes its final prediction. (see p. 302)

603
The Roman Senate ceases functioning after more than a thousand years.

1297
The giant moa, also known as the "giraffe bird," becomes extinct on the South Pacific islands later known as New Zealand, its natural habitat.

1502
Columbus leaves on his fourth and last voyage to the New World. (see p. 303)

1503
Alexander VI, the last pope to have children, dies. (see p. 304)

1543
Having loved — or at least gotten married — and lost five times, King Henry VIII of England takes his last wife, Catherine Parr.

1564
(Feb. 16) Swiss divine and reformer John Calvin (1509-1564) preaches his last sermon although in great pain and dies three months later.

1566
(July 1) Super-seer Nostradamus, having foreseen the Great Fire of London, the French Revolution, and the rise and fall of Napoleon, makes his final prediction: his own death. (see p. 305)

1567
The Roman Catholic Church ends its traditional practice — some say corruption — of selling indulgences.

1581
(March 25) For the last time in European Catholic countries, New Year's Day falls on this date. In 1582, the Gregorian Calendar moves it to 1 January.

1627
The last auroch, an ancestor of modern cattle, dies in a Polish game preserve.

1649
The "elephant bird," also known as *Aepyornis*, a large flightless bird similar to the

293

moa, becomes extinct on the island of Madagascar. Eggs of this creature measure thirteen-by-nine-and-a-half inches and contain an estimated two gallons.

1669
The last meeting is held by nations of Hanseatic League (formed in 1241), an organization of medieval towns seeking to establish trade security.

1681
The last dodo is seen on the island of Mauritius, its native habitat.

1687
Death of John Alden (born 1599), last survivor of those who signed the Mayflower Compact.

1709
After its union with the English Parliament, Scotland stops making her own coins.

Before 1719
Sir Ewen Cameron of Lochiel, called "The Ulysses of the Highlands," is credited with shooting the last remaining wolf in Scotland.

1737
England's Court of Chivalry, founded in the fourteenth century, sits for the last time.

1751
(March 25) For the last time in England, New Year's Day falls on this date. England finally accepts the Gregorian Calendar, so that New Year's Day of 1752 falls on 1 January.

1760
The solitaire, a large bird, becomes extinct. (see p. 305)

1768
Steller's sea cow, a giant mammal relentlessly hunted for food, becomes extinct.

1773
It is the last year during which Harvard students are listed in the school catalogue according to their social position.

1774
Virginia's House of Burgesses (established in 1619) sits for last time as colonists prepare for war with Britain.

1776
(June 25) British explorer Captain James Cook begins his last voyage. He dies in 1779.

1781
Thomas McKean of Delaware becomes the last delegate to sign the Declaration of Independence — five years after the other members of the Continental Congress.

1784
(June 3) Last sitting of U.S. Congress at Annapolis, Maryland, capital since 26

November 1783 of the new nation.

1788
(Oct. 21) Last meeting of the U. S. Continental Congress takes place in New York. The last president of the body is Cyrus Griffin.

1791
(Feb. 24) Tireless clergyman and letter-writer John Wesley writes his final epistle, declaring his belief that the fight against slavery must be relentlessly pursued. (see p. 307)

1792
Denmark abolishes the slave trade.

1805
(Dec. 31) The last day of the French Revolutionary Calendar, 10 Nivose, An XIV, ushers out a revolutionary (but confusing) experiment.

1808
(Jan. 1) Further importation of slaves is forbidden in the United States.

1810
Serfdom is abolished in Prussia.

1811
(Aug. 14) Paraguay abolishes slavery.

1813
Great Britain issues its last gold guineas.
Sweden abolishes the slave trade.

1814
Holland abolishes the slave trade.

1816
(March 24) A tireless preacher, the second bishop of the Methodist Episcopal Church in America, Francis Asbury preaches his last sermon at seventy. (see p. 308)

1824
United States presidential nominations are made by caucus system for last year. In the future, presidential candidates are selected by political party conventions.

1832
The issuance to soldiers of a daily liquor ration by the U.S. Army is abolished.
(Nov. 14) Death of Charles Carroll of Carrollton (1737-1832), last survivor of those who signed the Declaration of Independence. On the historic day, Carroll was selected at the last minute to sign the document.

1833
(Aug. 23) Slavery is abolished in the British colonies.

1834
(Feb. 28) The last descendant of Oliver Cromwell, Susan Cromwell, dies at the age of ninety.

1835
By act of Parliament, the

practice of bear-baiting is forbidden in Great Britain.

1842
1842 is last fiscal year beginning on 1 January. On 26 August 1842, the beginning of the fiscal year is changed to 1 July.

1844
(June 4) The last great auks are hunted down and killed on the island of Eldey, near Iceland. (see p. 308)

1847
Brook Farm, an experiment in communal living that began in 1841, closes its doors.

1850
The Bethlemite Order of Guatemala, a nursing community founded in 1650 to care for patients with infectious diseases, becomes extinct.

1855
In existence since 1133, the last Bartholomew Fair is held at Smithfield, England, on St. Batholomew's Day.

1856
First coined in England in 1351, the groat (with a value somewhat higher than a penny) is discontinued.

1857
The United States stops issuing half-cent coins.

1858
The British East India Company, in operation since 1600, is dissolved. Its duties — to exploit and manage foreign nations in the East — are taken over by the British government.

1860
The nation loses its last nickel shave and dime haircut when prices are raised to six and twelve cents at Tony Delight's in Chicago.

1861
Russian Tsar Alexander II issues an edict abolishing serfdom in his nation.
The ship *Australia* returns from Sumatra with the last full cargo of pepper discharged at Salem, Mass.
The Pony Express goes out of business after less than two years' operation.

1863
Almack's Club, founded in 1764, closes in London.

1865
(July 13) New York's volunteer firemen put out their last big blaze. On 31 July, the city changes the fire department to paid professional status. (Dec. 31) This is the last day slavery is legal in the United States.

1868
Hara-kari is abolished in Japan.
The last House of Commons sits in the United States. The body had been formed in

1776 as the lower house of the North Carolina Legislature.

1870
The last legal Jewish ghetto in Rome is abolished.
The Vermont Council of Censors, in operation since 1777, is abolished.

1872
(Dec. 12) The last Labrador duck, a species which once ranged from Canada to Philadelphia, is shot down over Long Island.

1873
The United States stops making the three-cent piece (in use since 1852) and the two-cent piece (since 1864).

1876
The last pure-blooded Tasmanian dies at the age of seventy-six.

1878
The United States stops making the twenty-cent piece, in use since 1875.

1879
The last of the southern bison herd is killed by U. S. hunters at Buffalo Springs, Texas.
The Oneida Community, whose followers are known as "The Bible Communists," is dissolved after thirty years of existence.

1883
(Aug. 12) The last quagga, a relative of the zebra, dies in a Dutch zoo. (see p. 309)

1888
Slaves in Brazil are set free.

1890
(March) Birmingham, England, the last major city to have a bell-crier, retires this vestige of the Middle Ages. (see p. 310)

1892
The last major cholera epidemic sweeps the United States.

1897
Zanzibar formally abolishes slavery.
(Dec. 31) Brooklyn's last day as a city brings to an end the administration of Mayor Frederick W. Wurster. (see p. 310)

1900
(Dec. 1) The last Guadalupe Island caracara, a large brown hawk, is killed.

1904
The last Louisiana parakeet is seen, the birds having been hunted down to supply the demand for caged birds.

1909
The last Indian head penny is minted.
The last meeting is held by the American Colonization Society, which nearly a century before said it had the answer to the slavery problem: send the slaves back to Africa.

1912
(Oct. 30) Common drinking cups are used on interstate trains for the last time.

1914
(Sept. 1) Martha, the last of America's two billion passenger pigeons, dies in the Cincinnati zoo. (see p. 312)

1916
(March 25) Considered the "last caveman," Ishi, sole survivor of the last wild Indian tribe of North America, dies.

1917
After 300 years, the last gold sovereign is struck in Great Britain.

1918
(Feb. 21) The last striking green and yellow Carolina parakeet, an old male named Incas, dies in the Cincinnati Zoo.
Mississippi becomes the last state in the U.S. to enact a compulsory education law.

1919
(June 18) The last horse-drawn fire engine runs in Baltimore.

1922
(Dec. 20) The last horse-drawn fire engine runs in New York City.

1923
(Feb. 5) The last horse-drawn fire engine runs in Chicago.

1927
(Dec. 31) Philadelphia's only horse-drawn fire engine makes its last run.

1928
Mrs. Elizabeth Lewis, last surviving member of the coronation party of Queen Victoria in 1837 — she was a nine-year-old flower girl — dies in New Kirk, Wales, at the age of 100.

1929
Large-size U.S. dollar bills are issued for the last time.

1931
Encarncion Mamaxe, 106, last of the tribe of Sobaipuris Indians, dies in the San Xavier del Bac Mission, Arizona.

1932
America's most famous criminal lawyer, Clarence Darrow, handles his last big case at the age of seventy-five. (see p. 314)

1933
The United States goes off the gold standard.
The race of prairie chicken or North American grouse known as the heath hen becomes extinct, the last survivor passing away at Martha's Vineyard, Massachusetts. (see p. 316)
William Dick (Makwa Monpuy or Maq-Uva-pey), the last man who can speak the Mohican language, dies at the age of seventy-six.

(Dec. 5) The last day of Prohibition ushers in a new era of less drinking for Americans. (see p. 331)

1934
(June) The U. S. Army stops delivering the nation's airmail. (see p. 327)
America's last gold coins are circulated.

1940
(Feb. 1) "First Class" is abolished on the Metroplitan and District Railways, thus elmininating all fare distinctions on London public transport systems.

1942
Created at the height of the Depression to provide work for idle thousands, the Civilian Conservation Corps is dissolved.

1948
(Jan. 12) Mahatma Gandhi, tireless leader for Indian independence, begins his last fast to protest his government's policy in the India-Pakistan confrontation. (see p. 318)
(June 30) It's the last day New York's subway can be ridden for a nickel.
(Nov. 29) The social condition of "untouchability" is officially abolished in India.

1950
(Sept. 21) Mrs. Mabel Young Sanborn, eighty-seven, the last of Mormon leader Brigham Young's fifty-six children, dies.

1951
(July 26) Segregation comes to an official end in the U.S. Army with the disbanding of the 24th Infantry Regiment, the last all-black unit in the armed forces. (see p. 320)

1952
John Thomas Moore, last surviving witness to the Wright brothers' 1903 flight, dies. (see p. 313)

1953
(Aug. 12) The death of Augustus Van Horne Stuyvesant brings an end to the line established by Peter Stuyvesant in the seventeenth century.
(Nov. 11) America observes her last Armistice Day. By an act of 24 May 1954, the holiday is changed to Veterans' Day.

1955
(Sept. 26) The last two surviving birds known as Euler's flycatcher, die in Jamaica during Hurricane Janet.

1958
(July 31) The last three-cent first class letters are delivered in the U.S.

1960
(Jan. 12) A waitress named Christina Erdlen becomes the eleventh and last wife of oft-married playboy Tommy Manville. (see p. 322)

(Dec. 30) For the last time since 1279, the farthing is legal tender in Great Britain.

1963
(Jan. 1) Philadelphia's traditional Mummers parade features "blackface" marchers for the last time. In 1964, the tradition is banned by a court order, after a suit by civil rights groups.
(September) The last Eskimo curlew is shot by a hunter on the Isle of Barbados.

1964
(Feb. 1) Timed postmarks are used for the last time in the U. S. (see p. 328)
Raymond Doan Vinh Na Champacak becomes the seventh and last husband of much-married heiress Barbara Hutton. (see p. 321)
(Nov. 23) For the last day, Latin is the official language of the Roman Catholic liturgy, conversion to the vernacular taking place on 29 November.

1965
(April 27) The Supreme Court of the United States announces that it is breaking a century-old tradition of announcing its decisions only on Mondays. The announcement is released on a Saturday.

1966
(June 9) Great Britain's Boy Scouts grow up by dropping the word "boy" from its name and doing away with short pants.
(June 30) Mississippi's last day of prohibition removes it as the only dry state in the nation.
(Nov. 18) The last meatless Friday is celebrated — or suffered through — ending a 1,000-year-old tradition for Roman Catholics.

1967
(April 27) Manhattan's last icehouse closes, the "victim of an illusive progress, practical and unsentimental."

1968
(July 1) Slot machines that pay off in cash are abolished in Maryland.
(Dec. 16) King Ferdinand and Queen Isabella's order banning all Jews from Spain is declared void after 476 years.

1969
(May 9) Two hundred Catholic saints lose their feast days as the church drops their names from the new liturgical calendar.

1970
(July 31) The 283-year-old "rum ration" tradition ends in the British Navy. (see p. 324)

1971
(Jan. 3) The last cigarette ad seen on American television gets on the air by mistake. (see p. 324)
(Feb. 15) Ending a 1,000-year monetary tradition,

Great Britain abolishes the shilling in favor of the decimal system.

Prohibition ends in India, though some people still drink furniture polish out of habit, instead of liquor.

1972
(Nov. 13) The tradition requiring Etonians to wear top hats is ended.

(Dec. 19) Apollo 17 has a successful splashdown and is the last of the moon mission series.

1973
(Jan. 12) The last all-male bastion falls as the venerable Harvard Club votes to admit women to its once-sacred inner sanctum.

Australia ends its racially discriminating immigration policy.

1977
(June 30) The last Railway Post Office in the U. S. goes out of service. (see p. 329)

1979
(Oct. 2) Charlie Smith, 137, who claims to be America's last slave, dies.

1980
Santiago, Chile, remains the last major city (with four million people in the metropolitan area) to have an all-volunteer fire department.

(May 8) Smallpox, the scourge of mankind for centuries, is declared eradicated at a World Health Organization ceremony.

The Last February 30th

The shortest month of the year for many centuries, February (meaning "to purify") was one of two months added to the calendar during the reign of Numa Pompilius (715-673 B.C.), the second king of ancient Rome. Before January and February were added, the year consisted of 10 months and 304 days, and consequently was always getting out of sync with the seasons.

King Numa Pompilius' adjustment brought about a year consisting of 7 months with 29 days, 4 months with 31 days, and February with 28, for a grand total of 355 for the year.

Losing 10 days annually produced such chaos by the time of Julius Caesar 7 centuries later, that another complete calendar revision was undertaken. In order to catch up with natural events, Caesar consulted an Alexandrian astronomer named Sosigenes. One result was the year 46 B.C., which had 445 days in it and was called the "Year of Confusion." The extra days were placed after February and November.

Having put the seasons back in order, Caesar then fixed the normal length of each year at 365 days. February, which had a standard length of 29 days, was given a thirtieth every 4 years under this new arrangement beginning in 45 B.C.

Incredibly, these new rules were somehow misinterpreted following the death of Julius Caesar in 44 B.C., February being considered a leap year month of thirty days every third year instead of every fourth, as Caesar had ordered. Thus, by 8 B.C., when Augustus was emperor, the seasons were three days off schedule, not enough to create havoc but a situation that could create problems if it was allowed to continue for another couple of centuries.

Never one to put off dealing with a situation, Augustus eliminated three leap years from 8 B.C. to 8 A.D. so the calendar could catch up, then replaced the month of Sextilius with August and, in order to have his namesake month be a big one, stole a day from February, reducing its normal length from 29 to 28 days.

The last 30-day February, then, was during the year 11 B.C. Since that distant time, February has been perennially short changed.

The Delphic Oracle's Last Prediction

For nearly a thousand years, the Delphi Oracle was situated on the slopes of Mount Parnassus, where, according to Greek myth, Apollo fought and killed a she-dragon in a cave below the city. Also according to legend, the decomposing body of the dragon emitted a stench which, when inhaled, rendered the inhaler capable of making prophecies. After several people were killed as a result of inhaling the gases, going into convulsions and falling into the fissures, it was decided to have a single priestess sit on a tripod above the rising gases and make predictions. Before long, the Pythia, the priestess intermediary to the oracle, was quite famous.

During the early years of the Delphic Oracle's existence, it established a record of siding with the invaders in every major war — with Xerxes I in the fifth century B.C., with Philip II of Macedon in the fourth century B.C., and in the Peloponnesian Wars, it spoke on the side of Sparta. The oracle's record for accuracy was helped by phrasing answers so they could be taken a number of ways and, then as now, the successes tended to be remembered more than the failures. Naturally, a donation of sacrificed animals or gold helped the Pythia give the visitor's problem the respect it deserved.

A favorite of the nation Lydia, whose king, Croesus, periodically showed up with gold and jewels in exchange for information, the Delphic Oracle lost that valuable customer when it wrongly advised him to invade Persia during the sixth century B.C. The Romans, who came later, paid little attention to the Delphic Oracle's predictions, but did respect its money-making ability. About the same time (60 A.D.), the Roman historian Plutarch described how the prophetess, instead of going into a trance, ran screaming toward the exit and died within a few days.

The Delphic Oracle had lost nearly all of its credibility when it was visited in 363 A.D. by Roman Emperor Julian, whose mission was to banish Christianity from the empire by rejuvenating the powers of the various pagan gods. Julian asked the Oracle if such a plan had any merit. To his surprise, the priestess replied that the Delphic Oracle would never make another prediction.

The prophecy came true. After a silence of twenty-seven years, the Delphic Oracle was destroyed by Emperor Theodosius I in 390 A.D.

Columbus' Last Voyage

It was the first voyage of Christopher Columbus that made him famous, of course. Legends have grown up around it, especially the one telling how Queen Isabella of Spain pawned her jewels to finance the voyage. In fact, she even had to borrow some money from King Ferdinand.

At any rate, the famous first voyage began on 3 August 1492, Columbus and eighty-seven others sailing on the *Santa Maria*, *Nina*, and *Pinta*. The purpose of the trip was to reach the spice-laden East by sailing west. As an example of the efficiency with which the expedition was planned, the interpreter who was sent along, one Luis de Torrez, spoke Hebrew, Latin, Greek, Spanish, Arabic, Coptic, and Armenian, but not Chinese, which was presumably the language of those they would meet. Three days after the ships set sail, the *Pinta* lost her rudder. And on 15 September, a meteor fell into the sea not far from them. Not long after this, the men began to murmur but Columbus hung on until Friday, 12 October, when land was finally sighted. The natives called the island Guanahani, but Columbus named it San Salavador.

Columbus' second voyage, in 1493, was a more ambitious undertaking, with a crew of 1,500 and 17 ships. After exploring the West Indies further, Columbus was sick for five months, recovering just in time to put down a native uprising and send back five shiploads of Indians to be used as slaves.

Columbus' third voyage, which began in 1498, resulted in the discovery of South America but not the Chinese spices everyone had been looking for all along. The amount of gold brought back by the explorer obviously disappointed the King and Queen, also, so Columbus sailed once again.

For his fourth and final voyage, he left Spain in 1502 with 150 men and 4 ships. Arriving at Central America, he sailed along the coast, hoping to find the mouth of the Ganges River. When he couldn't locate it, he returned with some tobacco, bananas, Indian corn, cocoanuts, palm oil, an American dog, a rabbit, several lizards, a stuffed alligator, and 6 Indians.

Older than his years at fifty-four, Columbus died on 20 May 1506. Had he been more of a writer like Amerigo Vespucci, a Florentine who wrote a graphic account of his voyages which somehow gave the impression he had discovered the New World, the Western Hemisphere today might consist of the continents of North and South Columbus.

The Last Pope with Children

In the early days of the Roman Catholic Church, it was not mandatory for the pope to be celibate; in fact, one pope, Hormisdas (514-523), was the father of another pope, Silverius (536-537); and Pope Gregory I (The Great), who reigned from 590 to 604, was the great-grandson of Pope Felix III (483-492).

Still another pontiff, Adrian II (867-872), was married before he ascended the papal throne and had a wife and family. Lame, one-eyed, and gray-haired, Adrian was a tragic figure. Refusing to adopt celibacy or renounce his family, he encouraged them to live at the Lateran Palace with him. Later, when his wife and daughter were abducted, Adrian called for help from France's Emperor Louis II. A punitive expedition was arranged,but when the abductor heard of it, he killed Adrian's wife and daughter and vanished.

The last pope to have children (albeit illegitimate ones), and acknowledge them, was Rodrigo Borgia, who became a cardinal in 1456 (while still in his twenties), vice chancellor of the Roman Church in 1457, and dean of the sacred college in 1476. During these early years before he became pope in 1492, Borgia had four children by Vanozza de Cataneis, a woman who happened to be married to someone else. When two of these illegitimate youngsters grew up to be the notorious Cesare and Lucrezia Borgia, the pope (Borgia took the name Alexander VI) quickly earned an even gaudier reputation. Word got around that Alexander had been elected by a corrupt conclave but nothing was done to remove him from office, even after he showed favoritism to his children by spending papal funds to further their careers.

The strongest voice raised against Alexander was that of Girolamo Savonarola, a spiritual leader who had previously attacked the influential Medici family. When Savonarola criticized Alexander in 1497, the pope excommunicated him and threatened to extend the interdiction to the entire city of Florence if he didn't stop preaching. Eventually Savonarola and two of his disciples were arrested and tortured. When Savonarola, under pain of torture, confessed to being a false prophet, Alexander allowed him to be executed.

The papacy survived "the Borgian pope," but after the reign of Alexander VI (which ended in 1503), more attention was given to the moral background of the man ascending the chair of Peter.

Nostradamus' Last Prediction

Acclaimed even today as one of the foremost seers in the history of the world, Michel de Nostradame, known as Nostradamus, lived from 1503 to 1566, and was amazingly accurate in many of his predictions.

In 1555, he published *Centuries*, a book of rhymed prophecies. Some of them, such as that which foresaw the great fire of London, were amazingly specific:

> "The blood of the just shall be dry in London.
> Burnt by the fire of 3 times 20 and 6.
> The ancient dame shall fall from her high place,
> Of the same sect many shall be killed."

During the famous conflagration of 1666, the statue of the Virgin Mary atop St. Paul's Cathedral did, indeed, fall.

Nostradamus was also very specific in predicting the death of Queen Elizabeth in 1603, the fact that Louis XV's love for luxurious living would lead to the French Revolution, as well as the rise and fall of Napoleon (even mentioning Elba). Yet many of the verses could pertain to one of many similar events, such as:

> "The Slavic people in a warlike hour
> Will be so highly lifted up by their ideals,
> That they will change a prince,
> And bring forth a person of lowly birth to rule."

which could refer to the Russian Revolution of 1917 — as claimed by hindsight — or any other southern European revolt against monarchy, which occurred in abundance during the early years of the twentieth century.

Nostradamus' last prediction was about himself. On the night of 1 July 1566, his pupil, Chavigny, bid Nostradamus goodnight, to which the seer replied: "Tomorrow at sunrise I shall not be here."

The next morning he was found slumped at his workbench, dead, apparently of natural — and predictable — causes.

The Last Solitaire

Like the dodo, the solitaire (*Pezophaps Solitarius*) was confined to a small area in the Indian Ocean, specifically the island of Rodriguez.

A strip of land only ten miles long and four miles wide, Rodriguez was untouched by white men until 1690, when a group of French Huguenot refugees landed there. On hand to greet them was a flightless bird slightly less than three feet tall, the male colored a

305

brownish-gray, the female brown with a white breast. The male had a distinctive knob of bone on each wing which it used for self-defense.

One of the Huguenots, Francis Leguat, mentioned in his diary published in 1708, a bird "which goes by the name of solitary, because 'tis very seldom seen in company, tho' there are an abundance of them."

Faced with the same problems as the dodo — inability to fly and capability of laying only one egg a year — the solitaire was unable to protect itself from dogs and other animals which inevitably followed human settlers. It became extinct about 1760.

The Last of Steller's Sea Cow

Until 1740, the giant mammal that came to be known as Steller's Sea Cow (*Hydrodamalis Stelleri*) was one of nature's best-kept secrets. Three decades after making man's acquaintance, the species was probably extinct.

This mysterious creature was discovered during the third Russian-sponsored expedition to determine if American and Asia were connected by land. When the chief surgeon fell ill, a German professor named Georg Wilhelm Steller was signed for the trip, which left from Russia in 1741.

Less a surgeon than a naturalist, Steller was delighted at spotting a gigantic "sea cow," which was twenty-eight to thirty-five feet long and twenty-two feet thick about the region of its navel. In place of teeth, the animal had two flat loose bones on each side of its mouth for grinding up seaweed. Its other features consisted of small eyes and ears and heavy facial bristles on the lower jaw so thick according to Steller, "that they resemble quills of fowls."

From a distance, Steller said the sea cow resembled the fabled mermaid, although no account ever described the woman-fish as having thick whiskers or a twenty-two foot waist.

Gentle and lacking a strong survival instinct, the sea cows always tried to save one of their own if it were hooked. This, obviously, made them easy to catch. In addition their meat was excellent and the larger creatures weighed up to 7,000 pounds each. In August, 1742, the explorers returned home with the news that Alaska and Russia were not connected by land but that an excellent source of meat could be found in those frigid waters which subsequently came to be known as the Bering Sea.

In 1746, Steller died at age thirty-seven, after describing the sea cow, a branch of the sirenian family, in his book *De Bestris Marinis* (*On Marine Animals*).

Decades of butchery followed Steller's discovery, and the sea cows were wiped out by 1768. While they were at it, the enterprising hunters also extinguished the spectacled cormorant (a plump, glossy, green bird described by Steller). An expedition sent to bring back sea cows in 1783-84 saw none at all, but in 1962 the Russian whaling ship *Buran* spotted a group of large marine animals, about twenty to twenty-four feet long, in shallow water off a cape northeast of Kamchatka. Whether or not they were Steller's sea cows is a mystery, since no specimens were captured and the mammals apparently are extinct.

John Wesley's Last Letter

The founder of Methodism, John Wesley (1703-1791) spent a half-century traveling and preaching the gospel of personal salvation through faith in Christ. His itinerary covered 250,000 miles with 40,000 sermons along the way, many of them in the open air before hostile crowds.

Often he was not received kindly in a community by the local clergy, who felt threatened by Wesley's philosophy that stated redemption was a matter that could be solved by man and God without the formal structure of the Church. Occasionally, mobs were incited to harass Wesley, but he accepted the danger as part of his job. "When struck by a stone, he would wipe the blood from his face and continue preaching," biographer John Langley Hall wrote. "Church bells were rung to drown his voice, he was pelted with stink bombs, and on one occasion a man was even bribed to shout, 'fresh salmon!' as a tasteful temptation to desert him." Wesley's rule was always to look a mob in the face.

A well-educated man with an Oxford manner of speaking who identified with the poor, Wesley was not a genial shepherd who suffered in silence. Once he declared that "nine-tenths of the men in England have no more religion than horses," and that the clergy "are the pests of the Christian world, the grand nuisance of mankind, a stink in the nostrils of God."

Wesley wrote incessantly in a style that Sir Leslie Stephen said went "straight to the mark without one superfluous flourish." Frequently he earned enough on his cheaply produced books to give away as much as 1,400 pounds a year. He also wrote letters, at least nine heavy volumes of them during his long lifetime, many of which display his genuine concern for social welfare and the souls of his fellow men.

He was still preaching and writing hours before he died. On the evening of 23 February 1791, he delivered a sermon in Mr. Belson's house at Leatherhead, then retired to read a tract concerning Gustavus Vasa, a black man who had been kidnapped and sold into slavery.

The next morning he wrote his last letter. It was to William Wilberforce, an English reformer who had been elected to Parliament in 1780 and was an energetic opponent of slavery. It read:

"Dear Sir...Reading this morning a tract by a poor African, I was particularly struck by that circumstance, that a man who has a black skin, being wronged or outraged by a white man, can have no redress; it being a law in all our Colonies that the oath of a black against a white goes for nothing. What villainy is that! that He who has guided you from youth up may continue to strengthen you in this and all things in the prayer of, dear sir, your affectionate servant..."

On 2 March 1791, Wesley died in his house on City Road in Leatherhead at the age of 87.

Francis Asbury's Last Sermon

The second bishop of the Methodist Episcopal Church in America, Francis Asbury dedicated himself to the ministry in 1771, when there were only 400 Methodists in North America. For the next forty-five years he crisscrossed the wilderness of the new United States, spreading the word. Traveling 5,000 to 6,000 miles annually, he introduced the circuit rider system, enduring extreme hardships despite a chronic throat disease that made it difficult for him to breathe and speak loudly.

By 1816, the year of Asbury's death at the age of seventy, there were 214,000 Methodists in the United States being served by 2,000 ministers.

Often delivering a half-dozen sermons a day, Asbury could preach on just about any topic or verse of scripture—and at considerable length. He was still active on 24 March 1816, just a week before he succumbed to tuberculosis and general debility. Arriving at the Old Methodist Church in Richmond, Virginia, Asbury was in such a weakened condition that he delivered the last sermon of his life lying on a table.

His subject was *Romans*, IX, 28: "For he will finish his work, and cut it short in righteousness: because a short work will the Lord make upon the earth..." The sermon lasted nearly an hour.

Asbury died on 31 March, at Spottsylvania, Virginia, a much-venerated man. The city of Asbury Park, New Jersey was named after him.

The Last Great Auk

A member of the penguin family, the Great Auk (*Pinguinus impennis*) was about two feet tall, had a dark brown head, and was extremely clumsy.

Once found in the northern sections of Russia, Canada, and the United States, the Great Auk began to disappear once it was discovered its body consisted of a good layer of meat covered by fat that was useful as fuel. In addition, the collarbone of the auk made an excellent fishhook. Even worse for the auk, it was easily hunted, often stretching itself prone on rocks, oblivious to anyone who approached.

Thus hunters often just dropped a gangplank from a fishing boat to a rock, walked over to the auks and knocked them on the head. By the nineteenth century, the bird was confined to Greenland, Iceland, and several nearby islands. The last auk on the island of St. Kilda, Scotland, was killed in 1821.

Fate was not kind to the auk. Seemingly safe on the remote islands at the southwest tip of Iceland (known as "the auk rocks"), the birds lost their safest haven, Geirfugl Island, when it disappeared during an earthquake in 1830.

Realizing that only a few Great Auks were left, museum directors around the world put out the word that they needed the birds for stuffing. This assured that the species would become extinct; any time an Icelander needed some money, he merely paddled over to the island of Eldey, killed an auk and sold it to a museum. Thus, between 1830 and 1844, the few remaining auks were reduced to extinction. On 4 June 1844, a bird collector named Carl Siemsen hired Jon Brandsson and Sigwrdr Islefsson to kill the last two Greak Auks.

Since that time, auks and auk eggs have become highly treasured and expensive items. In 1934, two eggs and two skins were purchased by Captain Vivian Hewitt (first aviator to fly the Irish Sea, in 1912) for a total of $7,245. This, added to his previous collection, made him the world's greatest private collector of auk material.

In 1971, the director of the Natural History Museum of Iceland paid $9,000 for a stuffed auk. Six years later, a specimen which had been bought in 1837 for five pounds was sold by the University of Durham for 4,200 pounds.

The Last Quagga

The quagga resembled an unfinished zebra, with stripes on its head, neck, shoulders, and part of its trunk. The rest of its body was a light chestnut color with white legs.

Found on the South African plains from the Cape of Good Hope as far north as the Vaal River, the quagga was first mentioned in 1685 by a man named Tachard. He referred to it as a "wild ass." Others, equally in the dark concerning the animal, thought it was a female zebra. In any event, man's normal greed took over, and soon the quagga was much in demand for shoes and meat.

In 1811, naturalist William John Burchell described a quagga hunt, which was one of unrelieved slaughter by Dutch settlers. By then the quagga was already in danger of becoming extinct but no thought was given to domesticating them. Sixteen specimens were shipped to European zoos during the nineteenth century, but no breeding programs were set up. In the meantime, the last wild quagga was shot about 1870.

The London Zoo's male and female, purchased in 1851 and 1858, respectively, failed to produce any offspring. The male had a fit of rage in 1864 and died soon afterward of injuries caused by his rampage. Eight years later, the female, the only living quagga ever photographed, died of old age.

Two other females outlived her: one at the Berlin Zoo dying in 1875, the last, a resident of the Amsterdam Zoo, dying 12 August 1883.

The Last Bell-Crier

A cliche of period movies, the typical bell-crier was pictured walking through old-time towns, shouting something like, "Twelve o'clock and all's well." In fact, the main duty of the bellman was not to provide time and news reports, but to make sure everyone had a lantern lit so that the street was properly illuminated. Thus, the usual cry in the night was, "Hang out your lanterns!" or "Look to your lanterns!"

In 1556, during the reign of Queen Mary, Alderman Draper of Cordwainer Street added the touch of saluting those who were still on the street with rhymes suitable to the festivals and seasons of the year. Later, criers began to make announcements relating to lost objects, sales by public auction or private contract, as well as comments relating to weddings, christenings, and funerals.

Daily newspapers gradually replaced the bell crier during the eighteenth and nineteenth centuries. The last city to give up its officially salaried crier was Liverpool, England, which retired Francis George in March 1890, after a career of 60 years.

During his decades on the street, Geroge restored 130,000 stray children to their parents and walked before fifty-three Liverpool Mayors on civic occasions.

His salary at the time of his retirement was twenty-five pounds a year.

Brooklyn's Last Day as a City

Although being mayor of Brooklyn was not the same as having a kingship, during the nineteenth century it was nearly as prestigious in many ways. Once a neglected suburb of New York City, Brooklyn absorbed many nearby settlements and villages such as Flatbush, New Utrecht and Gravesend until, just before the Civil War, it was the third largest city in the nation.

By 1890, Brooklyn's population was 806,343, a jump of nearly a quarter-million over the figure for 1880. In 1891, the Republican vote in Brooklyn was larger than that of the entire state of Vermont, double that cast in Oregon. In fact, the city in 1892 had more registered voters than seventeen states in the nation. The fourth largest industrial city in the United States, in a single week in 1886 the tonnage of ships at Brooklyn's piers totaled 45,199 as compared to 11,933 for New York City. One half of the sugar consumed in the U.S. was refined in Brooklyn; only Chicago did a larger business in dressed meats; nearly all of the east coast oil, aside from the facilities in New Jersey, was refined in Brooklyn.

Despite all this industrial activity and resultant prosperity, Brooklyn during the late nineteenth century was still basically a quiet and charming community proud of its greenery and churches. Thus when talk began to be heard that it would be "advantageous" for New York City to annex Brooklyn (the term used was "consolidation"), the reaction in Brooklyn was one of stunned amusement. When proponents of consolidation pointed out that it would be disastrous if Chicago surpassed New York in population and became "the commercial metropolis of America," a situation that could be averted only by adding Brooklyn's population to that of New York City's, few in Brooklyn were impressed, least of all the hometown paper, the *Eagle*, which noted on its editorial page that:

> Brooklyn is a city of homes and churches.
> New York is a city of Tammany Hall and crime government.
> Rents are twice as cheap in Brooklyn as in New York and homes are to be bought for a quarter of the money. The price of rule here is barely more than a third of what it is in New York.
> Government here is by public opinion and for the public interest. If tied to New York, Brooklyn would be a Tammany suburb, to be kicked, looted and bossed as such...

Against this background, Frederick W. Wurster became the twenty-fifth (and last) mayor of Brooklyn in 1897. Born in Germany in 1850, he came to America at the age of seven and went into the trade of his father, who had opened an iron and spring factory. Not a professional politician, Wurster entered the cabinet of Mayor Charles A. Schieren as fire commissioner. In 1896, he ran for Mayor, promising if elected to run the city on "a business basis."

His first problem after being elected, as it turned out, was whether or not there was to be a city of Brooklyn at all. By 1897, proponents of consolidation had given up trying to convince Brooklynites to join New York voluntarily. The new tack taken was to put the matter of consolidation to a vote by the entire greater New York area. Wurster opposed the idea, naturally, vetoing a bill that was eventually passed on a state level.

In 1897, voters went to the polls to decide the issue. New Yorkers, predictably, favored consolidation, by a margin of 96,938 to 59,959. Brooklyn's vote was so close that the first tally was not known for a month. Eventually it turned out to be 64,744 in favor and 64,467 against, an unexpected number of voters in Brooklyn's outer wards apparently choosing consolidation because they owned pieces of undeveloped real estate.

Brooklyn's last day as a city was 31 December 1897. On that New Year's Eve, Wurster held an open house at City Hall and reminded his audience that Brooklyn was not a "penniless bride." Meanwhile, a crowd gathered outside, watching silently as the minute hand of the clock pushed its way toward midnight. Before the last stroke of the New Year had sounded, the shivering spectators added their cheers to the din of exploding firecrackers and shrieking factory whistles. The American flag dropped only to reappear a few seconds later flanked by the municipal ensigns of the two cities which had just become one.

Wurster returned to private business, becoming a trustee, director, and incorporator of several banking institutions of Greater New York before dying at Belgrade Lakes, Maine, on 25 June 1917.

The Last Passenger Pigeon

On the morning of 24 March 1900, a small boy in Ohio sighted down the barrel of his BB gun and sent a pellet smashing into the brain of a big red-breasted, blue-backed bird. He had just killed the last passenger pigeon ever to be sighted in the wild.

Incredibly, only three decades before, a mass nesting of passenger pigeons in Wisconsin had covered 750 square miles, for they were once the most plentiful bird in America. Each year, they swept across the central and eastern United States and back again in soaring migratory waves that sometimes darkened the entire sky. They could fly for twenty hours without stopping, with bursts of speed up to ninety miles an hour.

Yet, though elegant and graceful in flight, they were slow and stupid on the ground. When they settled down to feed, they would funnel down out of the sky so close together a single shotgun blast once killed 187 of them. In 1672, some English hunters caught them with nets. It was possible to walk close enough to strike them with poles. Another factor contributing to the passenger pigeon's demise was the fact that females laid only one egg a season.

Ironically, the bird that man was to render extinct in so short a time saved the pilgrims in 1648, when the Massachusetts colonists had no food other than passenger pigeons. Later, in 1736, the birds sold in Boston at six for a penny, for "pigeon pie" was a delicacy and with an estimated 5 billion passenger pigeons in the country, there seemed no danger of eliminating the species.

Early in the nineteenth century, in fact, Scottish-American ornithologist Alexander Wilson watched a flock 250 miles long pass over Kentucky. A few years later, John James Audubon described another flock, also over Kentucky, as a "torrent of life." According to his account, the pigeons took three days to pass, blotting out the sun. A roost on the ground was 40 miles long and three miles wide.

As agriculture spread across the Midwest, farmers poisoned or killed the passenger pigeons because they were a nuisance—a single flock could strip a field of corn in a few hours. Hunters gradually took care of the rest. Finally, only three passenger pigeons remained, all in the Cincinnati Zoo when the last wild bird was shot in 1900. The last of these, whose name was Martha, died on 1 September 1914, at the age of twenty-nine.

Since the species was extinct, her body was frozen in a 300-pound cake of ice and shipped to Washington, D.C., where she still perches under glass in the Smithsonian Institution, a plumed monument to man's destructiveness.

The Last Witness to the Wright Brothers' Flight

Thursday, 17 December 1903, dawned cold and cloudy at Kitty Hawk, North Carolina. A strong north wind blew at better than twenty miles an hour, making it a poor day for Orville and Wilbur Wright to attempt another flight with their crate-like flying machine.

They had been seriously working at manned flight since 1899, when they first built a box kite to test their aeronautical theories. A glider followed, then innumerable tests and frustrations as they tried to locate and adapt a gasoline engine for their machine. There was a broken propeller shaft...then another...an aborted flight...discouragement, and then the resolve to try again.

At ten o'clock that Thursday morning, the men at a nearby lifesaving station saw the Wrights' signal that they were going to try again. Those who were free walked over to help out. John Daniels, Bill Pough, and Adam Etheridge were joined by W.C. Brinkley, a local resident who had become interested in the Wrights. Finally, along came seventeen-year old John Thomas Moore, who lived about three miles down the beach.

Soon the men and the boy hauled the spider web of struts and wires to the starting point, placing it on a dolly. Orville lay down in the cradle amidships, incongruously dressed in a suit, tie, and starched collar. The engine sputtered, roared, moved slowly down the track, then up...up it rose, above the ground, moving against the force of gravity with its own power for 120 feet in 12 seconds.

As the flight almost simultaneously began and ended, no one cheered. Nor did the conversation concern itself with the participants being at a historic event or even the future of aviation. Young Moore, in fact, seemed more interested in a bucket of eggs and a hen he had found down the beach, especially when one of the men pulled the youngster's leg saying the hen laid eight to ten eggs a day.

313

Three more flights followed that day, the longest one 852 feet — nearly a sixth of a mile — before a sudden gust of wind grounded the crude ship after it had been airborne for fifty-nine seconds.

The events of 17 December 1903 subsequently marked a turning point in the technological history of the world. The seven who were there went their different ways and the Wright brothers went on to glory and success. Gradually the witnesses died away, Orville surviving until 1948.

Finally, on a March day in 1952, the last witness to the historic Wright Brothers flight, John Thomas Moore, sixty-five, died of a self-inflicted gunshot wound.

Clarence Darrow's Last Case

The most famous criminal lawyer in Amerian history, Clarence S. Darrow, was able to boast that in a hundred or more murder cases, no client of his had ever died on the gallows or in the electric chair.

A fighter for so-called "lost" legal causes, Darrow was also an ardent champion of personal liberty and the improvement of working conditions. An agnostic, he was also a fierce opponent of bigotry and capital punishment, even when it was obvious that the perpetrator of a heinous crime was unrepentant. "Everybody is a potential murderer," he once said. "I've never killed anyone, but I frequently get satisfaction reading the obituary notices."

Born on 18 April 1857 in the little town of Kinsman, Ohio, Darrow resisted pressure from his father to become a minister, studying law instead and was admitted to the bar at the age of twenty. His first nationally famous case was tried in 1894, when he defended Socialist leader Eugene V. Debs, who had been arrested on a conspiracy charge. Debs was acquitted.

Darrow then went on to defend some of the most notorious people of his day. Darrow successfully defended William D. "Big Bill" Hayward, the McNamara brothers (charged with the 1911 bombing of the *Los Angeles Times* building), Nathan Leopold and Richard Loeb (for the 1924 thrill slaying of fourteen-year-old Bobby Franks), and, in perhaps his most widely known case, John B. Scopes for teaching evolution in violation of Tennessee law.

Darrow's last major case came in 1932, when he was seventy-five years old. Typically, he defended someone accused of a monstrous crime, in this instance U.S. Navy Lieutenant Thomas H. Massie, who early that year was indicted for the "honor slaying" of Hawaiian Joseph Kahahawai, Jr. in Honolulu.

The Massie case began in September of 1931, when the naval officer's wife was abducted and assaulted by five men, one of whom was later caught and identified as Kahahawai. The trial that followed was a sensational one, partly because it pitted a native son against an American naval officer, many of whom were resented by Honolulu's population. During the three-week trial, feelings ran high. While the jury was out for a marathon ninety-seven hours, the judge once had to break up a fight between a pair of angry jurymen. Despite strong evidence against Kahahawai and his cohorts, the jury was a hung one and acquittal followed.

That did not end matters, of course. In December of 1931, one of Kahahawai's friends was picked up by "Navy men" and beaten. A note delivered soon afterward to a U.S. submarine base nearby contained the threat that, "We have raped your women and will get some more." Between 12 and 18 December 1931, a half-dozen assaults on Navy men were reported. Then, on 9 January 1932, the body of Kahahawai was found. He had been beaten and shot to death. The finger of guilt pointed to Lt. Massie, his mother-in-law, Mrs. Granville Fortesque, and a Navy enlisted man, Edmond J. Lord. All three were charged with first degree murder.

Popular sentiment ran against the Americans. "People who take the law into their own hands always make a mess of it," wrote the *Star-Bulletin*, Honolulu's only English language afternoon newspaper. "Especially is this true when the misguided ones are from the ranks of those sworn to protect the Constitution and laws of our country..." A statement signed by thirty-nine pastors and religious workers of the city condemning the assault was issued by the Honolulu Inter-Church Federation.

Against this background, Darrow began his by-now-familiar defense of the underdog. His plea, a time-tested one, was that Massie was insane at the time of the crime's commission, that months of worry following the rape of his wife had worn down his normally rational thought processes to the point where he snapped. To combat this strategy, the prosecution brought in Dr. Paul Bowers of Los Angeles, who, based on his long record of psychiatric practice, testified that in his opinion Massie was sane at the time Kahahawai was shot. Demonstrating that he had lost little of his skill despite his age, Darrow was able to dismiss Dr. Bowers' entire testimony with a minimum of verbiage:

"Tell me, doctor," he asked, "Do you expect to be paid by the prosecution for coming here to Honolulu and testifying?"

"Why, yes," Bowers stammered. "Of course."

"That's all," Darrow said.

A murmur of astonishment that passed through the courtroom indicated that Darrow's attack, however illogical, had impressed both the jury and gallery.

Darrow's closing arguments to the jury were rather less succinct, taking four hours and twenty minutes. In demanding mercy for the defendants, he equated leniency with national honor and love of homeland, at one point charging that sending Massie to prison "would place such a blot on the fair name of this island that all the Pacific Ocean couldn't wash it away."

Alternating between outrage and gentleness, he concluded by asking the jury to consider that, "Every life is shaped by fate and what the individual has to do with it is probably very small. So take this case with kindness and understanding toward the living as well as toward the dead."

Shortly afterward, the jury returned with a verdict of manslaughter, a decision which could carry a heavy prison sentence but did not in this case. Through Darrow's machinations following the trial, Massie's sentence was eventually commuted to one hour in jail. The "great defender" had triumphed once again.

During the remaining five years of life left him, Darrow never stopped working for the underprivileged and under-represented. On 11 March 1938, he performed his last public act in a long career, driving to the Illinois State Penitentiary to appear as a witness before a subcommittee of the Parole Board. On that occasion, he pleaded for the release of Jesse Bings, a seventy-one-year-old black man serving a one-to-ten year sentence for embezzlement.

Two days later, Darrow died at the age of eighty.

The Last Heath Hen

The race of prairie chickens or North American grouse known as the heath hen (*tympanuchus cupido cupido*) was once plentiful in the New England states, ranging as far south as the Potomac River. But the birds had an unfortunate habit of remaining close to their nests during the breeding season, making them (and their offspring) easy targets for the Pilgrim fathers.

As early as 1791, the New York State Legislature passed a law prohibiting the shooting of heath hens during mating season, but there was little enforcement. As a result, the bird was gone from New York by 1870, its declining numbers retreating to the island of Martha's Vineyard, Massachusetts. Even there, the heath hen population decreased until 1907, when it was estimated that just seventy-seven remained in existence.

A genuine endangered species, the heath hen of the early twentieth century then faced a new danger: that they would be hunted by collectors eager to sell them to museums or ornithological collectors. "As a result," the *New York Times* editorialized on 31 May 1900, "scientific persons who ought to be more than a little ashamed of themselves are offering the natives of the island from $25 to $30 apiece for specimens of the doomed race." When preservationists called for laws to help save the heath hen, some were enacted, but the magazine *Forest and Stream* still viewed the situation with despair. "We may enact the most stringent laws and provide the most perfect theoretical scheme of protection," it remarked, "but so long as it shall be true that a heath hen in the hand will be worth $25 to its captor, the birds will be taken to the very last one."

In fact, it didn't turn out that way. Protective efforts increased the size of the heath hen flock to nearly 300 by 1915. But a year later, a forest fire destroyed practically all the birds. As a result, by 1927 the species was down to a grand total of eleven males and two females. A year later there were just two birds left.

By 1933, it was all over for the heath hen, its obituary appearing in the 21 April issue of the *Vineyard Gazette*. Composed by the paper's owner, Henry Beetle Hough, the farewell paragraph struck a poignant note. "To the heath hen, something more than death has happened, or rather, a different kind of death," he wrote. "There is no survivor, there is no future, there is no life to be recreated in this form again...There is a void in the April dawn, there is expectancy unanswered, there is a tryst not kept..."

The Last Mohican

James Fenimore Cooper's turgid novel notwithstanding, the Mohican (or Mohegan) Indians have never really become extinct, although they are very close to it. Currently, about twenty-five of them live on a small reservation in Connecticut.

Supported in their conflicts with American settlers by the British, the Mohicans became one of the most powerful Indian tribes in America, then quickly declined during the eighteenth century. Selling most of their land, they accepted a reservation on the Thames River in southwestern Connecticut.

If the term "last" refers to the the final Indian speaking the Mohican language, then the last of the Mohicans was William Dick (Makwa Monpuy or Maq-Uua-pey), who learned the melodious tongue from his grandmother. When Dick reached the age of 75, a University of Chicago anthropologist had him recite the tribal vocabulary, or as much of it as he could remember. Dick recalled about 300 words. He died in November of 1933, at the age of 76.

Norman Thomas' Last Run for President

If all of the votes cast for Socialist candidate Norman Thomas were added together, the last election he could have won was that of 1852, when the population of the United States was about 25 million. The unfortunate thing for Thomas was that he ran during the twentieth century — 6 times — when it was necessary to get 20 to 25 million votes.

The most active runner for the Presidency in American history, Thomas was called a radical during the 1920s and 1930s when, as a Socialist candidate , he espoused such ideas as unemployment insurance, minimum wage laws, old age pensions, and health insurance. Later, when Franklin Roosevelt's New Deal made many of Thomas' proposals law, socialism's appeal to the working class began to diminish. "It was often said that Roosevelt was carrying out the Socialist Party's platform," Thomas reflected. "Well, in a way it was true — he carried it out on a stretcher."

Also often called a communist, Thomas received almost as much disrespect from Russians as Americans. Leon Trotsky once remarked that, "Norman Thomas called himself a socialist as a result of misunderstanding." Thomas explained that the main thrust of his philosophy was not a communism-versus-capitalism situation, but a democracy-versus-totalitarianism struggle. In 1959, he predicted that, "If we and the Soviet Union escape war in the next thirty years, we'll both wind up practically with the same economic system. I emphasize the word economic. It will be the welfare state writ large. I hope we don't lose our democracy and I hope Russia will get more."

Thomas' first run for President was in 1928, and since the nation was prosperous, he received only 267,420 votes. Four years later, during hard times, he received 884,781 votes, the highest he ever garnered. Contending that true socialism had never been approached, Thomas was an also-ran in 1936, 1940, 1944, and 1948. His last campaign produced 140,260 votes.

Thomas was also an unsuccessful candidate for governor of New York, mayor of New York City (twice), state senator, alderman, and congressman. Despite his lack of success as a campaigner, he was a respected figure when he died on 19 December 1968, at the age of eighty-four.

Gandhi's Last Fast

One of the most respected figures in modern history, Mohandas Karamchand Gandhi (1869-1948) devised a philosophy of non-violent resistance from reading Tolstoy, Thoreau, the New Testament and Hindu scriptures. He called it "Satyagraha" — truth or soul-force.

An Indian nationalist rather than a social revolutionary, Gandhi organized strikes and boycotts to attack British rule. His most frequently used weapon was the fast, which he first used in 1918 when the British passed the Rowlatt Act perpetuating wartime curtailment of Indian civil liberties. Another fast, in 1920, led to Gandhi's arrest for sedition. He was sentenced to six years' imprisonment. Upon his release in 1924 he became president of the Indian National Congress, which gave him the opportunity to speak in favor of women's rights, prohibition, and personal hygiene.

During the following decades, Gandhi led several notable strikes by fasting—in 1929, to plead for independence; in 1932, protesting the treatment of India's Untouchables; in 1933, from May 8-29, again for the Untouchables; in 1943, while in prison for expressing civil disobedience against the British. Released May 1944, this was the last jail term of Gandhi, who spent twelve years of his life behind bars.

Although known as Mahatma ("great soul") and a very serious social reformer, Gandhi was a pleasant man with a quiet sense of humor. Referring to his frequent jail sentences, he once remarked, "I always get the best bargains from behind prison bars." Another time he poked fun at himself by urging an acquaintance to "never take anything for gospel truth even if it comes from a Mahatma."

In August 1946, the British asked Gandhi to form a new government in India, but, a year later, allowed India and Pakistan to be partitioned. Gandhi, who saw the action as something that would further divide the Muslim population of Pakistan and India's Hindu majority, fasted in sorrow at the ill-will generated by Britain's decision.

Then, in 1948, India and Pakistan drifted toward war in Kashmir. Religious feelings ran high as a result of massacres in the Punjab. Sikh and Hindu refugees demanded revenge against Pakistan and were forcing Moslems out of their homes, As war and riots threatened, Gandhi the pacifist put most of the blame on Sadar Vallabhbhai Patel, his longtime friend and boss of the Congress Party. Patel, urging a "get tough" policy with Pakistan, blocked passage of a financial agreement between the two nations, which caused war fever to increase in Pakistan, whose prime minister exclaimed: "Every Pakistani is an atom bomb in himself."

Because most Hindus favored Patel's position, Gandhi's last fast, which started on January 12, 1948, was unpopular with many Indians who wanted war. At 79, Gandhi was in no condition to fast long. Worried doctors hovering over him thought he might not live longer than two weeks.

Some Indians did not even know why the little man was fasting. Those who did sometimes added a jarring note. At one point, as Premier J. Nehru was approaching from his car, a crowd of Sikhs and Hindus began to shout: "Let Gandhi die!" Nehru emerged from his car crying, "How dare you say that? Kill me first! " He then chased the dissidents down the street as Gandhi dozed on.

By the third day of his fast, Gandhi was too weak to walk the 100 yards from the home of C.D. Birla, where he fasted, to his prayer service. Physicians reported that the religious leader was weakening by the hour, that his kidneys were not functioning properly.

At this point, when it seemed that Gandhi would die in his battle against war and hatred, Indians rallied to his cause. Meetings were organized and processions formed around the motto: "Save Gandhi's Life." Post office employees stamped every letter mailed in New Delhi with the line: "Keep communal peace and save Mahatma Gandhi." Finally, after Gandhi had gone without food for 121 hours, a group of Hindu, Moslem and Sikh leaders agreed to allow Moslems in India freedom to worship, travel and keep their own houses—one of Gandhi's conditions for ending the fast. At the same time, the Indian government agreed to reinstate the financial agreement with Pakistan.

The tension having eased considerably, Mahatma Gandhi accepted a glass of orange juice mixed with dextrasol, signifying the end of his fast. "If today's solemn pledge is fulfilled," he said with a chuckle, "it will revive with doubled force my intense wish to live a full span of life—at least 125 years."

Two weeks later, on 30 January 1948, Gandhi was shot and killed by Nathuram Godse, a 37-year old Hindu who viewed pacifism as a threat to Indian independence. Before he died, Gandhi blessed his assassin.

The Last Segregated U.S. Army Unit

For nearly a century following the Civil War, American military units, like bathrooms, schools, and other facilities across the nation, were "separate but equal." Blacks were allowed the privilege of fighting and perhaps dying for their country, but only if they remained in the place assigned for them by their white superiors.

The segregated military system started during the Civil War, when manpower was needed but many Northern leaders felt that whites and blacks would not fight side by side. A number of all-black units displayed excellent fighting qualities by wars end.

America's most venerable black unit, the 24th Infantry Regiment, was organized at Fort McKavett in Texas in 1869. It won its first battle honors in the frontier campaigns against the Indians and achieved its greatest fame as one of the units that stormed San Juan Hill at Santiago, Cuba, in the Spanish-American War. The 24th Infantry was also the first black unit to get into the Pacific Theatre of War in 1942. It fought the Japanese in the Solomon Island chain, in the Marianas, and at Okinawa. In 1946, it joined the occupation force in Japan.

During World War II, black leaders in America led a relatively quiet but aggressive fight for equality, wringing promises from white leaders that segregation would end after the war if blacks agreed to support the mobilization effort. (This "gentlemen's agreement" led, among other things, to the desegregation of major league baseball.)

Moving with all deliberate speed, the War Department had another conflict on its hands by 1950, when communist North Korea invaded South Korea. Needing more manpower—and still not having ended segregation—the U.S. Army finally took the big step on 26 July 1951. On that date, the 24th Infantry Regiment was disbanded and black soldiers integrated into other units of the Army.

Barbara Hutton's Last Husband

"Spring must be here. Barbara Hutton is doing her husband-
cleaning."
—Bob Hope

Woolworth heiress Barbara Hutton was the female counterpart of
Tommy Manville. A rich and spoiled playgirl who changed husbands as often as her wardrobe, Hutton provided lots of entertainment for the American public in the process.

Less jovial and outgoing than Manville, Barbara Hutton tended
to be depressed and withdrawn when a marriage failed, which may
explain why she went to the altar four times less than Tommy.

Her first marriage took place in June, 1933, at a Russian cathedral in Paris. The husband was a phony Georgian prince who said
his father had been a general in the Czar's army. Actually, according to one observer, "Prince" Mdivani was nothing more than the
"scion of a distinguished line of sheepherders."

Nevertheless, Hutton called herself Princess Barbara and gave
Mdivani a $50,000 annual allowance. He responded by insulting
her publicly with lines such as "Why can't you be sleek like a
European? You're fat as a pig." They were divorced on 13 May
1935. "I shall never marry again," Miss Hutton said.

Twenty-four hours after the divorce was final, she was married to
Count Court Hangwitz-Reventlow. When that marriage ended,
Barbara decided she had had enough of specious royalty and needed
the real thing. Husband number three turned out to be film actor
Cary Grant, who took to eating his meals in bed whenever Barbara
invited her friends over for dinner. That marriage lasted three years.

In 1947, free once again, Barbara met another chunk of royalty,
Prince Igor Troubetzkoy of Lithuania, who just happened to be
exchanging dollars for francs in a French park. Some said that
Troubetzkoy was more than a little shady but Barbara didn't care.
They were married on 1 March 1947, at which point disintegration
set in. Not long afterward, the prince was demanding $3 million for
a divorce settlement and Barbara was calling him "the meanest man
in the world." Eventually Troubestzkoy settled for $1,000 a month
for life as the price of bowing out of Barbara's life.

Single again in 1951, the 39-year-old Barbara took up with the
notorious Dominican playboy-diplomat Porfirio Rubirosa, whom
Zsa Zsa Gabor said was "to lovemaking what Tiffany is to
diamonds." Barbara never said whether she agreed or not. The
marriage took place on 30 December 1953, after which the bride
took to bed with a broken ankle and the bridegroom went out to
celebrate. The couple were separated seventy-three days later.

Another royal figure became husband number six. This was
Baron Gottfried Von Cramm, an international tennis star who dis-

321

claimed his right to the title. In 1961, he also disclaimed his right to Miss Hutton.

The heiress' last husband, Raymond Doan Vinh Champacak, was, in her words, "a beautiful young Indonesian prince." The wedding, which took place in 1964, was also the most exotic. Barbara wore a green and gold sari-type gown, a gold ring on each big toe, gold anklets, and had the soles of her feet painted red.

A bit more than two years later, on 4 December 1966, Barbara had to be carried into the plane leaving Tangier, Morocco, for Mexico City, where she was headed in order to obtain her final divorce. Friends of the fifty-four-year-old Miss Hutton said she had made a settlement of more than $3 million to free herself from the Laotian artist, who promptly faded into obscurity after his stint as last husband of the perennially lonely heiress.

Retiring to the exclusive Beverly Wilshire Hotel in Los Angeles, Miss Hutton died there on 12 May 1979 at the age of sixty-six, a very rich woman unable to solve her lifelong problem of how to share her existence with one man for more than a few years.

Tommy Manville's Last Wife

The son of the founder and chairman of the Johns-Manville asbestos corporation, playboy Tommy Manville used marriage as a means of personal publicity. He once hung a sign over the entrance to his mansion that read: "Beware. Marrying Manville lives here." He did his best to live up to the legend, taking eleven brides between 1911 and his death in 1967.

He was just 17 years old in 1911 when he met chorus girl Florence Huber under the marquee of Wallack's Theatre at Broadway and 46th Street in New York. Five days later, she was the first Mrs. Manville.

Surprisingly, the marriage lasted eleven years. For his second wife, Tommy married his father's 23-year-old secretary Lois Arline McCoin, on October 1, 1925. Later, Miss McCoin said: "Tommy never enjoyed being married. For him, the fun was in the chase. I took exactly three days to realize it."

By 1931, the year of his third wedding, friends of Tommy Manville were betting on the length of the marriage. Babe Ruth, who gave it a month, was closest, the breakup occuring after thirty-four days.

After wife number four departed in 1937, Manville said, "never again!" But in November, 1941, another buxom blonde became Mrs. Manville number five. She lasted seventeen days. Wife number six lasted two months but the seventh Mrs. Manville established a record for brevity, leaving in just eight hours. By this time, Manville had become a national joke. For example, an Idaho farmer wrote to

Tommy, "My brother is in a mental institution. They ought to let him out and put you in."

Three more wives followed, one of the marriages actually ending by something other than divorce when the eighth Mrs. Manville was killed in a car accident. "We have been friends," Tommy said of his wife at the crash scene.

Only months later, he was married again.

The eleventh and final Mrs. Manville, a waitress named Christina Erdlen, obtained the title on 12 January 1960, when Tommy was sixty-six. The marriage lasted until 9 October 1967, when Manville died.

By then, it was estimated that Manville had spent more than $1.25 million on divorce settlements. "Every penny was well spent," he said once to Ed Sullivan during a TV interview. "I know some of the biggest men in the country who spent a lot more on hobbies and ended up with a lot less."

The Last Meatless Friday

For more than a thousand years, Roman Catholics refrained from eating meat on Fridays, the custom becoming church law during he reign of Nicholas I, who was pope from 858 to 867 A.D.

The penance rule had many exemptions. Travelers on trains and airlines were not required to refrain from eating meat; military personnel and dependents living with them were exempted; and in Spain, Catholics stopped the penance in 1089 in recognition of the Moors' defeat. Nevertheless, a majority of the world's Catholics prepared fish and other substitutes with grim once-a-week regularity....until 1966.

In February of that year, Pope Paul VI ruled in an apostolic decree that prayer or charitable works might be substituted as penance instead of fasting and abstinence, thus authorizing national bishops's conferences to make their own decisions.

In Italy, the ban on eating meat on Friday was lifted the following August. Canada authorized its Catholics to eat meat on Fridays on 14 October 1966. French bishops issued a similar decree several days later. Mexico and the African republic of Upper Volta were next to fall in line.

On 18 November, the United States joined the list of nations dropping the tradition, the official end to the ban to be 2 December. But because November 25 was the Friday after Thanksgiving—a day when Catholics were traditionally exempted from the penance—the last meatless Friday in the U.S. was actually 18 November 1966.

Fish dealers who were interviewed about the possible economic consequences seemed unworried if not somewhat hostile. Said a spokesman for the National Fisheries Institute, "It is a long time since the seafood industry of the United States depended upon the observances of religious duties for its welfare."

The Last Rum Ration

For nearly three centuries, British sailors looked forward to their daily tot of rum, a tradition that began in 1687. Previously, beer had been the official alcoholic beverage of the Royal Navy, but when it was soon discovered that Jamaican rum did not go bad, it replaced beer. In 1731, the official daily rum ration for each man was fixed at a half pint in two equal tots.

Nine years later, Admiral Edward Vernon ordered the rum ration diluted with water in order to prevent drunkenness. The mixture of rum and water was nicknamed "grog" because of Vernon's penchant for wearing a type of cloak known as a grogram in foul weather. Drunken dizziness was soon known as "grogginess."

In 1824, the rum ration was reduced to a quarter-pint daily. Further erosion occurred in 1850, each man being given an eighth-pint before the midday meal. Meanwhile, in the United States Navy, temperance advocate Rear Admiral Andrew Hull Foote became the first to eliminate the rum ration on his ships. Finally, in 1914, U.S. Navy Secretary Josephus Daniels ordered that Welch's grape juice be served in place of rum on all vessels.

The tradition lingered in the British Navy until 31 July 1970, when the rum ration was ended for good. Royal Navy officials said that the 283-year old habit was "inappropriate" in a modern "instant response" Navy.

At Portsmouth, solemn music was played as officers gathered around a black-draped barrel in a coffin to sip their last measure.

Last TV Cigarette Ad

In January of 1967, a lawyer named John F. Banzhaf III asked the Federal Communications Commission (FCC) an embarrasing question: Considering the mounting evidence linking cigarettes with cancer and heart disease, shouldn't there be time on the airwaves to tell people not to smoke?

Six months later, the FCC directed the commercial broadcast industry to air one anti-smoking spot for every three cigarette ads it ran. Eventually, this led to the Public Health Smoking Act of 1970 which banned all cigarette advertising from radio and television after 1 January 1971.

The final day of programming before the blackout produced a monster smoke screen of last-minute smoking commercials. Philip Morris went on a $1.25 million binge on New Year's Day, filling the Dick Cavett, Johnny Carson, and Merv Griffin shows with ads. The traditional football bowl games were also loaded.

At midnight, the cigarette ads promptly disappeared—for twenty-four hours and forty minutes. Then, at precisely 12:40 a.m., 3 January 1971, during the movie *Crack in the Mirror* being aired on ABC-TV, New Yorkers suddenly saw and heard a thirty-second spot for Vantage cigarettes. A spokesman for the network said "human error" was responsible for the ad's getting on the screen.

The Last All-Male Ivy League University Club

During the 1960s, most of the Ivy League university clubs founded during the nineteenth century gave into the inevitable by eliminating their men-only rule. The Yale Club, for example, began admitting women in 1969; the Princeton Club, in 1963.

By 1972, only the Harvard Club remained an all-male bastion. "The hens ought to be allowed to peck at each other," one elderly member remarked. Another member, from the class of 1958, expressed fear that allowing women in would convert the 107-year-old club into "another East Side singles bar."

On May 4, 1972, with the black-gowned, grim-visaged features of thirteen past presidents gazing down at them from the mahogany-paneled walls of Harvard Hall, some 2,500 club members put the matter to a vote.

The result was 1,654 in favor of allowing women to join, 854 against. Because of the requirement that two-thirds of the membership had to favor a resolution for it to pass, the nays had won by a narrow margin of eighteen votes.

"The Harvard man had never feared to stand alone," shouted a tweed-jacketed member after the result was known. "This is a bastion to the madness of the outside world."

Others were not so jubilant. Even as the members were voting, two groups moved against the bastion. The New York Civil Liberties Union announced that it had filed suit against the Harvard Club, seeking revocation of the group's liquor license on the grounds that the state was encouraging discrimination. Mrs. Eleanor Holmes Norton of the New York Commission on Human Rights sent a two-page letter to the club calling for an end to its all-male policy.

An uneasy truce followed the May vote. In August, the club allowed women to have lunch in its main dining room, thereby reversing a time-honored rule requiring a separate entrance, dining room, and bar for women except for special occasions.

Then, on 12 January 1973, another vote was held, this time 2,097 to 695, in favor of admitting women. Albert H. Gordon, the outgoing president, accepted the result philosophically. "Sure, it would be nice to go back thirty years," he said, "but who can do that?"

The Last Case of Smallpox

An infectious disease which at its worst caused death and at its most benign left the victims scarred with pock marks, smallpox was around nearly as along as mankind. The mummy of Egyptian Pharaoh Ramses V, who died about 1160 B.C., shows he had smallpox in his youth.

Some well-known historical figures carried off by smallpox were Rebecca Rolfe (nee Pocahontas), who died in 1617 at the age of twenty-two; Holy Roman Emperor Josef I, who succumbed to the disease in 1711; and Russian Czar Peter II, who died at fourteen, on his wedding day in 1730. During the eighteenth century, smallpox killed 60 million Europeans. George Washington's Continental Army in the northern states had 5,500 cases out of a total of 10,000 men, which led the general to ask Congress for approval to innoculate the entire army.

By the late eighteenth century, the innoculation process was known but was a matter of some controversy. In 1718, Lady Mary Wortley Montagu, the wife of the British ambassador to Turkey, published "Innoculation Against Smallpox," which described how a small amount of smallpox pus could be inserted into a well person in order to produce immunization through a mild case of the disease. In order to dramatize the process, Lady Montagu had her five-year old daughter innoculated in the presence of some leading physicians, who were so impressed they recommended the process to King George I. After testing it further on charity school children and prison inmates, the King had two of his own grandchildren innoculated.

The bad news was that sometimes the innoculation process didn't work because of crude techniques or because people failed to understand that innoculation could not halt the disease once it had started.

The controversy raged until the end of the century, when Dr. Edward Jenner proved that injecting a person with cowpox provided immunity against smallpox.

As a result of Jenner's experiments, many nations started immunization programs in schools, gradually eradicating the disease. In 1949, the last case of smallpox in the United States was recorded. Innoculation continued until 1971, when it was stopped. That same year, South America was declared rid of the disease.

In lesser-developed countries, smallpox continued to break out despite continuing innoculation programs carried on by the World Health Organization. In 1967, India's Health Ministry reported that fifteen of the nation's seventeen states were plagued by smallpox and that some 4,000 people had died of the disease during the first three months of the year. All told, 2 million people died of smallpox throughout the world in 1967, but prevention became so efficient that by 16 October 1977, scientists were able to report that the last case had been discovered in Somalia.

The Last of the Pony Express

Beginning with a bang and dying with a whimper, the Pony Express (official title: Central Overland California and Pike's Peak Express Company) was established slightly more than a decade after the gold rush of 1849 changed California from a remote Spanish-American outpost to a bustling but isolated section of the United States. During the spring of 1860 a trail was laid out between St. Joseph, Missouri, and Sacramento, California, passing through 119 stations over a distance of 1,966 miles.

On 3 April 1860, amid much hoopla, the first Pony Express rider, Johnson William "Billy" Richardson, departed St. Joseph at exactly 7:15 p.m. while James Randall rode eastbound from San Francisco. Eleven days later, the last of thirty westbound riders, William Hamilton, arrived at San Francisco to the accompaniment of a brass band playing, "See, The Conquering Hero Comes." Thereafter, for about eighteen months, the Pony Express averaged ten days per delivery at a cost of between two dollars and ten dollars per ounce of mail, some 34,753 pieces of correspondence being transported.

During its existence, the Pony Express employed more than 200 riders, including William F. "Buffalo Bill" Cody and James B. "Wild Bill" Hickok. The firm distributed Bibles to all its riders and prohibited drinking and the use of foul language.

Predictably, Indian uprisings often slowed the deliveries, with one disturbance bringing mail delivery to a halt from the latter part of May 1860 to the end of June. Winter also lengthened the delivery time, although eventually service was increased from weekly to bi-weekly. The fastest time managed by the Pony Express was in November of 1860 when news of Abraham Lincoln's election victory was carried from Fort Kearny, Nebraska, to Fort Churchill, Nevada — then the terminus of the long-distance lines under construction by the Western Union Telegraph Company — in just six days.

The coming of the transcontinental telegraph spelled doom for the Pony Express and, when the eastern and western lines were joined near Salt Lake City on 26 October 1861, the service was discontinued. Those riders carrying mail at the time made their final deliveries in November.

The Last U.S. Army Air Mail

The development of air mail was slowed by World War I, but not enough to prevent the United States Army Air Corps from noisily inaugurating the first flights near the end of the war. On 15 May 1918 a large crowd assembled at Potomac Park near Washington,

D.C. for the debut of what was then called the U.S. Aerial Mail Service. Included in the audience was President Woodrow Wilson, who waited with increasing impatience as pilot George L. Boyle tried unsuccessfully to start his Flying Jenny. After twenty minutes and Wilson's departure, the crowd broke into jeers. The crew suddenly remembered that no fuel had been put into the plane. From that point on, with the exception of the pilot becoming lost and having to land in a Maryland pasture, the debut was a complete success.

The Army carried the mail until 10 August 1918 when, in accordance with the nation's free enterprise philosophy, contracts were awarded to private carriers. A disastrous period followed, as thirty-one of the first forty pilots hired met their deaths in plane crashes. The coming of the Depression, however, put the Army Air Mail Corps back into the airmail business in 1934.

Hampered by inexperience, lack of funds, and obsolete planes, the men of the Army Air Mail Corps suffered enormously during the spring of 1934. At Byrd Field, Virginia, pilots shivered in drafty hangars, cooked meals over outdoor fires, and slept on bare mattresses. Officers often had to lend money to enlisted men for food, and one radio operator in Chicago went two days at his post without a bite to eat. Altogether, Air Corps men went into personal debt to the tune of $250,000 in order to keep the mail flying. By 23 April 1934, Lt. Thurman A. Wood became the thirteenth fatality in two months when he crashed in a rainstorm after setting out from Chicago for Omaha after dark.

Faced with an impossible situation, the government returned the air mail routes to private carriers shortly thereafter. The last regular U.S. Army route, the Chicago, Pembina and North Dakota line, was flown in June 1934.

The Last Timed Postmark

Until 1 February 1964, postmarks of the United States Postal Service contained the time of day—within thirty minutes—that a piece of mail passed through each station. This nineteenth century practice was a monument to the speed of delivery—then. Thus, a letter addressed to the Reverend John H. Goucher (founder of Goucher College, Baltimore) from Bishop W. F. Mallalieu of Auburntown, Massachusetts, left Boston on 14 September 1908 with a 3 p.m. postmark. It arrived at 10:30 a.m. 15 September, just nineteen-and-a-half hours later. Such speed in those days, according to students of the early U.S. Post Office, was by no means rare. All for the price of two cents, it should be added, and without a Zip code to guide the letter on its way.

Six years after Postmaster General Arthur Summerfield's "greatest period of postal progress" was slated to begin, the Post Office decided to do away with the half-hourly cancellation time on its post-marks. The reason given was that recording the time on each letter necessitated a manual operation that slowed down the speed of mail delivery.

What was not said was that as the Post Office bureaucracy became more and more lead-footed, a mere thirty minutes one way or the other in the delivery of a letter was totally irrelevant.

The Last Railway Post Office

In 1838, Congress declared all railroads to be post roads and provided for making direct contracts for delivery of mail by rail. Several decades later, the process evolved whereby a car on many trains was equipped so that clerks could sort the mail as the car moved from city to city. On 7 July 1862, the first of these Railway Post Offices was established on the Hannibal and St. Joseph Rail-road. The idea caught on to such an extent that most railraoads had such service by the turn of the century.

Stories abound concerning the efficiency of typical RPO crews. In April 1947, L.B. Parker of Hinkley, California, wrote a thank you note to clerks on San Francisco and Barstow (Santa Fe RR) train #23, saying: "...I want to pat you guys on the back. That niece of ours, Dolores, received letter April 3, mailed April 2, addressed 'Hinkel,Calif.' You fellows are artists..."

Artists or not, the RPO crews soon discovered that with the decline of the railroads, their services were no longer profitable. The last Railway Post Office departed from Washington, D.C. bound for New York City on 30 June, 1977. After its run, the RPO system was discontinued.

The Last of Three English Coins

With a currency system based on twenty-shilling pounds, twenty-one shilling guineas, farthings which changed in value and size, and a multiplicity of "ha'pennies" and "tuppenny pieces," it was inevitable that Great Britain's money would undergo radical change in the twentieth century. When that change occurred, several tradition-al monetary units saw their last days.

Farthing
"Oranges and lemons, say the bells
of St. Clement's,
You owe me five farthings, say the
bells of St. Martin's."

By an act of Parliament, the childhood ditty known to generations of British children became obsolete on 31 December 1960. As of 1 January 1961, the coin was no longer legal tender in Great Britain.

,When it was first minted in 1279, a farthing could purchase a whole chicken or a pound of beef. Beginning as a silver coin, it was devalued in the seventeenth century and was made of copper. In 1684 a tin farthing was issued with a small copper plug in the center. Later a bronze farthing circulated, but by the early twentieth century it was already a children's coin good only for purchasing the cheapest piece of candy. "Don't bother with the change," most shoppers and shopkeepers said when a few farthings were involved. Thus, in an age of consistently rising inflation, the farthing was clearly an anachronism.

Gold Guinea

First struck in 1663 during the reign of King Charles II, the guinea was so named because gold imported from the Guinea coast of West Africa was used in making the coin.

Stamped on the coins was the figure of a small white elephant, an allusion to the arms of the Royal Adventurers, a company which established trade with Africa. Later, a castle accompanied the elephant in honor of Sir Robert Holmes who, on 8 August 1666, captured 160 Dutch merchant vessels containing bullion and gold dust from Cape Coast Castle in Guinea. (For foreigners who have travelled to London and wondered about it, this explains the origin of the "Elephant and Castle" underground station in that city.)

The value of the gold guinea fluctuated until December 1717, when it was fixed at twenty-one shillings. In 1813, the last gold guinea was issued, its place being taken in 1817 by the silver sovereign. Nevertheless, the "guinea" remained a part of Britain's currency system for more than 150 years after it was last struck, chiefly used in reckoning professional fees, prices for works of art, racehorses, or landed property. It was not restricted to these uses, of course. One reason the term guinea had such a long life was that , being one shilling higher than a pound, it allowed an automatic five percent increase in the price of a commodity without the buyer's being more than subliminally aware of it.

A couple of short-lived variations of the coin were issued during the eighteenth century, notably the quarter-guinea in 1718 and the third-guinea of 1787.

Shilling

No one has ever been able to discover exactly how, when, or why the British decided to divide a pound of silver into 20 shillings. A bother to foreigners and even some natives, the quaint monetary system lasted at least a thousand years until the day of reckoning (some said, much easier reckoning), which arrived on 15 February 1971.

Despite preparations that went back nearly a decade, some were not quite prepared for the changeover from shillings, half pennies, and sovereigns into a decimal pound made up of 100 pence. Many of the Commonwealth nations had already made the switch to the decimal system in the 1950s and 1960s, leaving Great Britain virtually alone.

When the changeover finally arrived, it was not as bad as many feared. British humorists synthesized the situation very well: one cartoon in *Punch* showed a man saying to his wife: "Pull yourself together, Mary. You just can't stay in bed till it's all over..." Another, in *The Evening News*, had a tradesman saying to his employer: "It couldn't be simpler, boss. I'm just not giving any change at all." In fact, many Britishers avoided early contact with the new monetary system by staying away from stores as much as possible. Some grumbled that merchants would use the occasion to slide prices up.

Many did, although there were exceptions. It was all a matter of comparing. The price of the *Sunday Times* actually came down, as did the cost of a telephone call. Public toilets rose in cost from one old penny to one new one.

Nevertheless, at the end of a week, Plantagenet Palliser would have been proud of the way Britons were adjusting to the whole thing. A central figure in Anthony Trollope's political novels of the nineteenth century, Palliser was the sad Prime Minister who spent a great deal of time wondering how he could bring about the decimalization of Great Britain's monetary system.

That it had been accomplished in only slightly more than a century probably would have surprised and delighted him most of all.

The Last of Prohibition

At thirty-two minutes and thirty seconds after five o'clock, Eastern Standard Time, on 5 December 1933, the dry era came to an end.

It was a Wednesday afternoon, thirteen years, ten months, eighteen days and a few hours after the "noble experiment" began. With great solemnity, delegate S. R. Thurman cast his vote and the gavel came down in the State Capitol at Salt Lake City, as Utah became the Thirty-sixth state to ratify the 21st Amendment repealing the prohibitive 18th.

At 5:33, the news reached Joe Weber, half of the Weber and Fields comedy team, who was sitting poised with a glass of champagne at the Astor Hotel in New York City. Swirling his drink as the cameras clicked and rolled, he declared himself the first legal drinker. Simultaneously, writer-critic Benjamin DeCasseres was performing the same cermony (but with scotch) across town at the Waldorf-Astoria, a news-ticker at his elbow.

The final formalities quickly followed, At 5:49:30, the Acting Secretary of State proclaimed prohibition at an end, forgetting to sign the papers in his excitement. A bit more than an hour later, President Franklin D. Roosevelt signed Presidential Proclamation 2065, thus making it official.

Celebrations in various cities took many forms. In New Orleans cannons were fired for twenty minutes. In Baltimore H. L. Mencken said that "it is not often that anything to the public good issues out of the American politicians. This time they have been forced to be decent for once in their lives." He then bellied against the Rennert Hotel bar and downed a glass of Repeal Beer for the assembled.

Elsewhere across the nation, celebrants buried prohibition effigies in coffins, electrocuted them or hanged them from flagpoles.

For some besides the diehard "drys," the end brought a touch of sadness. The Association Against the Prohibition Amendment celebrated its hard-won victory and then voted to disband.

But the last day of national prohibition did not mean liquor was legal all across the United States. In fact, anti-drinking laws in several states remained in force. As the years passed, however, most were repealed.

By the late 1950s, only Oklahoma and Mississippi remained as "dry" states. (In fact, it was possible to circumvent the law in both states, either by drinking in private clubs, buying bootleg booze, or carrying one's own liquor in a brown bag into a restaurant.)

Oklahoma's dry law had come with statehood in 1907. Those favoring legal drinking tried six times to have the prohibition repealed, and were finally successful after more than a half-century. On 7 April 1959, Oklahoma voters gave repeal a margin of about 80,000 votes. Drinking became legal at 10 a.m.. 1 September 1959.

Mississippi then remained the last bastion of the "drys." Dating from 1908, the anti-drinking law was the last one to be passed in the nation. Efforts to repeal it were defeated in 1934 and 1952. During the "dry" period, however, such a strong black market existed that the state levied and collected a nineteen percent tax on illegal liquor. In 1965, an average of 19,385 gallons of illegal liquor was consumed in every Mississippi county. This led Governor Paul B. Johnson, Jr. to say that "Mississippi without a shadow of a doubt is the laughing stock of the nation as far as its so-called prohibition farce is concerned." If the law was not repealed, he warned in 1966, he would inforce it strictly and "dry up this state like the Sahara."

Finally, voters in Mississippi got the message. On 1 July 1966 the last dry state in the nation became wet.

The Last American Slave

Naming a "last" American slave depends a great deal on the rules. Legally, tens of thousands simultaneously became last slaves on 1 January 1863 when Abraham Lincoln published his Emancipation Proclamation.

At least one slave remained in a state of voluntary servitude for thirty years after all others were freed in the United States. He was Anderson Whitaker, a slave owned by Nathan Whitaker of Scott County, Virginia. Nathan Whitaker was an invalid suffering from a severe form of inflammatory rheumatism; not wanting to be left alone, he proposed to Anderson that if he remained with him until he died, the house and property would be his. The black man agreed, remaining at the house and doing chores until August 1893, when Nathan Whitaker finally died.

When the contents of his master's will were revealed, Anderson Whitaker was chagrined to learn that he had been left nothing but an old horse worth about thirty dollars. He brought suit against old man Whitaker's heirs but was informed that a verbal contract could not bind where real estate was involved. Thus America's "last" slave ended up with much the same reward as his fellow sufferers.

On 5 October 1979, a gentleman claiming to be the last surviving slave died in a nursing home in Bartow, Florida. Describing how he had been brought to the United States from West Africa, Charlie Smith said he was twelve years old in 1854, when a slave-master coaxed him onto a ship docked in Liberia by telling him there were "fritter trees on board with lots of syrup."

Sold in New Orleans to a Texas rancher, Smith said, "I never saw Momma again."

Whether Charlie Smith lived to the age of 137, thus making him the last slave (or former slave) is a matter of conjecture. On the one hand, Social Security officers once turned up documents showing that Smith had been sold in New Orleans in 1854. On the other hand, officials for the *Guinness World Book of Records* stated in 1979 that Smith was dropped from the 1980 edition of their book (as one of the oldest living men) because a marriage certificate had been discovered which proved he had been born after the Civil War.

In the event Smith is permanently discredited, the title of "last American slave" would probably go to Sylvester Magee, who died on 15 October 1971 in Columbia, Mississippi, at the age of 130. Claiming that he had been brought as a slave in 1860 by plantation owner Hugh Magee and that he had helped bury the dead during the siege of Vicksburg, Sylvester Magee's evidence was supported by slave-trading records in addition to a family Bible, since destroyed, that had a handwritten note giving his birthdate as 26 May 1841.

If neither Magee or Smith measure up to historians' demands for accuracy, it is likely we will never know the identity of America's last surviving slave. What is certain is that the future is unlikely to produce few new claimants.

The LKA Game

One form of mental exercise involving "lasts" could be built around persons, places, and things which have changed their names, thus creating a question as to when they were "last known as...." For example, when was the American holiday, now called "Veterans' Day" last known as "Armistice Day?"

The answer: America's last official "Armistice Day", which had been celebrated annually every 11 November since 1918, was in 1953. The following year, Congress changed the holiday's title to "Veterans' Day" in order to honor all former servicemen rather than just those who served in World War I.

The question for New Yorkers who think they know a lot about their city might be: When was "The Avenue of the Americas" last known officially as "Sixth Avenue?" The precise answer is 11:24:59 a.m., 2 October 1945, just one second before the street's name was changed during a burst of Pan-American euphoria.

Nostalgia buffs of persons with reasonably good memories will see that the "Last Known As" game extends into many areas. Indeed, entire nations have changed names. To cite but a few: Iran was LKA Persia in 1935; Thailand was LKA Siam in 1949; Sri Lanka was LKA Ceylon in 1972; Botswana was LKA Bechuanaland in 1966; and, of course, Kalaallit Nunaat was LKA Greenland in 1979.

Structures or complexes have been quite susceptible to the name-changing habit, also. Hoover Dam, for example, was LKA Boulder Dam in 1947; New York's Brooks Atkinson Theatre was LKA the Mansfield Theatre in 1960; Rutgers University was LKA Queens College in 1825; Colgate University was LKA Madison University in 1890; and Princeton University was LKA the College of New Jersey in 1896.

Aside from women getting married or men adopting an alias to confuse the law or hide their identity, people have changed their names. Muhammad Ali, as nearly everyone knows, was LKA Cassius Clay in 1964; the basketball great Abdul Kareem-Jabbar was LKA Lew Alcindor in 1971.

Sports teams, for one reason or another, have also adopted new names or nicknames. Just in the area of baseball — who now recalls that the Chicago Cubs were LKA the "Orphans" in 1898? That the Pittsburgh Pirates were LKA the "Alleghenys" in 1889? That Boston's Red Sox were unashamedly LKA the "Puritans" in 1906 and Cleveland's Indians LKA the "Molly McGuires" in 1914? To complete the baseball cycle, it is necessary only to add that the New York Yankees were LKA the "Highlanders" in 1912, that the Cincinnati Reds were LKA the "Red Legs" in 1945, the Philadelphia Phillies LKA the "Blue Jays" in 1944, and the Houston Astros LKA the unwieldy "Colt 45's" in 1964.

In the area of commercial identification, it boggles the mind of even the staunchest trivia expert to produce the dates when Exxon was LKA Esso, Arco was LKA Atlantic, USAIR was LKA Allegheny Airlines, or Carter's Little Pills LKA Carter's Little Liver Pills.

Cities, of course, are easier to remember, especially since most of their names changes involve a certain amount of ceremony or at least political upheaval. In 1664, for example, the British threw the Dutch out of North America, a significant act which produced a number of name changes. Thus New York was LKA New Amsterdam that year, and Albany was LKA Port Orange.

The dissolution of the Ottoman Empire and proclamation of the Turkish Republic during the 1920s brought about the renaming of the capital city of Istanbul, which was LKA Constantinople in 1930.

Russia's 1918 Revolution produced the hero Vladimir I. Ulyanov, also known as Lenin, and as a result a veritable flood of cities and towns changed their names in his honor. Thus Leninogorsk was LKA Ridder in 1940; Leninsk-Kuznetsk was LKA Kolchigino in 1925; Leninabad was LKA Khodzhent in 1936; Leninakan was LKA Aleksandropol in 1924; and Ulyanovsk (cleverly avoiding the crush by adopting the hero's real name) was LKA Simbirsk in 1924.

Adopting a hero's name as the basis for a city's new identification can be dangerous, however, introducing an element of risk and instability in the LKA game. A Communist party official named Kliment Voroshilov, for example, was honored in 1935 when the cities of Lugansk and Nikolsk-Ussuriski changed their names to Voroshilovgrad and Voroshilov. In 1957, however, Soviet Premier Nikita Khrushchev linked Voroshilov with the "anit-party" faction he was intent on denouncing and the former hero of the Revolution suddenly became *persona non grata*. Soon people in the two cities noticed that they were receiving letters addressed to Lugansk and Nikolsk-Ussuriski once again.

The "de-Stalinization" of the late 1950s wrought considerable changes in Soviet Union road maps. After Lenin died, Josef Stalin became the most powerful man in Russia and during the 1920s and 1930s numerous factories, streets, collective farms, towns, and cities were given variants of his name. There was the huge steel city of Stalinsk (formerly Kuznetsk); the Ukrainian mining center of Stalino; the capital of the Tadzhik Republic, Stalinobad; Stalinogorsk in central European Russia, and Staliniri in the Georgian Republic. In addition, the highest mountain in the Soviet Union, Garmo Peak, was named Stalin Peak in 1933.

But the most famous city was Stalingrad, the drab but celebrated industrial center on the Volga River where the Nazi advance had been checked and then hurled back during World War II. Last Known As Tsaritsyn in honor of the ruling calss in 1925, when its name was changed in honor of Stalin, Stalingrad in 1961 was a symbolic name mentioned in the same breath as Midway, Waterloo, Actium, Hastings, Gettysburg, and El Alamein.

Then came "de-Stalinization," at first just a series of hints that the former Premier was not always perfect. These were followed by stronger charges, Khrushchev leading the agitation. Soon lesser officials, writers, and ordinary citizens who wanted to ingratiate themselves with the party joined the chorus urging that Stalin's name be expunged from honor rolls and public buildings. At the 22nd Soviet Communist Party Congress, one of the speakers was Darya Lazurkina, who as one of the multitude banished by Stalin in 1937 had survived nearly 20 years of prison, hard labor, and exile. Attributing her survival to having had periodic conversations with the late Lenin, she proclaimed to the 5000 delegates that only the day before Lenin had told her: "It is unpleasant for me to lie next to Stalin, who caused the party so much harm."

That night, while Moscow slept, a motorcade of jeeps and official Red Army vehicles drew up before the massive red-and-black marble mausoleum which contained the mummified corpses of Stalin and Lenin. After soldiers sealed off the square from the populace, Stalin's body was removed and reburied behind the Mausoleum in a cemetery reserved for third-class heroes of the Revolution, including U.S. comrade John Reed. As a climax to the bizarre ceremony, a vase of twelve white chrysanthemums was placed on the new grave of the man recently declared a mass murderer and false prophet.

The action set off a wave of anti-Stalinism in the U.S.S.R and its satellites. In Warsaw a disc jockey who obviously did not know the score played a cantata by Aram Khachaturian dedicated to Stalin and was promptly fired. From East Berlin's Stalinallee to a Paris suburb's Rue Staline, street signs were changed and statues torn down. In Stalingrad itself, signs in the railroad station bearing the former Premier's name were taken down, as was that on the front of the Stalingrad Hotel. In addition, a large statue of Stalin in the central Square of Fallen Fighters mysteriously disappeared. Letters to the editors of the city's newspapers demanded that a new name be provided for the city. Because of its location astride the Volga River, someone suggested the title Volgograd, a choice sufficiently uninspired to please everyone.

While this agitation was taking place, the city of Stalinsk renamed itself Novokuznetsk, Stalinobad became Dushanbe, Stalino's name was changed to Donetsk, and Stalin Peak was changed to Mount Communism.

Communist leaders in Stalingrad acted quickly, also. Saturday, 11 November 1961 was the last day that famous city was known as Stalingrad before changing its name to Volgograd.

Lest Americans think they are above this political fickleness, however, it should be pointed out that the historic rocket-launching site in Florida was "last known as" Cape Canaveral in 1963, before popular sentiment changed its name to Cape Kennedy. That situation lasted only a decade. As a result, the present-day Cape Canaveral was LKA Cape Kennedy in 1973, a distressing turn of events for those who feel plaques and street signs and names on maps insure immortality.

483 B.C.
Buddha (founder of Buddhism): "Decay is inherent in all component things."
428 B.C.
Anaxagoras (philosopher): "Give the boys a holiday."
399 B.C.
Socrates (philosopher, to a friend just after taking poison): "Crito, I owe a cock to Asclepius — will you pay the debt?"
323 B.C.
Diogenes (philosopher, asked why he wanted to be buried face downward): "Because everything will shortly be turned upside down."
286 B.C.
Chuang-Tzu (philosopher, asked about method of burial): "Above ground, I shall be food for the kites; below I shall be food for moles, crickets, and ants. Why rob one to feed the other?"
212 B.C.
Archimedes (Greek scientist, who had drawn figures in the sand to illustrate a theory just before being killed by Roman soldier): "Stand away, fellow, from my diagram."
29
Jesus Christ: "Into thy hands do I commend my spirit."
1142
Peter Abelard (philosopher): "I don't know! I don't know!"
1503
Pope Alexander VI: "Wait a minute."
1548
Gonzalo Pizarro (explorer, as he was stabbed): "Jesus!"
1645
Hugo Grotius (jurist): "Be serious."

1655

Pierre Gassendi (philosopher): 'I was born without knowing why, I have lived without knowing why, and I am dying without knowing either why or how.''

1702

Dominique Bouhours (grammarian): ''I am about to — or I am going to— die. Either expression is used.''

1719

Sir Samuel Garth (physician, to those gathered around his bed): ''Please, gentlemen, stand back and let me die a natural death.''

1728

Cotton Mather (religious leader): ''Is this all that I feared when I prayed against a hard death? Oh, I can bear this! I can bear it!''

1742

John Baptiste Dubos (historian): ''Death is a law and not a punishment. Three things ought to console us for giving up life. The friends whom we have lost; the few persons worthy of being loved whom we leave behind us, and finally the memory of our stupidities and the assurance that they are now going to stop.''

1773

The Earl of Chesterfield (upon seeing friend come into room): ''Give Dayrolles a chair.''

1776

Julie de Lespinasse (society woman): ''Am I still alive?''

1777

Albrecht von Haller (physiologist, felt his own pulse): ''Now I am dying. The artery ceases to beat.''

1783

Dr. William Hunter (physician): ''If I had strength enough to hold a pen, I would write how easy and pleasant a thing it is to die.''

1790

Adam Smith (economist): ''I believe we must adjourn the meeting to some other place.''

1798

Giovanni Jacopo Casanova (adventurer): ''Life is a wench that one loves, to whom we allow any condition in the world, so long as she does not leave us.''

1804

Immanuel Kant (philosopher): ''It is enough.''

1806

Edward Thurlow (judge): ''I'll be shot if I don't believe I'm dying.''

1809

Dr. Adam (rector of the High School of Edinburgh): ''It grows dark, boys... you may go.''

1818

Abigail Adams (wife of U.S. President John Adams): ''I am ready to go, and — John, it will not be long."

1822
Mrs. David Garrick (widow of the great actor, offered a cup of tea by her nurse): "Put it down, hussy! Do you think I cannot help myself."

1825
Pauline Bonaparte (sister of Napoleon I): "I always was beautiful."

1825
Bernard Germain Etienne de la Ville, Comte de Lacepede (Naturalist, to his son concerning a manuscript on which he was working): "Charles, write in large letters the word END at the foot of the page."

1831
Georg Wilhelm Hegel (philosopher): "Only one man ever understood me... and he didn't understand me."

1832
Leorges Leopold Cuvier (zoologist): "Nurse, it was I who discovered that leeches have red blood."

1832
Evariste Galois (mathematician, shot in a duel): "Don't cry, I need all my courage to die at twenty."

1833
Marc-Antoine Careme (cook, while sampling food): "These are good but prepared too hastily. You must shake the saucepan lightly — see, like this...."

1857
Auguste Comte (philosopher): "What an irreparable loss."

1858
George Combe (phrenologist): "I should say I was dying — and I am glad of it."

1863
Joseph Harvey Green (surgeon, felt his own pulse): "Stopped...."

1878
William M. (Boss) Tweed (politician): "Tilden and Fairchild — they will be satisfied now."

1882
Charles Darwin (anthropologist): "I am not in the least afraid to die."

1887
Henry Ward Beecher (religious leader): "Now comes the mystery."

1890
Sir Richard Francis Burton (explorer): "Chloroform — ether — or I am a dead man."

James Croll (physicist, asked for whiskey): "I don't there's much fear of me learning to drink now."

1895
Louis Pasteur (scientist, offered a glass of milk): "I cannot."
1903
Abram S. Hewitt (industrialist, pulling tube from his mouth while in oxygen tent): "And now I am officially dead."
1912
Lawrence E. G. Oates (explorer, just before leaving tent in Antarctic): I am just going outside and may be some time."
1913
J. P. Morgan (financier): "Don't baby me so."
1914
Pope Pius X (when Emperor Franz Josef came to ask blessing for the Austrian armies): "Get out of my sight! Away! Away! We grant blessing to no one who provokes the world to war!"
1915
Booker T. Washington (educator): "Take me home. I was born in the South, I have lived and labored in the South, and I wish to die and be buried in the South."
1916
Elie Metchnikoff (bacteriologist): "You will do my post-mortem? And look at the intestines carefully, for I think there is something there now."
1922
Alexander Graham Bell (inventor): "...So little done. So much to do."
1928
Clarence Walker Barron (financial editor and publisher): "What's the news?"
1932
William S. Thayer (physician): "This is the end and I'm not sorry."
Nicholas Johnson (ship captain): "Turn my face to the sea."
1934
Marie Curie (scientist): "I want to be left alone."
1949
John Tettemer (monk who sought release and subsequently married, asked if he wanted a priest): "Good heavens, no!"
1957
Ronald Knox (clergyman, asked if he would like to have part of New Testament read to him): "No... awfully jolly of you to suggest it, though."
1961
Carl Gustav Jung (psychiatrist, to his son): "Quick, help me get out of bed. I want to look at the sunset."

A Last Word

This book is not intended to be the last word on lasts. Most readers, particularly those with a special interest in one of the topics covered here, no doubt have already thought of their own lasts which were not included in this book ("How dare you leave out John Carroll's last movie!" "Nothing about George Halas' last game with the Bears?").

Lasts, of course, occur every day and I can but apologize for those that were overlooked or had to be eliminated because of space requirements.

If the reader feels that - to coin a phrase - there a future in lasts, at least to the extent that the author and publisher should be informed what juicy items were left out of this book, he or she is encouraged to drop us a line with the pertinent data. Credit will be given to contributors for information used in any sequels.

Regardless of what the future holds, I hope this book has proved useful and interesting. If readers have the occasion to repeat any of the facts or anecdotes contained herein, it is my hope (as well as the completion of a creative impulse mentioned in the introduction) that they will say they read it here first.

Index